INSIDE THE POEM

ESSAYS AND POEMS IN HONOUR OF
DONALD STEPHENS

Edited by W.H.New

Toronto
OXFORD UNIVERSITY PRESS
1992

Oxford University Press, 70 Wynford Drive, Don Mills, Ontario M3C 1J9

Toronto   Oxford   New York
Delhi   Bombay   Calcutta   Madras   Karachi   Kuala Lumpur
Singapore   Hong Kong   Tokyo   Nairobi   Dar es Salaam
Cape Town   Melbourne   Auckland   Madrid

and associated companies in
Berlin   Ibadan

This book is printed on permanent (acid-free) paper   .

Canadian Cataloguing in Publication Data

Main entry under title:

Inside the poem

Includes bibliographical references.
ISBN 0-19-540925-6

1. Canadian poetry (English) - 20th century -
History and criticism.   2. Canadian poetry (English) -
20th century.   3. Stephens, Donald G. (Donald
Graham), 1931-   .   I. New, W. H. (William Herbert),
1938-   .

PS8155.I58 1992   C811'.54   C92-094935-5
PR9190.5.I58 1992

Design by Heather Delfino
Printed in Canada

Contents

Preface

This book honours Donald Stephens, who taught Canadian literature at the University of British Columbia from 1958 to 1988. In particular, it honours his love of poetry and his extraordinary skill as a teacher, his commitment both to the art of literature and to his students. For in the classroom, as well as through his publications, Donald Stephens encouraged other readers to enjoy poetry too, helped his students develop the skills they needed to get "inside the poem," asked them to respond—and then to examine why they responded as they did and to consider the consequences of their judgments. Sensitivity to language, sensitivity to cultural context, sensitivity to personal experience: each of these had its place in interpretation. By urging his students to develop their responsiveness, he enabled them to see better and to read the world afresh. And he also encouraged them to write. In this book, some of his former students, together with several colleagues and many friends—poets, critics, teachers, and readers—have gathered to write, and to write about, poems. (I was his first M.A. candidate, Tom Hastings his last—and his many other students include Pauline Butling, Elspeth Cameron, Sandra Djwa, Dick Harrison, Dorothy Livesay, Seymour Mayne, Linda Rogers, Lilita Rodman, Stephen Scobie, Christine Somerville, Gordon Turner, and Fred Wah.) Together we honour Donald Stephens, and in doing so we celebrate language and invite other readers to share in the pleasures of poetry.

W.N.

Phosphorescence, or, The Poem Within

"*Phosphorescence*," wrote Emily Dickinson, "Now, there's a word to lift your hat to . . . To find that phosphorescence, that light within, that's the genius behind poetry." But as with many another attempt to "define" poetry, the language here leaps abruptly into metaphor. "A poem is a meteor," says Wallace Stevens. "Poetry is a way of taking life by the throat," says Robert Frost. "Poetry is a verdict," says Leonard Cohen. Others try simile, but as a way of clarifying what poetry is, the difference in device proves no more effective, and sometimes less: when Sir Arthur Conan Doyle says that "Poetry is like the pemmican of literature," one is more mystified than enlightened, though the failure of the phrase more likely results from a lapse in Conan Doyle's vocabulary than from the diffuseness of his subject. On other occasions, writers reverse the process, assuming that the word "poem" is sufficiently specific and concrete to give shape to more abstract ideas, particularly politics: in a leap of cultural faith not easily shared outside his borders, Walt Whitman proclaims that "The United States themselves are essentially the greatest poem" (to which it is tempting to read Robinson Jeffers' lines as a reply: "the day is a poem but too much / like one of Jeffers's, crusted with blood and barbaric omens / Painful to excess, inhuman as a hawk's cry"). These examples merely suggest that politics is too narrow a container for poetry—and that a definition of the word "poetry" (or the activity, or the idea) still proves elusive.

Several other writers have attempted to animate the idea of poetry by lodging it metaphorically in experience. By this approach, its presence in the world is what grants a poem its validity, as though—recursively somehow—the vitality of the language exists because of a vitality in what is usually called "real life." Because of life, runs this implicit syllogism, there exists language; and language becomes "poetry" to the degree that it reconstructs life; hence the "real poetry" must exist in life rather than in language because to reverse the process would be to prefer a verbal imitation to the real thing. In this vein, Longfellow waxes nostalgic, declaring "Children" to be "living poems"; Henry Tomlinson waxes earnest, openly seeking ratification: "The reader who is illuminated is, in a real sense, the poem." The problem is that "reality" takes a multitude of competing forms, from ideas to things, faith to forensic science, imaginative constructs to emotional and social relationships, words and sights and sounds to representations of words and sights and sounds.

After such huge but essentially elliptical claims, it seems refreshing to hear Edgar Allan Poe talking of the "poem which is a poem and nothing more." (Shades of Wordsworth, shades of Gertrude Stein.) But this, too, is a definition, and it comes with assumptions attached. When Poe speaks of "nothing more," he is not disputing the value of imagery but questioning the necessity of a social *function* for art—so far as he's concerned, poetry can be written "solely for the poem's sake" and be more valuable than if it preached or taught or reformed. He's not dismissive; he's simply declaring that the vitality of language, rather than being dependent on the vitality of "society," is a phenomenon of a different order, recognizable and appreciable on its own terms, which are aesthetic, aural, visual, verbal. His 1850 comments in *The Poetic Principle* thus sound as contemporary as those of Wallace Stevens in *The Man with the Blue Guitar* (1937)— "Poetry is the subject of the poem"—or the premise behind a host of late 20th century self-reflexive works. "A poem should not mean / But be," wrote Archibald MacLeish in 1926, championing art's *existence* rather than its serviceability. Even those modern journalists who rely on the quick cliché to describe racers and hawks—"poetry in motion," "poetry in flight"—inferentially claim to understand MacLeish's principle, for by using the word as they do, they more or less intrinsically accept that poetry is as visceral an experience as athletics or music or pure mathematics: that it's a way of connecting with the world that somehow escapes the rationalist's efforts to define—despite Aristotle and the rest of the troop of definers. But as the definers would shrewdly observe, any system of aesthetics is a social construction; saying what is vital or appreciable about any art or experience engages the sayer with the priorities of Convention as much as with the incontrovertibilities of Truth. In any event, they might also add, it's hard to experience anything without attaching some value to it or placing some interpretation upon it—and such terms as *value* and *interpretation* are each determinations *of* a poem as much as derivations *from* one. *Reader, writer, writing,* and *reading* are a sometimes uneasy foursome—but all are necessary for a poem to *happen;* take one away and there's just an object, a deafness of spirit, a blank imagination, a dead shell.

There are plenty of readers who would answer MacLeish's assertion ("not mean, but be") with the challenge: "Be *what?*"—thus (perhaps deliberately) resisting his intention. It's easy to call them philistines. (When Marianne Moore writes "I, too, dislike it," they are the sort of readers—or more often non-readers— who would rush to agree, intent on disputing the value and very idea of poetry without waiting to recognize the "real toads" that sometimes live in her "imaginary gardens.") There are many poets, however, who, over the course of history, have also insisted on the necessity of *meaning,* though they have not uniformly refused to accept the possibility that meaning and being might sometimes be one. Those writers who shape poetry *as aesthetic design*—whether in syllables and cadences and visual patterns, or in stanzas and regular metres and rhymes—do not always agree with those who want design to perform an ethical or political function. Sometimes they want the design simply to "be" on the page, or to "be" in performance—to "be" in the sound of syllable or the visual arrangement of line and lines: in experiential effects rather than in moral or message. But the two groups of writer-readers are seldom as readily distinguishable from each other as their literary quarrels would lead one to believe. Even the desire for a "pure" art *apart* from the world is a comment *on* the world, and open attempts to teach and reform can often give a reader an aesthetic pleasure that is clearly distinct from an argument or message. Just as poems are not all beautiful, moral, pleasurable, or politically respectable, so designs and messages are not necessarily going to easily coincide. Plainly, a reader does not have to agree with an argument to find it beautifully expressed; finding something which is disagreeable or reprehensible to be beautiful, however—or something morally or politically admirable to be tritely worded and eminently dismissible—does open up other moral and aesthetic dilemmas. Such conflict is not without meaning. Dialectic and dialogue emerge from it. Consequences follow. Sometimes these dilemmas are even the stuff of poetry.

When Samuel Taylor Coleridge wrote in 1827 that "prose = words in their best order" and "poetry = the best words in their best order," he claimed to be simply uttering a homespun truth. But the little word "best" undermines such a claim, inasmuch as it raises questions about the validity of subjective evaluation. Whose version of "best" governs judgment? Are aesthetics and absolutism compatible? Is language—which is susceptible to the vicissitudes of fashion, to differences in time and place and social custom, and to the competing and often contrary claims of class and gender and convention—even reconcilable with *an* idea of *the* ideal, on which Coleridge so quiescently relies? Yet if poetry has value—whether as pleasurable artifact or as ethical example, whether as the distillation of emotion (as Keats would have it) or the escape from emotion (as Eliot claimed) and a distillation of "pure" intellect instead—does it not follow that such a value can be characterized and explained? Even if "best" is a relative determination, is it not a functional term within its own limits? Such questions ask not only about the language of poetry and commentary but also about the contexts within which poetry is written and read. For these contexts, too, shape a reader's understanding. Coleridge's "best" is shaped by the class structures of 18th and 19th century England, by the fact as well as the specifics of his own education, by his male assumptions about what is reasonable and ordinary, by his personal habits, by his desire *for* "value" in the first place; it is also *bound* by them. In this he is not, except in particulars, any different from any other writer. ("Poetry is my only way to truth," says Phyllis Webb.) Yet the *word* "best," because it looks like an absolute, is often accepted as though it behaved absolutely. Recognizing that it proclaims a version of value rather than a universal truth does not deny its use, but does acknowledge its boundaries. As with any other claim for *the* "best" or "most natural" form of expression— whether Matthew Arnold's "grand style" (the sort of language that is commonly referred to in the later 20th century as "poetic," meaning *not ordinary*, or *not familiar*) or the "ordinary" speech styles, the vernacular rhythms and populist vocabulary embraced by post-colonial writers around the English-speaking world—Coleridge's claim, on analysis, shows its inherent political presumptions.

Given these several fields of uncertainty, what can a book like this one do? One thing it does *not* do is attempt some alternative way of defining what a poem *is*—nor does it try to suggest that "the poem in Canada" is a single structure of a particular kind, equatable with one attitude, one message, one dimension of language, one political belief, one technique of composition. Rather, it stresses the diversity of poetry and the diverse ways of responding to it. It is a book about reading individual poems—and therefore about some of the possible ways of responding to a text. Somewhat more indirectly, it also seeks to show through the practice of critical reading how the "life" of poetry derives from interconnections between text and reader. In this book's dialogues, Canada is one recurrent context, language another. But the individual readers of the poems that are discussed here bring additional perspectives to bear upon the way they read, and the poets (though several are overtly aware of being influenced by the writers they in turn have read, the music heard, the paintings seen) are an independent lot. The result is not a set of absolute judgments but a series of separate engagements with design. The readers as well as the writers here, each wrestling with "phosphorescence," demonstrate the process of thinking as well as the results of thought; collectively they are concerned with words and the world—with the experience that gives rise to language, with the experience of language that gives expression to ideas and emotions and intangible understandings, and with the powers of association and interpretation that assign meaning and value, find significance in design, and animate the world of words.

The book contains four sections. The last of the four (a comment by the novelist David Watmough) is a personal tribute to Donald Stephens, whose interest in poetry provided the stimulus for this volume; the third is a collection of new poems by contemporary Canadian writers; the second is a series of readings of particular Canadian poems both past and recent; the first provides the texts of the poems that the critics in Part Two are responding to. Readers of this book, consequently, can begin with the poetry, with the critical commentary, or with the personal essay. They can respond directly to the design and ideas of the individual poems; and they can read along with the critics, poems in hand, engaging in a constructive dialogue about interpretation, meaning, and language.

Many differences in approach are apparent here. Some critics stress the social or historical contexts of poetry, as when Diana Brydon comments on the political function of Dionne Brand's writing (and of the teaching of poetry), or when Wilfred Cude argues the institutional implications of a Roy Daniells poem, or when Sandra Djwa traces the biographical influences on textual revisions of A.J.M. Smith's "The Lonely Land." Literary history is Mary Jane Edwards' subject; she investigates the issue of canonicity as it affects textual editing and historical judgment. Other critics—Nathalie Cooke writing about Pat Lane, W.H. New about Eli Mandel, Susan Rudy Dorscht about Fred Wah, Thomas Hastings about Earle Birney—concern themselves in part with the way a literary context shapes critical understanding. And while those writers are concerned with the way language works inside the text, others are concerned with the way language outside the text affects the shape and structure of a given poem's meaning. Elspeth Cameron writes a source study involving Earle Birney's "David"; Bruce Grenberg probes the critical history of Archibald Lampman's "The City of the End of Things," and uses it in part to explicate the logical structure of the poem. Some critics—Lilita Rodman, for example, examining in detail the verbal paradigms of a poem by Frank Scott—respond to the implications of design; others—such as Christine Somerville, writing on Margaret Avison—respond to ethical imperatives in literature; still others—Clara Thomas, for example, considering the poetry in a Carol Shields novel—raise questions about generic borders and definitions. Manina Jones brings Bakhtinian theory to bear on the language of Robert Kroetsch, demonstrating in part how certain kinds of linguistic structure underlie the poet's irony; Geoffrey Durrant illuminates the musicality of P.K. Page's lines; Dick Harrison reflects on the "documentary" character of Dorothy Livesay's work; Brian Trehearne considers the "dialectic of fame and scorn" that informs a poem by Irving Layton. The patterns of ideas that develop within poems also attract some commentary, as when John Hulcoop engages with the philosophical implications of Phyllis Webb's work, or when Pauline Butling examines the gender politics of Daphne Marlatt's language, or when Lorraine Weir explains the "number grids" of Wilfred Watson's work, or when George Woodcock reflects on the Darwinian frame of reference in Al Purdy's Galapagos poems. Frank Davey and Stephen Scobie focus on language itself, implicitly demonstrating how verbal associations within texts by Margaret Atwood and Phyllis Webb lead to verbal associations between each text and the reader. Laurie Ricou and Robert Bringhurst engage in a kind of dialogue about creativity, revealing the kinds of overlap that are possible when critic and poet connect. Poetry, in some cases, is criticism by intent; criticism, in some cases, becomes a kind of poetry in effect. From each of these approaches follow different kinds of conclusion.

Poems are not all written the same way, with the same expectations of a reader or the reader's world; and they can't all be read the same way. Reading poetry is as often a process of tuning in to the assumptions as of recognizing the "meanings" of individual words. So when a critic fastens on the political implications of a poem, the response suggests a need (perhaps in the critic, perhaps in the poet or the poem) for consequences, a determination that "value" is connected somehow with practical solutions to observed difficulties in society. Words such as "equality" or "democracy" or "application" or "action" are possible terms of approbation in such a discourse. (Poets are "the unacknowledged legislators of the world," said Percy Bysshe Shelley.) Critics concerned with sheer aesthetic design, by contrast, tend more to find value in the order of verbal and visual relationships—the resonant phrase, the pleasing arrangement, the "mastery" of form—and also in the explication of this order: their concern is to share their insight with another reader, though not necessarily to change behaviour or stir readers to action. One person might delight in "rapture," another in "faith," a third in "felicity," a fourth in "creative power"—Abraham Klein catalogues some of the options, for poets as well as critics, in "Portrait of the Poet as Landscape"—each term operating like a ritual bell of commendation. But the intake of breath that says *recognition* to some will say *convention* to others. Sometimes *any* response that involves an emotional reaction is deemed to be sentimental. But is it? Is intellectual density *preferable* to feeling, or intellectual familiarity enough to condemn a verse to the slag-heaps of literary history? The (indeterminate, and perhaps indeterminable) moment when the *creative* turns into the ("merely") *fashionable* certainly can affect a reader's reaction—but to what end? When is a poem dismissible for being "derivative," and when is it praiseworthy for echoing or alluding to another work? Some writers deliberately attempt imitation; others dismiss it. Some writers delight in parody; others condemn it. Some writers strive for regularity, symmetry, order; others eschew it. Which of them is "right"? Or, if there is no "right," does this mean that all reactions are equally valid, and that all language is "poetry"? Those critics who declare evaluative measures to be élitist will choose (instead of declaring comparative "worth") to probe the historical circumstances that give rise to value systems; or they will probe the implications of the value systems themselves; or they will probe the life or mind-set of the writer whose ideas emerge through writing. A commitment to such alternatives does not thereby free these approaches from judgment (no language is without its slant of expectation); in a sometimes elaborate fashion, however, the abstract examination of the implications of ideas replaces verbal design—or the more familiar qualities that sometimes are taken for "phosphorescence": musicality, emotional impact, sincerity, "organic form," classical "rigour"—as the working criterion of value.

And all these critical approaches are present in this volume: those that find value in the idea, those that find value in the pattern, those that find value in the social consequences of language, those that find value in the process of explication and communication, those that question the very idea of value, and those that insist upon value before all else. The poems and comments that follow will not resolve these apparent disparities; they will, however, suggest a lively range of possibilities. "Resolving" would run counter to the poetry here, for it would suggest fixed answers, solid boundaries, limited choices, and politically motivated safety of statement. "Responding to possibility," by contrast, implies enquiry, and implies uncertainty, even intellectual danger. Because enquiry can be both a challenge and a pleasure, reading "inside the poem" can be a creative process, for writer and reader alike.

W.H. New

Acknowledgments

The enthusiasm of the contributors made this book a pleasure to prepare; I greatly appreciate their willingness to participate in this venture, and their support, and the friendly co-operation of the owners of copyright material. I am grateful also to Wes Robertson, Leagh Manndel, and Lynda Miller, who typed the manuscript, and to Carol McConnell, who patiently checked sources and proof-read the text.

MARGARET ATWOOD. "Notes Towards a Poem That Can Never Be Written" from *Selected Poems 1966-1984*. Copyright © Margaret Atwood 1990. Used by permission of Oxford University Press Canada. MARGARET AVISON. "'Just Left' or 'The Night Margaret Laurence Died'" from *No Time*. Reprinted by permission of Margaret Avison. EARLE BIRNEY. "David" and "The Bear on the Delhi Road" from *Collected Poems* by Earle Birney. Used by permission of the Canadian Publishers, McClelland and Stewart Limited, Toronto. DIONNE BRAND. "Blues Spiritual for Mammy Prater" used by permission of the author. ROBERT BRINGHURST. "Sunday Morning" used by permission of the author. ROY DANIELLS. "Three lecture hours per week" used by permission of Laurenda Daniells. A.M. KLEIN. "Portrait of the Poet as Landscape" from *A.M. Klein: Complete Poems*, edited by Zailig Pollock, © University of Toronto Press, 1990. Reprinted by permission of University of Toronto Press. ROBERT KROETSCH. From *Seed Catalogue* is used by permission of the author. PATRICK LANE. "Winter 45" used by permission of Coteau Books and the author. IRVING LAYTON. "Whatever Else Poetry is Freedom" from *Collected Poems* by Irving Layton. Used by permission of the Canadian Publishers, McClelland and Stewart, Toronto. DOROTHY LIVESAY. From "Call My People Home" from *The Documentaries*. Used by permission of the author. ELI MANDEL. "The Madwomen of the Plaza de Mayo" is used by permission of Ann Mandel. DAPHNE MARLATT. From *Booking Passage* © Daphne Marlatt. Used by permission of Red Deer College Press. P.K. PAGE. "Portrait of Marina" © P.K. Page. Used by permission. AL PURDY. "Darwin's Theology?" used by permission of the author. F.R. SCOTT. "Audacity" from *Selected Poems* by F.R. Scott. Used by permission of The Canadian Publisher, McClelland & Stewart, Toronto. CAROL SHIELDS. "Lost Things" from *Swann* by Carol Shields © 1987. Reprinted with the permission of Stoddart Publishing Co. Limited, Don Mills, Ont. A.J.M. SMITH. "The Lonely Land" from *The Classic Shade*. Used by permission of the Canadian Publisher, McClelland and Stewart, Toronto. FRED WAH. from *Breathin' My Name with A Sigh* (Talonbooks, Vancouver 1981). Used by permission of the author. WILFRED WATSON. Epilogue to *Gramsci 1*, from *Gramsci x 3*. Used by permission of the author. PHYLLIS WEBB. "Krakatoa," "Spiritual Storm," and "The Mind of the Poet" from *Hanging fire*, © The Coach House Press, Toronto, 1990. Used by permission of the author.

PART ONE

Texts

Margaret Atwood

Notes Towards a Poem
That Can Never Be Written

For Carolyn Forché

I

This is the place
you would rather not know about,
this is the place that will inhabit you,
this is the place you cannot imagine,
this is the place that will finally defeat you

where the word *why* shrivels and empties
itself. This is famine.

II

There is no poem you can write
about it, the sandpits
where so many were buried
& unearthed, the unendurable
pain still traced on their skins.

This did not happen last year
or forty years ago but last week.
This has been happening,
this happens.

We make wreaths of adjectives for them,
we count them like beads,
we turn them into statistics & litanies
and into poems like this one.

Nothing works.
They remain what they are.

III

The woman lies on the wet cement floor
under the unending light,
needle marks on her arms put there
to kill the brain
and wonders why she is dying.

She is dying because she said.
She is dying for the sake of the word.
It is her body, silent
and fingerless, writing this poem.

IV

It resembles an operation
but it is not one

nor despite the spread legs, grunts
& blood, is it a birth.

Partly it's a job,
partly it's a display of skill
like a concerto.

It can be done badly
or well, they tell themselves.

Partly it's an art.

V

The facts of this world seen clearly
are seen through tears;
why tell me then
there is something wrong with my eyes?

To see clearly and without flinching,
without turning away,
this is agony, the eyes taped open
two inches from the sun.

What is it you see then?
Is it a bad dream, a hallucination?
Is it a vision?
What is it you hear?

The razor across the eyeball
is a detail from an old film.
It is also a truth.
Witness is what you must bear.

VI

In this country you can say what you like
because no one will listen to you anyway,
it's safe enough, in this country you can try to write
the poem that invents
nothing and excuses nothing,
because you can invent and excuse yourself each day.

Elsewhere, this poem is not invention.
Elsewhere, this poem takes courage.
Elsewhere, this poem must be written
because the poets are already dead.

Elsewhere, this poem must be written
as if you are already dead,
as if nothing more can be done
or said to save you.

Elsewhere you must write this poem
because there is nothing more to do.

Margaret Avison

Just Left *or*
The Night Margaret Laurence Died

Bare branches studded once with jewelled birds
Someone inexorably plunders
One by one till an
Impoverished wintry sky from hill to
Darkening hill reveals
Untreasured tree-spikes, almost only
(One bunched bird left
His eye aglimmer there).

Waiting, dim
Loneliness, place of
That withdrawing vision—
More than the well of light from
The first far planet—
Fills, fills, fills, fills.

Mutable mortal night
Blinds mortal day
Still to changelessness.

The perched, askew,
Will ruffle still as the day-ocean
Lips in and foams towards flood of
All emptiness exposed.

Earle Birney

David

I

David and I that summer cut trails on the Survey,
All week in the valley for wages, in air that was steeped
In the wail of mosquitoes, but over the sunalive week-ends
We climbed, to get from the ruck of the camp, the surly

Poker, the wrangling, the snoring under the fetid
Tents, and because we had joy in our lengthening coltish
Muscles, and mountains for David were made to see over,
Stairs from the valleys and steps to the sun's retreats.

II

Our first was Mount Gleam. We hiked in the long afternoon
To a curling lake and lost the lure of the faceted
Cone in the swell of its sprawling shoulders. Past
The inlet we grilled our bacon, the strips festooned

On a poplar prong, in the hurrying slant of the sunset.
Then the two of us rolled in the blanket while round us the cold
Pines thrust at the stars. The dawn was a floating
Of mists till we reached to the slopes above timber, and won

To snow like fire in the sunlight. The peak was upthrust
Like a fist in a frozen ocean of rock that swirled
Into valleys the moon could be rolled in. Remotely unfurling
Eastward the alien prairie glittered. Down through the dusty

Skree on the west we descended, and David showed me
How to use the give of shale for giant incredible
Strides. I remember, before the larches' edge,
That I jumped a long green surf of juniper flowing

Away from the wind, and landed in gentian and saxifrage
Spilled on the moss. Then the darkening firs
And the sudden whirring of water that knifed down a fern-hidden
Cliff and splashed unseen into mist in the shadows

III

One Sunday on Rampart's arête a rainsquall caught us,
And passed, and we clung by our blueing fingers and bootnails
An endless hour in the sun, not daring to move
Till the ice had steamed from the slate. And David taught me

How time on a knife-edge can pass with the guessing of fragments
Remembered from poets, the naming of strata beside one,
And matching of stories from schooldays. . . . We crawled astride
The peak to feast on the marching ranges flagged

By the fading shreds of the shattered stormcloud. Lingering
There it was David who spied to the south, remote,
And unmapped, a sunlit spire on Sawback, an overhang
Crooked like a talon. David named it the Finger.

That day we chanced on the skull and the splayed white ribs
Of a mountain goat underneath a cliff-face, caught
On a rock. Around were the silken feathers of hawks.
And that was the first I knew that a goat could slip.

IV

And then Inglismaldie. Now I remember only
The long ascent of the lonely valley, the live
Pine spirally scarred by lightning, the slicing pipe
Of invisible pika, and great prints, by the lowest

Snow, of a grizzly. There it was too that David
Taught me to read the scroll of coral in limestone
And the beetle-seal in the shale of ghostly trilobites,
Letters delivered to man from the Cambrian waves.

V

On Sundance we tried from the col and the going was hard.
The air howled from our feet to the smudged rocks
And the papery lake below. At an outthrust we baulked
Till David clung with his left to a dint in the scarp,

Lobbed the iceaxe over the rocky lip,
Slipped from his holds and hung by the quivering pick,
Twisted his long legs up into space and kicked
To the crest. Then grinning, he reached with his freckled wrist

And drew me up after. We set a new time for that climb.
That day returning we found a robin gyrating
In grass, wing-broken. I caught it to tame but David
Took and killed it, and said, "Could you teach it to fly?"

VI

In August, the second attempt, we ascended The Fortress,
By the forks of the Spray we caught five trout and fried them
Over a balsam fire. The woods were alive
With the vaulting of mule-deer and drenched with clouds all the morning,

Till we burst at noon to the flashing and floating round
Of the peaks. Coming down we picked in our hats the bright
And sunhot raspberries, eating them under a mighty
Spruce, while a marten moving like quicksilver scouted us.

VII

But always we talked of the Finger on Sawback, unknown
And hooked, till the first afternoon in September we slogged
Through the musky woods, past a swamp that quivered with frog-song,
And camped by a bottle-green lake. But under the cold

Breath of the glacier sleep would not come, the moon-light
Etching the Finger. We rose and trod past the feathery
Larch, while the stars went out, and the quiet heather
Flushed, and the skyline pulsed with the surging bloom

Of incredible dawn in the Rockies. David spotted
Bighorns across the moraine and sent them leaping
With yodels the ramparts redoubled and rolled to the peaks,
And the peaks to the sun. The ice in the morning thaw

Was a gurgling world of crystal and cold blue chasms,
And seracs that shone like frozen saltgreen waves.
At the base of the Finger we tried once and failed. Then David
Edged to the west and discovered the chimney; the last

Hundred feet we fought the rock and shouldered and kneed
Our way for an hour and made it. Unroping we formed
A cairn on the rotting tip. Then I turned to look north
At the glittering wedge of giant Assiniboine, heedless

Of handhold. And one foot gave. I swayed and shouted.
David turned sharp and reached out his arm and steadied me,
Turning again with a grin and his lips ready
To jest. But the strain crumbled his foothold. Without

A gasp he was gone. I froze to the sound of grating
Edge-nails and fingers, the slither of stones, the lone
Second of silence, the nightmare thud. Then only
The wind and the muted beat of unknowing cascades.

VIII

Somehow I worked down the fifty impossible feet
To the ledge, calling and getting no answer but echoes
Released in the cirque, and trying not to reflect
What an answer would mean. He lay still, with his lean

Young face upturned and strangely unmarred, but his legs
Splayed beneath him, beside the final drop,
Six hundred feet sheer to the ice. My throat stopped
When I reached him, for he was alive. He opened his gray

Straight eyes and brokenly murmured "over . . . over."
And I, feeling beneath him a cruel fang
Of the ledge thrust in his back, but not understanding,
Mumbled stupidly, "Best not to move," and spoke

Of his pain. But he said, "I can't move. . . . If only I felt
Some pain." Then my shame stung the tears to my eyes
As I crouched, and I cursed myself, but he cried,
Louder, "No, Bobbie! Don't ever blame yourself.

I didn't test my foothold." He shut the lids
Of his eyes to the stare of the sky, while I moistened his lips
From our water flask and tearing my shirt into strips
I swabbed the shredded hands. But the blood slid

From his side and stained the stone and the thirsting lichens,
And yet I dared not lift him up from the gore
Of the rock. Then he whispered, "Bob, I want to go over!"
This time I knew what he meant and I grasped for a lie

And said, "I'll be back here by midnight with ropes
And men from the camp and we'll cradle you out." But I knew

That the day and the night must pass and the cold dews
Of another morning before such men unknowing

The ways of mountains could win to the chimney's top.
And then, how long? And he knew . . . and the hell of hours
After that, if he lived till we came, roping him out.
But I curled beside him and whispered, "The bleeding will stop.

You can last." He said only, "Perhaps. . . . For what? A wheelchair,
Bob?" His eyes brightening with fever upbraided me.
I could not look at him more and said, "Then I'll stay
With you." But he did not speak, for the clouding fever.

I lay dazed and stared at the long valley,
The glistening hair of a creek on the rug stretched
By the firs, while the sun leaned round and flooded the ledge,
The moss, and David still as a broken doll.

I hunched to my knees to leave, but he called and his voice
Now was sharpened by fear. "For Christ's sake push me over!
If I could move. . . . Or die. . . . " The sweat ran from his forehead,
But only his eyes moved. A hawk was buoying

Blackly its wings over the wrinkled ice.
The purr of a waterfall rose and sank with the wind.
Above us climbed the last joint of the Finger
Beckoning bleakly the wide indifferent sky.

Even then in the sun it grew cold lying there. . . . And I knew
He had tested his holds. It was I who had not. . . . I looked
At the blood on the ledge, and the far valley. I looked
At last in his eyes. He breathed, "I'd do it for you, Bob."

IX

I will not remember how nor why I could twist
Up the wind-devilled peak, and down through the chimney's empty
Horror, and over the traverse alone. I remember
Only the pounding fear I would stumble on It

When I came to the grave-cold maw of the bergschrund . . . reeling
Over the sun-cankered snowbridge, shying the caves
In the névé . . . the fear, and the need to make sure It was there
On the ice, the running and falling and running, leaping

Of gaping greenthroated crevasses, alone and pursued
By the Finger's lengthening shadow. At last through the fanged
And blinding seracs I slid to the milky wrangling
Falls at the glacier's snout, through the rocks piled huge

On the humped moraine, and into the spectral larches,
Alone. By the glooming lake I sank and chilled
My mouth but I could not rest and stumbled still
To the valley, losing my way in the ragged marsh.

I was glad of the mire that covered the stains, on my ripped
Boots, of his blood, but panic was on me, the reek
Of the bog, the purple glimmer of toadstools obscene
In the twilight. I staggered clear to a firewaste, tripped

And fell with a shriek on my shoulder. It somehow eased
My heart to know I was hurt, but I did not faint
And I could not stop while over me hung the range
Of the Sawback. In blackness I searched for the trail by the creek

And found it. . . . My feet squelched a slug and horror
Rose again in my nostrils. I hurled myself
Down the path. In the woods behind some animal yelped.
Then I saw the glimmer of tents and babbled my story.

I said that he fell straight to the ice where they found him,
And none but the sun and incurious clouds have lingered
Around the marks of that day on the ledge of the Finger,
That day, the last of my youth, on the last of our mountains.

Toronto 1940

Earle Birney

The Bear on the Delhi Road

Unreal   tall as a myth
by the road the Himalayan bear
is beating the brilliant air
with his crooked arms
About him two men   bare
spindly as locusts   leap

One pulls on a ring
in the great soft nose   His mate
flicks   flicks with a stick
up at the rolling eyes

They have not led him here
down from the fabulous hills
to this bald alien plain
and the clamorous world   to kill
but simply to teach him to dance

They are peaceful both   these spare
men of Kashmir   and the bear
alive is their living   too
If   far on the Delhi way
around him galvanic they dance
it is merely to wear   wear
from his shaggy body the tranced
wish forever to stay
only an ambling bear
four-footed in berries

It is no more joyous for them
in this hot dust to prance
out of reach of the praying claws
sharpened to paw for ants
in the shadows of deodars
It is not easy to free
myth from reality
or rear this fellow up
to lurch   lurch with them
in the tranced dancing of men

Srinigar 1958 / Île des Porquerolles 1959

Dionne Brand

Blues Spiritual for Mammy Prater

On looking at 'the photograph of Mammy Prater an ex-slave, 115 years old when her photograph was taken'

she waited for her century to turn
she waited until she was one hundred and fifteen
years old to take a photograph
to take a photograph and to put those eyes in it
she waited until the technique of photography was
suitably developed
to make sure the picture would be clear
to make sure no crude daguerreotype would lose
her image
would lose her lines and most of all her eyes
and her hands
she knew the patience of one hundred and fifteen years
she knew that if she had the patience,
to avoid killing a white man
that I would see this photograph
she waited until it suited her
to take this photograph and to put those eyes in it.

in the hundred and fifteen years which it took her to
wait for this photograph she perfected this pose
she sculpted it over a shoulder of pain,
a thing like despair which she never called
this name for she would not have lasted
the fields, the ones she ploughed
on the days that she was a mule, left
their etching on the gait of her legs
deliberately and unintentionally
she waited, not always silently, not always patiently,
for this self portrait
by the time she sat in her black dress, white collar,
white handkerchief, her feet had turned to marble,
her heart burnished red,
and her eyes.

she waited one hundred and fifteen years
until the science of photography passed tin and

talbotype for a surface sensitive enough
to hold her eyes
she took care not to lose the signs
to write in those eyes what her fingers could not script
a pact of blood across a century, a decade and more
she knew then that it would be me who would find
her will, her meticulous account, her eyes,
her days when waiting for this photograph
was all that kept her sane
she planned it down to the day,
the light,
the superfluous photographer
her breasts,
her hands
this moment of
my turning the leaves of a book,
noticing, her eyes.

Robert Bringhurst

Sunday Morning

for Don McKay & Jan Zwicky

Moonset at sunrise, the mind
dividing between them. The teeth
of the young sun sink through the breast of the cloud.
And a great white pelican rests in the bay,
on his way from Great Slave Lake
to Guatemala.
The mind is made out of the animals
it has attended.
In all the unspoken languages,
it is their names.

To know is to hold no opinions: to know
meaning thinks, thinking means.
The mind is the place not already taken.
The mind is not-yet-gathered beads of water
in the teeth of certain leaves—
Saxifraga punctata, close by the stream

under the ridge leading south to Mount Hozameen,
for example—and the changing answers of the moon.
The mind is light rain gathered
on the ice-scarred rock, a crumpled mirror.

To be is to speak with the bristlecone
pines and the whitebarks,
glaciers and rivers, grasses and schists,
and if it is permitted, once also
with pelicans. Being
is what there is room for in that
conversation. The loved is what stays
in the mind; that is, it has meaning,
and meaning keeps going. This
is the definition of meaning.

What is is not speech.
What is is the line
between the unspeakable
and the already spoken.

Roy Daniells

"Three lecture hours per week"

Take care when you lift the little copper bottle
You do not wake the genie. He is drowned
In your old drugs and safely under throttle,
Darkened and deadened, all his powers bound.
Pour gently into the teaspoon's silver bowl
And give in lukewarm water thrice a week
The thick dark liquor that might incite the soul
But O take care he does not wake or speak.
Put the top back on quickly. He is a spirit
Able to raise your prostrate crew as kings
And priests that his imperial halls inherit
Filled with unspeakable and glorious things.
Able to wither you with one slight breath.
All they who bound him go down into death.

A.M. Klein

Portrait of the Poet as Landscape

I

Not an editorial-writer, bereaved with bartlett,
mourns him, the shelved Lycidas.
No actress squeezes a glycerine tear for him.
The radio broadcast lets his passing pass.
And with the police, no record. Nobody, it appears,
either under his real name or his alias,
missed him enough to report.

It is possible that he is dead, and not discovered.
It is possible that he can be found some place
in a narrow closet, like the corpse in a detective story,
standing, his eyes staring, and ready to fall on his face.
It is also possible that he is alive
and amnesiac, or mad, or in retired disgrace,
or beyond recognition lost in love.

We are sure only that from our real society
he has disappeared; he simply does not count,
except in the pullulation of vital statistics —
somebody's vote, perhaps, an anonymous taunt
of the Gallup poll, a dot in a government table —
but not felt, and certainly far from eminent —
in a shouting mob, somebody's sigh.

O, he who unrolled our culture from his scroll —
the prince's quote, the rostrum-rounding roar —
who under one name made articulate
heaven, and under another the seven-circled air,
is, if he is at all, a number, an x,
a Mr. Smith in a hotel register, —
incognito, lost, lacunal.

II

The truth is he's not dead, but only ignored —
like the mirroring lenses forgotten on a brow

that shine with the guilt of their unnoticed world.
The truth is he lives among neighbours, who, though they will allow
him a passable fellow, think him eccentric, not solid,
a type that one can forgive, and for that matter, forego.

Himself he has his moods, just like a poet.
Sometimes, depressed to nadir, he will think all lost,
will see himself as throwback, relict, freak,
his mother's miscarriage, his great-grandfather's ghost,
and he will curse his quintuplet senses, and their tutors
in whom he put, as he should not have put, his trust.

Then he will remember his travels over that body—
the torso verb, the beautiful face of the noun,
and all those shaped and warm auxiliaries!
A first love it was, the recognition of his own.
Dear limbs adverbial, complexion of adjective,
dimple and dip of conjugation!

And then remember how this made a change in him
affecting for always the glow and growth of his being;
how suddenly was aware of the air, like shaken tinfoil,
of the patents of nature, the shock of belated seeing,
the lonelinesses peering from the eyes of crowds;
the integers of thought; the cube-roots of feeling.

Thus, zoomed to zenith, sometimes he hopes again,
and sees himself as a character, with a rehearsed role:
the Count of Monte Cristo, come for his revenges;
the unsuspected heir, with papers; the risen soul;
or the chloroformed prince awaking from his flowers;
or—deflated again—the convict on parole.

III

He is alone; yet not completely alone.
Pins on a map of a colour similar to his,
each city has one, sometimes more than one:
here, caretakers of art, in colleges;
in offices, there, with arm-bands, and green-shaded;
and there, pounding their catalogued beats in libraries,—

everywhere menial, a shadow's shadow.
And always for their egos—their outmoded art.
Thus, having lost the bevel in the ear,

they know neither up nor down, mistake the part
for the whole, curl themselves in a comma,
talk technics, make a colon their eyes. They distort—

such is the pain of their frustration—truth
to something convolute and cerebral.
How they do fear the slap of the flat of the platitude!
Now Pavlov's victims, their mouths water at bell,
the platter empty.
                    See they set twenty-one jewels
into their watches; the time they do not tell!

Some, patagonian in their own esteem,
and longing for the multiplying word,
join party and wear pins, now have a message,
an ear, and the convention-hall's regard.
Upon the knees of ventriloquists, they own,
of their dandled brightness, only the paint and board.

And some go mystical, and some go mad.
One stares at a mirror all day long, as if
to recognize himself; another courts
angels,—for here he does not fear rebuff;
and a third, alone, and sick with sex, and rapt,
doodles him symbols convex and concave.

O schizoid solitudes! O purities
curdling upon themselves! Who live for themselves,
or for each other, but for nobody else;
desire affection, private and public loves;
are friendly, and then quarrel and surmise
the secret perversions of each other's lives.

IV

He suspects that something has happened, a law
been passed, a nightmare ordered. Set apart,
he finds himself, with special haircut and dress,
as on a reservation. Introvert.
He does not understand this; sad conjecture
muscles and palls thrombotic on his heart.

He thinks an impostor, having studied his personal biography,
his gestures, his moods, now has come forward to pose

in the shivering vacuums his absence leaves.
Wigged with his laurel, that other, and faked with his face,
he pats the heads of his children, pecks his wife,
and is at home, and slippered, in his house.

So he guesses at the impertinent silhouette
that talks to his phone-piece and slits open his mail.
Is it the local tycoon who for a hobby
plays poet, he so epical in steel?
The orator, making a pause? Or is that man
he who blows his flash of brass in the jittering hall?

Or is he cuckolded by the troubadour
rich and successful out of celluloid?
Or by the don who unrhymes atoms? Or
the chemist death built up? Pride, lost impostor'd pride,
it is another, another, whoever he is,
who rides where he should ride.

V

Fame, the adrenalin: to be talked about;
to be a verb; to be introduced as *The*;
to smile with endorsement from slick paper; make
caprices anecdotal; to nod to the world; to see
one's name like a song upon the marquees played;
to be forgotten with embarrassment; to be—
to be.

It has its attractions, but is not the thing;
nor is it the ape mimesis who speaks from the tree
ancestral; nor the merkin joy . . .
Rather it is stark infelicity
which stirs him from his sleep, undressed, asleep
to walk upon roofs and window-sills and defy
the gape of gravity.

VI

Therefore he seeds illusions. Look, he is
the nth Adam taking a green inventory
in world but scarcely uttered, naming, praising,
the flowering fiats in the meadow, the
syllabled fur, stars aspirate, the pollen

whose sweet collision sounds eternally.
For to praise

the world—he, solitary man—is breath
to him. Until it has been praised, that part
has not been. Item by exciting item—
air to his lungs, and pressured blood to his heart.—
they are pulsated, and breathed, until they map,
not the world's, but his own body's chart!

And now in imagination he has climbed
another planet, the better to look
with single camera view upon this earth—
its total scope, and each afflated tick,
its talk, its trick its tracklessness—and this,
this he would like to write down in a book!

To find a new function for the déclassé craft
archaic like the fletcher's; to make a new thing;
to say the word that will become sixth sense;
perhaps by necessity and indirection bring
new forms to life, anonymously, new creeds—
O, somehow pay back the daily larcenies of the lung!

These are not mean ambitions. It is already something
merely to entertain them. Meanwhile, he
makes of his status as zero a rich garland,
a halo of his anonymity,
and lives alone, and in his secret shines
like phosphorus. At the bottom of the sea.

Robert Kroetsch

from Seed Catalogue

I.

No. 176—*Copenhagen Market Cabbage:* "This *new introduction,
strictly speaking,* is in every respect a *thoroughbred,* a *cabbage* of
highest pedigree, and is *creating considerable flurry* among *professional
gardeners* all *over the world.*"

We took the storm windows/off
the south side of the house
and put them on the hotbed.
Then it was spring. Or, no:
then winter was ending.

> "I wish to say we had lovely success
> this summer with the seed purchased
> of you. We had the finest Sweet
> Corn in the country, and Cabbage
> were dandy."
> —W. W. Lyon, South Junction, Man.

> My mother said:
> Did you wash your ears?
> You could grow cabbages
> in those ears.

Winter was ending.
This is what happened:
we were harrowing the garden.
You've got to understand this:
I was sitting on the horse.
The horse was standing still.
I fell off.

> The hired man laughed: how
> in hell did you manage to
> fall off a horse that was
> *standing still?*

Bring me the radish seeds,
my mother whispered.

Into the dark of January
the seed catalogue bloomed

a winter proposition, if
spring should come, then,

with illustrations:

No. 25—*McKenzie's Improved Golden Wax Bean:* "THE MOST PRIZED
OF ALL BEANS. *Virtue* is its own reward. We have had *many expressions*
from *keen discriminating gardeners extolling our seed* and *this variety.*"

Beans, beans,
the musical fruit;
the more you eat,
the more you virtue.

My mother was marking the first row
with a piece of binder twine, stretched
between two pegs.

The hired man laughed: just
about planted the little bugger.
Cover him up and see what grows.

My father didn't laugh. He was puzzled
by any garden that was smaller than a
quarter-section of wheat and summerfallow.

the home place: N.E. 17-42-16-W4th Meridian.

the home place: one and a half miles west of Heisler, Alberta,
                 on the correction line road
                 and three miles south.

No trees
around the house.
Only the wind.
Only the January snow.
Only the summer sun.
The home place:
a terrible symmetry.

How do you grow a gardener?

> Telephone Peas
> Garden Gem Carrots
> Early Snowcap Cauliflower
> Perfection Globe Onions
> Hubbard Squash
> Early Ohio Potatoes

This is what happened—at my mother's wake. This
is a fact—the World Series was in progress. The
Cincinnati Reds were playing the Detroit Tigers.
It was raining. The road to the graveyard was barely
passable. The horse was standing still. Bring me
the radish seeds, my mother whispered.

Archibald Lampman

The City of the End of Things

Beside the pounding cataracts
Of midnight streams unknown to us
'Tis builded in the leafless tracts
And valleys huge of Tartarus.
Lurid and lofty and vast it seems;
It hath no rounded name that rings,
But I have heard it called in dreams
The City of the End of Things.

Its roofs and iron towers have grown
None knoweth how high within the night,
But in its murky streets far down
A flaming terrible and bright
Shakes all the stalking shadows there,
Across the walls, across the floors,
And shifts upon the upper air
From out a thousand furnace doors:
And all the while an awful sound

Keeps roaring on continually,
And crashes in the ceaseless round
Of a gigantic harmony.
Through its grim depths re-echoing
And all its weary height of walls,
With measured roar and iron ring,
The inhuman music lifts and falls.
Where no thing rests and no man is,
And only fire and night hold sway;
The beat, the thunder and the hiss
Cease not, and change not, night nor day.
And moving at unheard commands,
The abysses and vast fires between,
Flit figures that with clanking hands
Obey a hideous routine;
They are not flesh, they are not bone,
They see not with the human eye,
And from their iron lips is blown
A dreadful and monotonous cry;
And whoso of our mortal race
Should find that city unaware,
Lean Death would smite him face to face,
And blanch him with its venomed air:
Or caught by the terrific spell,
Each thread of memory snapt and cut,
His soul would shrivel and its shell
Go rattling like an empty nut.

It was not always so, but once,
In days that no man thinks upon,
Fair voices echoed from its stones,
The light above it leaped and shone:
Once there were multitudes of men,
That built that city in their pride,
Until its might was made, and then
They withered age by age and died.
But now of that prodigious race,
Three only in an iron tower,
Set like carved idols face to face,
Remain the masters of its power;
And at the city gate a fourth,
Gigantic and with dreadful eyes,
Sits looking toward the lightless north,
Beyond the reach of memories;
Fast rooted to the lurid floor,

A bulk that never moves a jot,
In his pale body dwells no more,
Or mind or soul,—an idiot!
But sometime in the end those three
Shall perish and their hands be still,
And with the master's touch shall flee
Their incommunicable skill.
A stillness absolute as death
Along the slacking wheels shall lie,
And, flagging at a single breath,
The fires that moulder out and die.
The roar shall vanish at its height,
And over that tremendous town
The silence of eternal night
Shall gather close and settle down.
All its grim grandeur, tower and hall,
Shall be abandoned utterly,
And into rust and dust shall fall
From century to century;
Nor ever living thing shall grow,
Nor trunk of tree, nor blade of grass;
No drop shall fall, no wind shall blow,
Nor sound of any foot shall pass:
Alone of its accursèd state,
One thing the hand of Time shall spare,
For the grim Idiot at the gate
Is deathless and eternal there.

Patrick Lane

Winter 45

The man without a name who reversed his snowshoes
and walked forward, head down, shoulders hunched.
The man who climbed the mountains
in the heart of winter, crossing the pass,
heading west into the snow.

The one they followed.

The many trails he made, each one
a perfect map, a calligraphy
for those who pursued him.
His turning upon himself,
an animal born into his own making,
crossing and recrossing his tracks.

This way, this way, they would shout.

Him walking, head down, shoulders hunched, moving
toward his own quick death, his breath
breaking sharp and hard,
entering,
leaving.

Irving Layton

Whatever Else Poetry Is Freedom

Whatever else poetry is freedom.
Forget the rhetoric, the trick of lying
All poets pick up sooner or later. From the river,
Rising like the thin voice of grey castratos—the mist;
Poplars and pines grow straight but oaks are gnarled;
Old codgers must speak of death, boys break windows,
Women lie honestly by their men at last.

And I who gave my Kate a blackened eye
Did to its vivid changing colours
Make up an incredible musical scale;
And now I balance on wooden stilts and dance
And thereby sing to the loftiest casements.
See how with polish I bow from the waist.
Space for these stilts! More space or I fail!

And a crown I say for my buffoon's head.
Yet no more fool am I than King Canute,
Lord of our tribe, who scanned and scorned;
Who half-deceived, believed; and, poet, missed
The first white waves come nuzzling at his feet;
Then damned the courtiers and the foolish trial
With a most bewildering and unkingly jest.

It was the mist. It lies inside one like a destiny.
A real Jonah it lies rotting like a lung.
And I know myself undone who am a clown
And wear a wreath of mist for a crown;
Mist with the scent of dead apples,
Mist swirling from black oily waters at evening,
Mist from the fraternal graves of cemeteries.

It shall drive me to beg my food and at last
Hurl me broken I know and prostrate on the road;
Like a huge toad I saw, entire but dead,
That Time mordantly had blacked; O pressed
To the moist earth it pled for entry.
I shall be I say that stiff toad for sick with mist
And crazed I smell the odour of mortality.

And Time flames like a paraffin stove
And what it burns are the minutes I live.
At certain middays I have watched the cars
Bring me from afar their windshield suns;
What lay to my hand were blue fenders,
The suns extinguished, the drivers wearing sunglasses.
And it made me think I had touched a hearse.

So whatever else poetry is freedom. Let
Far off the impatient cadences reveal
A padding for my breathless stilts. Swivel,
O hero, in the fleshy groves, skin and glycerine,
And sing of lust, the sun's accompanying shadow
Like a vampire's wing, the stillness in dead feet—
Your stave brings resurrection, O aggrievèd king.

Dorothy Livesay

from Call My People Home

ANNOUNCER:

This one was young; but he wanted the world
For others. A philosopher,
He accepted the blow, Pearl Harbor.
He learned the way of waiting.

THE STUDENT:

To be alone is grace; to see it clear
Without rancour; to let the past be
And the future become. Rarely to remember
The painful needles turning in the flesh.

I had looked out of the schoolroom window
And could not see the design, held dear
Of the shaken maples; nor the rain, searing and stinging
The burning rain in the eye.

I could not see, nor hear my name called:
Tatsuo, the Pythagoras theorem!
I could not think till the ruler rapped
On the desk, and my mind snapped.

The schoolroom faded, I could not hold
A book in my hand.
It was the not knowing; the must be gone
Yet the continual fear of going.

Yes, to remember is to go back; to take
The path along the dyke, the lands of my uncle
Stretching away from the river—
The dykeside where we played

Under his fruit trees, canopied with apples,
Falling asleep under a hedgerow of roses
To the gull's shrill chatter and the tide's recurrent
Whisper in the marshland that was home . . .

To be alone is grace; to see it clear
Without rancour; to let the past be
And the future become. Especially to remember
The habit of grace; chosen, accepted.

CHORUS OF NISEIS:

Home, we discover, is where life is:
Not Manitoba's wheat
Ontario's walled cities
Nor a B.C. fishing fleet.

Home is something more than harbour—
Than father, mother, sons:
Home is the white face leaning over your shoulder
As well as the darker ones.

Home is labour, with the hand and heart,
The hard doing, and the rest when done:
A rougher ocean than we knew, a tougher earth,
A more magnetic sun.

Eli Mandel

The Madwomen of the Plaza de Mayo

They wear white scarves and shawls.
They carry pictures on strings about their necks.
I have seen their faces elsewhere:
in Ereceira, fishermen's wives
walking in dark processions
to the sea, its roaring,
women of Ireland
wearing their dark scarves
hearing the echo of guns, bombs

Identities
the *desaparecidos*
lost ones
the disappeared

in the Plaza the Presidential Palace
reveals soldiers like fences with steel spikes
the rhythm of lost bodies
the rhythm of loss

A soldier is a man who is not a man.
A fence, a spike
A nail in somebody's eye.
Lost man.

Why are the women weeping?
For whom do they cry
under the orange moon
under the lemon moon of Buenos Aires?

"If only for humanitarian reasons
tell the families of the living
where are they
tell the families of the dead
what they need
what they deserve to know."

No one speaks.
The junta says nothing.
The *desaparecidos* remain silent.
The moon has no language.

Daphne Marlatt

---

from Booking passage

this coming and going in the dark of early morning, snow scribbling its thawline round the house. we are undercover, under a cover of white you unlock your door on this slipperiness.

to throw it off, this cover, this blank that halts a kiss on the open road. i kiss you anyway, and feel you veer toward me, red tail lights aflare at certain patches, certain turns my tongue takes, provocative.

we haven't even begun to write . . . sliding the in-between as the ferry slips its shoreline, barely noticeable at first, a gathering beat of engines in reverse, the shudder of the turn to make that long passage out—

the price for this.

we stood on the road in the dark. you closed the door so carlight wouldn't shine on us. our kiss reflected in snow, the name for this.

under the covers, morning, you take my scent, writing me into your cells' history. deep in our sentencing, i smell you home.

there is the passage. there is the *booking*—and our fear of this.

you, sliding past the seals inert on the log boom. you slide and they don't raise their heads. you are into our current now of going, not inert, not even gone as i lick you loose. there is a light beginning over the ridge of my closed eyes.

passage booked. i see you by the window shore slips by, you reading Venice our history is, that sinking feel, those footings under water. i nose the book aside and pull you forward gently with my lips.

a path, channel or duct. a corridor. a book and not a book. not *booked* but off the record. this.

irresistible melt of hot flesh. furline and thawline align your long wet descent.

nothing in the book says where we might head. my tongue in you, your body cresting now around, around this tip's lip-suck surge rush of your coming in other words.

we haven't even begun to write . . . what keeps us going, this rush of wingspread, this under (nosing in), this wine-dark blood flower. this rubbing between the word and our skin.

tell me, tell me where you are when the bush closes in, all heat a luxuriance of earth so heavy i can't breathe the stifling wall of prickly rose, skreek of mosquito poised . . . for the wall to break the wall that isolates, that i so late to this: it doesn't, it slides apart—footings, walls, galleries, this island architecture

one layer under the other, memory a ghost, a guide, histolytic where the pain is stored, murmur, *mer-mère*, historicity stored in the tissue, text . . . a small boat, fraught. trying to cross distance, trying to find that passage (secret). in libraries where whole texts, whole persons have been secreted away.

original sin he said was a late overlay. and under that and under that? sweat pouring down, rivers of thyme and tuberose in the words that climb toward your scanning eyes

She shouts aloud, Come! we know it; | thousand-eared night repeats that cry | across the sea shining between us

this tracking back and forth across the white, this tearing of papyrus crosswise, this tearing of love in our mouths to leave our mark in the midst of rumour, coming out.

. . . to write in lesbian.

the dark swell of a sea that separates and beats against our joined feet, islands me in the night, fear and rage the isolate talking in my head. to combat this slipping away, of me, of you, the steps . . . what was it we held in trust, tiny as a Venetian bead, fragile as words encrusted with pearl, *mathetriai*, not-mother, hidden mentor, lost link?

to feel our age we stood in the road in the dark, we stood in the roads and it was this old, a ripple of water against the hull, a coming and going

we began with . . .

her drowned thyme and clover, fields of it heavy with dew our feet soak up, illicit hands cupped one in the other as carlights pick us out. the yell a salute. marked, we are elsewhere,

translated here . . .

like her, precisely on this page, this mark: *a thin flame runs under / my skin.* twenty-five hundred years ago, this trembling then. actual as that which wets our skin her words come down to us, a rush, poured through the blood, this coming and going among islands is.

P.K. Page

Portrait of Marina

Far out the sea has never moved. It is
Prussian forever, rough as teazled wool
some antique skipper worked into a frame
to bear his lost four-master.
                              Where it hangs
now in a sunny parlour, none recalls
how all his stitches, interspersed with oaths
had made his one pale spinster daughter grow
transparent with migraines—and how his call
fretted her more than waves.
                              Her name
Marina, for his youthful wish—
boomed at the font of that small salty church
where sailors lurched like drunkards—would, he felt
make her a water woman, rich with bells.
To her the name Marina simply meant
he held his furious needle for her thin
fingers to thread again with more blue wool
to sew the ocean of his memory.
Now, where the picture hangs, a dimity
young island housewife with inherited
clocks under bells and ostrich eggs on shelves
pours amber tea in small rice china cups
and reconstructs
how great-great-grandpapa at ninety-three
his fingers knotted with arthritis, his
old eyes grown agatey with cataracts
became as docile as a child again—
that fearful salty man—

and sat, wrapped round in faded paisley shawls
gently embroidering.
While Aunt Marina in grey worsted, warped
without a smack of salt, came to his call
the sole survivor of his last shipwreck.

■ ■ ■

Slightly off shore it glints. Each wave is capped
with broken mirrors. Like Marina's head
the glinting of these waves.
She walked forever antlered with migraines
her pain forever putting forth new shoots
until her strange unlovely head became
a kind of candelabra—delicate—
where all her tears were perilously hung
and caught the light as waves that catch the sun.
The salt upon the panes, the grains of sand
that crunched beneath her heel
her father's voice, 'Marina!'—all these broke
her trembling edifice. The needle shook
like ice between her fingers.
In her head
too many mirrors dizzied her and broke.

■ ■ ■

But where the wave breaks, where it rises green
turns into gelatin, becomes a glass
simply for seeing stones through, runs across
the coloured shells and pebbles of the shore
and makes an aspic of them
then sucks back
in foam and undertow—
this aspect of the sea
Marina never knew.

For her the sea was Father's Fearful Sea
harsh with sea serpents
winds and drowning men.
For her it held no spiral of a shell
for her descent to dreams,
it held no bells.
And where it moved in shallows it was more
imminently a danger, more alive
than where it lay off shore full fathom five.

Al Purdy

Darwin's Theology?

—stand under the great sky round
            circling these islands
where the absence of a god
leaves a larger vacuum
than a presence could fill
with a presence
sea and sky completely occupied
by the non-existent monster

Galapagos Islands

F.R. Scott

Audacity

("Audacity is missing in Canada." The Times *30/11/59)*

They say we lack audacity, that we are middle class, without the
      adventurousness that arises from the desperation of the lower
      classes or the tradition of the upper classes.
They say we are more emphatically middling than any country
      west of Switzerland, and that boldness and experiment are far
      from our complacent thoughts.
But I say to you, they do not know where to look, and have not
      the eyes to see.
For audacity is all around us,
Boldness sits in the highest places,
We are riddled with insolence.

Do you want audacity?
Let me tell you—
Any day in Montreal you may hear the guns crack at the

noon-hour, as the police give chase to the bank-robbers

Who are helping themselves to the wealth of the land like the
French and the English before them, *coureur de bois* and
fur-trader rolled into one;

You may watch the patrol cars circle their beats to gather the
weekly pay-off from unlicensed cafés

Whose owners sell booze on the side to acquire the $15,000 they
need for the $25-permit;

You may learn the name of the distinguished Legislative
Councillor who controls the *caisse-électorale*

Into which rattles the coin that makes possible the letting of
contracts,

And who tips his hat to the priest

And is saluted respectfully in return;

You may marvel at the boldness of promoters of oil and natural
gas, men too quick for production, fixers and peddlers,

Getting their hands on concessions and rights, access to
underground treasures awaiting man's use in the womb of
our northland,

Playing the suckers and markets, turning their thousands to
millions, loading the pipe-lines with overhead that is paid by
the housewife who cooks her spaghetti,

Then solemnly demanding higher rates for sales of the product
(extra hot, natural gas!) before friends on the Board of
Control:

You may follow the hucksters and admen compiling their
budgets, planning the assault on "public opinion," setting the
poll-questions,

Writing editorials for weeklies, letters to editors, telegrams to
senators, articles for journals,

Day after day on the job of confusing the issue, baiting the
eggheads, laughing at the "culture kids" of CBC, fixing the
give-aways,

Posing as democracy's friends and admirers, while undermining
the concept of government and welfare,

Singing the praises of free enterprise that relies on high tariffs,
defence contracts and floor prices;

You may stand in awe at the audacity of journalists, twisting the
news items by headline and rewrite, blanking out truth,

Ponderously laying down the conventional wisdom in
unconventional English,

While a few owners gather dailies into chains run by gangs of
paid hack-men,

Then add on the radio stations and TV outlets, lest some glimmer
of free opinion escape them;

You may be amazed at the boldness of churchmen and ministers,
  meeting in synod and conclave and conference to spy out our
  sinfulness,
Who wax indignant over lotteries, horse-racing and the drink
  question, or, with Savonarola intensity,
Denounce crime-comics and short bathing-suits;
But all this is as nothing, not worthy of mention,
Beside the supreme, the breath-taking audacity
Of the great executives in their panelled boardrooms
Found at every point in the social structure where policy is laid
  down or decision taken,
Without whom no hospital can be opened, no charitable
  campaign launched, no church can engage a preacher and no
  university can build a building,
Daring to be omniscient, omnipotent, omnipresent, not to
  mention omnivorous—
These surely you can see in this Canada of ours, O London
  Times,
In this country that has the audacity to proclaim the "supremacy
  of God"
In its Bill of Rights?

Carol Shields

Lost Things
By Mary Swann

It sometimes happens when looking for
Lost objects, a book, a picture or
A coin or spoon,
That something falls across the mind—
Not quite a shadow but what a shadow would be
In a place that lacked light.

As though the lost things have withdrawn
Into themselves, books returned
To paper or wood or thought,

Coins and spoons to simple ores,
Lustreless and without history,
Waiting out of sight

And becoming part of a larger loss
Without a name
Or definition or form
Not unlike what touches us
In moments of shame.

A.J.M. Smith

The Lonely Land

(SECOND VERSION)

Cedar and jagged fir
Uplift accusing barbs
Against the grey
And cloud-piled sky;
And in the bay
Blown spume and windrift
And thin, bitter spray
Snap
At the whirling sky;
And the pine trees
Lean one way.

A wild duck
Calls to her mate,
And the ragged
And passionate tones
Stagger and fall,
And recover,
And stagger and fall,
On these stones,

(FINAL VERSION)

Cedar and jagged fir
uplift sharp barbs
against the gray
and cloud-piled sky;
and in the bay
blown spume and windrift
and thin, bitter spray
snap
at the whirling sky;
and the pine trees
lean one way.

A wild duck calls
to her mate,
and the ragged
and passionate tones
stagger and fall,
and recover,
and stagger and fall,
on these stones–

Are lost
In the lapping of water
On smooth, flat stones.

This is a beauty of dissonance,
This is a desolate splendour,
This resonance
Of stony strand,
This smoky cry curled over a black pine.
These are the poems of Canada,
Resinous scent of the balsam,
Cold sting
Of blown spray,
Cry of wild duck over Long Lake
When the wind bends the pines
South
And curdles the sky
From the north.

are lost
in the lapping of water
on smooth, flat stones.

This is a beauty
of dissonance,
this resonance
of stony strand,
this smoky cry
curled over a black pine
like a broken
and wind-battered branch
when the wind
bends the tips of the pines
and curdles the sky
from the north.

This is the beauty
of strength
broken by strength,
and still strong.

Fred Wah

From *Breathin' My Name with a Sigh*

(Arrangement of these excerpts by Susan Rudy Dorscht)

[EXCERPT 1]

my father hurt-
ing at the table
sitting hurting
at suppertime
deep inside very
far down inside
because I can't stand the ginger
in the beef and greens
he cooked for us tonight
and years later tonight
that look on his face
appears now on mine
my children
my food
their food
my father
their father
me mine
the father
very far
very very far
inside

[EXCERPT 2]

     mmmmmm

     hm

     mmmmmm

     hm

[EXCERPT 3]

mother
somewhere
remember
whoever
forever
to fly over
love her
pleases her
caress
close
careless
loss
most
moist
remove her
mutter
mummy
maybe
habit
added-up
puddled
mud
cleaver
pie
calamity
dust
wax
because of her
house
window
Saskatchewan
radio
air

yuhh	Yeh	Yeh	breath
			quiet
thuh moon			just
			Mary
			baby
huh^h	wu	wu	lady
			cream
unh	unh	nguh	swede
			more-to-me
w_____h			names
			remember
w_____h			her
			corrine
			kar en
			clean
			heart
			core
			remember you flying over me mommy
			outside a moist loss
			touch & float

Wilfred Watson

---

from *Gramsci x3*

EPILOGUE TO GRAMSCI 1

Lights *up to Tatiana. She has been writing letters. These have been to relatives and friends of Antonio Gramsci, informing them of his death on April 27, 1937. She has just finished a letter to Teresina and Edmea, which has been very difficult for her to write.*

Tatiana *reads*

Tatiana,	*1*	to
and	*2*	Teresina
Edmea,	*3*	sad
Your	*4*	greetings.
uncle	*5*	Nino

	died	6	Gramsci
	a	7	month
	today,	8	ago
9	May		

	the	1	twenty-seventh.
	release	2	His
	from	3	prison
	a	4	came
	few	5	days
	he	6	before
	died,	7	but
	authorities	8	the
9	hadn't		

	got	1	round
	complete	2	to
	the	3	formalities
	to	4	required
	discharge	5	him.
	will	6	I
	write	7	more
	I've	8	when
9	got		

	over	1	my
	physical	2	own
	weaknesses,	3	which
	minor	4	seemed
	as	5	long
	he	6	as
	was	7	being
	to	8	subjected
9	cruelties		

	which	1	were
	to	2	intended
	break	3	his
	but	4	spirit
	never	5	did.
	was	6	He
	arrested	7	in
		8	Rome
9	November		

eighth,	*1*	1926,
sent	*2*	and
to	*3*	the
of	*4*	island
Ustica,	*5*	where
prisoners	*6*	political
were	*7*	kept
house	*8*	under

9   arrest.

In	*1*	January
he	*2*	1927
was	*3*	transferred
prison	*4*	to
in	*5*	Milan.
May	*6*	In
1928	*7*	he
tried	*8*	was

9   at

Rome	*1*	and
to	*2*	condemned
twenty	*3*	years'
A	*4*	imprisonment.
medical	*5*	examination
him	*6*	revealed
to	*7*	need
medical	*8*	special

9   treatment

not	*1*	available
prison	*2*	in
and	*3*	recommended
He	*4*	clemency.
instead	*5*	was
to	*6*	sent
the	*7*	prison
at	*8*	hospital

9   Turi.

After	*1*	five
of	*2*	years
medical	*3*	neglect
he	*4*	there,
was	*5*	transferred

a	6	to
clinic	7	in
and	8	Formia

9   after

there,	1	to
clinic	2	another
in	3	Rome,
he	4	where
died,	5	just
his	6	before
release	7	from
not	8	custody,

9   just

afterwards,	1	as
I	2	intended.
will	3	write
length	4	at
later	5	and
spare	6	not
you	7	or
the	8	myself

9   truth. Your aunt Tatiana.

BLACKOUT

Phyllis Webb

"Krakatoa" and "Spiritual Storm"

for Dorothy Livesay and bill bissett

Hot magma
          indigo dawn
wild yelps
          of pure physics
crack open deep sea
buttocks thrust up love lava

world heart/broken/cardiac
arrest.
Krakatoa. Krakatau.

The small gods gather
for countdown, each lifts
a finger to the wind (quake,
tide, tsunami) tastes
the cost of all-paroxysmal
sexual storm, lid blown off,
creator creating, a whim,
wham of blowup on shores—
Java, Sumatra, Hawaii—
blasting away 2200 miles heard,
Krakatoan wind circling the dust
up high enough. Radiant

marvellous sunsets for years.
Spectacle. Le monocle de mon
oncle set flying into the eye
of the storm (*spiritual* for him,
timbre just right, *pinhead*).

God how I suffer to get this down as if I'd
been there watching the lava hit and run after
dogs and children and hens, cone island collapsing
into the sea. Always this me. Tourist, back-packed,
camera at ready, lens cap removed.

And the big gods come, finally, to the Pacific
for 36,000 dead, fallout, cinders, oracular
birth of Anak (child of) Krakatoa. Bad mouth.
Ash. Devolution. Darkness at noon.

So be it. So it was: May 20, 1883, "paroxysmal"
blast August 26, "climax" eruption August 27,
10 a.m. Masses of floating pumice near the
volcano so thick as to halt ships. Surrounding
region in darkness two and a half days.
Temperature world-wide lowered $0.27°$.
Plant and animal life gone five years.
Anak (child of) Krakatoa active into
the 1980's.

Genetic spleen

Time lapse backwards

Mortal fear
Cassandra
Nostradamus
"Sons of guns"

I cannot surprise you. Not with the blue jay's
return. Not with the velvet yellow of pansyface,
not with my held-back fire. Apocalypse. Every-
thing predictable in the book. Ominous ocean.
Glacier waterslide. Occult fecal blood's old
testament. Rotted bodies. Sun's eclipse.
Venus swinging below the moon.

Veracity. Storm, calm, dilemmas, ditch-jumps.
Capacity for wonder. The spring of the mouse-
trap sprung, we are caught—thus and so—in
this pose, shadowed beyond doubt. Fire hanging
back for a more effective, filmic test-site,
for desert bloom.

Phyllis Webb

"The Mind of the Poet"

Slippages, repeat performance, soundings profounder as
down we go for the third time through green waters,
pearl-diving, operatic; or dead poets brought back on
their knees second time around, gartersnakes splitting
through mind-burn, matter-disorders. Ho Hum. Jump-
ing bugs. What a parade of fancy-frees, scared shitless
half the time, sorrowing saints, dumb pets waiting for
the can to open. *Bird brains, eagle eyes, sad sacks,*
whose minds float on forgetfulness—to quartz, sapphire,
topaz, emerald-hard memory shards, spooky auditions,
Toad of Toad Hall greeting his guests at the door with his
white butler's gloves on.

PART TWO

Discussions of the Texts

What's in a Genre:
Margaret Atwood's "Notes Towards a Poem"

Frank Davey

The Margaret Atwood text "Notes Towards a Poem That Can Never Be Written" was published in 1981 in a book titled *True Stories* (65-70), in which the fourth page begins "Some of these poems have appeared in . . ." On four occasions here, genre conventions are foregrounded: three times affirmed—"Notes," "*these* poems," "*True* Stories; and once denied—"a Poem That Can *Never* Be Written." The text is published again in 1988 in an anthology titled *15 Canadian Poets X2* (409-11), which is identified by its editor as a "teaching anthology of twentieth-century Canadian poetry." In both publications the poem that can never be *written* is represented by "notes" which, if not "written" in the narrowest sense of the word, have at the very least been typeset, and classified as a "poem." This is a true story. Later an essay can be attempted, if not on the poem that can never be written, then on the notes which have been substituted for this poem, or have been presented with apparent success *as* a story or a poem.

■ ■ ■

The visual signs offered by "Notes Towards a Poem That Can Never Be Written" indicate "poem" somewhat more strongly than they indicate "notes." These signs include none of the signals of haste, incompleteness, or indecision that "notes" connote: no dashes, ellipses, over-writings, or erasures. Rather, they repeat the visual signs established by the surrounding "poems" of the two books they occur in. The lines are arranged in stanza-like units that, in the *15 Canadian Poets* anthology, resemble the stanzas of "Five Poems for Dolls" that precedes it. The lines in both texts stretch one inch to about four inches across the page. Roman numerals interrupt both, arranging the "stanzas" into sections which in one case appear to be the five "poems" of its title and which in the other are possibly separate "notes," or sections of notes. In *True Stories* the text is doubly marked as "notes towards" by being included in a ten-text section of the book also titled "Notes Towards a Poem That Can Never Be Written." These ten texts are visually and prosodically indistinguishable from all but one (a prose piece) of the 28 texts that constitute the remainder of what the back cover announces is "Margaret Atwood's ninth collection of poems."

Other signs in "Notes Towards a Poem" also offer intertextual suggestion that it may be a poem. It begins with a dedication, which "notes" rarely do but which literary texts do often. Its lines open in a syntax—"This is the place"—which is the syntax of the opening lines of numerous "poems" that bear the Margaret Atwood signature— "This is a photograph of me" (*The Circle Game*,

11), "This is before electricity" (*Procedures for Underground*, 7), "This is the one song everyone" (*You Are Happy*, 38), "This is what you changed me to" (30), "This is the plum season" (93). In the anthology this syntax is echoed not only in the opening of "Game After Supper," six pages earlier, but also in lines within the other eight "Atwood" poems the anthology includes: "This is no museum" ("A Women's Issue"), "This is not a smile" ("Five Poems for Dolls"), "This is not order" ("Progressive Insanities of a Pioneer").

■ ■ ■

The title "Notes Towards a Poem That Can Never Be Written" denies the possibility of a written text but appears to leave other possibilities open. "Written" appears to invoke a "speech/writing" dichotomy: the poem that can never be written may be envisaged, imagined, perhaps even spoken or shouted. It is being at least imagined here, foreseen: "notes" are being proposed "towards" it. It can be known other than through an act of full literacy. But the opening lines appear to move against such a possibility. "This is the place / you would rather not know about" they begin, "the place you cannot imagine." Three times these lines repeat "this is the place," affirming place over cognition and imagination—the place that can make one "not know" or "not imagine." What, however, is this "you" that cannot imagine—a generic "you" that signifies humanity-in-general, a "you-reader" addressed by the note-writing originator of the non-poem, or an intradiegetic "you" (one within the text, within the recounted event) whose being addressed by the note-writing subject is witnessed by a "third-party" reader? Does a reader encounter these "notes" in the second person or the third? Does the note-writer construct itself in the second person as well as the first?

■ ■ ■

Part two of the "Notes" begins "There is no poem you can write / about it, the sandpits / where so many were buried." There being "no poem" appears to mark a slight change from the title in which there was at least a poem which notes could be written "towards." Now there seems to be "no poem." But again, "poem" is modified—not "no poem" at all but "no poem *you* can write", or perhaps "no poem you can *write*." What began in the title as a dichotomy between "notes towards" that could be written and the poem that could not, and a covert dichotomy between the envisioned poem, perhaps even the oral poem, and the written, now appears to have taken on a third contrast: between a writing-subject that can write at least "notes towards" a poem, and even pass them off as a "poem" we are reading, and an intradiegetic "you" that can write "no poem." The three dichotomies overlap imprecisely: written notes vs. unwritten poem, oral/imaginary poem vs. [un]written poem, a "you" incapable of writing vs. a writer capable of writing the words we are reading. These imprecisions leave unanswered questions not only about the identity of "you" and about the subject position from which a reader encounters the text, but also about poetry itself: is a written poem more "real" than one envisioned in "notes" but never written?

or is a "poem that can never be written" unwritten because poetry itself is in-capable of representing the horror of political torture, its buried victims, "pain still traced on their skins"? The third of this section's four stanzas suggests that incapability may reside in the kinds of texts that "we" employ to consider such victims: "We make wreaths of adjectives for them, / we count them like beads, / we turn them into statistics & litanies / and into poems like this one." Like the "you" of the first stanza, this "we" is ambiguous, potentially signifying only people like the writing-subject, or the writing-subject and the reader, or the writing-subject and the intradiegetic you. But the signs associated with incapability are not at all ambiguous—they point directly to the conventionality of literature, its literariness: the classical praise of the laurel wreath, the religious gesture of the rosary, the secular twentieth-century faith in statistics. They imply another poem which is somehow not literary, not produced through discursive conven-tions, but somehow more authentically produced, perhaps even "unwritten," through some unspecified, textually unmediated process. All three—wreath, ro-sary, and statistics—point also to death, and associate it with literary convention. They are followed by a fourth sign, "poems," and abruptly the "notes towards a poem" have become one of "poems like this one." But what kind of poem is "this one"?—a failure, no more effective than wreath or rosary? "Nothing works" the next line reports. The "notes" may have inexplicably become a poem, but possibly not the one looked "towards" in the title.

■ ■ ■

In part three, the first- and second-person pronouns of the opening parts yield to an impersonal narration about a woman who lies on a "wet cement floor" under "unending light" wondering "why she is dying." It is this woman's body, the writing-subject announces, "silent and fingerless," that is "writing this poem." Which poem, however, is "this poem"—the text we are reading, the one that will "never be written," the deathly "non-working" poem of the preceding section, or the discursively unmediated one implied by the preceding section? Or are some of these the same poem? Or is the text indeed claiming this dying woman as its writer? The woman and the "poem that can never be written" are se-miotically related, it unwritten, she "silent and fingerless." But she is also, through oxymoron and metaphor, distinct from it and acting to negate its unwrittenness: "writing this poem."

■ ■ ■

Part four appears to recount the torture that the woman whose body "writes this poem" is undergoing. The subject searches unsuccessfully for metaphors to describe the torture—"it resembles an operation / but it is not one / . . . / Partly it's a job / . . . / Partly it's an art." In its failure, the note-writer dem-onstrates the limitations of the kind of poetry considered in part two. It also suggests that art itself may harbour or conceal moral corruption: what is being done to the woman is "partly . . . like a concerto," and "partly it's an art."

If torture can be in part a concerto or an art, it may perhaps also be in part a poem.

■ ■ ■

Part five shifts to the first person singular. The subject responds to someone— perhaps the intradiegetic "you" from before—who has accused it of flawed vision: "why tell me then / there is something wrong with my eyes?" This subject now presents its vision as if it also were conditioned by torture: "this is agony, the eyes taped open / two inches from the sun. / . . . / The razor across the eyeball / . . . / It is also a truth." It addresses its interlocutor as if it, in contrast, had only indirect experience of physical abuse: "What is it you see then? / Is it a bad dream, a hallucination? / Is it a vision?" Here what appeared to be the diegetic situation of the first parts of the poem, a privileged, untortured subject attempting vainly to write a poem about a helpless, silent, fingerless victim of politically motivated torture, seems reversed. It is the victim that now occupies the text's subject position, and who addresses a naively troubled and privileged intradiegetic you: "Witness is what you must bear."

■ ■ ■

At the opening of the text, its geographic and political site was the torture chamber, and implicitly the oppressive, illiberal "country" of the torture chamber. "This is the place / you would rather not know about, / . . . / this is the place that will finally defeat you // where the word *why* shrivels and empties / itself. This is famine." At the beginning of the sixth and final section, another major but concealed change occurs: the site changes to one far away from torture and violent political abuse, although the demonstrative pronoun—"this"— remains the same. "In this country you can say what you like / because no one will listen to you anyway, / it's safe enough, in this country you can try to write / the poem that can never be written." The shift works to re-confirm the writing-subject of the text as the "safe" untortured spectator who appeared to be the writer of the opening section, but it also subverts the specificity of the demonstrative. "This" can apparently denote either place, the unsafe or the safe, the place of torture or the place of immunity from torture. These two "places" construct the dichotomy that this concluding section develops: between a liberal country that has the appearance of political freedom because no one listens to anything that is said, and an "elsewhere" (hitherto, in part one, "this place") where words have the power both to inspire courage and to provoke extreme violence. The momentary ambiguity of "this" participates in a generalized ambiguity that recurs throughout the text: an ambiguity about who is speaking or writing, a torture victim or a privileged onlooker; about who is being addressed, a torture victim, a privileged onlooker, or the reader; and about what text we are reading, "notes towards a poem," the perhaps discursively unmediated poem the notes aimed "towards," the futile "poems like this one" of part two, or the "this poem" of the final section: "Elsewhere, this poem is not invention. / Else-where, this poem takes courage."

■ ■ ■

The moral dilemma of the writer in the final section, free to write anything because nothing written from a comfortable, liberal democratic subject position is taken seriously, appears to lie behind much of this ambiguity. The poem "that can never be written" is among other things a poem that, if written, could have consequence, both to change society and to bring retribution upon the writer. The "notes towards" of the title indicate how distant the writing-subject believes itself to be from such a possibility. At the same time the writer is unwilling to give up the attempt, and so begins writing what is formally, in line and stanza structure, a "poem." But after the opening gesture of "notes towards," how can this text gain the standing of a poem?

The strategy the note-writing subject adopts involves appropriation, disguise, and ambiguity, in which the boundaries between notes and poem, writer and victim, and reader, victim, and writer, are rhetorically obscured. If the writer's text can claim authorship by the torture victim, or speak back to the safe-from-torture writer in the voice of the torture victim, it can perhaps claim standing as a poem. If the text can be made to obscure whether its addressee is itself, its reader, or the torture victim, it may be able to effectively erase the difference between the liberal and oppressive societies, and to appear to have a "right" to speak on behalf of subjects which it otherwise understands it is unable to represent—"Nothing works. / They remain what they are." If it can blur the boundaries between its own mere "notes" and the poem those notes envision (or between them and the poem the torture victim, "elsewhere," might have written), or even imply itself to be textually identical to that poem apart from their relative positions in space—"Elsewhere, this poem is not invention. / Elsewhere, this poem takes courage"—it might be able to assume at least quasi-status as a poem. If the writing-subject can blur the difference between its own words and those of the victim, perhaps it can even become the victim, appropriate its subject position, and relatively painlessly take for itself the victim's painfully acquired clarity of vision—"The razor across the eyeball / . . . / Witness is what you must bear."

A sort of rhetorical envy informs this ambiguity. The "notes" both foreground the modesty of the writer who would not claim priority over the suffering-earned poetic standing of the victim, and announce envy of the poem they would move towards; they both envy and hide themselves behind "this poem" which the dying and fingerless woman writes. The writing-subject envies the torture that qualifies the dying woman to write a poem that, untortured, the writer will "never" be qualified to write. The writer even envies the "country" of oppression, where words are consequential and poems are writable, and laments its own: "In this country you can say what you like / because no one will listen to you anyway."

■ ■ ■

The dilemma enacted in "Notes Towards a Poem That Can Never Be Written" is presented as the dilemma of the contemporary writer in First World democracies: the writer who possesses great freedom to write and power to publish, but achieves little political impact through this power; who covets the plight of the Third World victim as a means of recovering political impact, but has at best dubious authority to represent (politically and aesthetically) the victims of the horrendous oppression which occurs "elsewhere"—but from which the First World believes itself, for the moment at least, insulated. How can this writer speak "on behalf of" the systematically electro-shocked, raped, and mutilated political prisoner, both when her or his own "safe" position in culture, politics, literature, and discourse is so different from the position of that victim, and when even to presume to speak "on behalf of" may be to commit a colonizing act of impersonation. Even if the poem envisaged in the title is construed as a possible, socially mediated text and not as some unmediated and hypothetical entity beyond discourse, it can "never be written" both because its potential writer is dying and because its available writer is an alien to its intertexts.

Nevertheless, "Notes Towards" not only gets written and published, but becomes, in its own rhetoric as well as in the contexts provided by Oxford University Press, the poem it "never" could be. The text that is an "invention" and has not taken "courage" to write has become what Bowering has called the "poem for high school anthologies" (Barbour and Scobie, 38). Its writing-subject, which at the beginning could only hope to write "notes," has legitimated itself through a series of rhetorical moves that culminate in its being able to claim the same "painful" vision as that possessed by a victim's mutilated eyes. The main device in this process is ambiguity of pronoun reference—the obscuring of who is speaking, of how many positions "you" may include, and of where "this" place may be. Part five, with its blurring of first- and second-person pronouns, and with its paradoxical statements about the clarity of blurred vision, finally blurs any separation between the writer's vision and that of the victim. The concluding statement, "Witness is what you must bear," is made readable as a self-aggrandizing statement about the speaking-subject of the poem we are reading as well as an ironically figurative statement about the tortured woman. The speaking-subject here is able to take on the authenticity of having been tortured—the "razor across the eyeball"—"eyes taped open / two inches from the sun"—without suffering any of the incapacitating consequences. In a sense, the statement accomplishes an exchange of positions between the speaking-subject and the victim: as the woman's actual torture becomes figurative, the speaking-subject's vicarious or sympathetic pain becomes the literal "witness" that she must bear. The victim may die but the writing-subject acquires acute moral vision. This is accomplished by the transformation of physical torture into a metaphor for the paradoxically acute moral vision of the speaker. If one translates this process into an economic model, the victim's pain becomes—despite the deference the note-writer has tried to show towards the unwritable poem of the victim's suffering—the raw material for the note-writer's new vision, and her unwritable poem the occasion for the writer's notes to be seven times ambiguously termed "this poem."

Perhaps the most intriguing aspect of "Notes Towards a Poem That Can Never Be Written" is the effort the speaking-subject makes to have its appropriation and conversion of the victim's physical suffering into its own aesthetically usable pain seem morally acceptable. It is primarily the marks of modesty and deference that the subject gives the text—an intermittent insistence that the text is only a poor attempt, mere notes, mere "adjectives," something uncourageous that "invents" and "excuses" itself—that carries the burden of this effort. Although the text is repeatedly made to call itself a poem, it remains governed throughout by the title, "Notes Towards," so that each assertion that it is a "poem" remains incomplete and contradictory. The writer has it self-critically compare itself— "poems like this one"—to the "unworking" conventions of "beads," "statistics & litanies." In the concluding sixth section the writing-subject speaks cynically of the discourse of its own "country," and suggests that its own lengthy text may be paradoxically still unwritten: "Elsewhere you must write this poem / because there is nothing more to do." But the paradox points at least as much in the other direction: a text has indeed been written, the demonstrative "this" of "this poem" has been provided with a referent; something other than notes has been assembled out of notes towards a poem that the writer began by proposing, perhaps astutely, could never be written.

Works Cited

Atwood, Margaret. *The Circle Game*. Toronto: Anansi, 1966.

———. *Procedures for Underground*. Toronto: Oxford, 1970.

———. *True Stories*. Toronto: Oxford, 1981.

———. *You Are Happy*. Toronto: Oxford, 1974.

Barbour, Douglas, and Stephen Scobie, eds. *The Maple Laugh Forever*. Edmonton: Hurtig, 1981.

Geddes, Gary, ed. *15 Canadian Poets X2*. Toronto: Oxford, 1988.

The Shadow of Death:
Margaret Avison's "Just Left *or* The Night Margaret Laurence Died"

Christine Somerville

When paging through Margaret Avison's *No Time* (1989), I chanced upon "Just Left *or* The Night Margaret Laurence Died." The double title evoked for me the shock of the January morning in 1987 when I heard that Laurence had died of cancer, and the memory of the warm tributes from other Canadian writers. But Avison's poem is not written as a personal elegy; instead, it meditates unconventionally on mortality, loss, and grief. In her earlier "New Year's Poem" (*Winter Sun*, 1960), Avison recorded the everyday details that define the change of year and fix it in memory; the opening image is a bare branch, a drying remnant of the old year: "The Christmas twigs crispen and needles rattle / Along the windowledge." That death rattle of needles contrasts with the vitality of the previous week, when the now empty rooms held "perfumes, furs and . . . seasonal conversation." In "Just Left," the empty branch reappears, evoking the sorrow of sudden loss: "Bare branches studded once with jewelled birds / Someone inexorably plunders / One by one till an / Impoverished wintry sky from hill to / Darkening hill reveals / Untreasured tree-spikes, almost only." The stark branches emphasize the contrast between past and present, never sharper than immediately after a death. Here the theft of birds—many separate thefts that have taken place one at a time—unsettles the emotions. "Plunders," which implies robbery and violation, arouses a sense of outrage, especially because this act is perpetrated by "Someone" unseen. Is God the plunderer? If so, He is inexorable in taking these birds, and the arbitrary way in which He exercises His power over life and death is chilling.

Archetypally, the singing bird stands for the poet, the human singer; appropriately, the bird in the poem is mute, a reminder both that Laurence's voice has been stilled, and that the bereaved poet is silenced by the suddenness of her death. The bird recalls Laurence's short story cycle, *A Bird in the House* (1970), in which the young protagonist, Vanessa MacLeod, encounters the superstition that "a bird in the house means a death in the house" (86). "Just Left," however, depends on contrast between present and past. The coloured birds that were plundered from the branches contrast sharply with the "One bunched bird left." The image vividly conveys the compounding losses of old age as contemporaries die one after another.

Nevertheless, the bird's open eye is a point of light in the stanza, and for Avison the Christian poet, light is closely associated with the Son of God, the Light of the World. (The masculine "His," referring to the bird's eye, suggests the Holy Ghost, often depicted as a dove.) Despite the darkness of night, the bird remains awake, keeping a vigil through the night of Laurence's death. Since in Christian iconography the human soul takes the shape of a bird that flies away from the body at death, the image of the bird refers also to Laurence's soul. And yet the stanza is pervasively sorrowful. The adjective "bunched" not only describes how the bird huddles on the branch, but also emphasizes its loneliness, its loss of the warmth of companions.

Part of the appeal of this poem derives from its portrayal of the Christian struggling to accept death. The voice is that of a companion in sorrow, not a superior who has gained the high ground of unswerving belief. Unlike Kimberly, whose faith makes everyone uncomfortable in Alice Munro's short story "Labor Day Dinner" because for her "all the arguments have already been won" (156), Avison portrays the inner argument as one that is never settled. Although the poem suggests that spiritual comfort is accessible in the midst of sorrow, Avison gives grief full weight. The poem closes upon "all emptiness exposed" rather than an affirmation of the Resurrection. The title is key, however, since it places the poem in the immediate aftermath of Laurence's death, too soon for the speaker to be consoled.

So far as I know, Avison and Laurence were not close friends, but Laurence's death must have had special significance in that they belonged to the same generation and were both Christians committed to a social gospel of service to others. But as a writer, Laurence concerned herself with the details of the individual personality, while Avison strives to transcend the personal in search of universal truth. "Just Left" is a landscape without human figures. Laurence features in the title but not in the body of the poem, and Avison does not appear at all as grieving poet. Instead, the poem presents the wrench of sudden absence by means of a nightscape that enables the reader to experience sorrow and loss without another consciousness intervening. According to Gail Fox, Avison strongly dislikes what she calls the "confessional mode" because it tempts the poet to indulge in self-pity. In "Dancing in the Dark" (56-7), Fox tells how Avison hates "therapeutic writing," the use of poetry for relieving personal feelings, and has frequently advised her to "Forget the I's." This maxim applies equally to Avison's aesthetic and religious principles. She sees her task as a "plunge" that immerses her in dangerous waters, as the title of her essay "Muse of Danger" makes clear. She warns that the most profound religious experience may not translate into profound poetry, and the Christian poet needs to think as much about metre as about faith (147).

"A poet chooses to accept the full halo of values in the words he uses" (148), she writes in "Muse of Danger," and "No potential effect of any word is irrelevant to the poem where it occurs" (149). Both statements suggest that it is worth exploring various possible meanings of the first part of the title, "Just Left." If "left" is in the active voice, the phrase means that the leave-taking has occurred very recently; if "left" is in the passive, the emphasis falls on the speaker's sense of having been abandoned. "Just left" also implies an abrupt departure without warning or time to say goodbye. Taken by itself, the word "just" also becomes problematic, perhaps suggesting that Laurence's death depletes the world of her justice or goodness. Similarly, the adverb "still" can mean "motionless," which suggests death; but it can also mean "constantly," which suggests God's changeless, eternal love. Even the title of the collection, the ambiguous *No Time*, may be variously interpreted to mean "no more time," "unconcerned with time," or "eternal."

Avison effectively borrows from older poetic forms. Behind "Just Left" she sketches the faint outline of a Petrarchan sonnet. The first two stanzas construct an octave and a sestet, though after the opening line (in iambic pentameter); the metre breaks down, the lines grow shorter, and two more stanzas are added as a coda. Still, the basic pattern links the poem to such precursors as Hopkins, whose Terrible Sonnets evoke a similar mood of desolation. In "Just Left," the harsh phrase "untreasured tree-spikes" transforms the tree branches into cold metal spikes, recalling Christ's Cross and nails. The coined word "untreasured" points again to Hopkins and his "unleaving" in "Spring and Fall," and the "Margaret" of Hopkins' poem, who sees in the falling leaves intimations of her own death, adds another gloss upon Laurence's death. In effect, the "unleaving" is a reminder, through the shared Christian name, that the death of one *Margaret* prefigures the death of the other.

In a rapid transition, however, Avison shifts attention from the desolate "tree-spikes" to the glimmering eye, the tiny point of light that illuminates the scene and replaces the bare image of absence with the wakeful image of presence. Empty trees are not all there is, but are "almost only," which for Avison is an important distinction. So long as someone remains to mourn, death has meaning. The closing lines of "'Anti-War' or 'That we may not Lose Loss'" (*No Time*, 45) declare that the minimum requirement, "the least blessing," is this: "to cherish in want on earth / the dignity of one significant death." The bird's open eye implies the presence of an onlooker who sees, and thereby confirms, the ultimate value of each life.

Another mood shift occurs between the first and second stanzas. Anger gives way to passivity and numbness, as suggested by the truncated first three lines with their broken syntax and enjambment. By removing all unnecessary words, Avison rids the lines of nearly all the weak stresses so that the heavy stresses fall in a series: "Waiting, dim / Loneliness, place of / That withdrawing vision." Set apart by commas, the phrases are free-floating rather than anchored to a noun they are to modify. As R.J. Merrett has shown, Avison's syntax is unpredictable because she is convinced that "what makes sentences meaningful is the desire to interpret them" (82). In the opening lines of this stanza, the fragmentation of syntax and the foreshortened run-on lines suggest the incoherent speech brought on by the shock of this death. At the midpoint, however, more regular rhythm returns and the line lengthens. Finally, the stanza culminates in a series of words linked by alliteration, "first, far, fills," the last of which is triumphantly repeated four times, "Fills, fills, fills, fills," approaching through its cadence the resolution of the traditional sestet. Nevertheless, the fractured syntax frustrates attempts to parse the sentence and decide what flows in to fill the void. Both loneliness and light are possibilities, but the focus of the stanza rests on emptiness longing to be filled, and the word "more" promises that the longing will be satisfied.

The "first far planet" may refer to the moon, which was classed as a planet in the Ptolemaic system. "Planet" (from the Greek *planetes*) means "wanderer," and the planets were the heavenly bodies that changed places in relation to the fixed stars. The associations of the moon with womanhood, and the planets with wandering, enrich the poem by linking Laurence's death with the ancient cosmos. In modern terms, the "first far planet" probably refers to Venus, the bright planet known as both the evening star and the morning star (Kals, 69), especially since the poem develops contrasts between darkness and light, night and morning. But the precise identification of a particular planet is less important than the implication that light flowing from any planet, rather than being self-generated, is reflected light from the sun, itself representing the Divine light. The sestet closes on a note of rapture which is the apogee of the poem, but the poem does not end here. The two stanzas that follow form a coda which plunges back into the darker mood of the beginning: "Mutable mortal night / Blinds mortal day / Still to changelessness." Although the imagery has darkened once again, the lines also offer comfort by suggesting that grief is a misunderstanding by (blind) mortal men who cannot see that death is not the end of human life. As Avison explained in her preface to "The Jo Poems," gradually grief goes beyond the darkness of desolation and we experience "a refreshed shining out of the person clear now of time, and unforgettable" (*No Time*, 14). Although grief ultimately renews our memory of the dead, the process of healing is gradual; therefore, when morning finally comes, the mood of sorrow returns.

In the last verse, the hiatus of night ends and the everyday world "Lips in and foams toward flood of / All emptiness exposed." Descending abruptly from the spiritual to the physical plane, the tidal image of water that "lips in" enacts a return to mortal time. Although Laurence's life has ebbed away in the night, for the survivors, the tide flows in once again. That flood also suggests the flood of words about to pour forth about Laurence, and implies reluctance to have the silence of the night come to an end. The entire stanza has a faintly ironic tone; the phrase "the perched, askew" is perhaps a slight dig at the literary establishment, whose distress over the death of Laurence is viewed sardonically. "All emptiness exposed" implies not only the emptiness of a world without Laurence, but also the spiritual and intellectual emptiness of those who have outlived her.

In its ironic comment and irregular metre, the last quatrain runs counter to the shadow form that Avison has used when composing this poem. One explanation is that she set up the sonnet in order to break its rules, as a way of showing grief overpowering formal constraints. But this would oversimplify her web-like weave of form and feeling. Probably the sonnet was one of several models that she had in mind. It has been suggested that the seven lines that she added in the poem's coda are as important structurally as the first fourteen (van Rijn). Symbolically, the number seven represents perfect order. There are seven days of the week, seven notes on the musical scale, seven planets in the Ptolemaic system; therefore, although the mood of desolation persists, the seven-line coda implies that Laurence's death is still part of the divine pattern since the perfect order that testifies to God's presence in the universe is reaffirmed. Effectively, the added seven lines illustrate the tension between the ideal of Christian hope and the reality of human despair.

Since "Just Left" dramatizes a spiritual struggle between grief and hope, irregular versification mirrors the tension between these two emotions. Nevertheless, this treatment of the theme of mortality need not imply a darkening of Avison's spiritual vision, a reversal of what critics saw in *The Dumbfounding*, "a deepening of religious experience and a reconciliation to the physical world" (Geddes, 576). Just as the Christian story incorporates birth, death, and rebirth, Avison, as Christian poet, incorporates this cyclical pattern both in the individual poem and in the entire collection. Perhaps the word that is needed to describe the poems in *No Time* is not "meditative" but "devotional." Even in dark moments, Avison never loses sight of the wonder of creation. She understands what Margaret Laurence's Hagar took a lifetime to discover in *The Stone Angel*: "I must always, always, have wanted that—simply to rejoice" (292). Like the chiaroscuro technique of light enclosed by darkness in Rembrandt etchings, Avison's light imagery attracts attention away from the surrounding darkness, affirming that hope presses back the shadow cast by death.

Works Cited

Avison, Margaret. *The Dumbfounding*. New York: Norton, 1966.
———. "Muse of Danger." Kent, 144-9.
———. *No Time*. Hantsport, N.S.: Lancelot, 1989.
———. *Winter Sun*. Toronto: Univ. of Toronto Press, 1960.
Fox, Gail. "Dancing in the Dark." Kent, 55-7.
Geddes, Gary, ed. "Notes on the Poets." *20th-Century Poetry & Poetics*. Toronto: Oxford, 1969: 575-6.
Hopkins, Gerard Manley. "Spring and Fall." *The Poems of Gerard Manley Hopkins*. Ed. W.H. Gardner and N.H. MacKenzie. 4th ed. London: Oxford, 1967: 88-9.
Kals, W.S. *Stars and Planets: The Sierra Club Guide to Sky Watching and Direction Finding*. San Francisco: Sierra Club, 1990.
Kent, David, ed. *"Lighting up the Terrain": The Poetry of Margaret Avison*. Toronto: ECW, 1987.
Laurence, Margaret. *A Bird in the House*. 1970; Toronto: Seal, 1981.
———. *The Stone Angel*. 1964; Toronto: McClelland & Stewart, 1968.
Merrett, Robert James. "Faithful Unpredictability: Syntax and Theology in Margaret Avison's Poetry." Kent, 82-110.
Munro, Alice. "Labor Day Dinner." *The Moons of Jupiter*. Toronto: Macmillan, 1982: 134-59.
van Rijn, Mary. Letter to the author. 20 August 1991.

Earle Birney's "David" and the *Song of Roland:* A Source Study

Elspeth Cameron

Ironically, Earle Birney was not sanguine about the success of "David,"[1] the poem which, more than any other, was to ensure his reputation as a major poet. "I've just finished a narrative of about 275 ll., about mountain climbing in the Canadian Rockies," he wrote on 24 April 1941 to James McLaughlin, the editor of the American journal *New Directions*, who was compiling an anthology of contemporary verse. "E.J. Pratt, the only 'known' Canadian poet," Birney continued:

> thinks it's swell, but he can't suggest a place that would take it. The material is strange for an easterner, and the west has no magazines. The form is an assonantal five-beat stanza, abba—and nobody has, apparently, written in that form, so it's out! And the damned thing tries to be understandable and tragic and pictorial, and nobody but a duffer would want to read that kind of thing nowadays.[2]

Birney's peevishness stemmed from his disappointment that E.J. Pratt, though exuberantly enthusiastic about the poem, thought it too long for his *Canadian Poetry Magazine*. It seemed to Birney, however, that a more sophisticated editor like McLaughlin might be more likely to publish it. In a letter a month later, by which time he had compressed his poem from 275 to 184 lines, he wrote: "I am honestly trying 'new directions' of my own in "David," and I hope that you will find it good enough for your anthology."[3]

"David" was indeed a "new direction" for Birney. It was the result of an idiosyncratic fusion of an astonishing number of exotic elements—some personal, some literary—the twelfth-century *Song of Roland* among them. "David" owed much, of course, to Birney's mountaineering experiences as an adolescent in Banff, Alberta, and to climbing accidents he had heard of or read about there and in the coastal mountains near Vancouver, where he climbed during his undergraduate years at the University of British Columbia.

Among his literary sources, Birney directly acknowledged three narratives: Archibald MacLeish's Pulitzer prize-winning saga of the conquest of Mexico by Cortés, *Conquistador* (1932), and Stephen Vincent Benét's Civil War epic, *John Brown's Body* (1928), as well as the *Song of Roland*, a *chanson de geste* based on Charlemagne's crusade against the Saracens in northern Spain.[4]

Aside from these acknowledged literary influences, there is sufficient evidence to conclude that Birney's poem also owed much to Scottish long poems, such as Burns' classic romp "Tam o' Shanter" and Hugh MacDiarmid's philosophical and political musings in *A Drunk Man Looks at the Thistle* (1926) and "The Glass of Pure Water" (1937)[5]; and, closer to home, the narratives of Pratt himself, particularly "Brébeuf and his Brethren," which Birney had fulsomely praised as the poem of the year in September 1940 (*Canadian Forum*, 80), only a month or so before he began writing "David."

Of "David"'s specifically named literary antecedents, however, the most surprising is probably the *Song of Roland*. MacLeish and Benét were Birney's contemporaries, North Americans whose narratives had proven popular and successful. But *Roland* was a work remote in time, language, and sensibility; it was eight centuries since the Old French heroic epic had eulogized events that took place three centuries before that. For this reason, the case of *Roland* and the unique influence it may have on a modern poem is intriguing.

Birney encountered the *Song of Roland* in the course of his highly specialized training as a Chaucerian scholar. Though it is not clear exactly when he first read the poem, his capacity to read it in the original Old French versions was acquired in 1936 at the University of Toronto where he studied Old French, Old Norse, Gothic, and Anglo-Saxon, languages which comprised the minor in Germanic Philology and Linguistics for the Ph.D. he completed that year. That he knew the poem intimately, along with the main body of critical literature which interpreted it, is clear from his undated lecture notes[6] on "Romance," "The Epical Tradition in Old English and Middle English," and "*Romans de France.*"

The most extensive notes on *Roland* consist of a one-page outline which mentions the historical basis of the poem (the Battle at Roncevaux in 778, in which Charlemagne's rearguard, returning from a successful expedition against the Moors in Spain, is ambushed and destroyed by Basque mountaineers); a list of eight characters of which Roland is the "only one individualized," a "tragic epic hero" whose "glorious fault [is] an excess of soldierly zeal"; and comments about the treatment of content ("national religious epic—la douce France & a holy war, monotonous repetition of incident, elementary epic characterization, and passion for [the] marvellous"). Elsewhere among notes that repeat some of these points, Birney observes that *Roland* is the "Carolingian counterpart of the Grail theme."

The only aspect of the *Song of Roland* that Birney clearly admits drawing on is the form of the poem. In a letter responding to literary critic Desmond Pacey's request for information to be used in his forthcoming book about Canadian poets,[7] Birney wrote, "In 'David' itself I am conscious of minor formal influences of the *Song of Roland* and *Conquistador*."[8] Precisely what Birney meant by this statement (which Pacey did not refer to in his book) is not entirely clear, and he does not elaborate by example. He may, for instance, have meant that the formal influences from both sources was "minor"; or he could have meant that the influence was not necessarily minor, but that it stemmed from minor, as opposed to major, formal elements in these two antecedents.

Certainly, a comparison of "David" with *Roland* reveals many formal similarities—both major and minor—and suggests, beyond these, that Birney's poem may owe more to this literary source than these purely formal characteristics.

Although *Roland* is roughly twenty times longer than "David," and is, consequently, much greater in scope and complexity, formal similarities are numerous. Both poems describe a simple Rise-Climax-Fall pattern. Though *Roland* develops a binary plot-line (Brault, 49-51) and "David" a single story, the Ascent/Death of the Hero/Expiation story provides an overall structure within which minor episodes are presented with—to borrow Gerard Brault's description of *Roland*—a "geometric" effect (Brault, 76-7). The *Song of Roland* is made up of *laisses*, or stanzas, which present self-contained scenes where stylized attitudes and gestures "convey abstract ideas in visual terms" (Owen, 31). Though Birney's poem differs formally in that he regulated his stanzas to four lines each, whereas in *Roland* the *laisses* vary in length from fewer than five lines to over twenty; and Birney grouped his stanzas into five numbered sections (presumably to echo the five acts of classic dramatic tragedy), whereas *Roland*'s *laisses* simply follow one another, both poems have the same effect of presenting a variety of scenes through one or more stanzas without transitional links. In both poems, too, each stanza, or *laisse*, is unified by assonance: in *Roland* by the use of the same vowel (usually) in the last word of each line, in "David" through an a-b-b-a pattern.[9] Birney lengthens the five-beat decasyllabic line standard of *Roland* to a five-beat line of usually twelve or thirteen syllables.

This technical comparison of formal elements cannot, however, do justice to the suppleness of either *Roland* or "David." Though Birney, like the author of *Roland*,[10] presents a succession of self-contained, memorably simple, unlinked scenes, the effect in both poems is "an impression less of individual 'frames'" punctuated by laconic dialogue "than of a running film strip synchronised with a resonant, pulsating and evocative sound track" (Owen, 31). This is due partly to the fact that the *Song of Roland* was in all likelihood, as its title suggests, a poem to be sung or chanted by *jongleurs*, and that many of its formal elements (such as assonance, strong rhythms, epithets, and formulaic phrasings) were intended as mnemonic devices or musical cues. As D.D.R. Owen observes:

> in modern terms, the structure of the poem might be called symphonic. It has distinct movements, and between and within them are the tonal variations: lyrical passages alternate with rousing periods of full orchestra; there are the crescendos and diminuendos, changes of pace and key within the general flow; and of great importance are the continual statements and re-statements of themes and phrases, which bind the whole composition together and strengthen its formal unity. (29-30)

It is for reasons such as these that the *Song of Roland* is considered the greatest *chanson de geste*.

Birney, possibly because of his advanced linguistic training, was able to imitate this peculiarly "oral" vividness of *Roland*. Like its twelfth-century antecedent (and unlike either *Conquistador* or *John Brown's Body*, both of which seem more literary and less emphatic to the ear), "David" has striking auditory effects (its pounding rhythms, modulating pace, and proliferation of onomatopoetic and alliterating words, for example) and seems meant to be read aloud. In fact, its first impact on a wide audience was in a radio airing on 4 January 1942, a month after the poem's original publication in *The Canadian Forum*.[11]

Aside from these formal common denominators between *Roland* and "David," there are a number of ways—some rather important—in which Birney's poem may have been influenced by this *chanson de geste*. But before turning to these, some clear dissimilarities must be noted. Because these are manifold and significant, Birney's "David" can in no way be understood to be modelled on the *Song of Roland*, nor to copy or parody it. Aside from the striking differences in length and complexity already mentioned, the *Song of Roland*, unlike "David," aggressively vindicates Christianity, not only in theme but also in texture (events in *Roland* are commonly understood to be deliberate parallels of Biblical happenings, for example); it is—to use today's terminology—explicitly nationalistic and racist, glorifying France at the expense of the Muslim Saracens; it develops a story involving several minor characters, different settings, and the movements of large groups; and it takes for granted a connection between "heroism" and military prowess.

Only one section of *Roland*—the middle section concerning the ambush in the mountain pass of the rearguard led by Charlemagne's nephew Roland, his death, and the death of his comrade-in-arms Oliver—can be seen as a source for elements other than formal ones in "David." This climactic section presents a debate between Roland and Oliver about whether or not Roland should sound his horn to call Charlemagne and the troops proceeding through the pass ahead of them to return and help. Oliver urges Roland to do so; Roland refuses, on grounds that his honour would be sullied. In the ensuing battle, the French, who are vastly outnumbered by the Saracens, go down to bitter and bloody defeat. When defeat becomes inevitable, Roland and Oliver debate again about whether or not Roland should sound his horn. Oliver now argues against blowing it; Roland, wounded and desperate, sounds the horn with such force that his temples burst and bleed. Oliver is mortally wounded and dies, to Roland's great distress. Then Roland himself dies in battle.

Even from this thumbnail sketch a number of echoes in "David" can be detected. Among these, one of the most striking is the quality of friendship between two young men. The relationship between Roland and Oliver in the *Song of Roland* is frequently hailed as the finest example of *compagnonnage*, a relationship defined by D.D.R. Owen as follows:

> Two young men, not related by birth . . . might freely pledge to each other loyal comradeship and brotherhood in arms. Their pact was not necessarily formal; but its effect was to link the knights' destinies as firmly as any feudal tie or even blood connection . . . neither history nor legend offers any more illustrious pair of [such] companions than Roland and Oliver. (11)

According to C.M. Bowra, such a friendship is "a partnership of a special kind," possibly the highest order of love possible between humans: "The participants share both dangers and glory, and the honour of one is the honour of the other . . . A hero's love for his friend is different from his love for his wife or his family, since it is between equals and founded on an identity of ideals and interests" (65). There is more than a hint of such *compagnonnage* between David and Bob as they move up and away from "the ruck of the camp" into a shared idealism. Peter Aichinger notes a parallel between David and King Arthur, and between Bob and Sir Bors, but the parallel between the two mountaineers and Roland and Oliver is more convincing.[12] David, like Roland, leads and teaches his companion in ways that have overtones of a chivalric code of behaviour; and the affection and loyalty demonstrated under duress is of an exceptionally rarified sort.

Like the *Song of Roland*, too, "David" focuses on a single hero. By Bowra's definition, the hero of epic and romance "differs from other men by his peculiar force and energy":

> [H]e has an abundant, overflowing, assertive force, which expresses itself in action, especially in violent action. . . . [T]he great man must pass through an ordeal to prove his worth and this is almost necessarily some kind of violent action, which not only demands courage, endurance, and enterprise, but, since it involves the risk of life, makes him show to what lengths he is prepared to go in pursuit of honour. . . . [T]he story passes from the record of bold achievements to something graver and grander and suggests dark considerations about the place of man in the world and the hopeless fight which he puts up against his doom. . . . The splendour which irradiates a hero in the hour of defeat or death is a special feature of heroic poetry. (97, 48, 118, 128)

Despite some obvious differences in content—mountain-climbing, though risky, is by no means the same thing as a battle—there is much in "David" that could have been suggested by such characteristics of heroic poetry in the *Song of Roland*. That we are to focus on a central hero, the meaning of his attitude to life, and the significance of his death, is implied by the title.[13] The aura surrounding David, which gives the impression that he is exceptional, particularly in terms of his "courage, endurance and enterprise," resembles our impressions of Roland. "[M]ountains for David were made to see over." Certainly the violence and horror of David's accident and death equals that of Roland and Oliver's deaths in battle. The sense of a terrible waste of splendid young manhood, and, beyond that, a sense of "dark considerations about the place of man in the world," is common to both poems. As in many heroic poems—*Roland* among them—the story in Birney's poem centres on an ethical test in which the hero must make an "agonizing choice" (Brault, 104) for which he must accept responsibility. That Birney locates this aspect of his source not in David, the character who most resembles Roland, but in Bob, who resembles Oliver, is an interesting twist that does not in any way diminish the connection between the two poems.

More than one commentator on the *Song of Roland* has noted its author's "art of adapting the background to the tone and temper of events." One of the main ways in which this correspondence is struck is by relating Roland and Oliver's climbing of the Pyrenees to their ascent into the abstract code of chivalric honour, national pride, valour, and loyalty. *Roland* dramatizes, through its scenery, the heights to which Roland aspires, and, through the use of panoramic vistas, suggests the aristocracy of the fellow-knights, the spiritual dimension of their crusade, and the magnitude of their far-reaching ambitions. As Brault observes, *Roland's* narrative moves "literally from elevation to elevation, the story reverberating from peak to peak, as it were, like the sound of the hero's oliphant

[horn]" (81). Birney may have derived some aspects of this technique from *Roland* (Pacey found Birney's irregular lines and anapestic rhythms "well chosen to give the effect of climbing" [306]), though his personal mountaineering experience and his other formal source, *Conquistador*, are so thoroughly intertwined that specific influence is impossible to discern. Certainly, if he drew on *Roland*, he outdid that source both in his majestic description of the Rockies and in the way in which his mountains, valleys, lakes, and swamps *are* his theme and characters. This amplification can be seen by comparing parallel passages from the two poems:

> Halt sunt li pui e li val tenebrus
> Les roches bises, les destreiz merveillus.

> [The mountains are high and the valleys are shadowy,
> The rocks dark, the defiles frightening.]

> (*Song of Roland, laisse* 66, ll. 814-15)

> The peak was upthrust
> Like a fist in a frozen ocean of rock that swirled
> Into valleys the moon could be rolled in.
> ("David," II, ll. 17-19)

In several small details, too, there are echoes of *Roland* in "David." The episodes of the "skull and the splayed white ribs of a mountain goat" and the suffering "wing-broken" robin which David kills, though clearly used by Birney as foreshadowing, correspond roughly to the several scenes of carnage on the battlefield at Roncevaux. The most salient feature of the description of Oliver's death is the lance that pierces his chest right through from back to front, a blow that may have suggested the "cruel fang / Of the ledge thrust in his back" that David endures. And Oliver's inadvertent sword-blow to Roland's head, struck when Oliver cannot see because he is bleeding so much, and the poignant dialogue in which Roland forgives his friend for mistakenly attacking him, may have suggested the central incident of David, when Bob slips because he is "heedless / Of handhold" and unwittingly causes David's fall when David loses his balance as a result of reaching out to steady his friend. Certainly Roland's remorse and distress at Oliver's death (caused ultimately by Roland's refusal to sound his horn for aid) anticipates Bob's guilt and grief at David's death.

Why Birney used the *Song of Roland* as a source for "David" poses an interesting literary challenge. His engagement with early Germanic literatures in preparation for the Ph.D. and his ongoing use of these works in his university teaching kept the *Song of Roland* fresh in his mind. But in his own life, too, there was a curious parallel to the twelfth-century poem; Birney had been serving on a crusade as intense and far-reaching as Charlemagne's. For close to a decade, he had devoted himself to Trotsky's cause as a member of the Independent Labour Party in anticipation of a new world order to be ushered in by the Fourth International. Birney had joined the "Church" (as the Trotskyist movement referred to itself) in 1933, after sampling a number of left-wing political organizations in the early 1930s, and had dedicated his energies to speeches, reading groups, arrangements for speakers, and the dissemination of party publications, with nothing less than missionary zeal. His abandonment of Trotskyist politics in January 1940 as a result of Trotsky's endorsement of Russia's invasion of Finland the previous November constituted a wrenching disillusionment. "I have broken with POLITICS," he wrote to a friend at the time.

> For a while I carried on a fight against the Old Man's [Trotsky's] Finnish policy— he wanted the Reds to win, at the same time piously "condemning" the invasion. But I finally had to face a lot of ugly facts I had been forced to admit for along [sic] time: that the Old Man's organization is growing as bureaucratic as the next one, that up here the whole organizational approach is quixotic and suicidal . . . I still think the ultimate choice is socialism or barbarism. But as for me, I've spent more than eight year's [sic] leisure time, and sacrificed more than I care to think of, for [a cause] that seems pretty futile now. . . . My spare time, if I can find any, is going to be writing, and not political writing . . . you know me well enough to know that a break like this doesn't come easy, not without a lot of thought.[14]

Though Birney had dabbled in poetry and short story writing since he was an undergraduate at UBC in the mid-1920s, it was only in the winter of 1940-41 that he turned his best energies to creative writing, as if to fill the vacuum left by abandoning "POLITICS."

It was out of this clear turning point in his life that "David" and most of the other poems that would eventually be collected in *David and Other Poems* (1942) were forged. This context suggests that "David" was an expression of the end of youthful idealism: "That day," as Bob puts it, "the last of my youth, on the last of our mountains." The *Song of Roland* may have suggested itself as a model partly because the high point of Birney's Trotskyist experience was the visit he and his fellow-traveller Ken Johnstone (using their party pseudonyms, Comrade Robertson and Comrade Alexander) paid to Trotsky in Hønefoss, Norway, in November 1935: like two fellow-knights sworn to a chivalric code, they were received at court and sent onwards in the great crusade. There was a more subtle parallel, too, between the two Trotskyites and Roland and Oliver. Just as Oliver's sister is Roland's fiancée, Johnstone's sister was Birney's wife.[15] And the *Song of Roland* may have seemed appropriate, specifically, because Birney intended to treat it both seriously and ironically: seriously, in that *Roland* captured the uplifting spiritual euphoria of naive youthful commitment and the special bonding that tied compatriots to their crusade; ironically, in that surviving the loss of idealism (as Bob does, whereas Roland and Oliver do not)[16] means carrying on in a real world no longer glorious, but diminished and ugly. Even in defeat and death, Roland and Oliver vindicate idealism; their honour is not only un-sullied, but augmented. But Bob, whose "agonizing choice" evokes an act of mercy-killing, which may represent a higher moral order shared by David, but is, none the less, a "crime" and may represent reversion to a lower moral order, must carry forward the burden of a shameful self-knowledge which is profoundly repellent.

Birney recognized that "David" would probably strike contemporary readers as old-fashioned. Hence his remark to McLaughlin that "nobody but a duffer would want to read that kind of thing nowadays." As he explained further to E.K. Brown, on submitting it to the *University of Toronto Quarterly*, the poem was "written in conscious antipathy to the fashionable obscurancy, the Audenian didactics and the pedantic allusiveness of the sons of Eliot."[17] He was disappointed, but not surprised, that Brown didn't accept it, that McLaughlin found its form "too traditional,"[18] and that poet Kenneth Rexroth in San Francisco suggested sending it to England since "the market for such literature is almost entirely English."[19] It was the *Song of Roland*, more than any of Birney's other literary sources, that caused his poem to "lapse," as he put it regretfully, "into the cliché of melodrama."[20]

Yet the experiment was bold, and ultimately successful. By going back to the *chanson de geste*, Birney brought to Canadian poetry a refreshing vigour achieved through oral effects and the restoration of English words to their roots in early Germanic languages. Partly intent on making a mark for western Canadian poetry—which he thought of as non-existent in any modern sense— he turned naturally to a classic poem of national self-glorification as a model for what he called gently "western nostalgia."[21] And, in adapting an aristocratic, chivalric brotherhood to a contemporary ethical situation, he signalled, as he intended, a new voice in Canadian poetry:[22] a voice paradoxically romantic and realistic, at once intelligent, secular, philosophical, democratic, and passionate.

Despite the many self-deprecating comments Birney made to friends ("I'm a rather lightminded beginner";[23] "I've somewhat shamefacedly published a little"[24]) as "David" found its way to its audience, it was not long before the poem was acclaimed as a classic on its own terms. Birney, at his lowest ebb after "twelve tantalizing personal letters of rejection"[25] for "David"'s publication, wrote to Frank Wilcox, a former University of British Columbia professor:

> most of my verse, as you might guess, stinks. . . . Some of it is so bad that I put it out anonymously. One effusion ["David"] that I acknowledge will appear in the Canadian Forum next week, but I doubt if I will send it to you. It is a piece of ornate melodrama, and I would have you think better of me than that I published it.[26]

But once the poem was published and broadcast by radio, it was quickly appreciated in terms such as these by poet James Wreford Watson, who wrote to Birney without having any idea who he was:

> I was very attracted to ["David"], arrested and elevated. It has something of the grand manner about it, with all the classical virtues of austerity, architecture and abstraction, and yet with an organic structure and a vital freedom that fuses content and form in a very organic way. . . . As for the verse itself, it strikes me both for its discipline and its freedom. . . . The trick of carrying one verse over into the other, the clever use of assonance, the organic variation of rhythm, the nice choice of words impress me with a mastery of the best from the classical and romantic traditions, and their fusion into something original, necessary and in advance of them.[27]

Notes

[1]"David" was first published in *The Canadian Forum*, which did not please Birney, because he had been literary editor of the journal until December 1940 and suspected that it was accepted there for that reason. The version I use in this article is the first version to appear in book form in *David and Other Poems*.

[2]Earle Birney to James McLaughlin, letter 24 April 1941, Birney Collection, Thomas Fisher Rare Book Collection, University of Toronto.

[3]Birney to McLaughlin, 23 May 1941, Birney Collection, Toronto.

[4]The text used here is the "Oxford" text generally accepted by scholars as the most authentic version. The edition used is Brault.

[5]For a full exploration of these influences, see my "The Influence of the Scottish Long Poem on Earle Birney's 'David'," *British Journal of Canadian Studies* 7.1 (1992): 59-73.

[6]See Box 79, Birney Collection, Toronto.

[7]See Desmond Pacey, *Ten Canadian Poets. A Group of Biographical and Critical Essays* (Toronto: Ryerson, 1958).

[8]Birney to Pacey, 4 Feb. 1957, Birney Collection, Toronto.

[9]It is worth noting here that MacLeish uses a 3-line assonantal stanza with an a-b-a pattern in *Conquistador*, and links his stanzas assonantally by using the "b" vowel from each stanza as the "a" vowel in the following one. In other words, Birney's form in "David" is a hybrid, merging the self-contained assonantal *laisses* of *Roland* with some aspects of the more structured stanzas of MacLeish's *Conquistador*.

[10]Despite much scholarly speculation, the author of the *Song of Roland* is unknown, though, because of the poem's last line "Ci falt la geste que Turoldus declinet" ("Here ends the story that Turoldus tells"), he is usually referred to as Turoldus.

[11]Lacey Fisher read "David" for the Western Canada Network of CBC radio at 10:15 p.m. (Pacific Coast Time), Monday, 4 Jan. 1942.

[12]Aichinger writes: "in Part VII all these boyish things are left behind and a new note of high seriousness creeps in. David becomes the 'chevalier sans peur et sans reproche' who has undertaken many adventures with his squire (Bob) but who must now go forth to dreadful and final battle with the Finger. As he passes, 'the quiet heather flushed' like a maiden blushing for her warrior knight. David yodels at the mountain sheep and sends them fleeing as a brave knight would drive in the enemy's pickets and sound a defiant trumpet challenge to the enemy himself" (89).

[13]In fact, among Birney's acknowledged and probable literary influences, all but *Conquistador* use proper names in their titles: *John Brown's Body*, "Tam o' Shanter," "Brébeuf and his Brethren," and the *Song of Roland*.

[14]Birney to Hilton Moore, 29 Jan. 1940, Birney Collection, Toronto.

[15]Though the marriage had been annulled almost at once, Birney and Sylvia Johnstone were still technically married at the time Birney and Johnstone visited Trotsky.

[16]That Birney intended this clear difference between *Roland* and "David" is suggested by Bob's words when he trips on his way down the mountain and back to the camp: "but I did not faint," for much is made of the fact that Roland faints on seeing his dead friend, Oliver.

[17]Birney to E.K. Brown, 30 May 1941, Birney Collection, Toronto.

[18]McLaughlin to Birney, 5 July 1941, Birney Collection, Toronto.

[19]Kenneth Rexroth to Birney, 5 Sept. 1941, Birney Collection, Toronto.

[20] Birney to G.G. Sedgewick, 5 April 1942, Birney Collection, Toronto.

[21] Birney to Frank Wilcox, letter n.d. [probably mid-May] 1941, Birney Collection, Toronto. Even the notion of "western nostalgia" may have been suggested by the *Song of Roland*, which nostalgically glorifies events that occurred three centuries earlier.

[22] Birney had explained in his letter of 30 May 1941 to Brown: "what I want most to see in Canadian letters is poetry which is not following English or American fashions, however timely, but is striking out for itself."

[23] Birney to Brown, 30 May 1941, Birney Collection, Toronto.

[24] Birney to Wilcox, letter n.d. [probably mid-May] 1941, Birney Collection, Toronto.

[25] Birney to Sedgewick, 5 April 1942, Birney Collection, Toronto. The rejections, as listed by Birney in his copy of *David and Other Poems*, Birney Collection, Toronto, were from: *Sewanee Review, Atlantic Monthly, Penguin New Writing, Poetry* (Chicago), *Queen's Quarterly, Twice A Year, New Directions, New World, National Magazine, University of Toronto Quarterly,* and *Horizon*. The twelfth was *Canadian Poetry Magazine*.

[26] Birney to Wilcox, 20 Nov. 1941, Birney Collection, Toronto.

[27] James Wreford Watson to Birney, 3 March 1942, Birney Collection, Toronto.

Works Cited

Aichinger, Peter, *Earle Birney*. Twayne's World Authors Series. Boston: Twayne, 1979.

Benét, Stephen Vincent. *John Brown's Body*. New York: Rinehart, 1928.

Birney, Earle. "Canadian Poem of the Year." *The Canadian Forum* (Sept. 1940): 180. Rpt. in Birney, *Spreading Time: Remarks on Canadian Writing and Writers, Book I: 1904-1940*. Montreal: Véhicule, 1980: 51-2.

———. "David." *The Canadian Forum* (Dec. 1941): 274-6.

———. *David and Other Poems*. Toronto: Ryerson, 1942.

Bowra, C.M. *Heroic Poetry*. London: Macmillan, 1952.

Brault, Gerard J., trans. and ed. *The Song of Roland: An Analytical Edition* (2 vols). University Park and London: Pennsylvania State Univ. Press, 1978.

MacDiarmid, Hugh. *A Drunk Man Looks at the Thistle*. Edinburgh: Blackwood, 1926.

MacLeish, Archibald. *Conquistador*. Boston: Houghton Mifflin, 1932.

Owen, D.D.R., trans. *The Song of Roland*. Bury St. Edmunds: Boydell, 1990.

Pacey, Desmond. *Ten Canadian Poets: A Group of Biographical and Critical Essays*. Toronto: Ryerson, 1958.

Earle Birney's Equivocal Dance: The Cultural Politics of "The Bear on the Delhi Road"

Tom Hastings

I. BIRNEY ON THE DELHI ROAD

During November and December of 1965 Earle Birney presented a series of broadcasts for the CBC program "The Best Ideas You'll Hear Tonight," in which he discussed the nature of the creative process. Published a year later as *The Creative Writer*, the aim of these seven half-hour talks was, writes Birney, "to say some things about all the arts, and about useful creativity in general" (2). Birney therefore uses the occasion to survey his own artistic identity as well as the state of Canada's cultural and social identity on the eve of its centennial. Committed to the project of nation-building in each of his capacities as Canadian poet, professor, and citizen, Birney explores the fledgling state of the Canadian writing scene in the mid-1960s, the role of the artist in contemporary Western society, and the "mad" process of creative writing. To illustrate his comments, Birney frequently describes his own writing experiences, retrospectively explaining the genesis of some of his best-known poems. As Birney writes, "My experiences are all I have to be certain about. . . . I've been impelled—impelled sometimes merely by one acute sense impression, which started a chain of recalls back to an experience which, I could now apprehend, was emotionally important for me" (15-16). The result—what Birney calls an attempt "to unravel a poem of my own and say how and why I wrote it" (24)—is both a model for reading his poetry and a point of departure for the interpretation of many of the poems he mentions.[1]

As an illustration of his own process of poetry-writing, Birney chooses to "unravel" one of his best known travel poems, "The Bear on the Delhi Road." In the process of describing the "acute sense impression" which led to the composition of "The Bear on the Delhi Road," Birney not only adumbrates his own critical principles, which configures his literary *œuvre* according to his critical values at that time, but also reveals his authorial intentions, thereby directing future interpretations of the poem and exposing the poem to a critical judgment of success or failure in achieving that intention, be that intention laudable or in some way questionable. Since my reading of "The Bear on the Delhi Road" will take Birney's own critical comments as a point of departure, it is worth quoting the passage at length:

> In the summer of 1958 I had a glimpse of a bear and two Kashmiri men on a roadside in northern India—seen from my passing car. It was a strange sight, of

course, but it haunted me for reasons far beyond oddness. The bear was huge, shaggy, Himalayan. It must have been captured high up in the cool mountains and purchased by these men with perhaps the savings of their lifetime, and they had been walking with it hundreds of miles through mountain passes down to the terrible mid-summer hot plains, brutally training it for dancing as they went, so they could make a living exhibiting it in Delhi. But it wasn't just the bear's wretchedness, it was the two men's; it was their fearful, dumb hopping around the bear. Bear and men pursued me for fourteen months till I could find the leisure on a Mediterranean Island, and the mood,—and then in two hours the words came and the bearish rhythm and the images with which to lay those three ghosts, which were I think also the ghosts of my own multitudinous guilt feelings, as a well-fed western tourist in a world of unimaginable poverty and heat and dusty slaving. Even then it took a dozen later sessions of tinkering and touching to get it said well enough for those special spectres to stop spooking me. And now all that's left is a very different desire, a very mild and fading one, to use my personal spell to raise those ghosts among others—among you, if you will listen. (16)

As Birney explains, "The Bear on the Delhi Road" is to be understood as, first, his anti-colonialist effort to come to terms with his own position as a well-off Westerner travelling in a world that ruthlessly discriminates between those who have privilege and those who do not; and, second, as his effort to raise the consciousness of his readers by representing his personal experiences in the East. Birney's critical comments therefore suggest that "The Bear on the Delhi Road" may be read as an anti-Orientalist text, a text that struggles against received notions of the East as naturally inferior, impoverished, and alien. However, a number of Birney's critical comments expose an ambivalence in his anti-Orientalist gestures. In particular, Birney's efforts to assuage his guilt as a privileged Western tourist by questioning the very structures of Western privilege are predicated upon an exoticization of the Indian, who is commodified as an 'other' through which the Westerner, as self, comes to understand his or her own identity. Birney thus repeats the very Orientalist structures he had intended to place under examination.

Much of Birney's poetry is informed by a strong geographic element. Travel and the importance of one's experience in an alien landscape define the shape of Birney's work. Indeed, *The Collected Poems of Earle Birney* are subdivided by geographical location, with Birney's travel experiences in the Far East supplying a significant number of the collection's poems. This fact alone implicates Birney in the cultural logic of the West's Orientalism. According to this logic, says Edward Said in *Orientalism*,

> Everyone who writes about the Orient must locate himself *vis-à-vis* the Orient; translated into his text, this location includes the kind of narrative voice he adopts, the type of structure he builds, the kinds of images, themes, motifs that circulate in his text—all of which add up to deliberate ways of addressing the reader, containing the Orient, and finally, representing it or speaking in its behalf. (20)

Birney's relationship to the Orient, as presented in *The Creative Writer*, is one that self-consciously seems to acknowledge his Western privilege. References to his "passing car," his comfort, his eventual "leisure on a Mediterranean Island," and his healthy, "well-fed western" identity are opposed to the Kashmiris' discomfort and "unimaginable poverty," their hard work, "wretchedness," and "dusty slaving." Their "fearful, dumb hopping" suggests an inanimate, stagnant nature that is the antithesis of Birney's animated, creative nature, which accords him the mobility and leisure to enjoy a dozen "sessions of tinkering and touching." Birney's creative process here has a play-like quality for him; as he says, "poetry is . . . a kind of intricate and infinite play" (*Creative Writer*, 17). This poem, as a poem, connotes the leisure that was necessary for its creation and is the most immediate marker of the difference in class between Birney and the objects of his musing.

The poem, for Birney, is ultimately a means of dealing with the guilt provoked by the contrast between his leisure and the Kashmiris' labour. He imagines this economic contrast in cultural terms by identifying himself as a Westerner against the Kashmiri Easterners who represent everything the West is not. In the process of assuaging his guilt, he reinscribes the superiority of his Western position by the very language he uses to define and assuage this guilt. Thus, while acknowledging his "multitudinous guilt feelings" as a "well-fed western tourist," he describes the cause of that guilt feeling, the sight of the two Kashmiri men and the Himalayan bear from a passing car window, in phantasmagoric terms that not only exoticize them, but empty them of their humanity. The men and bear are described as "ghosts" which seem to haunt him relentlessly: "Bear and men *pursued* me for fourteen months" until I could "get [the poem] said well enough . . . to stop [the] spooking" (my emphasis). In psychoanalytic terms, these ghosts or spooks are uncanny in that they combine a sense of the alien (as exotic humans, as supernatural pursuers) and of the familiar (as thinly disguised projections of his *own* feelings of guilt *vis-à-vis* the East).[2] The desire to "lay those three ghosts" to rest suggests that expiating his guilt requires that the image of the Kashmiris transcend its everyday, historical meaning (Kashmiris as working men) to convey a meaning of mythic import (Kashmiris as suffering humanity). The ideological nature of this transcendence is evident in Birney's phrase, "these special spectres": a "spectre" is a "thing that is thought to be seen but has no material existence" (*OED*), and in this passage the Kashmiris are seen as an image, but they have no material existence of their own.

By "no material existence" I mean that the Kashmiris are a figure of the "wretchedness" of the East, a figure in which two Indian individuals and a bear are synecdochal metaphors representing a supposed truth about the entire East to which they belong. But this concept of the "East" as a totality does not in fact exist except as a discursive projection of the Western imagination, functioning to articulate the identity of the West to itself and for itself. The encounter with the East is for Birney an encounter with his own privilege, and instills in him a sense that to be a Westerner is to be morally complicitous with the apparatuses that oppress the East. Birney effectively concedes this point when he writes that the "glimpse" of the Kashmiris and the bear is the ghost of his own "multitudinous guilt feelings, as a well-fed western tourist" in northern India. The role of the Kashmiris in the passage is therefore to be what Terry Goldie would call "essential non-participant[s]": their presence is necessary insofar as it allows Birney to mitigate his own uncomfortable feelings of privilege (14). The composition of "The Bear on the Delhi Road" is this act of personal mitigation: "it took a dozen later sessions of tinkering and touching *to get it said well enough* for these special spectres to stop spooking me" (my emphasis).

Colonial discourse appears in this passage even in the form of what is perhaps an unintentional allusion to race in the term "spook," which is a colloquial pejorative term for Black people.[3] The poem unwittingly participates in racial stereotyping through which, writes Homi Bhabha, the "colonial power produces the colonized as a fixed reality which is at once an 'other' and yet entirely knowable and visible" (199). According to Robert Young, in *White Mythologies*, this production of the colonized "constitutes only a partial representation of him: far from being reassured, the colonizer sees a grotesquely displaced image of himself. Thus the familiar, transported to distant parts, becomes uncannily transformed . . ." (147). Birney's account of his creative process as it manifests itself in writing "The Bear on the Delhi Road" thus corresponds with Bhabha's conceptualization of the production of the colonial subject in two ways. First, Birney creates a partial representation of the Kashmiris (as wretched) that ignores their full humanity, and second, he finds in the distant 'other' an image of himself (as guilty). In this correspondence lies the justification for situating Birney *in* colonial discourse, despite the anti-Orientalist gestures he makes.

The inscription of colonialist discourse in the passage is further marked by the use of a rhetoric of speculation. The initial description of the bear and the two men immediately establishes this evaluative tone: "It was a strange sight, *of course*" (my emphasis). The phrase constitutes a double gesture in which he codes the scene both as *exotic* (bear and man together!) and as *domestic* (for India, exotic *is* normal). Furthermore, the conjectural tone of the passage not only undermines the authority of Birney's representation of the Indian scene, but also highlights the degree to which the poem's declared "historical" referentiality is suspect. Describing the bear, Birney writes: "It *must have been* captured high up in the cool mountains and purchased by these men with *perhaps* the savings of their lifetime" (my emphasis). The inconsistency of *necessity* and *possibility* reveals Birney's role in putting into narrative form the scene he witnesses. Although he only gets a quick "glimpse" of the "fearful, dumb hopping" of the men and their bear from a "passing car," he expands this single moment in time and space to encompass the many miles from the Himalayas to Delhi and the many months of the journey. Birney's employing of this "glimpse" in this manner appropriates the Kashmiris' agency by making them subject to a history he invents for them. To this extent, Birney enacts the logic of representation that Said identifies in Gustave Flaubert's treatment of his mistress, Kuchuk Hanem: she "never spoke of herself, she never represented her emotions, presence, or history. *He* spoke for and represented her" (6; Said's emphasis). It is in this sense that Birney "represents" the Indian men.

To claim, as I do, that for Birney the creation of the poem works to alleviate his conscience does not, of course, directly address the question of whether Birney adopts an anti-Orientalist or a (neo-) colonialist discourse. In order to deal further with this distinction, it is consequently necessary to suspend the question of praise or blame. The very possibility that Birney could travel extensively in Asia, as well as the existence of numerous travel poems recording these trips, locate Birney's poetry within a discursive field predicated on Orientalism because, as Said explains, Orientalism depends upon a "flexible *positional* superiority" in which the "Westerner" was "in, or thought about, the Orient because he *could be there*, or could think about it, with very little resistance on the Orient's part" (7; Said's emphasis). One symptom of this "positional superiority" in Birney's numerous travel poems is unease about being a Western traveller in the East. In "A Walk in Kyoto," for example, he qualifies his gaze upon Japan as a "phallic western eye"; in *The Creative Writer* he generalizes to say that poets are "trailed by the spectres of their experiences" (28). Birney's effort to mark his "positionality as [an] investigating subject" (Spivak, 296) seems to acknowledge a potentially complicitous role in the production of knowledge *vis-à-vis* his placement within a specific institution (Western patriarchy) and a certain class (bourgeois traveller). Yet his effort in good faith to situate himself too often results in a form of Western solipsism.

This solipsism is apparent in Birney's invocation of the traditional humanistic *topos* of the poem as touchstone of universal brotherhood. In the "Preface" to his *Selected Poems 1940-1966*, Birney writes, "my poems are the best proof I can print of *my humanness*, signals out of the loneliness into which all of us are born and in which we die, affirmations of kinship" (xii; my emphasis). If his poetry proves *Birney's* "humanness," then it fundamentally represents a journey into the self, regardless of the variety of locales. "Affirmations of kinship" of "all of us" articulates a classical liberal humanism which subordinates the recognition of cultural difference to a kind of universalism that unquestioningly treats Western values as the norm.

Even at the moment of framing his poetry with generous sentiments, and despite his own intentions, Birney demonstrates how "the Orient has helped to define Europe (or the West)," how Orientalism "has less to do with the Orient than it does with 'our' world" (Said, 1, 12). Again, this is not so much a choice Birney makes as it is a condition which he lives. In this sense, his poetry is an important barometer of the historical moment in which it was created; Birney's poetry embodies the cultural politics of the conjuncture at which he stood as a witness on the Delhi Road. To return to Said: "any and all representations, because they *are* representations, are embedded first in the language and then in the culture, institutions, and political ambience of the representer" (272; Said's emphasis). Birney elliptically names his "political ambience" when he considers his poem as an act in the world intended to have certain effects. His "desire," "mild and fading" though it be, is "to use [his] personal spell to raise those ghosts [of guilt feelings] among others—among you, if you will listen" (*Creative Writer*, 16). With this line he introduces a reading of his poem for his radio audience; and to specify what place the raising of guilt has in defining what is for Birney "our world," it is necessary to read "The Bear on the Delhi Road" in terms of "guilt-raising" as a symbolic resolution of the contradictions implicit in his creative endeavour.

II. "THE BEAR ON THE DELHI ROAD"

In "The Bear on the Delhi Road," acoustic, visual, and spatial patterns imbue the poem with a performative quality which reflects Birney's dictum in *The Creative Writer* that "successful" poetry should be "something inescapably auditory as well as visual" (72).[4] The poem disrupts its own ontological status as either script or presumed utterance, demanding equally the attention of the eye as well as the ear.[5] Playful modulations of the word "Bear," for example, give rise to various interwoven acoustic and visual patterns.

Visually, the digraph ea from "bear" appears sixteen times in the poem, creating a repeated visual pattern for the eye to follow: "Bear," "Unreal," "bear," "beating," "leap," "great," "teach," "peaceful," "bear," "wear," "wear," "bear," "reach," "easy," "reality," "rear." Two acoustic patterns with slight variation emerge from this visual ea pattern. The first sound pattern is that of words that rhyme with "bear." Bear is pronounced (bār) and the corresponding International Phonetic Alphabet vowel symbol is (eə): bear/ air/ spare/ bare/ wear/ berries. The second sound pattern that emerges from the visual ea pattern of the word "bear" is the vowel sound as in the word "unreal." "Unreal" is pronounced (ŭnrēal) and the corresponding International Phonetic Alphabet vowel symbol is (i): The/ teach/ deodars/ reality/ Unreal/ peaceful/ easy/ rear/ these/ beating/ free/ leap/ reach. The euphonic presence of these vowel sound patterns, (eə) and (i), is disrupted by the poem's cacophonic k and b sound patterns of alliteration: k: flicks/ stick/ clamorous/ kill/ crooked/ Kashmir/ galvanic/ claws/ locusts; b: body/ beating/ ambling/ about /brilliant/ berries/ fabulous/ bald/ both. Minor patterns of alliteration further disrupt the poem's patterns of assonance and consonance: the b in "beating" and "brilliant," the l in "locusts" and "leap," the t in "great" and "mate," the f and k in "flicks" and "stick," the k in "clamorous" and "kill," the l, r, and ch in "lurch," the l and v in "alive" and "living," the f in "four" and "footed." The rhythmically uneven distribution of vowel patterns with alliterative consonant patterns in the poem intimates the presence of a discordant music—a "bearish rhythm"—that, by implication, is the same music as that which accompanies the bear and men in their dance (*Creative Writer*, 16).

Both men and bear are described by words whose sounds express or reinforce the sound they denote through onomatopoeia. The man "flicks   flicks" at the bear with a stick and the men want the bear to "lurch   lurch" with them as they "dance."

In sympathy with the auditory accompaniment *to* the dance itself, as implied by the narrative *of* the dance in the poem, is an erratic visual (s)pacing of single words and groups of words that represent the poem's meaning through visual effects. In particular, the unusual typography of the first stanza mimics the bear's awkward attempts, its "fearful, dumb hopping," to stand on its back legs and walk in a human-like manner (*Creative Writer*, 16). Just as the bear takes several solid and sturdy steps and then loses its balance, taking several fragmented and disjointed steps, so the irregular (s)paced lettering of the poem expresses this movement: "Unreal   tall as a myth / by the road the Himalayan bear / is beating the brilliant air / with his crooked arms / About him two men   bare / spindly as locusts   leap." The first line of this stanza is broken, but the movement of the following three lines is secure, as if the bear has found its footing but then loses its step again in the last two broken lines.

The interrelatedness of formal and semantic aspects of the poem identifies Birney with a literary modernism that attempts to co-ordinate aural and visual patterns. "Why not," says Birney, "give the eye as much as it can use to extend the experience of the poem?" (*Creative Writer*, 72). Implicit in this modernist insistence on integrating a visual emphasis into poetics is the doctrine of "spatial form," in which the poet effects in the reader's imagination a timeless spatialization of the poem's linear sequence of words.[6] The poem bears the mark of a retrospective spatialization of narrative in its closing epigraph, "Srinagar 1958/Île des Porquerolles 1959," in which the difference in year and the two locations obliquely suggest an allegory of composition by which the Asian experience (in Srinagar) is cast into a final poetic form once Birney regains his European perspective (from a French island in the Mediterranean). The result is an iconic poem that spatializes "the tranced dancing of men."

This dancing takes place against the backdrop of a journey through a space in which what is behind (i.e., the past) is associated with positive qualities, and what is ahead (i.e., the future) with negative ones. In abstact terms, there is a movement from high to low; in geographic terms, from mountain to city; and in cultural terms, from the "fabulous hills" to Delhi's marketplace of entertainment. The "bald alien plain" on which they stand is, then, most notably a place of transition. The medial aspect of the poem is figured in a metaphoric exchange of qualities between the bear and the Kashmiris. Both are described in similar colloquial expressions, as "mate" and "fellow." The bear is anthropomorphized when described as beating its "arms," and the Kashmiris are animalized when they are described as being "bare / spindly as locusts." The bear/ bare homonym encapsulates this exchange; the difference between the bear's "shaggy body" and the Kashmiris' thin bodies is rhetorically glossed over by this figure. By the end of the poem the Kashmiris have gained some of the bear's mythic quality, while the bear has acquired some of the banality of human identity.

The implication of this mutual exchange is that identity itself has a dance-like quality. The surfeit of verbal constructions reiterates the physical and metaphoric movement found throughout the poem. The first stanza begins in the progressive tense ("is beating") to express continuing action; figuratively, there is a suggestion that the bear beats out a tune in the air. In stanza three, the action of the two men leading the bear is expressed in the main verb "led," which is attached to an auxiliary verb "have," just as the bear is attached to the two men. Infinitive verbs convey a sense of abstract timelessness: "to kill," "to teach," "to dance," "to wear," "to stay," "to prance," "to paw," "to free," and "to lurch." The combination of stasis and movement conveyed by the dance motif at this grammatical level is summed up by the universalizing movement from "him to dance" to "they dance" and, finally, "the tranced dancing of men."

The European perspective Birney attains from the Île des Porquerolles under-writes the universalizing of the Kashmiris' condition of wretchedness. To indicate sympathy with the men for whom "it is no more joyous . . . / in this hot dust to prance," Birney makes a gesture no doubt intended to be universally inclusive (despite the gendered collective noun "men") by calling the Kashmiri dance the "tranced dancing of *men*" (my emphasis). This elevation of the scene into an expression of a human condition represents an attempt to resolve the poet's felt contradiction. He wants to identify with the wretched men (I share your pain), yet is conscious of his own complicity as a Westerner in, if not creating, then at least not forestalling, their misery, a complicity spoken by the poet's aesthetic and geographic distance from the subjects at the end of the poem.

By representing the Kashmiris' condition as universal, Birney forges a chiasmus-like relationship with them: as a man, he is a tranced dancer, therefore he shares their "wretchedness"; they attain the ability to signify the immanence of the uni-versal in the particular, of the sacred in the profane. The poet's relationship with the Kashmiris is structured like that of the Kashmiris' relationship with the bear; in each case there is a mutual exchange of qualities, and this recuperates the loss associated with the medial space in which they move, by qualifying that loss as a greater gain.

At a rhetorical level, this qualification is possible because the word "tranced" can mean both "abject suffering" and also "ecstatic detachment." Birney thus displaces the contradiction inherent in his position as a writer onto the liminality of the word "tranced." Resolving his positional contradiction by representing it through the synthesizing powers of the word "trance" is an act determined by his political self-awareness, the cultural politics of modernism, and the fortuitous duplicity of a word.

Yet there is a further element which determines the choice of "trance," imbued as it is with spiritual resonance—namely, Birney's sustained concern with Can-ada's national identity and with developing national myths.[7] This poem, ostensibly about India, is an Asian detour which helps its author determine where *here* is by determining where it is not. W.H. New argues that the "reaffirmation of imaginative power" Birney seeks "could only come after recognizing Canada's geographical/mental relationship with Asia as well as with Europe" (264). The poem evinces this relational effort in its meditation on the identity of the men and the bear, a meditation that ends with the enigmatic pronouncement, "It is not easy to free / myth from reality."

Successive appearances of the terms "myth" and "reality" in the poem trace the same descent/ascent movement—a loss of a transcendent vision followed by the recuperation of this loss through a redemptive immanence—as is contained in the term "tranced dancing." The phrase "galvanic they dance" suggests that actions take place involuntarily as though controlled by nervous convulsion through the automatistic effects of material progress, the locus of which in the poem is the city of Delhi, where the men will make "their living" by exhibiting the bear. Opposed to the oppressive reality of the modern condition are the marvellous qualities of the bear's Himalayan associations, which make the animal "tall as a myth." This opposition supports an initial, naïve reading of the problem of freeing "myth from reality" as analogous to the difficulty of separating gold from dross. Yet, for the bear the Himalayas are a pleasant reality—it has a wish "forever to stay / only an ambling bear / four-footed in berries." This passage suggests that the positions of "myth" and "reality" on a hierarchy of value, far from being inherent to the concepts themselves, are contingent on the way the terms are mapped onto the opposition between necessity (the forces of history that deprive the individual of freedom) and possibility (the availability of choices that constitute freedom). The phrase "free myth from reality" in this sense suggests the difficulty in opening up a space of freedom in the realm of necessity. It is thus a formula expressing the conundrum that the phrase "tranced dancing" solves; all men share in the euphoric immanence of the possible even while appearing to be controlled by outside forces.

It is the historical circumstances of the poem that make the connection between this abstract, displaced articulation of the redemptive potential of myth and Birney's nationalism. He effectively uses the Kashmiri scene to affirm an existential acceptance of limitation and the creative potential of Canada's *lack* of myths. As W.H. New concludes, "The Asian experience . . . lets Birney also discover his ability to reconcile history and myth and to face the idea of 'Nothing' with equanimity. Finding 'nada' within 'Canada' can therefore become for him in return a kind of cosmic joke" (266). New makes the link between the poem's thematic treatment of history and Birney's literary nationalism by suggesting the moral of the tale: "Silence and absence become curiously positive virtues" (266). New is right to locate Birney's representation of historicity most centrally in the poem's notion of negation. It is in the Kashmiris' very determination by the forces of history and in their lack of choice that they participate in history conceived of as the effect of humanity's collective will.

But to get the rest of the story we must ask at whose expense Birney tells this "cosmic joke" affirming the nothingness that dwells within Canada. Even to pose this question is to shift the poem's meaning from an affirmation of Canada's postcolonial possibilities to an act not untouched by the violence of defining the self by writing over the Asian "other." Ultimately, it is in this double gesture that we must locate the poem's value as Birney's *active* voicing of the cultural politics that result from his own determination *by* history *as* Canadian nationalist, *as* modernist, and *as* a liberal who conscientiously attempts to represent the complicated pathways of sympathy uncovered in the act of travelling. Contrary to the acceptance suggested by New's tone of affirmation and sought in Birney's hopeful invocation of his "personal spell . . . if you will listen" (*Creative Writer*, 16), however, it must be acknowledged that for us today "The Bear on the Delhi Road" stands as a completely equivocal monument to the nature of modern Canada's encounter with a non-European culture.[8]

Notes

[1] Birney's choice of the verb "unravel" to describe his critical project embodies a double meaning that he seems unaware of. While "unravel" can indicate an active effort "to disentangle" something, it can also mean "to come undone," suggesting an agency beyond one's control (*OED*).

[2] On the uncanny see Freud (399).

[3] As Henry Louis Gates, Jr. notes in his introduction to *"Race," Writing and Difference*, the use of the term "race" is problematic for its essentialist implications, i.e., its suggestion that such a term can refer exactly to some material phenomenon. I am aware that my use of the term "race" is open to question; nevertheless, I can find no other term that is not equally essentialist.

[4] In *The Creative Writer*, "The Bear on the Delhi Road" *is* punctuated, as it is in *The Bear on the Delhi Road* (1973) and *Ice Cod Bell or Stone* (1962), where it was first published. In this paper I am analysing a version of the poem that *does not* have any punctuation as this is the accepted copy text in anthologies, and is the one that Birney himself seems to recognize as such in *The Collected Poems of Earle Birney* Vol.2 (1975). The version of "The Bear on the Delhi Road" in *The Creative Writer* is conventionally punctuated, although this goes against Birney's discussion of his new experiments with radical forms of punctuation (i.e., blank spaces or no punctuation) in another one of his talks (see "Experimentation Today," 72). However, a version of the poem that appeared in *Selected Poems 1940-1966* the same year as *The Creative Writer* (1966) does not have any punctuation and contains this comment by Birney: "Belatedly but willingly influenced by contemporary trends, I've come to surround my pauses with space rather than with typographical spatter" (ix). My quotations of Birney's poem are from *The Collected Works of Earle Birney*.

[5] For a discussion of text as script and utterance, see Garrett Stewart's *Reading Voices* in which he discusses the "somatic and referential dimension" of the "acoustics of textuality" (11).

[6] The relationship of historicism to spatial form within a Modernist framework is discussed in Joseph Frank's "Spatial Form in Modern Literature." According to Frank, "the dimension of depth has vanished from the plastic arts . . . [P]ast and present are seen spatially, locked in a timeless unity which, while it may accentuate surface differences, eliminates any feeling of historical sequence by the very act of juxtaposition" (653).

[7] Such concern with myth and/as national identity is reflected in a poem like "Can. Lit." where Birney writes, "it's only by our lack of ghosts / we're haunted." Birney's interest in supernatural figures such as ghosts, spooks, spectres, and valkyries constitutes an interesting, and, I believe, unexplored thematic element in his work.

[8] I wish to thank Paul Brophy and Leslie Arnovick for their generous advice and valuable comments.

Works Cited

Bhabha, Homi. "Difference, Discrimination, and the Discourse of Colonialism." *The Politics of Theory*. Francis Barker et al., eds. Colchester: Univ. of Essex, 1983: 198-211.

Birney, Earle. *The Bear on the Delhi Road*. London: Chatto and Windus, 1973.

———. *The Collected Poems of Earle Birney*. 2 vols. Toronto: McClelland and Stewart, 1975.

———. *The Creative Writer*. Toronto: Canadian Broadcasting Corp., 1966.

———. *Ice Cod Bell or Stone*. Toronto: McClelland and Stewart, 1962.

———. *Selected Poems, 1940-1966*. Toronto: McClelland and Stewart, 1966.

Frank, Joseph. "Spatial Form in Modern Literature: An Essay in Two Parts." *Sewanee Review* 53 (April 1945): 221-40, 433-56, 643-53.

Freud, Sigmund. *Introductory Lectures on Psychoanalysis*. James Strachey, trans. and ed. New York: W.W. Norton, 1966.

Gates, Henry Louis, Jr., ed. *"Race," Writing and Difference*. Chicago: Univ. of Chicago Press, 1986.

Goldie, Terry. *Fear and Temptation: The Image of the Indigene in Canadian, Australian, and New Zealand Literatures*. Montreal: McGill-Queen's Univ. Press, 1989.

New, W.H. *Articulating West: Essays on Purpose and Form in Modern Canadian Literature*. Toronto: New Press, 1972.

Said, Edward. *Orientalism*. New York: Vintage, 1979.

Spivak, Gayatri Chakravorty. "Can the Subaltern Speak?" *Marxism and the Interpretation of Culture*. Cary Nelson and Lawrence Grossberg, eds. London: Macmillan, 1988: 277-313.

Stewart, Garrett. *Reading Voices: Literature and the Phonotext*. Berkeley: Univ. of California Press, 1990.

Young, Robert. *White Mythologies: Writing History and the West*. New York: Routledge, 1990.

Reading Dionne Brand's
"Blues Spiritual for Mammy Prater"

Diana Brydon

For the past two years I have been teaching Canadian poetry in the context of issue-oriented courses designed to interrogate the construction and representation of postcolonial women's identities, rather than in the more conventional context of a course specifically organized around genre and nation. Such a focus can change our understanding of Canadian poetic traditions, shifting attention from continuity to disruption and from homogeneity to heterogeneities. Students who may once have seen a poem as an object foreign to their lives may find themselves re-experiencing poetry as a process in which they as readers are invited to become intimately and painfully, as well as pleasurably, involved. Such involvement happens when the focus shifts from "Literature" as an entity to be studied and valorized as the achievement of the great ones among us, to writing as one of the most powerful discursive modes for constructing ourselves in relation to our communities and our environment; and to reading defined as active participation in those discursive processes.

My course, "Reading Women in the Postcolonial Context," advertised itself as "designed to introduce students to the study of contemporary feminist theory and a wide variety of women's texts, encouraging them to bring theory and reading practice together in a co-operative and questioning spirit." We began by considering the multicultural, postcolonial nature of Canada—moving from exploratory readings in work by women (First Nations and immigrant), from our own culture—out into readings in poststructuralist feminist theory, and then on into some of the different postcolonial contexts of other parts of the English-speaking world.

The twenty-four students who took the course came with varying backgrounds and levels of expertise in critical practice. For most of them, this course was their first encounter with poststructuralist theory. We used Chris Weedon's *Feminist Practice and Poststructuralist Theory* to provide us with our initial orientation and then as a touchstone for our progress throughout the course. Her call for a "theory of the relation between language, subjectivity, social organization and power" (12) became our working agenda.

Dionne Brand's "Blues Spiritual for Mammy Prater" reformulated those relations for us in a particularly powerful way. Deceptively simple in language and construction, it initially appears completely accessible to the reader, only to throw that sense of accessibility into question through its self-conscious re-enactment of the scene of reading. Brand's speaker describes the moment of her own interpellation as Black woman, implicated in African-American diasporic history, as she finds herself captivated, in "turning the leaves of a book," by the eyes of an old Black woman in a photograph. The White reader of Brand's poem finds herself outside this interlocking gaze, participating vicariously in its emotional intensity but outside the "pact of blood across a century" and the cultural traditions it has generated.

We readers "see" the photograph only through Brand's construction of her own complex response to it. In its focus on describing Brand's encounter with the image of an individual ex-slave woman, the poem forestalls our bringing of our own cultural responses to slavery into play, allowing Brand space to establish her own perspective. This is an important tactical move. In my experience, most White students bring to Black writing a complex mixture of emotional expectations based on guilt, fascinated horror for the evils of slavery, and a genuine curiosity about cultural difference. Such emotions, left unexamined, may lead unwittingly to further objectification of the very other they wish to embrace in compensation for the past process of victimization. Brand's poem prevents the bringing into play of such emotions by establishing immediately her own, and Mammy Prater's taken-for-granted, subjectivity and agency. They determine the terms on which they will be read, not defiantly in opposition to those who would see victims, but as a matter of dedication to truth and clarity in reconstructing an important moment of recognition. That recognition, of the complex ties that bind the poet to Mammy Prater, reminds Brand of her cultural heritage as a Black woman in North America, and, implicitly, of the ways in which that cultural memory has contributed to the construction of her own sense of identity and of the choices open to her, through history and language.

The poem names itself as "blues spiritual," a culturally specific Black American mode of signifying, born in resistance to slavery, pride in difference, and in communal, oral forms of expression. It employs many of the organizing principles of the blues, specifically repetition and call and response patterns, adapting them within its own framework as written artifact.

It is written for Mammy Prater, a real person, an ex-slave, whom the author knows only through her photograph—that is, through another culturally constructed representation. The name Mammy Prater, itself, carries symbolic resonances. Prater suggests "prating," a form of speech usually associated with women and children, designating chatter, idle talk to little purpose. A prater, then, is a chatterer. It seems an ironic name for a person who speaks only through the silence of a photograph, a person whose perspective and voice have been silenced through history and the law, yet it also seems appropriate that in this poem the poet will see an important message in what has previously been misunderstood, denigrated, and overlooked, a message she initially sees as coded only for her but that she shares with her readers through the course of the poem.

"Mammy" incorporates the dominant American stereotype of the Black woman. Selma James describes the mammy as "a mythologised Black woman" (94), whose "fulfilment in life came from serving the white family" (95), yet who paradoxically proved to be "the living contradiction to all the racist stereotypes and myths against Black people, that we were sub-human, that we were stupid, that we were savages" (96). Brand's Mammy Prater exploits that contradiction, focusing on the power rather than on the servility of this mammy. Derogatory cultural stereotypes are interrogated and dismantled through the poet's re-reading of an apparently straightforward photograph and its caption.

"Blues Spiritual" is a poem about agency, about acting and being acted upon, about acting in history and in art. The poem is prompted into life by the act of looking, locating its beginning in the speaker of the poem finding her attention arrested by the eyes in a photograph of Mammy Prater, "'115 years old when her photograph was taken.'" The structure of representation within which photographs usually operate sets up a subject/object relation, in which the viewer looks and the photographed object is looked at. Furthermore, within our patriarchal symbolic structure, the gaze is always male, so that even if the watcher is female, looking itself is already constructed for her in terms of the objectifying male gaze. Brand's poem, however, defies these conventions, to make Mammy Prater the taker rather than the taken of this photograph, and eventually to establish a reciprocal gaze, woman to woman, between Mammy Prater and the speaker of "Blues Spiritual." This gaze has given rise to the poem, which reconstructs that moment of origin. The poem metaphorically reproduces the call-and-response pattern of the blues. Brand reconstructs the photo's "call," including its silent message in her elaborated "response." The poem begins and ends with the call of the photograph; Mammy Prater's call initiates the poet's meditation on how that call interpellates her through reconstructing imaginatively the history and identity of Mammy Prater, an ancestor figure.

Mammy Prater is constructed as the subject who waits, transforming waiting itself through the force of her will. If there is play here on the double meanings of waiting as serving and waiting as anticipation of change, then the emphasis falls on the latter, conceiving it as active rather than passive, as the energy and will-power required to "avoid killing a white man" rather than as the passive endurance of time and suffering. Her waiting is so intensely powerful in its silently reproduced photographic image that it "calls" to the poet from beyond the grave. Six times we are told "she waited," and each time the waiting takes on more power.

Repetition, a central structural principle of the blues, is more than a literary or musical device: it embodies a world view that recognizes the inevitability of repetition as a natural principle instead of suppressing repetition in search of progress, or movement away from the ground of being. James Snead suggests that Black culture highlights repetition, "often in homage to an original generative instance or act" (218). In this poem, Mammy Prater's eloquent waiting, expressed through the call of her eyes to the poet, provides this generative instance. Snead further points out that repetition is essential to improvisation, showing the "desire to rely upon 'the thing that is there to pick up'" (221). Brand's poem can be understood as an improvisation upon the paradoxical theme of Mammy Prater's silent call.

Against our commonsense understanding that a photographer "takes" a photograph and that what is photographed is "taken," Brand's poem insists that

Mammy Prater herself "waited until it suited her / to take this photograph and to put those eyes in it." Those eyes repetitively engage the poet-onlooker, and then, through that speaker's mediating words, they address us, in our role as readers. My students heard the first person voice, the I, behind every mention of Mammy Prater's eyes. The link here between subjectivity and seeing does seem to be central. Mammy Prater focuses her call through the medium of her eyes, using her body to speak what slavery prevented her from writing or saying.

For Brand, the photograph becomes Mammy Prater's "self-portrait"; the unknown photographer becomes "superfluous" to her triumphant assertion of her own subjectivity through the means that were to hand. Brand's narrator's reading of the photograph sees and recreates a character who turns her own body into a work of art with a message to convey—"she perfected this pose." Her history, her pain and her survival, may be read in her eyes but is also present, in a more contradictory form, in the "etching" on her body, etching left on the gait of her legs by the fields she worked, etching over which she had no control but which in the photograph becomes the material with which she works: "she sculpted it over a shoulder of pain." Although the poet can recognize that this "shoulder of pain" is "a thing like despair," she sees too that Mammy Prater could never have acknowledged despair and survived the degradation of "the days that she was a mule." (For those familiar with Jamaican English, "mule" takes on further derogatory reference: barren women are called mules. By failing to bear children, they forfeit their right to be considered human within their community. This word fuses the double burden of Mammy Prater's identity: to white slave-owners, she is a mule because she is Black, but she also risks demotion to the subhuman among her own people if she fails to meet their cultural expectations of women.) Although treated as if she were subhuman, her body transformed by that drudgery, Mammy Prater retains the signs of her humanity in her eyes, which speak the I of a human self who never relinquished the right to determine her own destiny and control her own body.

At this point in the poem, the syntax becomes unclear. The line "deliberately and unintentionally" may modify the action of the fields on Mammy Prater's body or the nature of her waiting, or—more logically perhaps, but less suggestively—the etchings may be left deliberately and the waiting may be unintentional. But how can the waiting be described as unintentional here, when the entire first and last verses of the poem insist that it is deliberate? The effect of such a line, however one decides to read it (and there seems to be no definitive reading), is to focus attention on the indefinite itself and to force consideration of a paradox: in what ways may an action be both deliberate and unintentional? The line pushes the reader into a mode of thinking beyond dualities. The preceding lines have made it impossible for the reader to think of Mammy Prater as either a victim or a triumphant survivor. Megan Stitt, one of the students in our class, points out that "Brand creates here a conflict that, unresolved, makes you think." Mammy Prater's control over history ("she planned it down to the day / the light") and over her own body ("her breasts / her hands") coexists with the lack of control implied by her "days as a mule" (Stitt, 5).

Because it was forbidden to teach slaves to read and write, she was probably illiterate, yet she contrived to write, metaphorically speaking, a message in her eyes that "her fingers could not script" but that the poet would instantly understand.

The construction of Mammy Prater's subjecthood being enacted here may be illuminated by recourse to the distinction often made between race, which is increasingly being recognized as having no ontological reality, and racism, which self-evidently exists. Similarly, although slavery clearly existed, it does not follow that slavery produced slaves. If those human beings designated slaves by those who held power over them refused to see themselves through their "master's" eyes, as slaves (as mules), then their self-definition as human beings produces a paradox for the slaveholders but not for themselves. Brand's poem tells us that Mammy Prater had to wait one hundred and fifteen years for technology to perfect "a surface sensitive enough / to hold her eyes" so that the viewer of her image might see her as she saw herself. It suggests that Mammy Prater's faith that eventually such communication could be achieved operated as a sustaining fiction through the dark years when she was misread or not even "seen" as a person at all. The poet too, the poem suggests, clings to her necessary fictions. She needs to believe that this message was planned especially for her, despite the casual "turning the leaves of a book" that first led to this momentous "noticing." This mutual need to see and be seen connects the two women across more than a century.

This need is intimately related to the historical legacies of imperialism and slavery. Cornel West writes that "The modern Black diaspora problematic of invisibility and namelessness can be understood as the condition of relative lack of Black power to represent themselves to themselves and others as complex human beings, and thereby to contest the bombardment of negative, degrading stereotypes put forward by White supremacist ideologies" (27). These problems were exacerbated for Black women. As the title of a now-classic text puts it, *All the Women Are White, All the Blacks Are Men, But Some of Us Are Brave*; neither Black Studies nor Women's Studies were initially capable of seeing Black women as having their own subjectivities based on their own experiences of gender and race as inseparable. In "Blues Spiritual for Mammy Prater," the Black woman subject is both seen and named. But Brand's poem goes far beyond merely replacing the negative stereotypes with positive Black images; it attempts to change the relations of representation.

Brand has written that "All the Black people here have a memory whether they know it or not, whether they like it or not, whether they remember it or not, and, in that memory are words such as land, sea, whip, work, rap, coffle, sing, sweat, release, days . . . without . . . this . . . pain . . . coming . . . We know . . . have a sense . . . hold a look in our eyes . . . about it . . . have to fight every day for our humanity . . . redeem it every day" ("Bread," 52-3). The poem "Blues Spiritual" dramatizes a moment when that memory pushes itself forward into consciousness, making itself felt once more in all the immediacy of a physical experience.

Through the communal affirmative repetitions of the blues ("she waited / she waited . . . to make sure / to make sure . . . she knew / she knew . . . she waited . . . to write in those eyes what her fingers could not script . . . her eyes"), we are invited to share in the poet's reconstruction of a human face from a brutal past. As readers, we are denied the position of voyeur. We never see the photograph. What we see is the potential for realigning the sight lines of how we look at other people and how we construct our understanding of what we see in relation to ourselves. It is important for us to understand this poem within the context established by the title of the collection in which it appears, *No Language Is Neutral*. The poem makes itself a gift for Mammy Prater, in exchange for the gift of Mammy Prater's inspiring photograph. It is "for" Mammy Prater, implicitly "against" those who would see her and use her as a mule and those who simply would not see her at all. In taking this interested stand, the poem insists that we understand poetry as a culturally significant act, capable of creating as well as reflecting and maintaining community values.

As bell hooks reminds us: "There is a radical difference between a repudiation of the idea that there is a black 'essence' and recognition of the way black identity has been specifically constituted in the experience of exile and struggle" (hooks, 29). There is no question of a Black "essence" in "Blues Spiritual" but there is a carefully articulated understanding of the ways in which Black women's identities have been constituted through history and language. Brand writes as a poet who grew up in Trinidad and now lives in Toronto. Her cross-cultural position as poet, as well as the boundary-crossing subjects she chooses to address, question the systemic pressures that shape and mis-shape our subjectivities as people defined through categories such as gender, ethnicity, class, or nation. Her poetry, whatever its explicit subject matter or setting, explores questions of crucial interest to Canadians today. Although ostensibly addressing what some might see as an American (i.e., U.S.) topic, "Blues Spiritual for Mammy Prater" speaks directly to our Canadian obsessions with cultural continuities and identity formation, refusing simplistic embracings of "essence" in favour of more complicated explorations of subject construction. According to Chris Weedon, in feminist post-structuralist criticism, "The central focus of interest becomes the way in which texts construct meanings and subject positions for the reader, the contradictions inherent in this process and its political implications, both in its historical context and in the present" (167). This is the approach I have tried to elaborate here, but it is also the process I see at work in "Blues Spiritual for Mammy Prater," creating a *mise en abîme* effect in which Brand focuses on the ways in which the photo of Mammy Prater constructs meanings and subject positions for her persona as reader. I have also focused on the ways in which Brand's persona constructs meanings and subject positions for us—myself and you, my readers— as readers. In enacting such a process, Brand ensures that we must live and think both inside and outside the poem. "Blues Spiritual for Mammy Prater" lures us deep into the heart of its poetry only to show us the multiple ways in which poetry is continuous with the world.

Works Cited

Brand, Dionne. "Blues Spiritual for Mammy Prater." *No Language Is Neutral*. Toronto: Coach House Press, 1990: 17-19.

———. "Bread Out of Stone." *Language in Her Eye: Views on Writing and Gender by Canadian Women Writing in English*. Libby Scheier, Sarah Sheard, and Eleanor Wachtel, eds. Toronto: Coach House Press, 1990: 45-53.

Ferguson, Russell et al., eds. *Out There: Marginalization and Contemporary Cultures*. New York: New Museum of Contemporary Art, and Cambridge, Mass.: MIT Press, 1990.

hooks, bell. *Yearning: Race, Gender, and Cultural Politics*. Boston: South End Press, 1990.

Hull, Gloria T., Patricia Bell Scott, and Barbara Smith, eds. *All the Women Are White, All the Blacks Are Men, But Some of Us Are Brave: Black Women's Studies*. Old Westbury, N.Y.: Feminist Press, 1982.

James, Selma. *The Ladies and the Mammies: Jane Austen & Jean Rhys*. Bristol: Falling Wall, 1983.

Snead, James. A. "Repetition as a Figure of Black Culture." Ferguson et al., 213-32.

Stitt, Megan Perigoe. "A Touch of History in *No Language Is Neutral*." Student Essay for English 410, Guelph University, submitted 28 Nov. 1991.

Weedon, Chris. *Feminist Practice and Poststructuralist Theory*. Oxford: Blackwell, 1987.

West, Cornel. "The New Cultural Politics of Difference." Ferguson et al., 19-38.

Robert Bringhurst's "Sunday Morning": A Dialogue

Robert Bringhurst and Laurie Ricou

I. WHITE PELICAN, BLUE JAY   ROBERT BRINGHURST

For Laurie Ricou

Blue flash in the alder, then in the evergreen. The Steller's jays are leaping like manic acrobats through the conical, fragrant brain of the Douglas-fir. Here today, gone today, no promises, no knowing whether the same tree will be full or empty tomorrow.

I have heard it said that the critic is to the poet as the ornithologist is to the bird. It isn't so. The poet is a mind without a skull to keep it covered, standing on one leg, gesticulating, dumb. Dumb when the wind is still, at any rate, and often monotonous when it blows. If the critic is the ornithologist, the poem is the bird and the poet is the tree.

And if the critic is like most ornithologists of the moment, she is an honourable woman or he is an honourable man: intelligent, quiet, alert, and slow to malice. Even if the enlightened ornithologist feels professionally obliged to shoot the bird, measure its eyeballs and its bones, and examine its stomach contents in the lab, he or she is unlikely to be carrying a chainsaw.

But what can the tree do when the ornithologist, hesitant to shoot the bird and eager for other sources of information, comes to the tree with his bundle of hewn and seasoned questions?

—*Cyanocitta stelleri* was seen to emerge from your branches. Are you responsible for this poem? Was it hatched in your embrace? And if it was, was it hatched in a nest that had been built there by others of its kind?

—Sir, we have a riddle here in the forest: If a word is spoken without a tree to hear it, is there anything it can mean? But in this case, even after I have heard you, I do not know what to say. Trees, as you know, are never weaned. Their eyes are shut, their faces underground. Their brains accrue between their legs; their minds are open to the weather. Many small thoughts bore into the wood and take up residence and breed. Large thoughts come and go and leave no record. If the sun shines and the rain falls and the rain has not been poisoned, and if no one cuts us down to make those packing crates for humans you call houses, I am happy. If the rain turns sour and the smog grows thick, I die. But even if I knew the answers to your questions, how could I discuss the private lives of my tenants, former tenants, visitors, friends?

—Well, what about this pelican? Do pelicans roost in trees?

—To the best of my knowledge—you are the ornithologist, remember—

pelicans roost on water. But do you know Octavio Paz's poem *Piedra de sol*, which opens and closes with trees made of water?

> *un sauce de cristal, un chopo de agua,*
> *un alto surtidor que el viento arquea,*
> *un âbol bien plantado mas danzante,*
> *un caminar de río que se curva,*
> *avanza, retrocede, da un rodeo*
> *y llega siempre . . .*

—Would you be willing to translate that?

> —a willow of crystal, a poplar of water,
> a tall fountain that the wind heels over,
> a tree, deeply rooted but still dancing,
> a riverbed, a channel that meanders,
> advances, retreats, pirouettes,
> and is always arriving . . .

—I have a poem here entitled "Sunday Morning" and circumstantial evidence that indicates you wrote it. It includes a great white pelican, the sun, the moon, a saxifrage, a mountain, Guatemala, Great Slave Lake, two kinds of pines, and a considerable clutter of abstractions. Or it includes words that symbolize all these. It is a page and a half long and lives in a book. Is it a bird? Are you a tree?

—It sings and I don't. At least, it makes a noise—like a breeding pelican or a jay—that I call singing.

—Did you write it?

—I don't know. It came together in my mind, my limbs. (In you, those may be different; in me, they are the same.) I saw it, heard it, felt it, thought it, tasted it. I began to mumble, to stutter, like a piece of old machinery trying to sing. I was ashamed, I suppose, of my own incoherence. So I kept at it until I could speak a few clear phrases. After a time, I even grew fond of them. Then, so as not to forget them, I wrote them down. But I'm misleading you if I sound like Mackenzie King. It was no more uncanny than meeting someone in the street, knowing the face and having trouble recalling the name. It was much like that, but more involved, and it went on longer.

—How long?

—Weeks, I suppose, of fairly continuous consternation. At a lower intensity, it goes on even now, after six or seven years. I don't have all the words right yet, and never will. The text is as hard as a rock, yet if I turn it in the light, some phrases often seem to change. Bits here and there. Deliberate irresolutions, perhaps. Since it isn't a neoclassical composition, it doesn't have a cadenza.

—Why the title "Sunday Morning"? Is this an allusion to a poem of the same name by Wallace Stevens? to the CBC radio program? to Christian worship?

—If those allusions seem significant to you, I'm willing to take the blame. In my opinion, the most important source of the name is simple fact. It was

Sunday morning when I saw the pelican. But if I had seen the pelican on Wednesday night, I might have looked for a name of a different kind.

—So there really was a pelican?

—There was a solitary pelican, afloat among the goldeneyes and scoters, on the outer harbour of Vancouver, on a Sunday morning in the fall. Vancouver, as you know, is not on the flyway of the great white pelican. In a six-year vigil by that water, where none would be expected, that's one of two white pelicans I saw.

—Could you be sure it was a pelican?

—I've seen many on the river between Great Slave Lake and Athabasca, where they breed, and in the south, where they spend the winter, and a few en route between. But I was the stray on those occasions; I was the visitor. On this occasion—speaking of strictly impersonal events, you understand, in personal terms—the pelican came to me.

—Did you compose the poem at once, after seeing the pelican?

—Not that I know of. It was a very busy time. Other visitors, in addition to the pelican, were passing through town. Don McKay, Jan Zwicky, Gary Snyder, Les, Murray and other friends came and went within two or three weeks, equally far from their usual flyways. Most of them stayed only a few days. But of all those conversations, which were many and intense, the wordless one with the pelican is the one that stayed most vividly in my mind. And I contributed nothing to it: nothing but intent inaction. The pelican had been gone for weeks or months before I found my tongue.

—What about the other proper names in the poem: *Saxifraga punctata*, Mount Hozameen?

—Other fragments of the truth, come to roost in the tree or stand with it, in honour of the pelican. Bristlecone pines, from the Shoshone and Paiute country in Nevada. Whitebark pines from the Rockies and Cascades. Dotted saxifrage from Mount Hozameen, which is a long, toothy ridge in the Interior Salish country, on the B.C./Washington line. Glaciers and rivers, and glacier-scraped granite and grasses and schists. The immensely delicate, persistent little flowers that grow in the palms and fists of the rock, and the intricate, sensuous hardness of the stone. Reminders that beauty is not of our making. Reminders that beauty requires our respect far more than our protection.

Whitebark pines are very *pretty* trees, as most sub-alpine species are. They're as flexible as yogis. You can tie their limbs in knots, and that's how they outwit the mountain snowloads and the wind. They carry their needles in bundles of five, like a wild rose or a human hand. And they depend on other creatures, not as intermediaries in actual copulation, as flowering plants so often do, but as midwives performing a kind of Caesarean section. Whitebark cones don't open of their own accord. They wait for Clark's nutcracker—a long-billed cousin of the whiskeyjack, the Steller's jay, the crow—to pry them open and eat the seeds. What passes intact through the nutcracker's guts—along with whatever he spills in his greed, unless it is eaten by ptarmigan, grouse, grey jays, winter wrens, and rosy finches, or by marmots and picas and voles—is what seeds the new generation.

Bristlecone pines aren't pretty at all, but they are extraordinarily beautiful. They don't grow very tall, but the oldest ones go back about 5,000 years, which is to say they are the oldest individual, independent living beings in the world. What may have been the oldest of them all—the senior-most sentient being on the planet—was deliberately felled with a chainsaw in 1964 by a scientist, so-called, who couldn't wait to count the rings.[1]

—None of this is in the poem.

—All of it is implied in the poem by the naming of these trees. Their names have meaning, more and deeper than the names of London or Jerusalem or Hadrian or Keats or Waterloo.

The two species—whitebarks and bristlecones—meet in the Ruby Mountains, in western Nevada. I hope sometime to find a high basin where both of them are growing side by side.

—It sounds as though the theme of the poem is trees.

—The theme of this confession seems to be trees. I, as a tree, am inclined to speak about other trees. The theme of the poem, I think, is what it says: that the mind is made out of the plants and animals it has watched, touched, smelled, thought and listened to, that being consists in speaking with other species of beings; that meaning is persistence, and that meaning in the end is what we love; that what-is is more than language; that language is a charming metaphor, but *out there* and *in here* and the arteries and veins and nerves which bind them are still present, functional, meaningful, even when language disappears.

—You appear to disagree, not only with the view that language is the womb and substance of poetry, but also with the view that poetry can't be paraphrased.

—Sometimes the best paraphrase is word-for-word restatement with a few repeats, ad libs, and shifts in intonation. Maybe the salient difference between poetry and prose is that a paraphrase of the former is apt to be longer than the original, not shorter. But some aspects of poetry are highly resistant to paraphrase, and those aspects are predominant in certain kinds of poems. Homer's thought is very sensuous, very musical, yet his poetry is far more accessible to paraphrase than Poe's. I would rather not be limited to paraphrase. At the same time, I would rather not be Poe.

—Paz speaks, in the poem you were quoting earlier, of the "brilliance of misery shining like a bird / that petrifies the forest with its singing . . ."

— . . . *fulgor de la desdicha como un ave / petrificando el bosque con su canto* . . . It is a long and brilliant poem, like a quetzal's tail. Certainly more deserving of discussion than this tattered piece of verse you say is mine.

—Not many of your poems carry personal dedications, but "Sunday Morning" is dedicated to Don McKay and Jan Zwicky. Would it be rude of me to ask why?

—Both of them are friends, and both are poets I admire. Don has taught me a great deal about the skill and the *philosophy*, let us say, of watching birds.

Jan has taught me just as much about music, language, and the ancient craft of thinking that links the two. But the link, again, is simple fact. They came to visit, as I mentioned, only a few days after the pelican. Both of them would have loved to see the bird, but he chose not to hang around. By Sunday night, the pelican had gone.

It's true, as you say, that I've been stingy with dedications. And there might have been more to the dedication in this case. The trip on which the saxifrage revealed itself so potently was one I made with other friends: the lichenologist Trevor Goward and the Pound scholar Anne Tayler. I think it was Anne who guided me to the saxifrage, in its full, diminutive glory in the early morning, wearing necklaces of tears.

Be that as it may, the poem became a gift for Don and Jan: an epithalamium of sorts.

—A poem in honour of marriage.

—No, not quite. I would like to live—and maybe they would too—in a world in which conventions such as marriage could be trusted. That is to say, a world where human custom and community didn't expropriate far more than they can give. Such communities do exist, of course—some that are incompletely conquered, and others that have more or less seceded from the general plan to leave nothing on earth beyond the reach of human currency and control. But the community I belong to, like it or not, as a colonial North American, is impotent, directionless, and atomized, while the world I spend my time in, for the most part, is a world where humans trespass one at a time.

We live in the ruins of what was once a functioning whole—where humans were surrounded, outflanked, and outnumbered by pines, pelicans, jays, and others who gave the human presence its boundaries, its shape, and its means of perspective. Even in these ruins, people can and do, of course, still come together. They can honour one another and worship one another. But what can marriage mean where there is no one who can sanction or perform it? Men and women, like humans and pelicans, gesticulate and talk across a barrier, with everything to say and minimal means to say it. But when the primal marriage between humans and the world has broken down, what can the secondary marriages between individual men and women do? Many have crumbled, of course. And some hide out in other forms and under other names, as if they were waiting for the end of the interregnum.

—Why, then, do you call it an epithalamium?

—In fact, a *thálamos* isn't a wedding, it's an inner room—could be a bedroom or a kiva or a vault, or the inner sanctum of a shrine, or the inner chambers of meaning and being, which none of us can dismantle, and which none of us has built.

—You said you had nothing to say about the poem.

—I have nothing to say about the poem. I have this to say about the poem: The poem is not the text. It is not the words. Our minds are trees. The trees we climb and walk beneath are minds, and they are open. The forest is the green cerebral cortex of the world. The poem in this case, finding no tree big enough or open enough, stood offshore for a day—longer than most of them pause among us—and then continued on its journey, asking nothing from you or me.

II. SAXIFRAGA PUNCTATA, RAVEN   LAURIE RICOU

For Robert Bringhurst

The raven beats its way up to the hydro line and sits mocking me. *Hwock. Hwock.* The sound is, perhaps, not speech. But it stays in the mind. It has meaning.

I have lived fourteen years on the West Coast, where raven's outlaw adventures explain the migration of the salmon and the location of the mountains. *Hwock.* But I've never learned to tell the difference between a crow and a raven. I have shared Bill Reid's sculpture "Raven and the First Humans" with a circling group of amused and amazed students. We were walking through the Museum of Anthropology to study writing in British Columbia. I have sat and stared at those four and a half tons of cedar for twenty solitary, stunned minutes. I have learned that the cedar is still alive. And I've learned that I need to learn the difference between crow and raven.

—*Corvus corax.* Its law is my song. When I hear readers puzzling about my language, I think about birds. I sense that the poem is to the critic as the bird is to the ornithologist.

—I've heard often enough that in order to take the measure of a poem, the critic has to kill it. I remember, too, that Audubon killed many birds to get the detail of those paintings. But the poem is alive *in the mind.* I don't believe any critic can kill it. Nevertheless, I like the metaphor enough that I would want to change it only slightly. The critic is the birder, trying to catch the poem on the wing: "the observation of birds can be many things—a science, an art, a recreation, a game or a sport, an environmental ethic, or even a religious experience" (Peterson, xi). The birder-critic, who must pay close attention to the nuances of marking, has first to be quietly patient. As Roger Tory Peterson tells it, birding is also a way to know trees and rocks and seas and all that weaves itself into habitat. And maybe a third aspect of the analogy is crucial: "guessing at birds, imagining things you haven't (quite) seen, pursuing illusions, and making a fool of yourself are all parts of the game" (Connor, 239). The critic as raven.

—Couldn't you just watch, or listen, without writing it all down?

—Birders need to keep notes not just for the gratification of enumerating sightings. They need the record for its cumulation (Connor, 245, 247): their journals allow them (force them) to reconsider the accuracy of their sightings; they provide a context within which to identify the "real" (that is, the most subtle) discoveries. Birding is a group activity, pursued in the company of others who can confirm your sighting. The critic keeps the company of print. But the birder also has to be a good listener, adept at hand signals, and have Sunday mornings freed into idleness. The birder believes that to be is to speak with pelicans.

—You asked me to talk about "Sunday Morning." It seems *un*typical of my poems.

—Well, it's untypical in that, yes, it's not so explicitly erudite, not so overtly allusive, as "Some Ciphers" or *Hachadura*. In that sense, I suppose, it's a Sunday morning poem, the poem where you play rather than work, if that's a distinction I can make, or dream rather than think (to use a distinction you apply to Stevens). But it combines species names and biological, geographical particulars with abstracts, ambient pronouns, and copula constructions. So it's typically cerebral in that sense. The poem as brain teaser: how do you say the unsayable. You tempt the idea of absence and negativity as reified somehow. (See Budick and Iser.)

You open by focusing on the literal experience of that surprising white pelican. Then you develop that observation, not by noting the bird's 10-foot wingspan, or red eyelids, nor by introducing the historic association of pelican with Christ, but by attentive balancing of gnomic abstractions such as we might find in Jan Zwicky's *Wittgenstein Elegies* (1986): "To know is to hold no opinions: to know / meaning thinks, thinking means." The passage holds the mind by its chanting the single note (five times) "ō." This double aphorism may try to teach that complete knowledge depends on setting aside the prejudices and feelings our culture has induced. But that single paraphrase won't do, because the pun obliges us to hear each "know" as "no," and vice versa. Similarly "thinking means," not only reminds the reader that "thinking" is its own purpose and significance, but that knowing involves discovering methods (means of doing things) and discovering balance between extremes (cf. arithmetic means).

Speaking of balance, you've written here a paradox followed by a chiasmus, or, perhaps, a chiasmus crossed over by another chiasmus. And, hence, the doubled dialogue of this discussion—your invented "crossing over," crossing over mine, echoes the four parts of "Sunday Morning," and, I think, a key rhetorical strategy in most of your poetry.

—You're beginning to sound more like academic than birdwatcher. What do you think the moon and sun have to do with all this?

—The poem is about migration. I keep trying to warn my students (which is to say myself) away from such imprecisions as "is about," but because your poetry honours such constructions, I will let it stand. The pelican has veered from its normal migration route, which lies several hundred kilometres inland. Cosmic migrations, if more predictable, figure aviary migrations. Moonset, for example, coincides with sunrise once each lunar month, at the new moon. The conjunction of sun, a stationary heavenly body (at least relative to earth), which is perpetually seen as mobile, and a continuously circling moon which only shows one face, is a paradigm of migration. The poem enacts a condition of moving between limits, of living in the spaces between.

—It wasn't designed this way, but I realize now that "Sunday Morning" may be a misleading title, sending critics off to Wallace Stevens looking for allusions that don't exist.

—At least the day of the week is significant. Even to people unattached to an institutional church, Sunday morning is often the time of the week to be a little less concerned with the busy-ness of doing, a little more concerned to touch the people who matter most in their daily lives: Sunday mornings offer a little more time just to stare and wonder. As much as with Stevens' "Sunday Morning" (whose incidental lines—"The day is like wide water, without sound"— seem more relevant than the over-ripe exoticism of the whole), I associate your poem with Phillip Larkin's "Church Going," and its surprised discovery of a slightly awkward reverence within the self. The polished intelligence of your syntax will slip into colloquialism—"the mind is made *out* of the animals"—as if to register an uneasy humility.

—So Stevens doesn't have much relevance here?

—Mostly by contrast, I think. Your distinction in the review in *Fine Print* between Pound, whose poems are "systems of references, pointing excitedly to persons, places, things, and texts outside themselves, which the reader really is asked to investigate," and Stevens' "more rabbinical . . . explicat[ion of] a central core of thought" suggests first an analogy between Bringhurst and Stevens. Your poems, too, read like "a complex algebra of simple terms" (Bringhurst 1986, 79). But I can't just *listen* to your poems and be satisfied. I need to find out, because your poems (e.g., "Anecdote of the Squid," "A Lesson in Botany") often contain their own evidence that *you* needed to find out about persons, places, and things, and that finding out made the poem.

—I think of the poem as an epithalamium, but that term describes the occasion, or tone of the poem, rather than its form.

—Your lines, certainly, seem to have no pattern to them, other than the un-pattern of the mind's drifting in a Sunday morning reverie. Your third line, for example, which stretches through 11 monosyllables and 3 prepositional phrases, finds no correspondence in the doubled doublets found in the third line of the third stanza.

But your structure of stanzas—three 10-line stanzas followed by a compact final stanza of 4 short lines—is argumentative. You have there something like an expanded Shakespearean sonnet form marking three stages—I would label them setting (or occasion), exposition, and resistance—followed by a pithy, witty paradox that sums up and sends your reader back through the poem, back to look at the *line*, back to consider the puzzles of transcribing in mute type the mysteries of the speaking voice going out of existence.

Perhaps the form draws more on the koan; the emphasis, that is, falls on a Zen sense of riddle. The poem as a whole performs the riddle of the individual sentences. The final line of the first stanza, for example, begins with an unattached "it." The usage signals that—fundamentally—the line cannot mean. *Something* "is"; something has being and existence, but *what* that something is is a mystery. Linguists would call this "it" an ambient pronoun—suitable for a poem which wanders off the normal paths of migration.

Meaning, ontology, is provided by absence; we learn what is *not*, but what *is* is left unstated, left to guess work. So the structure of the whole poem *promises* a three-part sequence of development, followed by resolution, but gives us tri-angulation framing a puzzle of the absent and unexpressed.

—But as a critic interested in regionalism, you must find Pound and Stevens rather remote from Mount Hozameen.

—To equate a regional approach with reductiveness is a refuge for the de-racinated. The best regional writing reads Heidegger through Hozameen, Kyoto through chitons. Your work has strong affiliations with other Northwest poets. You have often noted your connection with Gary Snyder and his respect for Zen traditions/relationships (Bringhurst 1989, 189). I think you also share a sensibility with Richard Hugo, particularly with his calm deliberation over the natural phenomenon made abstract—for example, in a line like "To know is to be alien to rivers" (Hugo, 68), where predicating is so crucial to mystery. And to this regional grouping, such as critics like to assemble, I would add Kim Stafford's fusion of medieval learning and the talky anecdote, and the geo-poems of David Wagoner.

—Well, these are all poets who, like Don McKay, don't say "tree" and "bird," but white pine, red pine, loon, or Blackburnian warbler. I think academic critics get obsessed with language *qua* language, and miss the granular, fecund detail which the poem is curious about.

—I often say something similar to my students. If I were reading "Sunday Morning" with them, however, I would want them to think not only about the minor miracle of a pelican off its flight path, but also about the challenge that Snyder, Stafford, Wagoner, and you accept in writing in contact with the Northwest's flora and fauna: the obligation to respect, and sometimes to incorporate the "enigmatic, poignant and beautiful narrative[s]" of the aboriginal peoples (Bringhurst 1990, 39). You once acknowledged the importance to your writing of an even earlier stage of human culture, with an implicit question:

> . . . it pleases me sometimes to ask whether our paleolithic descendants [ancestors] could make sense of some of my own poems if they heard them . . . I like to ask whether it [a poem] is fit to be thought about next to a glacier-scarred stone or the limb of a mountain larch or a grassblade, or fit to be listened to with kingfishers and finches. (Bringhurst 1989, 187-8)

With such an apparently a-linguistic touchstone in mind, you ask three things of your language. Of course, you ask it to tell some story, some extended leisurely and circling narrative which will require a patient listener. And you ask it to evoke the mnemonics of an oral tradition: in "Sunday Morning" this element is most evident in the mesmerizing repetition of the formula "the mind is . . ."

—I do think that the spiritual capital of the north Pacific coast is Haida Gwaii (Bringhurst 1990, 34). But in honouring it, I prefer contemplation to mesmerism. Can we talk about the saxifrage and the pines?

—Yes. But first, think a little more of the call of the raven. I know you admire Inuit throat-singing for its derivation from bird calls (Bringhurst 1989, 194). I would not place this poem quite in the category of throat-singing, but I do know that hearing Robert Bringhurst read affects the hearing of the poem on the page. That rolling, resonant bass, with the eyes almost closed, creates reverence for each word it touches. Hence the learned Latin taxonomies and the colloquial throwaways about the trivia of daily existence are in performance fused in one voice. That's what I find mesmerizing.

The third demand you make of your language is that each word, especially the words for plants, animals, and places, is expected to tell a story. Again this interest in the micronarratives in single words reminds me of a Native American writer:

> "But you know, grandson, this world is fragile."
> The word he chose to express "fragile" was filled with the intricacies of a continuing process, and with a strength inherent in spider webs woven across paths through sand hills where early in the morning the sun becomes entangled in each filament of web. It took a long time to explain the fragility and intricacy because no word exists alone, and the reason for choosing each word had to be explained with a story about why it must be this certain way. That was the responsibility that went with being human, old Ku'oosh said, the story behind each word must be told so there could be no mistake in the meaning of what had been said; and this demanded great patience and love. (Silko, 35-6)

—But I suspect my shifting from one register to another, from proper names to abstracts, from oracular assertion to casual cliché, hides the story behind each word.

—It deprives the reader of much context for reading the poem as an anecdote recounting a personal experience. I don't get much sense of a persona, the way I do in Al Purdy. But setting the proper nouns in a context of abstractions tied up with linking verbs, you are insisting that the physical and breathing things of the world are profoundly to be thought about. And, to reverse the movement, you are claiming that the way to deep thinking is through the plants and rocks.

Pay attention to a bristlecone pine, you seem to be saying, and you will discover a story. And the story is the mind's map—it shows a way to think about things. Whitebark pine (*Pinus albicaulis*), first of all, with its "light-gray to yellowish-brown" colour and its lying "flat on the rocks" (Farjon, 33) recalls the white pelican that sets the poem to wondering. It's an often twisted and blasted tree that grows exceedingly slowly in harsh climates. So, too, is the bristlecone pine (*Pinus aristata* and *Pinus longaeva*), a species which draws its life from the most adverse conditions. Taking time, outside the reading of the poem itself, to find out about the plants and animals suggests some of the implicit patterns in the poem. The bristlecone's habitat, at elevations of 7,000 to 12,000 feet in eastern California, Colorado, Nevada, and Utah, extends the arboreal geography of the poem south along the migration path of the pelican.

To equate *being* and "speak[ing] with the bristlecone / pines" recognizes that each tree *writes* by its very living, recording on its "tree-ring calendar whatever environmental conditions prevailed during each year of its life" (Mirov & Hasbrouck, 12-13). The bristlecone articulates an extraordinarily precise climatology, extending over 4,600 years; this record in turn allows us to read other stories, about the construction of pueblos, for example (Schulman, 355). More radically, examination of cores from bristlecone pine has necessitated changes in the fundamental assumptions of radiocarbon dating, and, hence, a drastic revision of notions of direct Egyptian and Mycenean influence upon the Bronze and Iron Age cultures of Europe (Ralph & Michael, 559).

Perhaps more directly significant in an epithalamium is the bristlecone's unusual method of procreation. As with the whitebark pine, the Clark's nutcracker is the essential bird—so the two trees of the poem are linked in an unexpected way (albeit undetected by the casual reader). Nutcrackers remove seeds from the bristlecone's cones, and store what they don't eat in shallow sub-surface caches. This habit provides the dominant method of regeneration in the most extreme and difficult sites. This object lesson in ecology is, of course, implicit, but it underpins the epithalamium: mutual dependence between organisms is here a condition of both individual and social well-being.

—Pelican is not exactly conventional in a wedding-poem either.

—Its rarity on the Coast (and even there, it prefers fresh water) makes its sighting inherently precious. But you may have had in mind the breeding habits of the American White Pelican (*Pelecanus erythrorhynchos*) which are gregarious—they don't take a single mate. On Sunday morning you encounter the oldest living trees and the largest living birds. Both the twisted trees, and the "bulky" birds with their "extensible sac of skin capable of holding at least 3 gallons of water" (Leahy, 556), may seem, at first, ridiculous. But ridicule turns to awe when we see the bird fly or discover how long the tree has survived. An odd metonymy brings together bird and tree. And confuses names:

> Aristophanes in *The Birds* uses the word for both a woodpecker (the joiner bird) and a water bird of the pelican sort. The original Greek word is from *pelekus*, "axe," and hence its aptness as a name for the woodpecker. Its application to the waterbird is probably a reference to the size and shape of the bill. *Pelekus*, in turn, is collaterally related to the Sanskrit *parasu*, which also means "axe." (Gruson, 27-8)

Axe cuts trees. Curiously, the pelican is linked etymologically, if obliquely, to the trees it overflies in its migration.

—The ingenuity of that line of inquiry seems excessive. It's at such a point that I feel the focus on language refusing the literal experience which motivates the poem.

—Perhaps the pelican fits in a more direct, if more ironic, way, for its voice is scarcely significant. A bird-watcher can often depend for identification on listening. The invisible and unseen is identified by sound. The pelican, however, is "unspoken": its repertoire of "hissing, blowing, groaning, or grunting" is almost never heard in the presence of humans ("Pelicans," 165-6). Between the unspeakable and the already spoken.

You might also be thinking of the pelican as symbol of piety. Certainly the conventional mythical associations of the bird fit with the reverent tone of the poem. But I am more interested in that rather Darwinian image in lines 2 and 3, which puzzled me until I discovered this story of self-sacrifice:

> The principal myth concerning the pelican is that the parent bird, if unable to find food for her brood, pierced her breast with the tip of her bill and fed the youngsters on her own blood, and that is how the bird is figured in the earliest pictures of it. It was because of this belief that the pelican was chosen as an emblem of charity and piety and became a favourite heraldic emblazonment. There is a different version

of the story according to Bartholomew. Writing in 1535 he says that the young pelicans smite the parents in the face, whereupon the mother retaliates, hitting them back and killing them. Then, on the third day, the mother smites herself in the side until the blood runs out onto the bodies of her youngsters, bringing them to life again.

These two stories may have arisen because in feeding its young the parent presses its bill against its neck and breast in order to make the contents of the pouch more readily available to the young, who thrust their bills into the pouch to take the food. The red tip on the common pelican's mandible may also have made the story more plausible. ("Pelican," 1728)

Many of my poems draw on myth and folklore, of course, but as much as this poem is yours to reinvent, I want to bring you back here to biology and ecology. I am interested in the unexpected interdependence of glaciers and rivers, grasses and schists.

—Yes. But I think I've said enough. I don't want to push your patience any further.

—But I suspect you've done more research on *Saxifraga punctata* than on any other part of the poem, because it stands out there in the middle of the poem in all its Latinate taxonomic strangeness.

—You're correct. I could go on about its signature, its medicinal qualities, its flowering (like bristlecone) in the harshest of conditions. I am especially intrigued that the plant is part of the riddle: *Saxifraga punctata*, for all the precision of its Latin nomenclature, is misnamed. No such distinct species exists (Webb & Gornall, 52). At the core of the poem, in all its fragile and special beauty, is an absence, a plant by another name.

But I don't want to say much more, because *Saxifraga punctata* reminds me that what I actually like best about your poems is that they are as likely to send me to a botanical garden as to the *Encyclopedia of Poetry and Poetics*. I called Judy Newton, at the UBC Botanical Garden, and she told me to come to read the books on saxifrages, the amazing 440 intricately differing species of them (Webb & Gornall, 1)—the variation reminds me of the study of snowflakes. When I got there, Judy said she might have a sample, and sure enough, there it was—gathered in 1971. Would I like a photocopy? I didn't know you could photocopy saxifrage, but when I saw Judy with tiny tweezers lift the dried *saxifraga punctata* from the folder and place it reverently on the glass, I thought I understood something about your poem and the connections it establishes with places.

Notes

[1]The firsthand account of this event is Donald R. Currey, "An Ancient Bristlecone Pine Stand in Eastern Nevada," *Ecology* 46.4 (1965): 564-6. The story is amplified somewhat by Galen Rowell in *High and Wild* (San Francisco: Sierra Club, 1979), 99-105.

Works Cited

Bringhurst, Robert. "Off the Road: Journeys in the Past, Present and Future of Canadian Literature." *Best Canadian Essays 1989*. Douglas Fetherling, ed. Saskatoon: Fifth House, 1989.

———. Review of *Wallace Stevens Poems*. *Fine Print* 12.2 (April 1986): 79, 119.

———. "That Also Is You: Some Classics of Native Canadian Literature." *Canadian Literature* 124-125 (Spring-Summer 1990): 32-47.

———. "Unraping the World: The Poetry of Don McKay." *Lines* 95 (January 1986): 87-90.

Budick, Sanford, and Wolfgang Iser, eds. *Languages of the Unsayable: The Play of Negativity in Literature and Literary Theory*. New York: Columbia Univ. Press, 1989.

Connor, Jack. *The Complete Birder: A Guide to Better Birding*. Boston: Houghton Mifflin, 1988.

Farjon, Aljos. *Pines: Drawings and Descriptions of the Genus Pinus*. Leiden: E.J. Brill/ W. Backhuys, 1984.

Gruson, Edward S. *Words for Birds: A Lexicon of North American Birds with Biographical Notes*. New York: Quadrangle Books, 1972.

Hugo, Richard. *Making Certain It Goes On: The Collected Poems of Richard Hugo*. New York: Norton, 1984.

Lanner, Ronald M. "Dependence of Great Basin Bristlecone Pine on Clark's Nutcracker for Regeneration at High Elevations." *Arctic and Alpine Research* 20.3 (Aug. 1988): 358-62.

Leahy, Christopher. *The Birdwatcher's Companion: An Encyclopedic Handbook of North American Birdlife*. New York: Hill and Wang, 1982.

Mirov, Nicholas T. & Jean Hasbrouck. *The Story of Pines*. Bloomington & London: Indiana Univ. Press, 1976.

"Pelican." *The International Wildlife Encyclopedia*. Vol. 13. Eds. Maurice Burton and Robert Burton. New York: Marshall Cavendish, 1969: 1724-8.

"Pelicans." *Grzimek's Animal Life Encyclopedia*. Vol. 7. Ed. Bernhard Grzimek. New York: Van Nostrand Reinhold, 1972: 163-9.

Peterson, Roger Tory. "Foreword." Connor, xi-xiii.

Ralph, Elizabeth K., and Henry N. Michael. "Twenty-five Years of Radiocarbon Dating." *American Scientist* 62.5 (Sept./Oct. 1974): 553-60.

Schulman, Edmund. "Bristlecone Pine, Oldest Known Living Thing." *National Geographic* 113.3 (March 1958): 355-72.

Silko, Leslie Marmon. *Ceremony*. New York: Viking Press, 1977.

Webb, D.A. and R.J. Gornall. *Saxifrages of Europe: With notes on African, American and some Asiatic Species*. London: Christopher Helm, 1989.

Zwicky, Jan. *Wittgenstein Elegies*. Coldstream, Ont.: Brick Books; Edmonton: Academic Printing, 1986.

Going Down into Death:
A Reading of "'Three lecture hours per week'"

Wilfred Cude

Roy Daniells composed "Three lecture hours per week" at a time when our academic institutions were embarking on a period of almost giddy expansion, and he acknowledged with dismay the professional and ethical hazards of that uncertain venture. The world of the poem, as the title indicates, is the ever-increasing domain of academe: "three lecture hours per week" was the stock phrase terminating each course description in every Canadian university's undergraduate calendar of the era. The stolid prose of the title provides a grim preamble to the formality, economy, and precision imparted by the Shakespearean sonnet form, the structure used for the text's stately flow of words. This treatment, encompassing an ultimately frightening modern reality within the confines of a highly traditional presentation, is beautifully adapted to the subject of current academic life.

"Take care," the speaker exhorts at the poem's opening, "when you lift the little copper bottle / You do not wake the genie." The transition from the title to this sentence is abrupt, spiriting us from the humdrum workaday schedule of the contemporary university undergraduate into the fabulous realm of Aladdin and the magic lamp. But are we really in the realm of Aladdin and the lamp? At this point, as befits a poem on the subject of teaching, questions proliferate. Who is the speaker? To whom does the speaker address these words? What, exactly, is the nature of this genie? And how on earth could there be any possible connection between the world of "three lecture hours per week" and a "little copper bottle" that apparently contains some sort of genie? The answer to all these questions will emerge slowly, as we patiently follow the speaker through fourteen lines of provocative thought.

As the speaker continues, with measured phrases that convey sombre and sometimes terrifying images, we discover that there is indeed a link between the classroom and the bottled genie. The speaker is clearly a person of considerable experience, someone familiar with the process of handling this particular genie. The process itself is fraught with danger, for the speaker insists upon caution and seems apprehensive about the prospect of the genie's escape. The person addressed in the poem would appear to be a novice in the exercise of authority, someone having custody of the genie's bottle, access to inhibiting substances that induce passivity, and command of a "prostrate crew," yet still requiring instruction in managing all three. According to the speaker, there is a ritual that must be followed precisely in these matters, a ritual to be painstakingly executed "thrice a week." It is this almost tongue-in-cheek qualification, recasting and echoing the title, that provides us with the necessary link between the mirrored domains of the poem.

Despite the intriguing implications both of the speaker's fears and the novice's situation, the mysterious presence of the genie most fully challenges our imagination. After all, considerable forces have been used to keep him under restraint: the solid copper of the bottle locking him in, the rather nasty influence of "old drugs" that leave him "drowned," and the virtually paranoid attitude of those entrusted with his custody. But all these forces taken together can only serve to keep him quiescent; and he remains, the speaker warns, even under such rigorously depressing conditions, "a spirit / Able to raise your prostrate crew." Once out of that bottle, this genie can transform those unfortunates into "kings / And priests that his imperial halls inherit," a menacing prospect since those same halls are "Filled with unspeakable and glorious things." At the end of the third quatrain, therefore, we are provoked into asking: is there anything analogous to this actually to be found in the classrooms of a modern university?

Of course there is. Every lecturer recognizes that spirit, the spirit of knowledge conjured by uncounted generations of scholars, all dreamily wandering through the many groves of academe. Truly unleash that spirit in the classroom, though, and your students will be students no longer. They will have no time or tolerance for a due sense of deference, since other concerns must occupy them. They will become, at the very least, your peers, and perhaps even your superiors, themselves reaching out towards the unspeakable—or the glorious. What they will then touch, or will then do, remains totally beyond your control. Revising history, reappraising art, recasting political, social, or economic conventions, penetrating the atom, numbering the galaxies, tampering with the essence of life, or unravelling the fabric of time itself: some students, yes, even your students, inspired by knowledge, driven by knowledge, could accomplish as much—or more. To seriously confront this vision is to invite second thoughts on the advisability of freely letting slip that wild spirit, that frighteningly unmanageable genie. Thus enters, insidiously whispering in the mind, the speaker of Roy Daniells' poem.

It is important to appreciate exactly why Daniells chooses to have the campus realities summarized by a speaker of a characteristically peculiar practicality. We might speculate extensively on the identity of this speaker, who could be a high-ranking administrator, a full professor, a senior lecturer, or possibly even a graduate student or a senior undergraduate. In all probability, this speaker is male, for the campuses of the era were still very much dominated by men: and it is therefore conceivable that the speaker might also be Daniells himself. Yet none of this matters as much as the fact that the speaker is an old academic hand, someone who has observed the existing system shrewdly, intensively, and carefully, someone who feels impelled to instruct a silent and presumably deferential novice in the guileful craft of teaching a university course. There is a sophisticated irony here, one that intensifies as the poem unfolds: the speaker's advice is derived from real knowledge, and is driven by real knowledge—and is thus infused with the same spirit that so terrifyingly haunts the poem. Is the speaker himself aware of this irony? That is the question lurking behind the advice of all three quatrains, not to be addressed until the couplet, and perhaps not to be answered even then.

According to the speaker, the "genie" entrapped within that "little copper bottle" is fortunately rendered comatose, held "safely under throttle" by the "old drugs" of a profession long schooled in stultifying the splendours of the universe. Rather than risk the release of such a formidable "spirit," thereby hazarding a confrontation with whatever a newly consecrated congregation of "kings" and "priests" might devise, the speaker urges his auditor to dole out in each class tiny measures of the same noxious mixture that keeps the genie "darkened and deadened." This treatment, the speaker implies, will have the same impact on the "prostrate crew" as it does on the genie: they will remain comfortably prostrate, offering no threat to anybody, including the speaker, the novice instructor, and themselves. The recommended dosage is just one teaspoon, rather nervously administered "thrice a week," a mocking reprise of the modern university calendar's standard prescription.

Significantly, throughout all three quatrains, the speaker is adamant in counselling the continued confinement of the genie. His fear of that spirit is apparently only matched in intensity by his scorn for the prostrate crew of students, whom he nonchalantly consigns to a potentially permanent condition of dependency. Yet the speaker's contempt for these poor creatures, would-be wizards of power that must be spoon-fed, is tellingly moderated by the details that he furnishes. The spoon itself is "silver," suggesting that the students are nonetheless a privileged group; and the edifices of thought that they might command, should the genie slip free of all those institutional constraints, are admittedly palaces of wonder "filled with unspeakable and glorious things." Tragically, though, the speaker will not countenance any attempt to attain the glorious—not if it also means, as any serious venture into the halls of thought necessarily must, confronting the unspeakable. Obsessed with security and comfort, he advocates the dissemination of depressant drugs, very much after the manner of a pusher pandering to a junkie's addiction. The spoon, not in the least disguised by the metal of its composition, is a tarted-up tool required for the fix: any heroin addict would understand that ghastly nuance only too well.

By the end of the third quatrain, Daniells' estimation of the prevailing academic system has been conveyed in a blunt, direct, and uncompromising manner. "The thick dark liquor that might incite the soul," immediately watered down to a tepid habit-forming nostrum, is symbolic of the sterile formulas evolved by pedants across the centuries to enervate the spirit of knowledge. We might think of leaden exposition overburdened with footnotes, wearisome stuff inlaid with latinized filigree, tags of "*ipse dixit*" and "*quod erat demonstrandum*" underscoring the trivial and the commonplace. This sort of sludge flows out of the same workmanlike copper bottle that confines the genie; but it has been tampered with, diluted past potency into a mere sedative, and now constitutes an alien substance. It is not the genie, it is not even of the genie, it is instead the subtle poison that muffles him up—and with him, after their own exposure to the noxious fluid, the hapless students enrolled in the class of a lack-lustre academic.

Having thus sketched out for us the insidious doctrine governing far too much of academic instruction, a doctrine he intimates was both practised and preached in the intellectual community to which he had devoted so many years, Daniells alters the tone of the sonnet to conclude with a dramatic reversal. The first line of the couplet might be read as underscoring the message of the previous twelve lines; but the second line throws everything that was said into doubt, introducing the possibility that it was all intended ironically, as advice on how *not* to proceed. The genie, the speaker reminds his auditor in a sharp sentence fragment, is "able to wither you with one slight breath." So consistent is that sentiment with what has gone before, we might not remark that it is offered as a contingency, rather than a certainty: the genie is capable of withering an instructor, but that does not mean he will do so. What does remain beyond any misconstruction, though, is the sombre simplicity of the speaker's last sentence. "All they" who leave the genie "bound," we are told with cold finality, "go down into death." That swift conceptual turn is comparable to the finest in the tradition of the Shakespearean sonnet. Anyone can persist in choosing a secure but debilitating technique to cope with knowledge, intent upon diverting students from the hazards and the rewards of free inquiry; but such a betrayal of the teacher's trust is itself a form of punishment, inevitably dooming the perpetrator to spiritual extinction.

Is this, notwithstanding the urgency of virtually everything the speaker has said, the sonnet's real message? As scholars, we must concede that sheer logic eliminates any other conclusion. On the one hand, there are two possible consequences of ignoring the counsel proffered by the speaker throughout the body of the poem: letting slip the genie means freeing a host of kings and priests, who might then traffic in the glorious—or the unspeakable. The first of these consequences is what all teachers should desire, were it not for the inhibiting fear of the second. On the other hand, however, there is nothing but dead certainty, brutally annunciated by that same speaker in the last line: follow the counsel, confine the genie, and accept destruction. Upon mature reflection, we must turn away from the certainty of death, and take our chances with what the genie and our students might create. The thoroughly darkened diction of the speaker reinforces this conclusion, since it binds up the articulated persuasion in implicit dissuasion, inviting us to recoil from the practices so harshly expressed. The rhyme of "bottle" with "throttle," for example, attaches the genie's place of confinement to the ugly result of keeping him there. By the end of the poem, pounded by such diction, we have already acquiesced in the force and justice of the last line.

Over the decades, our profession has largely disregarded the insights that Daniells so cogently delineated. But no longer. In an essay entitled "These hours have 50 minutes," written for the 28 May 1988 edition of *The Globe and Mail*, another Canadian professor of English restates similar themes in compelling prose. Philip Milner looks carefully at the perversity inherent in stultifying students with exercise after exercise, each designed to elicit ostentatious busywork, and all fashioned to conform rigorously with the absurdly diminished measure of the undergraduate calendar. "An academic year has eight months," he caustically points out. "A week has five days. An hour has 50 minutes." Within the confines of this calendar, students are deterred from genuine scholarship by repeated dosages of pure pedantry. "Each tick of the clock is measured, dissected, and pretended to be something larger than it is," Milner protests. "Could anyone except a baffle of university administrators have created such a calendar? We faculty and administrators deserve the misshapen fruit—Coles Notes and the BS Unlimited Term Paper Co. are representative examples—that the system we operate has spawned." Milner finishes by contrasting that misshapen campus fruit with the more natural produce of a northern Nova Scotian garden. "The growing season has its own cycle," he remarks, delicately reminding us with this most germane symbol that human minds should also be permitted unhampered growth. "You can't rush things in a garden" (D6).

Neither Daniells nor Milner could now be dismissed as merely another crank fulminating about teaching from the periphery of Western scholarship. Increasingly, out of the very centre of the North American academic community, more voices are joining the chorus calling for teaching reforms. Listen to Charles J. Sykes, a journalist who published the scathingly titled bestselling *ProfScam: Professors and the Demise of Higher Education* late in 1988. Across the entire United States, he charges, professors have "abandoned their teaching responsibilities and their students," fabricating instead an intellectual milieu in which "bad teaching goes unnoticed and unsanctioned and good teaching is penalized" (5). Listen to Page Smith, founding Provost of the University of California at Santa Cruz and author of several prize-winning studies of history, who published the disturbingly titled *Killing the Spirit: Higher Education in America* early in 1990. "The strange, almost incomprehensible fact is that many professors," he remarks in wonder, "just as they feel obliged to write dully, believe that they should lecture dully" (211). Listen especially to Bruce Wilshire, professor of philosophy at Rutgers University, who published the hauntingly titled *The Moral Collapse of the University: Professionalism, Purity, and Alienation* late in 1990. "The neglect of teaching in the university is an ominous symptom," he warns. "I believe it signals a weakening of our will to live." In what might almost be regarded as an unconscious paraphrase of Daniells' main point, he insists that "if we do not nurture our young and identify with them, we forfeit any hope in the regeneration and continuation of the species; we are walled up defensively within the confines of our egos and our momentary gratification. But this means we are not fully alive ourselves" (225).

Precisely so. "All they who bound him go down into death." And we academics will only be deluding ourselves, should we continue to pretend that nobody is listening to such voices. "If government officials, employers or the public at large come to believe, as they apparently already suspect . . . that the teaching and learning mandate of the universities is taking second place to other activities on the part of faculty," admonishes Dr. Stuart Smith, reporting his findings on academic reform, "they will not respond favourably to the financial needs of these institutions" (33). There is more than one way, it would seem, to go down into death; and institutions, as well as individuals, can face destruction through a mindless adherence to the *status quo*. Let's not, therefore, misconstrue the message we are hearing. Quite simply, the system yielding some fine instructors did not yield nearly enough of them; the norm, regrettably, has been captured by Roy Daniells. This is a situation that must change. And until it does, "Three lecture hours per week" should be required faculty reading on every campus.

Works Cited

Milner, Philip. "These hours have 50 minutes," *The Globe and Mail* (20 May 1988): D6.

Smith, Page. *Killing the Spirit: Higher Education in America*. New York: Viking, 1990.

Smith, Stuart L. *Report: Commission of Inquiry on Canadian University Education*. Ottawa: Association of Universities and Colleges of Canada, 1991.

Sykes, Charles. *ProfScam: Professors and the Demise of Higher Education*. Washington: Regnery Gateway, 1988.

Wilshire, Bruce. *The Moral Collapse of the University: Professionalism, Purity, and Alienation*. Albany: State Univ. of New York Press, 1990.

Reading A.M. Klein's
"Portrait of the Poet as Landscape"

Mary Jane Edwards

A.M. Klein's "Portrait of the Poet as Landscape," composed in 1944-5, was first published in the Montreal magazine *First Statement* in its issue of June-July 1945. The poem was entitled "Portrait of the Poet as a Nobody," was divided into seven parts, and had twenty-eight stanzas and 175 lines. After this appearance, Klein, working on the tearsheets from *First Statement*, revised the poem. He rewrote several lines, and he cut Part III, thus omitting two six-line stanzas structured in the style of Anglo-Saxon verse that described the poet as a "Skop of the sales-force, bard of their booty," who sold his gift with words to "mongers and martmen" (*First Statement*, 5). The new version, entitled "Portrait of the Poet as Landscape," and composed of six parts, twenty-six stanzas, and 163 lines, was first published in July 1948 in Klein's collection *The Rocking Chair and Other Poems*. Reprinted several times, it has appeared most recently in *Complete Poems*, the scholarly edition of Klein's poetry prepared by Zailig Pollock and published in 1990 as part of *The Collected Works of A.M. Klein*. "Portrait of the Poet as Landscape" thus is, and has been, available in various texts and contexts. The purpose of this essay is to read what has been called Klein's most important poem in some of these textualities.

I first read "Portrait of the Poet as Landscape" in 1955-6 in a little anthology called *Longer Poems for Upper-School, 1955-1956*. I was attending Grade Thirteen at the Galt Collegiate Institute and Vocational School in Galt, now Cambridge, Ontario, and my English teacher was Frank Ferguson. He was—and is—*the* Mr. Ferguson whom Peter Gzowski frequently praises, and his explication of "Portrait of the Poet as Landscape" was a model for both instructors and learners. Contemplating such matters as the poem's imagery, rhyme, rhythm, structure, and tone, we worked our way through it deliberately and slowly. Poetry was words, and words were to be enjoyed for their sensuality as well as their sense. And appreciate them we did! I remember our admiration for the alliteration in such a phrase as "zoomed to zenith" (*Longer Poems*, 24) and for the assonance and onomatopoeia in a line like "How they do fear the slap of the flat of the platitude!" (*Longer Poems*, 25). I was particularly taken with the repetition of "o" sounds and the triumph and tragedy that one could hear in them as they were combined in varying chords and melodies.

I do not remember how much attention we paid to the critical commentary on "A.M. Klein" and "Portrait of the Poet as Landscape" that concluded the volume. My friend, whose copy of *Longer Poems* I borrowed for this reminiscence, has "Excellent notes" written in pencil on one page of this section, but otherwise it is unmarked. Since the title page states that the notes were prepared by Roy H. Allin and Alan F. Meiklejohn, two secondary school teachers, there was little apparent reason to consider their explanations as special. In an article published in 1984, however, D.M.R. Bentley pointed out that some of the notes on "Portrait of the Poet as Landscape" in *Longer Poems* were actually "suggested by Klein himself" (42). On the one hand, these notes, directed as they were at teenagers, seem rather unnecessary now. On the other hand, Klein's proposed explication of the phrase "dimple and dip of conjugation" (*Longer Poems*, 23)—"To the poet the inflections of the verb have all the beauty of a face shining and dimpling with laughter" (*Longer Poems*, 61)—and his comment on the lines "they [items] are pulsated, and breathed, until they map, / not the world's, but his own body's chart!" (*Longer Poems*, 27)—"The poet's aim is to feel in himself what all humanity feels" (*Longer Poems*, 65)—underline both Klein's love for language and his definition of the poet. All these notes, furthermore, point to Klein's interest in the gloss and, perhaps, his conviction that a good poem was itself a kind of sacred scroll deserving of annotation and explication.

I have also forgotten how we interpreted the last stanza of "Portrait of the Poet as Landscape":

> These are not mean ambitions. It is already something
> merely to entertain them. Meanwhile, he
> makes of his status [as] zero a rich garland,
> a halo of his anonymity,
> and lives alone, and in his secret shines
> like phosphorus. At the bottom of the sea. (*Longer Poems*, 28)

My friend has noted in the margin beside these lines that the poet finally has "no status in purely material world, but doing job becomes honour." We undoubtedly discussed, then, the poet's "status of zero" metamorphosing into "a rich garland" and "his anonymity" into "a halo" as possible indications of the poet as secular hero and religious prophet/saint. If we were convinced by the note, this one prepared by the two teachers, that the poet's position "At the bottom of the sea" "suggests that the poet is far from making his dreams come true" (*Longer Poems*, 65), our spin was probably pessimistic. But we were young and optimistic, and, from our religious training, we knew something about drowning into life, so we may well have preferred to give the ending a more positive twist.

What most fascinates me now about my initial encounter with "Portrait of the Poet as Landscape" is not how I read it, but in what context. For *Longer Poems for Upper-School, 1955-1956* consists of three selections: John Milton's *Paradise Lost*, Book I, ll.1-330; Robert Browning's "An Epistle Containing The Strange Medical Experience of Karshish, The Arab Physician"; and Klein's "Portrait of the Poet as Landscape." Given this triumvirate, it is not surprising that I harboured the illusion until very recently that I first studied Canadian literature when I read the poems of E.J. Pratt in my final year at university. Even though the note on Klein in *Longer Poems* clearly identifies him as a Canadian—it states wrongly, in fact, that he "was born in Montreal" (57)—the siting of Klein's elegy after Milton's epic and Browning's dramatic monologue located A.M. Klein and "Portrait of the Poet as Landscape" firmly in the canon of English literature. I have read the poem in other contexts since, but never, I think, with the same confidence in its—and our—place in the literary world.

I did not read "Portrait of the Poet as Landscape" again until the early 1960s. By then I had one of those historically grounded honours degrees in modern languages and literatures (English and French) from the University of Toronto, and I was studying for an M.A. in English at Queen's University. I was taking a course on James Joyce, but specializing in Canadian literature; my subject of concentration was modern Canadian poetry. It was in these contexts that I renewed my acquaintance with "Portrait of the Poet as Landscape." With my background in English literature, it was easy to see Klein's poem as a Canadian variation of such elegies as Milton's "Lycidas," as in fact Milton Wilson had already done in "Klein's Drowned Poet: Canadian Variations on an Old Theme." Through his allusions, Klein himself invites the specific comparison of his poem to Milton's. At the end of "Lycidas," the poet, "Sunk though he be beneath the watery floar," has not drowned. He has, instead, "mounted high," joined "the saints above," and become himself "the Genius of the shore" (*Milton*, 44). At the beginning of "Portrait of the Poet as Landscape," however, "Lycidas" has descended to earth to be confined in a room, perhaps even a cupboard, where he has been "shelved" (*Longer Poems*, 22), and at the end of the poem the poet, positioned as he is "At the bottom of the sea," seems to have drowned. In contrast to Milton's poet, then, Klein's—discarded and submerged as he remains—is dismal indeed.

My impression of Klein's marginalization of the artist in the modern world was further reinforced by another exercise in intertextuality that I undertook at this time. For, while my course on Joyce led me to read Klein's essays on *Ulysses*, my interest in modern Canadian poetry encouraged me to consider "Portrait of the Poet as Landscape" as a commentary on the conclusion to *A Portrait of the Artist as a Young Man*. At the end of the novel Stephen Dedalus flies off "to encounter for the millionth time the reality of experience and to forge in the smithy of [his] soul the uncreated conscience of [his] race" (253). As Icarus, he will of course soar too near the sun, his wings will melt, and he will drown. Although there is some indication in *A Portrait of the Artist as a Young Man* that Icarus will rise again to become Daedalus, the "old artificer" (253), the drowned poet of "Portrait of the Poet as Landscape" casts doubt both on this future and on Klein's optimism about the role of the artist as creator of conscience, or, for that matter, consciousness.

A different interpretation, however, was also available to me during this period. I read "Portrait of the Poet as Landscape" both as a discrete work of art and as the final poem in *The Rocking Chair and Other Poems*. In this context two observations are pertinent. First, the poems that precede "Portrait of the Poet as Landscape" in the volume introduce images that are repeated in this poem. Thus, for example, the description of the aboriginals in "Indian Reservation: Caughnawaga" is repeated in the image of the poet in "Portrait of the

Poet as Landscape" as someone "Set apart, / . . . with special haircut and dress, / as on a reservation" (*Rocking Chair*, 53). The "Orator" in "Political Meeting"— stirring up, through his "moods, tricks, imitative talk," the bird that rises as "the body-odour of race" (*Rocking Chair*, 15-16)—becomes in "Portrait of the Poet as Landscape" one of those impostors who impersonate the poet. And the diver in "Lone Bather," who is "bird . . . dolphin . . . plant" (*Rocking Chair*, 37), may be the alter, active ego of the lonely poet in "Portrait of the Poet as Landscape" who, after "An afternoon" of creation "far from the world" (*Rocking Chair*, 38), is re-creating himself "At the bottom of the sea." Second, throughout *The Rocking Chair* Klein looks at the landscape of Quebec (and, by extension, Canada) and at people and objects in that landscape. And Quebec, through images of geography and topography, is mapped out for the reader in a series of pictures—photographs, pastorals, and landscapes—that depict views, old and new, in and of the province. In the spatial iconography of the series of poems that make up *The Rocking Chair*, then, the portrait of the poet as landscape may be intended to indicate his ultimate importance as the seminal figure in the landscape, connecting human beings with nature and creating and preserving both. The final image of *The Rocking Chair and other Poems*, that of the poet rocking in the undulations of the sea, perhaps of eternal life, is powerful—and positive.

I received my M.A. from Queen's University in 1963 and my Ph.D. from the University of Toronto in 1969. Since the mid-1960s I have concentrated on early (pre-1880) Canadian literature, and I have specialized in prose rather than poetry. As a result, I have not paid much attention to "Portrait of the Poet as Landscape," its place in Klein's canon, and, finally, Klein's place in the literary world. As I look back now, what has happened to Klein and his reputation is nothing short of phenomenal. His work has been the subject of many articles and books, and in 1974 there was an A.M. Klein Symposium, one of the symposia in the "Re-Appraisals: Canadian Writers" series sponsored by the Department of English at the University of Ottawa. In "A.M. Klein and His Montreal," the introduction to the Summer 1984 issue of the *Journal of Canadian Studies*, that was dedicated to Klein, Zailig Pollock records that "it was as a result of the [Ottawa] Symposium that the A.M. Klein Research and Publication Committee was established to prepare a scholarly edition of Klein's Collected Works for publication by the University of Toronto Press" (3). My most recent reading of "Portrait of the Poet as Landscape" has been in the context of Pollock's two-volume edition of Klein's *Complete Poems* in *The Collected Works*.

This new reading of "Portrait of the Poet as Landscape" in *Complete Poems* has benefited, first, from all the criticism done on Klein. Although the poem itself is remarkably free of both explicitly Canadian and explicitly Jewish references, I see the poem now as an important work in the canon of Klein, who himself is a significant poet in the canon of Canadian literature in English, and, if one believes the title of Rachel Feldhay Brenner's book, *the* seminal writer of Canadian Jewish literature. This reading has benefited, second, from the contexts in *Complete Poems*. Through the inclusion of the "[Deleted Section]" from "Portrait of the Poet as a Nobody" immediately after the edited text of "Portrait of the Poet as Landscape" and through the "Textual Notes," I can recreate the versions of the poem at their various stages of composition and revision. In the "Explanatory Notes" I can read Klein's suggested notes from *Longer Poems for Upper-School, 1955-1956*. In the same section, through Pollock's notes, I can trace echoes from Milton and Joyce as well as from Dante, Gerard Manley Hopkins, Rainer Maria Rilke, Karl Shapiro, and William Butler Yeats, and I can link "Portrait of the Poet as Landscape" with Klein's poetry and his work as a whole. In *Complete Poems*, then, "Portrait of the Poet as Landscape" can be seen in a variety of contexts and intertextualities.

A note written by Klein just before he first composed "Portrait of the Poet as a Nobody" and reprinted by Pollock in the explanatory notes for "Portrait of the Poet as Landscape" not only provides a glimpse of the origin of the poem—"Describe being a poet. Who wants him in this age, the day of gasoline and oil"—but also gives both a source for the poem and clues for another reading of its final lines—"So many things still unpraised (See Natonek) still unlabelled by my words" (*Complete Poems*, 1000-1). In late 1943, as Pollock explains, Klein was reading *In Search of Myself*, a work recently published by the Czech writer Hans Natonek, that tells of his experiences as a Jewish refugee in the United States in the early years of World War II. Klein called *In Search of Myself* a "Sickly sentimental European story, broken by shrewd insights . . . To me useful for suggestions" (*Complete Poems*, 1001). One image that may have intrigued Klein was Natonek's association of the artist with water. At the end of *In Search of Myself* the narrator is rejoicing that he is "about to cast another book among the people, as a fisherman sinks his net into the ocean," and that, entering the American market, he has "a permit to one of the greatest, most extensive fisheries on earth" (258-9). In his excitement, he is drawn by "the strong tang of the ocean" (259) to the pier where his boat docked on his arrival in the United States. There, "a clean breeze" blowing about him "from the sea," he feels himself at "home" (261). The connotations of Natonek's ocean as the means to safety, salubrity, and succour may reinforce the affirmation in Klein's final image of the seascaped poet. Klein's drowned poet may also, of course, be his rather cynical answer to Natonek's optimism about his future as a writer in North America.

So many readings! Such interpretative possibilities! I celebrate the subtleties of "Portrait of the Poet as Landscape" that are revealed by siting this poem in *Complete Poems*, in *The Collected Works of A. M. Klein*, and in the canons of English literature, Canadian literature, and Jewish literature. And I am grateful to all the critics and scholars who recognized in Klein an important writer and in "Portrait of the Poet as Landscape" a challenging poem. We cannot go back, and even if we could, we would not give up our hard-won Canadian/English/ Jewish knowledge about Klein and his works. Still, I harbour a modicum of regret for the innocence—and, yes, ignorance—of Mr. Ferguson's Grade Thirteen English class of the mid-1950s where, confident in ourselves and spontaneous in our enthusiasms, we read "Portrait of the Poet as Landscape" simply, as it turns out, as a brilliant and provocative *essai* in the creativity and flexibility of language itself.

Works Cited

Bentley, D.M.R. "A Nightmare Ordered: A.M. Klein's 'Portrait of the Poet as Land-scape.'" *Essays on Canadian Writing* 28 (Spring 1984): 1-45.

Brenner, Rachel Feldhay. *A.M. Klein, The Father of Canadian Jewish Literature: Essays in the Poetics of Humanistic Passion.* Queenston, Ont.: Edwin Mellen Press, 1990.

Joyce, James. *A Portrait of the Artist as a Young Man.* 1916; rpt. Harmondsworth: Penguin, 1960.

Klein, A.M. *Complete Poems Part 2: Original Poems, 1937-1955 and Poetry Translations.* Zailig Pollock, ed. Toronto: Univ. of Toronto Press, 1990.

———. "Portrait of the Poet as a Nobody." *First Statement* 3.1 (June-July 1945): 3-8.

———. *The Rocking Chair and Other Poems.* Toronto: Ryerson, 1948.

Longer Poems for Upper-School, 1955-1956. With notes prepared by Roy H. Allin and Alan F. Meiklejohn. Toronto: Ryerson, 1955.

Natonek, Hans. *In Search of Myself.* Barthold Fles, trans., Sugden Tilley, ed. New York: Putnam's, 1943.

Patterson, Frank Allen, ed. *The Student's Milton.* New York: Appleton-Century-Crofts, 1933.

Pollock, Zailig. "A.M. Klein and His Montreal." *Journal of Canadian Studies/Revue d'études canadiennes* 19.2 (Summer 1984): 3-4.

Wilson, Milton. "Klein's Drowned Poet: Canadian Variations on an Old Theme." *Canadian Literature* 6 (Autumn 1960): 5-17.

Rooting the Borrowed Word: Appropriation and Voice in Kroetsch's "Seed Catalogue"

Manina Jones

"Once upon a time he was a gardener of the possible fruition." (Kroetsch, *Completed Field Notes*, 255)

LYRE, LYRE, PANTS ON FIRE

Robert Kroetsch's essay "Unhiding the Hidden" begins with an expression of the desire for—and the impossibility of producing—genuinely "original" writing in Canada, that is, writing rooted entirely in its place of origin, writing that speaks with a singular Canadian voice. "The particular predicament" of the Canadian writer, as Kroetsch describes it, is that he[1] doesn't really live in a new world, but inherits a pre-existent linguistic and experiential grounding from elsewhere: "he works with a language, within a literature, that appears to be authentically his own, and not a borrowing," but which, no matter how familiar it may initially seem, is in fact borrowed (17):

> The Roman writer borrowed a Greek word into a Latin context. The Canadian writer borrows an English word into an English-language context, a French word into a French-language context. The process of rooting that borrowed word, that totally exact homonym, in authentic experience, is then, must be, a radical one. (18)

Kroetsch reiterates the problem in his essay "No Name Is My Name": "The Canadian writer in English must speak a new culture not with new names but with an abundance of names inherited from Britain and the United States. And that predicament is in turn doubled—by the writing done in the French language in Canada" (51). Despite the "Adamic impulse" Kroetsch sees as characteristic of the literature of a "new place" ("No Name," 41), then, the Canadian writer is no Adam in a New World garden, speaking a pristine language and simply naming the world into existence; his predicament (the word is used in both essays) is that his language and his world are *prae-dicare*, already spoken forth.

Kroetsch's speculation on the problem of Canadian voice in both these essays fails to recognize a number of issues, not the least of which might include the different predicaments of Canadian writers whose first language is neither English nor French, or that of First Nations writers for whom the geography now designated as Canada is not a "new place" at all. What Kroetsch at least potentially does identify is a kind of postcolonial political struggle at the level of the sign.

Even more generally, his essays skirt the possibility that the Canadian writer's predicament is a particular version of every language-user's struggle with what Mikhail Bakhtin describes as the always "'already bespoke quality of the world,'" which is tied up with "the 'already uttered' quality of language" itself (331):

> Language is not a neutral medium that passes freely and easily into the private property of the speaker's intentions; it is populated—overpopulated—with the intentions of others. Expropriating it, forcing it to submit to one's own intentions and accents, is a difficult and complicated process. (294)

This "dialogic inter-orientation with the alien word," Bakhtin notes, significantly, is a condition of speaking that could have been escaped only by "the mythical Adam, who approached a virginal and as yet verbally unqualified world with the first word" (279). Bakhtin condemns poetry—implicitly lyric poetry, which presumes to speak with an individual voice, for a unitary consciousness and single intention—as the form least capable of evoking the dialogic process. The language of the (lyric) poet, according to Bakhtin, aspires to be Adamic, appears to be his own: "he makes use of each form, each word, each expression according to its unmediated power to assign meaning (as it were, 'without quotation marks') that is, as a pure and direct expression of his own intention" (285).[2]

Kroetsch's "Seed Catalogue" is a poem that is self-conscious about putting quotation marks and their equivalents into poetry. Quotation marks and various inferential agents[3] indicate the appropriation of the words of others from elsewhere and their insertion into the poem, drawing attention to—and celebrating—the *mediated* assigning of meaning, the *im*pure, *in*direct nature of expression. Shirley Neuman has described the conspicuously intertextual result of this strategy in Kroetsch's poetry. The "intertext" (Kroetsch's term) is "the space shared by the relations between different poetic texts in the frame of a larger 'Collected Poem.' The 'poem' exists in the lacunae and intersections between the different texts it holds in its space" ("Allow self," 115). "Poetic text" is, in the case of "Seed Catalogue," clearly a relative designation, since it encompasses much material that leads another life as discursive prose. "Seed Catalogue" is, in Neuman's term, a "collected poem," because it is a poem whose constituent elements are obviously collected from elsewhere.

INORGANIC GARDENING

Despite the garden imagery that permeates "Seed Catalogue," then, it is a text that resists the myth of organic form, according to which a poem grows "naturally" and homogeneously from the innate properties of its material and the personality of the poet. "Seed Catalogue" begins, for example, by drawing attention to the fact that it has already begun. It opens, not with the words of the poet, but with a citation from a seed catalogue advertising "Copenhagen Market Cabbage" (32), whose name reinforces its status both as a vegetable strain "foreign" to Canadian soil, and as an instance of the "alien word," an imported textual product. While the poem begins, naturally enough, with the label "I," the citation itself is tagged "No. 176," emphasizing a slippage or discontinuity between "inside" and "outside" texts.

Each textual component of the poem is, to use a figure associated with gardening, "grafted" onto the larger body. The term "graft" is employed in Arturo Schwartz's description of what he terms (recalling Dadaist practice in the visual arts) the "printed ready-made," an extract of a printed text introduced by the poet into his composition: "Such intervention is of botanic nature: it has affinity with the grafting practised by the gardener to modify the flower or fruit of a plant" (29). This intervention may be of a botanic nature, but it is not, strictly speaking, organic. Indeed, the method is also a "graft" in the sense that the poet illicitly "plays dirty" with the poetic conventions of both lyric voice and organic form.

In "Seed Catalogue," further, it is impossible to sustain an opposition between "rooted" and "grafted" texts. E.D. Blodgett identifies as dialogic—or what he terms "interdiscursive"—the effect of this strategy: "the various texts become commentaries for each other" (202). "Seed Catalogue," then, is a choric locus, or what Kroetsch calls a "shared book" ("Statement," 311), but not only because it is a communal document that incorporates other people's words. The individual word is opened up and multiplied, and lyric voice itself is exposed as a fiction. The poem thus provides a provocative response to the linguistic dilemma posed in the two Kroetsch essays cited at the beginning of this article: it is literally pro-vocative in its teasing out of a multiplicity of voices using the "inherited word." In "Seed Catalogue," Kroetsch, significantly, *finds* (rather than originates) a response precisely by the repetition of inherited language, with a significant difference. Instead of attempting to replace the borrowed word—repeatability, as Derrida demonstrates, is a feature of writing (179-80), so that replacing "used" language is an impossibility—"Seed Catalogue" suggests a re-placing or re-situating of it through citation. A citation is by definition a text that has precisely the same form as its historical antecedent; it is, in the words of "Unhiding the Hidden," a "totally exact homonym" that "reroots" the word by excerpting and contextually rerouting it.

In "The Moment of the Discovery of America Continues," Kroetsch describes the "translation" of the 1917 seed catalogue he found in the Glenbow archives in 1975 into the poem "Seed Catalogue" as one such rerouting/rerooting (11). This "idiomatic" movement, in which the poet is as much an interpreter of the given text as an originating speaker, is clearly one version of "homolinguistic translation," a poetic tactic Douglas Barbour identifies with the denial of the lyric impulse (58). In "Seed Catalogue" homolinguistic translation has the effect of producing a heterogeneous poetic voice which emanates, not from an "original" poetic speaker, but from within the already spoken or written local, communal language of the prairie town. "Seed Catalogue" repeatedly inquires into the origin and development of the poetic speaker—"*How do you grow a poet?*" (41, 42, 43, 44)—but as Blodgett comments in his discussion of Kroetsch's *The Ledger*, the appropriation of "outside texts" into the poem prevents the poetic totalization of language, the exclusive valorizing of voice as monologic presence (200), because the "origin" of the "text" is another text. Indeed, to return to the Edenic scenario proposed earlier, "Seed Catalogue" not only parodies the myth of the Fall, as Smaro Kamboureli observes (112), but also parodies by textualizing the myth of an Edenic, "original" language. The poem is writing about writing about the desire for, the imagination of, as-yet-unrealized gardens: "Into the dark of January / the seed catalogue bloomed // a winter proposition, if / spring should come, then" (33).[4] It is the seed catalogue, and not a garden that blooms forth here. The implied duplication of the poem's title ("Seed Catalogue"/seed catalogue) is a reminder—indeed, an epitome—of the textual, citational nature of the poem's affiliation with the "outside" that it literally reproduces. The title's doubleness also signals the ambivalent relationship between prosaic and poetic texts that "Seed Catalogue" sustains.

One response "Seed Catalogue" provides to the question *"How do you grow a poet?"* (42) consists of a list of prescriptions that again contra-dicts the idea of an original, Adamic lyric speaker. The list humorously indicates not only the obvious necessity that the poet's physical well-being be maintained, but also suggests the importance to the poet of an already written inheritance of language, and the pre-scripted nature of the linguistic utterance itself. "Seed Catalogue"'s prescriptions incorporate local wisdom about spiritual and physical health into the poem, re-reading and revaluing the "prosaic" regional idiom:

> For appetite: cod-liver
> oil.
> For bronchitis: mustard
> plasters.
> For pallor and failure to fill
> the woodbox: sulphur
> & molasses.
> For self-abuse: ten Our
> Fathers & ten Hail Marys.
> For regular bowels: Sunny Boy
> Cereal. (42)

The question *"How do you grow a gardener?"* doubles the query about growing a poet. The former question is followed earlier in the poem by a listing of seed-names (34), and the parallel implies a correspondence between poet and gardener, gardener's seeds and poet's prescriptions: words themselves. Indeed, the Derridean association between the Latin word for seed, *seme*, and the Greek for sign, *sema*, is persistently evoked in "Seed Catalogue." This is, significantly, a false etymology, an apparently original "root" connection that turns out to be a purely textual one.

When the question *"How do you grow a poet?"* is again posed, the response takes the form of another foregrounded prescription, the citation of a product testimonial from the seed catalogue: "'It's a pleasure to advise that I / won the First Prize at the Calgary / Horticultural Show . . . This is my / first attempt. I used your seeds'" (42). The seed catalogue is a publication that provides a kind of local forum—it places on display (in order to profit from) the statements of its community of correspondents. So too does the "Seed Catalogue," but the poem encourages a generically (at least) double reading. The happy gardener of the prose citation is, in effect, already a poet and doesn't know it ("advise" and "Prize," for example, are rhymes)—"Seed Catalogue" shows it. The gardener's "first attempt" at horticulture is not primal ("I used your seeds"), and neither is the poet's citational gesture original. The writer of the testimonial letter in the seed catalogue and its re-writer, the poet of "Seed Catalogue," achieve a "spectacular" success based, in effect, on the fruitfulness of someone else's prior seminal product . . .

NOW, *LIST*-EN HERE

. . . And on their own ability to tend seeds and attend to words, respectively. The poet in this context must be an avid listener to language: "My mother said: / Did you wash your ears? / You could grow cabbages / in those ears" (32). It should be noted that these lines are themselves a citation, a linguistic inheritance from the poet's mother—they are juxtaposed with a quotation from the seed catalogue (another vernacular inheritance) that describes the Copenhagen Market Cabbage in terms of genealogy: "[it] is in every respect a *thoroughbred*, a *cabbage* of *highest pedigree*" (32). The poet, because he has attended to the metaphorical resonances of the language of the catalogue, has recognized its "poetic" potential, "transplanted" it into the poem, and allowed it to grow in significance.

This passage about the poet's ears might elicit recollections of the poet in William Carlos Williams' *Paterson*, a similarly fecund character whose voice is also both interrogated and interrogatory: "His ears are toadstools, his fingers have begun to sprout leaves (his voice is drowned under the falls)" (83). Williams' poem is a kind of pre-text for "Seed Catalogue" in its "listening" to and poetic recitation of the language of locality, its use of unassimilated citations to generate a localized voice and sense of place. *Paterson* cites Ezra Pound's comment on Williams' refusal of formal closure in his poems: "Your interest is in the bloody loam but what / I'm after is the finished product" (37). The poets of both *Paterson* and "Seed Catalogue" have what amounts to a "dirty mind": they provide a fertile matrix for the growth of given germs of meaning. "Seed Catalogue"'s interest in the "growth of the poet's mind," as Shirley Neuman perceives, places it in relation to Wordsworth's *The Prelude* as well ("Allow self," 121). The poet's mind in Kroetsch's text, however, is not presented as the source of an integral voice, but as a locus of textual intersection.[5]

What does remain of the lyric impulse in "Seed Catalogue" is an openness to, and foregrounding of, what Northrop Frye calls lyrical "babble" (275), in everyday speech, a playful affirmation of the singing voice of language, its musical possibilities that border on nonsense: "I don't give a damn if I do die do die do die do die do die / do die do die do die do die do die do die do die do die do / die do / die do die do die do die do die do die do die do die / do" (40). The words of this silly—but memorable—little ditty are, ironically, about the defiance of death. Their musical sound functions typically as a mnemonic device, demonstrating the "death-defying" ability of language to survive over time through the significant poetic gesture of recitation. "Seed Catalogue" is not just a "collected poem," then; it is also a re-collected poem, in which recitation is a method of translating "then" to "now," of "seeding/time" (44), or growing a past: "*But how do you grow a poet? || Start:* with an invocation / invoke— // His muse is / his muse/if / memory is" (41). The word itself is a kind of muse, and voicing it is in itself both an inspiration and a remembering. Implicit in the word "muse," for example, is a connection between inspiration, the musical, mnemonic elements of language, and the poet's meditative musings: "no memory then / no meditation / no song (shit / we're up against it)" (41).

AN S-*CATALOGUE*-ICAL POETICS

The last lines of this passage seem to emphasize the poet's limitations, which are elaborated at length in the list that catalogues "the absence of . . ." various commodities and qualities in the prairie milieu (39). "Seed Catalogue," however, not only counteracts but subverts such limitations by producing what might be seen as a productively excremental vision (what more fertile place is there than up against shit?), in its poetically unconventional emphasis on the colloquial bawdy/body and its functions; in its formal recycling, via a citational strategy, of what might normally be considered a corpus of verbal refuse; and in its oral folk-tale or "bullshitting" impulse. Scatological imagery, for example, is used to describe the kind of record or trace that the poet leaves in his passage through the landscape:

> only a scarred
> page, a spoor of wording
> a reduction to mere black
>
> and white/a pile of rabbit
> turds that tells us
> all spring long
> where the track was. (43)

The poet of "Seed Catalogue" tracks down accounts of the past, leaving a literally documentary record that is the trace of a trace of a communal past: this is, notably, "a pile of rabbit / turds that *tells us*" (emphasis added). In a poem named for a seed catalogue, "spoor" inevitably resonates with the botanical "spore," and evokes the textual process of dissemination, a sowing/scattering-about of meaning, a planting that is limitlessly transplanted.

Early on in the poem, "Seed Catalogue" makes a connection between its sca-tological preoccupation, the notion of poetry as song, and the language of the seed catalogue:

> No. 25—*McKenzie's Improved Golden Wax Bean*: "THE MOST
> PRIZED OF ALL BEANS. *Virtue* is its own reward. We have had
> *many expressions* from *keen discriminating gardeners extolling our seed*
> and *this variety*."

Beans, beans,
the musical fruit;
the more you eat,
the more you virtue. (33)

Virtue, it would seem, is its own re-word. This popular children's rhyme about flatulence (which is, after all, like the folk tradition of the tall tale, an expulsion of "hot air") is (re)cited, and itself takes in the language of the seed catalogue, censoring the traditional last word of the verse in favour of the more decorous, but nonsensical "virtue." Few readers of the poem, however, would forget that the conventional last word is the musical word, the word that rhymes, "toot." Beans—and, by humourous extension, the linguistic endowment of the poet's past—are both extolled and re-told/tolled (or resounded), with a difference.

WHAT'S NEW?

In a 1978 article on Kroetsch's poetry, Susan Wood expresses what is essentially a dissatisfaction with the unconventional nature of this strategy, or what she calls Kroetsch's "wavering" in "Seed Catalogue" between prose and poetry, as well as his unwillingness "to transcend the prairie town reality, which he records in its flat colloquial language. . . . We've 'heard it' before, so what's new?" (36). Wood, in effect, restates the problem of originality, and relates it to the poem's indeterminate genre. One effect of the generic instability Wood identifies is the possibility that the "flat colloquial language" used might be seen as a kind of prose poetry in its ability to voice a prairie colloquy. It is not, according to the logic of the poem, necessary to "transcend" prairie town reality in order to read it as "poetic." In fact, "Seed Catalogue" offers the possibility that it is necessary only to repeat that colloquial language in a new context, to (aesthetically) frame it with quotation marks, to (poetically) re-cite it.

   The poem stresses its own reliance on the oral tradition of re-sounding old phrases and stories, a tradition in which the storyteller is not an "original," but remembers, elaborates on, and recontextualizes a legacy of stories: "—You ever hear the one about the woman who buried / her husband with his ass sticking out of the ground / so that every time she happened to walk by she could / give it a swift kick? // —Yeh, I heard it" (40). This "dirty" joke presents yet another twist on the botanical metaphor of "planting." Not only is the anecdote strategically "planted" in the poem by the canny poet, the joke is that finality is again spurned through an act of iteration, since the wife in the story always gets another kick at the can. As does the storyteller: the punchline of *his* joke is the listener's response, which draws attention to the context of reiterated telling. Or, to put it another way, response is, in this context, the "kicker."

RE-SEEDING HEIR-LINES

"Seed Catalogue" represents another incident in which the speaker's father tells and retells the story of his shooting at a badger, allowing the tale to conform, not simply to his original intention when he shot at the badger, but to his re-construction of intention with each recontextualized telling. In the first version of the story, the poet's father shoots at the badger, but misses and mistakenly hits a magpie. "A week later," however, "my father told the story again. In that version he intended to hit the magpie. Magpies, he explained, are a nuisance" (35). In the context of the oral folk-tale, intention is not simply a prior design, a predetermined, immutable meaning; it is, *pace* Wordsworth, a postludic act, a playful reinterpretation of the given verbal text. In the interview *Labyrinths of Voice*, Kroetsch points out both the importance of the linguistic inheritance of the past, and the danger of "the heirloom model for inherited stories," which suggests that the past is "a fixed thing": "I suppose that is one of the things print did to us: we suddenly have a fixed text. I'm still tempted by oral models where the story in the act of retelling is always responsive to individuals, to the place, to invention" (13). The re-telling of received stories in "Seed Catalogue" unfixes the given text, gesturing toward certain characteristics of the oral tradition, and placing the poet in what appears to be a long (story/genetic) line of prairie bullshitters. His recontextualized telling of the father's story allows yet another range of possible inflections, but it also allows the accents of his father's voice to remain: the badger "was digging holes in the potato patch, threatening man and beast with broken limbs (I *quote*)" (35, emphasis added).

Since "will" or intention is something shown to be less than final in the in-heritance of the past, the inclusion in the poem of a "last will and testament" must be seen as ironic indeed. What is inherited in that will, however, is not simply the material objects that it represents—"*To my son Frederick my carpenter tools*" (47)—but also the language of the document that is simultaneously pro-saically familiar and poetically defamiliarized. "Seed Catalogue" uses the materials at hand—the will, the seed catalogue, letters, and other inherited texts—in order to reconstruct and revalue the local past, a past on which the present community depends for its existence. It is significant, then, that when the question, "*How do you grow a prairie town?*" is posed, the response provided—"Rebuild the hotel when it burns down. Bigger. Fill it / full of a lot of A-1 Hard Northern Bullshitters" (40)—allies the notion of reconstruction with the exaggerating im-pulse of the tall tale as "bullshit." It also, significantly, names storytellers after a local variety of a seed ("A-1 Hard Northern").

The poet's father passes on the narrative tradition of the tall tale. It is his mother, however, who subtly alerts the poet—as well as the poem's reader—to the traces of semiotic multiplicity in the most mundane of expressions. The poet in/of "Seed Catalogue" listens carefully to the inherited words of the (m)other, the voice that is at once familiar and alien, and represents it: "Bring me the radish seeds, / my mother whispered" (33). "Radish" is a word whose root is "root," and "seeds" a word whose meaning is, at least in the false etymology already suggested, "meaning." "Seed Catalogue" represents a search for roots and meanings, and, inevitably, a search for roots *as* meanings. This "radical" approach means that the poem is not simply a nostalgic return to an original Garden, or even a garden, but rather, as the title of the larger work of which it is a part indicates, the prolific yield of a "field" of "notes."

Notes

I would like to thank Susan Rudy Dorscht for her valuable advice on this paper.

[1] The gendered pronoun is Kroetsch's. I have maintained it for the sake of consistency.

[2] For a discussion of the difficulties Bakhtin encounters in trying to maintain the ultimately untenable binary opposition novel/(lyric) poetry, particularly when his theories about the dialogized nature of consciousness and the internally dialogized quality of the word itself are taken into account, see Tzvetan Todorov's *Mikhail Bakhtin: The Dialogical Principle.*

[3] Julia Kristeva calls "inferential agents" words that mediate between the author's enunciation and that of others, such as "if, *as* Vergil *says* . . ." "and *thereupon* Saint Jerome *says*," etc. (see pp. 45-6). As E.D. Blodgett implies, spatial arrangement in "Seed Catalogue" might be considered an inferential agent, since it too designates the enunciation of others (202).

[4] All references to "Seed Catalogue" are in Kroetsch's *Completed Field Notes.*

[5] For more on *Field Notes* and autobiography, see both Neuman articles listed in the Works Cited, and Susan Rudy Dorscht's "On Sending Yourself: Kroetsch and the New Autobiography."

Works Cited

Bakhtin, Mikhail. *The Dialogic Imagination: Four Essays.* Caryl Emerson and Michael Holquist, trans., Michael Holquist, ed. Austin: Univ. of Texas Press, 1981.

Barbour, Douglas. "Lyric/Anti-Lyric: Some Notes About a Concept." *Line*, 3 (Spring 1984): 45-63.

Blodgett, E.D. "The Book, Its Discourse, and the Lyric: Notes on Robert Kroetsch's *Field Notes.*" *Open Letter*, 5th Series, 8-9 (Summer-Fall 1984): 195-205.

Derrida, Jacques. "Signature Event Context." Samuel Weber and Jeffrey Mehlman, trans. *Glyph I.* Baltimore: Johns Hopkins Univ. Press, 1977: 172-97.

Dorscht, Susan Rudy. "On Sending Yourself: Kroetsch and the New Autobiography." *Signature*, 2 (Winter 1989): 27-41.

Frye, Northrop. *Anatomy of Criticism: Four Essays.* Princeton: Princeton Univ. Press, 1957.

Kamboureli, Smaro. *On the Edge of Genre: The Contemporary Canadian Long Poem.* Toronto: Univ. of Toronto Press, 1991.

Kristeva, Julia. *Desire in Language: A Semiotic Approach to Literature and Art.* New York: Columbia Univ. Press, 1980.

Kroetsch, Robert. *Completed Field Notes: The Long Poems of Robert Kroetsch.* Toronto: McClelland and Stewart, 1989.

——. "The Moment of the Discovery of America Continues." *The Lovely Treachery of Words: Essays Selected and New.* Toronto: Oxford, 1989: 1-20.

——. "No Name Is My Name." *The Lovely Treachery of Words*, 41-52.

——. "Reciting the Emptiness." *The Lovely Treachery of Words*, 34-40.

——. "Statement by the Poet." *The Long Poem Anthology.* Michael Ondaatje, ed. Toronto: Coach House, 1979: 311-12.

————. "Unhiding the Hidden." *Open Letter*, 5th Series, 4 (Spring 1983): 17-22.

————, Shirley Neuman and Robert Wilson. *Labyrinths of Voice: Conversations with Robert Kroetsch*. Edmonton: NeWest, 1982.

Neuman, Shirley. "Allow self, portraying self: Autobiography in *Field Notes*." *Line*, 1.2 (Fall 1983): 104-21.

————. "Figuring the Reader, Figuring the Self in *Field Notes*: Double or Noting." *Open Letter*, 5th Series, 8-9 (Summer-Fall 1984): 176-94.

Schwartz, Arturo. "Contributions to a Poetic of the Ready-made." John A. Stevens, trans. *Marcel Duchamp: Ready-mades, etc. (1918-1964)*. Paris: le Terrain Vague, 1964: 13-41.

Todorov, Tzvetan. *Mikhail Bakhtin: The Dialogical Principle*. Vlad Godzich, trans. Minneapolis: Univ. of Minnesota Press, 1984.

Williams, William Carlos. *Paterson*. New York: New Directions, 1963.

Wood, Susan. "Reinventing the Word: Kroetsch's Poetry." *Canadian Literature*, 77 (Summer 1978): 28-39.

"The City of the End of Things":
The Significance of Lampman's Sound and Fury

Bruce L. Grenberg

Archibald Lampman's "The City of the End of Things" presents a poser for the reader-critic. Although frequently anthologized, and the object of numerous telegraphic critical comments, this poem, which was first published in 1895, has yet to receive a full critical analysis.

The most complete treatment of the poem (but only three pages long!) is that by L.R. Early in his book, *Archibald Lampman*. Early argues that the poem "presents an infernal apocalypse that is the logical end of urban corruption and mechanization," and suggests that the intense and compelling vision of the poem indicates the "strength of foreboding that lay behind the principled optimism of his essays" (99). James Steele finds in "The City of the End of Things" Lampman's "modernist anxiety about the social implications of industrialization" (Steele, 127) and leaves it at that. D.G. Jones argues that "it is the 'unreal city' that furnishes the demonic or nightmare side of Lampman's vision," with its "images of confusion and violence, hostility and isolation," and concludes that "it is the essential vacuity of such a world that characterizes the nightmare vision of 'The City of the End of Things'" (Jones, 116-17). One can scarcely argue with these summary views, but with little specific analysis of the poem's details of structure, imagery, and themes, Jones's judgments do little more than open the door to the poem's values. There are a number of other critical "one-liners" about the poem, usually in the context of some other thematic argument about Lampman's late-developing and ambiguous social consciousness, and usually suggesting a muted approval of Lampman's quasi-cryptic attack upon the industrialization, or urbanization, of his beloved Canadian nature.

Unfortunately, a persistent strain of inchoate Canadian nationalism further blurs the already limited critical assessment of Lampman's achievement as a poet. In 1976 Sandra Djwa finds G.H. Unwin's 1917 evaluation of Lampman as "good a description as any": "a native genius, moulded and ripened by a study of the masters of English verse, but distinctively fresh and Canadian" (Djwa, 113). In the same collection of essays, *The Lampman Symposium*, and in a similar tone, Bruce Nesbitt finds in Lampman a "defined . . . break with colonial romanticism" (Nesbitt, 109). And in characteristic bluntness Robin Mathews proclaims that "if Lampman cannot be understood by the British or the U.S. readers, the failure to understand is a function of imperial parochialism passing under the misnomer of cosmopolitanism" (Mathews, 123).

I think it is time to put this quasi-political posturing behind us, time to move beyond the self-answering question of whether or not Lampman is a significant

Canadian poet and ask whether or not Lampman is a significant poetic voice of the nineteenth century. For it is quite clear from the biographies that Lampman wished to be known and remembered as a poet—not merely as a Canadian who wrote poems. My purposes in this essay, therefore, have little to do with the grand claims and counter-claims about Lampman as a distinctly *Canadian* poet; rather, I shall try to read "The City of the End of Things" as a nineteenth-century poem within the well-established tradition of nineteenth-century "meditative-argumentative" literature, and I shall try to assess his accomplishment within those larger traditions of poetry that clearly meant so much to him, if not always to his apologists.

Indeed, one of the salient features of "The City of the End of Things" is its lack of any specific, let alone Canadian, locale or "identity." The "City of the End of Things," which is identified in the last line of the poem's first stanza, is referred to throughout the rest of the poem as "it." The repetitive use of the third person impersonal pronoun in itself establishes and maintains an indefinite quality to the city—a quality of indefiniteness and of dislocation that permeates the entire poem. The city has "no rounded name that rings" (6), its "roofs and iron towers have grown / None knoweth how high" (9-10), and "abysses and vast fires" (30) give shape without form to the palpable obscure of the cityscape.[1] Surely Lampman's conception is mythic rather than mimetic, for the poem has setting without place, temporality without history, and society without identity. By establishing this indeterminate "other-world," Lampman relieves us of our predispositions and allegiances towards our world and asks us to accept without question his conditional world of mythic vision, just as the writer of science fiction builds his other-worlds from the ground up and requires the reader to accept the terms of the new environment.

Lampman's mythic world is poetically captured at the moment of its dissolution, and the adjective most frequently applied by critics to the poem's tone and theme is "apocalyptic." That term is overused in general, and as applied to Lampman's poem it is inexact, and therefore dangerously misleading, for there are no angels of God in the poem and no anti-Christ, no "new heaven and a new earth," and certainly no "new Jerusalem, coming down from God out of heaven, prepared as a bride adorned for her husband" (Revelation 20-21). Further, there is in the poem certainly no sense of the original meaning of "apocalypse" as an uncovering of meaning or ultimate values. Rather, Lampman seems to go out of his way to dislocate his reader and obfuscate meaning at every turn, creating not apocalypse now, but uncertainty forever. In this regard, the poem might be viewed as an *anti*-apocalyptic poem, for it perpetuates no image of an ultimate order and purpose to a cryptic "reality," but instead offers a vision of a universe permeated by a disorder which is absolute in its sway.

All of this is not to say that Lampman does not have *his* purposes in the poem. The dream situation that he favours in so many of his poems becomes, in "The City of the End of Things," a nightmarish inversion of Victorian values that constitutes an anti-Utopia. The Romantic/Victorian dream of inevitable, if dialectical, progress (Comte, Hegel, Marx, Huxley) becomes in the poem a nightmare of irresistible regress. The nineteenth-century assumptions that science was necessarily progressive and that material well-being could produce a paradise on earth generate the darkest irony in the poem, in which the "multitudes of men, / That built that city in their pride" (49-50) have "withered age by age and died" (52).

Lampman, in this poem anyway, is clearly set against the received opinion of his time and his culture. But the poem is not simply a protest against the industrialization and urbanization of the western world, and it is not merely a plaintive conjecture on how or why western culture might be brought to ruin. Lampman's critical inquiry points to a much more formidable and resistant target than these. In "The City of the End of Things" he makes the absolute and all-encompassing assertion that all humankind is self-determined and inescapably self-doomed. Indeed, the salient feature of the poem is that Lampman poses no power, no authority, no purpose outside of humanity that can protect humanity from itself. And that grim conviction is the source of both the power and the tragedy in the poem's bleak vision.

Although "The City of the End of Things" has no explicit setting in time or place, and thus strikes the reader as almost featureless, or at best dimly featured, Lampman takes some pains to give the poem a balanced, almost geometric, structure. The eighty-eight-line poem is divided into two exact halves of forty-four lines, the first half of the poem dominated by a description and definition of a Tartarean anti-humanistic world of "measured roar and iron ring" (23) ruled by "fire and night" (26). Lampman's description of this world of "inhuman music" (24) and "abysses and vast fires" (30), guarded by Death, which would smite an unwary visitor "face to face, / And blanch him with its venomed air" (39-40), obviously owes a good deal to the first two books of *Paradise Lost*, and perhaps something to Browning's "Childe Roland," and Lampman also captures Milton's opening theme of the unending, unchanging horror of Hell by presenting his description in what might be termed a disembodied, but perpetually present, tense. The dominance of the present tense in the opening forty-four lines of the poem, in fact, rhetorically endows the world described with a pervasive and persuasive factualness that compels our acceptance even as we reject its inhumanity.

However unpalatable and monstrous the vision in the first forty-four lines of the poem, the last half of the poem conveys Lampman's true vision of horror. Beginning with line 45, Lampman shifts abruptly to the past tense and presents a mytho-historical perspective on the origins of nightmare. Here, he reveals that his city of dreadful night is the direct product not of any fiendish antagonist, but of humanity's highest endeavours:

> It was not always so, but once,
> In days that no man thinks upon,
> Fair voices echoed from its stones,
> The light above it leaped and shone:
> Once there were multitudes of men,
> That built that city in their pride,

> Until its might was made, and then
> They withered age by age and died. (45-52)

The first six lines of the passage echo, if faintly, Matthew 5:14: "Ye are the light of the world. A city that is set on an hill cannot be hid." And the Beatitudes of Matthew 5 are, we recall, specifically addressed to "the multitudes" (5:1), whom Christ admonishes in verse 16, "Let your light so shine before men, that they may see your good works, and glorify your Father which is in heaven." One might safely assume that Lampman, as the son of an Anglican clergyman, would be familiar with the Sermon on the Mount; what is not immediately clear is the purpose to which he puts his ironic inversion of Christ's message to the faithful—for an inversion it certainly is.

One could argue, of course, that Lampman's nightmare vision is that of a world without faith, a world in which "the salt have lost his savour" and "is thenceforth good for nothing, but to be cast out, and to be trodden under foot of men" (Matthew 5:13). In this context, the men "that built that city in their pride" (50) would be re-enacting Adam's original sin, and "The City of the End of Things" would stand as a conventional, even hackneyed, homily on the sin of pride and the inevitable fall of man. There might indeed be a residuum of this conventional Christian posture in the poem, but Lampman goes far beyond the simple irony of arguing that humanity has failed to follow the divine directive. Rather, his sardonic explanation for the origin of the city of the end of things rests upon his conviction and assertion that this dreadful city of night has sprung directly *from* the light of humanity's highest aspirations and, indeed, faith.

The entire poem, in both theme and image, is founded upon the antinomies of good bringing forth evil, light generating darkness, humanity spawning in-humanity. Thus, for example, the city of "fire and night" (26), of "the beat, the thunder and the hiss" (27), is seen as the direct, if distant, product of the original city where "the light above . . . leaped and shone" (48). Similarly, the "fair voices" which echoed from the stones of the original city (47) have not yielded to, but have *become*, the "iron lips" from which is blown "a dreadful and monotonous cry" (35-6). Summarily, "that prodigious race" (53) of titanic, heroic, original men has paradoxically produced a race that "are not flesh," that "are not bone," that "see not with the human eye" (33-4).

In "The City of the End of Things" Lampman thus presents not only a vivid diorama of humankind in the throes of dissolution, but also provides a poetic exegesis upon the causes of that dissolution. Clearly, the second half of the poem reflects Lampman's horror at the path taken by nineteenth-century industrial-ization and the specialization inherent in mass production, mass consumption. Given the nightmare world of the poem, the "End of Things" in the poem's title suggests an Aristotelian final cause of "things" that is categorically opposed to the optimism inherent in Victorian progressive, expansionist, materialistic thought. For Lampman, in the most overt sense, "things" simply destroy nature. The artifices of humanity, however well-conceived or well-intended, are ineluc-tably flawed, for they consume the nature which is necessary to their continuance.

By a simple, but irresistible logic, then, "things" for Lampman must inevitably consume nature and be in turn consumed themselves, their impermanence yielding to "the silence of eternal night" (75), where "Nor ever living thing shall grow, / Nor trunk of tree, nor blade of grass; / No drop shall fall, no wind shall blow, / Nor sound of any foot shall pass" (81-4).

Lampman is relentless, if not remorseless, in his analysis of the human dimension to this ecological nightmare. And we are reminded, and must remember always, that for Lampman there are no villains in the human drama, no Serpent and no Satan to blame for the Fall. The city of the end of things is founded by, and prospers under, the "fair voices" of a "prodigious race." These mythical giants of men that "built that city in their pride, / Until its might was made" (50-1) are clearly meant to depict the finest flowering of their culture, representing not only the best that has been thought and said, but the best that can be done by the human spirit. But consonant with the fundamental paradox of Lampman's dark vision, it is precisely the greatness of this endeavour that defeats itself. Just as artifice consumes itself by consuming nature, so extraordinary achievement destroys itself by outdistancing the culture it purports to represent. Again the logic is grim and irresistible: the extraordinary talents and achievements of the few are alienating and divisive forces that doom the culture. Thus, the "prodigious race" is depicted as withering "age by age" and dying (52), until "Three only in an iron tower, / Set like carved idols face to face, / Remain the masters of its [the city's] power" (54-6).

Clearly Lampman is attacking the specialization that characterized the Industrial Revolution, but his perspective is far different from, even opposed to, that of Marx. For Lampman focuses our attention upon the alienation, not of the worker from his work, but of the innovator from his innovation. Those extraordinary qualities and special powers that made the "three" the masters of their culture (the city), have inevitably set them apart from that culture and imprisoned them in an "iron tower" (54).

However dark this portrait of the human condition seems, in which our highest aspirations, even when achieved, lead to crushing defeat, Lampman has yet darker tints to his palette. For

> at the city gate a fourth,
> Gigantic and with dreadful eyes,
> Sits looking toward the lightless north,
> Beyond the reach of memories;
> Fast rooted to the lurid floor,
> A bulk that never moves a jot,
> In his pale body dwells no more,
> Or mind or soul,—an idiot! (57-64)

This is the idiot of *Macbeth* who stands sentinel over the sound and fury of Lampman's dark world, and he is also Milton's Death, that shape without form who guards the Gate of Hell. More importantly, he is Lampman's image of the ultimate destiny of "The City of the End of Things," and thus is akin to

Yeats's "rough beast" emerging from the *Spiritus Mundi* as our world's final nightmare.

Beginning with line 65, Lampman shifts tense yet again, this time to the future, and the poem becomes emphatically visionary. In this vision of the future, the three masters of the city also will "perish and their hands be still, / And with the master's [sic] touch shall flee / Their incommunicable skill" (66-8). From this point to the end of the poem, Lampman depicts a world dismantled, returning to its origins:

> A stillness absolute as death
> Along the slacking wheels shall lie,
> And, flagging at a single breath,
> The fires that moulder out and die.
> The roar shall vanish at its height,
> And over that tremendous town
> The silence of eternal night
> Shall gather close and settle down. (69-76)

Thus Lampman sets the stage for the poem's conclusion, and if he were writing "The City of the End of Things" as a conventionally "apocalyptic" poem, this is the point at which we would expect to hear something of the final judgment. It is precisely any final judgment, however, that Lampman withholds from the reader. The destroyed "City of the End of Things" might bear some resemblance to the destroyed Babylon of Revelation 18, but for Lampman there is no analogue to Revelation 19 with its "great voice of much people in heaven, saying, Alleluia; Salvation, and glory, and honour, and power, unto the Lord our God: For true and righteous *are* his judgments: for he hath judged the great whore, which did corrupt the earth with her fornication, and hath avenged the blood of his servants at her hand" (Revelation 19: 1-2). No God of vengeance or redress stands at the end of Lampman's poem. Only the "grim Idiot at the gate / Is deathless and eternal there" (87-8)—the "One thing the hand of Time shall spare" (86).

Because "The City of the End of Things" is notable for its scant and repetitive imagery (fire, darkness, shadows, towers, and halls), the haunting image of the Idiot in the concluding movement of the poem becomes all the more compelling and dominant. The Idiot's power, however, springs not from any awful attributes, but, indeed, from an almost total lack of definition. His is a "bulk that never moves a jot" (62), and "In his pale body dwells no more, / Or mind or soul . . ." (63-4). It is this shapeless, motionless, colourless, mindless, soulless Eidolon that serves Lampman as a fit emblem of vacuous, purposeless, valueless, ineffable being.

By the time we reach the end of the poem, we recognize—or should recognize, I think—that the entire poem has been built upon an illusion. The "end" of things presupposes a beginning, and to go from beginning to end implies at least movement, if not necessarily continuous progress. This illusion of passage is reinforced by Lampman's employment of present, past, and future tenses to convey the origin, enactment, and termination of human aspiration. In like manner, Lampman's choice of the relentlessly octosyllabic line with alternating rhyme, although somewhat tedious, does suggest a stringent, even rigid, order to the poem's thematic statement. But in the end, all these putative structures collapse upon themselves, just as the "City of the End of Things" collapses upon itself. And we are left in a Void—presided over by an Idiot.

In spite of, or perhaps because of, its grim pessimism, the centrality of "The City of the End of Things" to the Lampman canon is assured. The poem articulates Lampman's summary, if not final, engagement with the various and, as it turns out, contradictory claims made upon his imagination by Romantic naturism and heroism, Victorian optimism and materialism, and, more particularly, socialist political and philosophical assumptions about human aspiration, equality, and dignity. Like most poets, Lampman would not win a prize for systematic thought, but his naked honesty in confronting the demons of cultural contradiction that beset so many of his nineteenth-century contemporaries bespeaks the same kind of moral courage that we find in Coleridge, Melville, Browning, and Conrad. And that, I submit, is high praise indeed.

Notes

[1]"The City of The End of Things," *The Poems of Archibald Lampman* (1974). For ease of reference I cite line, rather than page, numbers in my text.

Works cited

Djwa, Sandra. "Lampman's Achievement." *The Lampman Symposium*. Lorraine McMullen, ed. Ottawa: Univ. of Ottawa Press, 1976: 111-14.

Early, L.R. *Archibald Lampman*. Boston: Twayne, 1986.

Jones, D.G. "Lampman's Achievement." McMullen, 115-120.

Lampman, Archibald. "The City of the End of Things." *The Poems of Archibald Lampman*. Duncan Campbell Scott, ed. Toronto: Morang, 1900; rpt. with introduction by Margaret Coulby Whitridge. Toronto: Univ. of Toronto Press, 1974: 179-82.

Mathews, Robin. "Lampman's Achievement." McMullen, 121-3.

Nesbitt, Bruce. "The New Lampman." McMullen, 99-110.

Steele, James. "Lampman's Achievement." McMullen, 125-8.

How Do You Read a Riddle?:
Patrick Lane's *Winter*

Nathalie Cooke

Patrick Lane's *Winter* sequence, a collection of forty-five poems entitled "Winter 1" through "Winter 45," seems to function like a charm or spell. Winter, the word and the idea, is central not only to the collection, but to the incantation as well. Lane draws his readers northward by the incantatory repetition of words, sounds, even letters—snow: the *s* as in ice, the *no* in north, the *w* in wind and winter.

But Lane breaks his own spell and thereby writes the sequence from the realm of charm to the realm of riddle. Luring his readers winter-ward, he also cautions them to be watchful; for as the many examples of lost and wandering figures in the *Winter* sequence suggest, becoming spellbound is dangerous—deadly. Indeed, winter is figured as a kind of trap, a benumbing place that disorients those who enter. The first poem of the collection both warns and invites the reader:

> Imagine a man
> walking endlessly and finding his tracks,
> knowing he has gone in a circle. Imagine
> his disappointment. See how he strikes out again
> in a new direction, hoping this way
> will lead him out. Imagine how much
> happier he will be this time with the wind
> all around him, the wind filling in his tracks. (1)

In part, the warning says that, in a region without signposts, instinct alone is not enough to ensure survival; one needs to come prepared. And, while the man in this poem is alone and therefore doomed, Lane's readers have the poet as a guide. The poem itself consequently serves as a directive, with its insistent invitation to "imagine." *See* the man, the poem urges, and imagine . . .

That Lane's readers *are* tempted to "imagine" is a function of the powerful magic of his poetic spell. Charmed, in part by the poem's insistence, and in part by the repetition of sounds, Lane's readers surely find themselves *s*eeing the *s*now *s*ifting in the holes where the man's feet were and thinking *h*ow much *h*appier *h*e would be. That is, Lane first draws his readers with the magic of charm, with its associations with "music, sound and rhythm" (Frye, 123), but then he calls upon them to witness the effects of the charm itself. The circling motion of the man lost in the snow enacts the movement of the spellbound mind.

Such a visual figuring of the winter charm, serves also to transform the nature of the charm itself. Indeed, the power of charm is precisely that its victims are unable to escape because they fail to recognize the need for escape. By contrast, as soon as the victims recognize the charm to be a kind of trap from which they must seek escape, they find themselves in the realm of *riddle* or *verbal trap*. "The riddle is essentially a charm in reverse," Northrop Frye argues. "It represents the revolt of the intelligence against the hypnotic power of commanding words" (137). Charm or riddle: it is a question of perspective.

■ ■ ■

In *Winter*, Lane incorporates his reader in this riddling sequence. But the reader's role shifts, for there are two levels of riddle operating in the text. Faced with the most obvious riddles of the collection—those which, as Susan Glickman notes, are both embedded within and signalled by the poems (120)—Lane's readers ponder the enigma together with the poet. When the poems themselves become riddles (or riddling poems), however, readers ask questions of the poems instead.

"Winter 8" engages the reader on both levels of riddle. Here, the poet is himself struggling to answer a riddle—the "second" one. Presumably, answering the first riddle was easy ("The answer to the first riddle was *snow*") but, as the first line of the poem announces, "The second riddle is more difficult." Consequently, in the poem's opening, the poet not only alerts his readers to the riddling nature of the poem, he engages their help in solving the "second" riddle. It is a formal "enigma": "*The absence of colour | is the colour of blue.*" Lane's readers (and perhaps my own as well) find themselves trying to solve the enigma. There are clues. The poet ponders a series of responses: he rejects "snow," "pondering the last couplet" (how is snow the colour of blue?); and then wonders about "love," "ice," "cold." As well, the *Winter* sequence provides other possible answers to the enigma: darkness, for instance, which turns the snow blue in "Winter 9."[1]

More troubling than the "second" riddle outlined in this poem, however, is the "first" one, precisely because it is not clear exactly what that first riddle is. Indeed, while the poet offers both the formal enigma and a series of possible answers *in* "Winter 8," he simultaneously distracts his readers from the enigmatic nature *of* "Winter 8." Ultimately, the riddle to which the reader must respond is that posed by the poem itself: what *is* the "first" riddle, and how does the poem function in relation to it?

One possible answer lies in the preceding poem, "Winter 7," which is not only a riddling poem, but is a riddle structurally. Here, the subject—an icicle—is never directly named, only described indirectly: as "the bare bone of winter," or "a small floating rib."

Alternatively, the "first" riddle might be the epigraph, taken from Phyllis Webb's poem "Sitting": "*sitting perfectly | still | and only | remotely human*" (102). The opening phrase of Webb's poem, "The degree of nothingness | is important," points to the poem's radical refusal of disclosure. Even the conventional disclosure of poetic riddle, in which the title supplies the referent missing from the poem itself,[2] is absent.

However, that the answer to Lane's "first" riddle is "snow"—as the musing poet reminds us in "Winter 8"—seems to rule out both these possibilities. Instead, then, I suspect that the "first" riddle is the title of the collection itself: "winter"; for, like the moving figures within the poems, the poems themselves circle, turn upon themselves. While "winter" connects these poems, "at once both symbol and metaphor, unique and ubiquitous," as Lane tells us in his Afterword, it is never fully defined. If the exact meaning of winter lies at the heart of these poems, that is, it is also concealed by them.

When the first of Lane's winter poems appeared in the April 1988 issue of *Border Crossings*, they were introduced by a four-line poem entitled, simply, "winter," which functioned as a kind of epigraph: "A beautiful space, / this place he has made out of nothing. / In a moment he will name it / the first of the many names for snow." Even here, of course, "he" (the unnamed namer) evades the final naming—and the absence of this epigraph in the final sequence puts off the "final naming" indefinitely. Nevertheless, the epigraph *does* provide a clue to the riddling nature of the collection: how can absence be defined or circumscribed?

Previously, Lane approached this conundrum by demanding that his readers participate in (indeed they are integral to) the act of fictional creation. In "There Is a Time," for instance, reader and poet "imagine" together, creating a world. The poet functions not as an artist or creator, but as a kind of director or guide. He makes suggestions: "Perhaps a child is ill . . .," "Perhaps it is winter . . ." In this poem, then, Lane's response to the question—how does one define a thing that is a no-thing?—is "imaginatively" (*OM*, 38-9).

In this *Winter* sequence, however, the reader moves behind the poet, following his imagining. Whereas the fictional woman in "There Is a Time" watches through the wood for her fictive man, the fictional man in "Winter 3" contemplates his own future imaginings: "It will be winter when they come. / He will sit with his back to the high window / and imagine their tracks in the snow, the circles / and arabesques, the sudden turns, the fallen angels. / He will follow them to the end of their tracks" (3). Here, the reader must follow the circles and arabesques of the winter creatures, and also the wanderings of the subject and the poet's mind. That is, the reader is distanced from the figures in this poem not only because they exist in the conditional tense (as fictional constructs), but also because they exist in the fictional future.

More often, readers of Lane's *Winter* have a curious sense of being belated witnesses. Indeed, in this shadow world, one can witness only fleeting traces of the wintry figures themselves: tracks left in snow before the wind fills them in (1); writing made illegible when a balloon deflates (22); ice soon melted by the chinook; moments of hesitation, transgression, transformation, available only through the mind—no, the eyes—of the poet-perceiver. Dermot McCarthy points to the movement in Lane's recent poetry from "vision to revision, a seeing again which is a seeing more completely." "Lane's poetry is now both a witness to the world of the object—the world of man and animal and nature beyond the self—and the world of the perceiving mind" (85). But the truly belated witness in *Winter* is not the poet so much as the reader. In "Winter 2," for example, Lane draws an implicit parallel between poet and photographer who, as if to emphasize the belatedness of his vision, is engaged in the act of remembering the moments captured in his thousand photographs of winter. "Each one is perfectly exposed, each one a pure / white with sometimes only the barest of shadows; / a fleeting, ephemeral grey that betrays / the image of who or what it was he took. / It pleases him to go through it slowly and remember" (2). As this passage also suggests, Lane primarily uses setting here as a way to articulate and explore absence.

What is the appropriate setting for an exploration of absence? Winter, the "pure white" of a snow-filled landscape, "with sometimes only the barest of shadows." Robert Frost's "Desert Places" and Wallace Stevens' "The Snow Man" are familiar examples of poets grappling with such issues within a spatial context. In both these poems, absence is described and experienced by the perceiving subject. "I am too absent-spirited to count," explains Frost's narrator. Here, the bleakest desert places are not part of the outside world (the blank "whiteness of benighted snow / With no expression, nothing to express," or the "empty spaces / Between stars—on stars where no human race is") but rather within the speaker himself. "I have it in me so much nearer home / To scare myself with my own desert places" (296). For Stevens's speaker, winter becomes a state of mind. "One must have a mind of winter . . . not to think / Of any misery in the sound of the wind." Stevens' speaker becomes one with the landscape. He "listens in the snow, / And, nothing himself, beholds / Nothing that is not there and the nothing that is" (54). For Frost and Stevens, then, the problematic leap between absence and presence is made by the perceiving subject who achieves a kind of emotional (in the case of Frost) or intellectual (in the case of Stevens) accommodation to external nothingness.[3] By contrast, in Lane's sequence, the tasks of seeing and thinking are usually divided between two different figures. It is in the comparison between these two modes of perception that the riddle— the liminal realm of comparison—lies.

I am not suggesting that Frost and Stevens do not engage their readers in a way that "activates the symbolic process," as Susan Edmunds would define the task of the riddler (43). Indeed, indicative of Stevens's interest in riddling throughout his *œuvre*, "The Snow Man" contains a formal conundrum or riddle based on "the punning use of words" (Bryant, 6). "Nothing himself," the perceiver, "beholds / Nothing that is not there and the nothing that is." However, Lane extends this "toying" with the rhetoric of negation. The very form of the riddle— where, as in traditional folk riddle the "referent of the elements is to be guessed" (Georges and Dundes, 116)—provides him with the fitting genre within which to enact absence.

Perhaps the most striking example of this enactment occurs in the last poem of the collection, "Winter 45," a riddle poem about one of the greatest Canadian historical enigmas: Albert Johnson. Here readers are invited not to answer the questions posed *within* the poem, but rather to ask questions *of* the poem. It is a poem of death. As in "Winter 1," a man is crossing the snow. This man, however, is not lost. He knows where he is going—to his "own quick death." Lane's readers, too, seem to have a clear sense of direction. They are pursuing this man, following his tracks through the poem, as his pursuers follow the "many trails he made, each one / a perfect map, a calligraphy / for those who pursued him" (45). Gone is the poet's invitation to "imagine," which was so insistent in the first poem of the collection. Instead, the verbs communicate action and direction. The man walks, climbs, makes trails, breathes hard, even as he moves towards his death. And his pursuers shout and follow. Lane's readers follow as well, relieved perhaps that this riddling poem appears to have an easy answer—at least for a Canadian audience.

After all, as Canadians, we know this particular story very well. Those of us who were not held captive to our radios in the winter of 1931-32 have nevertheless heard of the way the RCMP, aided by Wop May in his Bellanca aircraft, pursued Johnson for nearly two months through the harsh Canadian winter, losing three men before trapping and killing him on 17 February 1932. The RCMP victory was muted by the fact that they were never able to make a positive identification of the body. The man was wearing no identification at the time of his death; and the $2,410.00 found on the body, "ten times enough to pay for its funeral in that depression year" (Wiebe, "Death," 221), was never claimed. Johnson's capture, that is, did not provide the Canadian public with the name they sought.[4] Lane explains:

> He's so perfectly Canadian in who he is. He doesn't have a name. He's lived absolutely alone in an isolated world and he's essentially a pure survivor in the heart of the country. Americans would never invent a hero like that, but in our country these are our classic stories. (Wilson, B5)

The way in which Lane's poem emphasizes the enigma of Johnson also emphasizes the riddle form, for it points to the complex task of pursuit. Most obviously, the riddle structure of the poem is announced in the opening phrase— "The man without a name"—which draws attention to the absence at the poem's heart. Equally enigmatic are the clues to his identity—this man who "reversed his snowshoes / and walked forward" deliberately sets out to fool his pursuers, to throw them off the trail.

In terms of solving the poem's riddles, our identifying the man in this poem does not wholly constitute a successful search—for Johnson has become, through his various literary transformations, not just enigmatic but emblematic of the refusal to be named or defined. As Rudy Wiebe points out, "the man floating down the Peel River never called himself Johnson until a Loucheux Indian asked him 'Are you Albert Johnson,' and he said 'Yes'—though a day later it was obvious that he was not the Albert Johnson then being expected at Fort McPherson" ("Death," 244). Further, since the publication of Wiebe's article in 1978, Dick North has argued that the man was in fact Johnny Johnson, whose prison folder included, appropriately, the place of his birth as "Nowhere" (*Trackdown*, 172-3). Even more significant is the fact that North's pursuit of Johnson, decades after his death, is testimony to Johnson's transformation into the stuff of legend. And in legend, he is, ironically, nameless. "It was as if," North writes in his first book, "he had come from nowhere, and was a 'non-person'" (*Mad Trapper*, 47). As the structuring of Rudy Wiebe's short story, "The Naming of Albert Johnson," dramatizes, the moment of naming is also the moment at which the story ends.

A further transformation of Albert Johnson occurs in Robert Kroetsch's "Poem of Albert Johnson," where he becomes not only nameless outlaw turned symbol, but poet: Kroetsch turns his attention from the enigma of the man (and his actions) to the enigma of his message of survival.[5] Lane, too, seems to link Johnson with the figure of the poet, for the poet-guide of other poems in the *Winter* collection is notably absent in this last poem. Whereas earlier readers were asked to "imagine a man," in "Winter 45" a man appears without preface. "The man without a name," the poem begins. In this poem of hunt, in other words, we see only the hunters, and the man they hunt. Significantly, however, the activities of the man who heads into the "heart of winter" strikingly parallel those of the poet in this collection: "The many trails he made, each one / a perfect map, a calligraphy / for those who pursued him. / His turning upon himself, / an animal born into his own making, / crossing and recrossing his tracks." He defines himself clearly, providing "a perfect map," a "calligraphy." But what is the map of? the calligraphy for? The act of creation is transferred to the figure himself: "His turning upon himself, / an animal born into his own making." But what has emerged?

One answer has to do with a punning reference to Lane's earlier associations with the figure of the outlaw—the result of his powerful invective "To the Outlaw," as much as of his poetry itself. If readers are to associate the poet in this poem with the figure moving into the heart of winter, then, by analogy, their role comes dangerously close to that of the hunters. I say dangerously because, by such a pursuit, a tracking, they will inevitably bring the poet's movement to an end. But if they pursue the poet, as the hunters do the hunted, this poem concerns the poet's death as much as Albert Johnson's.

But I suggest that in "Winter 45," Lane is demanding that we "pursue" the activities of the poet in a different sense—not in order to track meaning, but rather to extend it. Here, those significant acts of imagining and witnessing are conferred directly on us, as readers. And we are being asked to strike out in a new direction. But what *is* that new direction? What is an appropriate metaphor for reading, a "Laneway"?

So far I have outlined the circling and turning tropes that are demanded by and figured in Lane's poems. But the movement in "Winter 45"—which does, literally, lead its readers out of the collection as a whole—seems more purposeful, directed. The man not only turns and returns, he reverses his footsteps. It is not, that is, a question of turning (a simple trope), but of *over*turning. Is "overturning" or "turning over" the figure of the movement of the mind as it follows, contemplates, and responds to a riddle? Certainly it is a helpful way of thinking about how we must answer a riddle: by going back to the same question from different angles, changing the direction of our thought process, overturning our established notions of logic. As well, it mirrors the challenge to meaning in the poetics of the line. In poetry, each line break allows the poet to turn meaning in upon itself. In "Winter 5," for example: "The sound of winter is made up of all," we read in the first line. And yes, we think, it is true: the wind, the snow, the sounds of silence. But Lane continues, "The sound of winter is made up of all / the things not there." And the meaning turns. So too, in Lane's poetry more generally, the meaning emerges from the turns. In the gaps and fissures of the line breaks, in the absences of the riddles, the enigmatic cracks—winter emerges.

Significantly, what slips through the cracks is neither an intellectual nor a conceptual notion of winter (such modes of perception must be overturned), but an emotional one. For all those creatures in this collection who are stilled by death, struck dumb by repetitive toil and extreme cold, whose tracks and traces are obliterated by wind and snow, we must surely feel a grief that this pictorial meditation does not permit. If, that is, as Bruce Whiteman suggests, the evidence of human endurance is largely erased by the snow (43), we find ourselves returning to this near-heroic endurance, celebrating it. We must overturn the poet's notion that the snow fills everything in, "leaving no room for despair." That may be the perspective of the man who is benumbed, snow-spellbound; but in the warmer world, we cannot help but feel for those who are trapped and lost, out in the cold.

■ ■ ■

It seems only appropriate that a sequence of poems about winter, written by a Canadian poet, should rephrase the question that still obsesses us: "Where is here?"[6] That the question is framed in metaphysical rather than in geographical or cultural terms, however, provides for a series of meditative lyrics. The answer, for Lane, is that "here" cannot be defined in terms of "geographical time and place," but rather of a "locus, a nexus that you can operate out of." Lane's setting for this collection, the prairies in winter (although this description seems almost too specific), seems to him a "forgotten place and a forgotten time. It doesn't exist in the larger political, economic, socio-cultural world, so consequently you can drop into this world and drop out of the other world" (Meyer and O'Riordan, 3). Strangely, then, by choosing to locate this riddling collection in a place that is out of place,[7] Lane poses the question "Where is here?" and leaves the reader to answer it.

The issues preoccupying Lane in this collection in particular, and in his recent poetry in general—the problematic relation between "word and world," absence and presence, even between such different modes of perception as the sensual, intellectual, philosophical, and emotional, for instance—cannot be easily resolved. Wrestling with "the endless tangle of objects, words, and ideas" (McCarthy, 85), the writer's role (as Lane sees it) is one of "constant witnessing" (Dale, 32), a process of continual transformation. The riddle, together with its tropes that turn and overturn meaning (paradox, metaphor, interrogation), provides Lane with an effective vehicle for the exploration—and enactment—of the mind's shifting relation to its world.

Winter not only collects riddling statements but also poses riddling questions that frame their own statements. As John Hollander observes in his exploration of the poetics of the question, the "very mode of interrogation is itself a trope" (13). In this belated literary age, he tells us, we have become sceptical of the authority of statement, so much so that the tentative exploration of the question carries an authority which makes us more comfortable.

> . . . in a late—which is to say, a literary—age, a questioning voice seems to hold more authority than a propounding one. It is in this condition of thoughtful read-ership—the one we think of as being modern in that, for example, doubt seems to be a necessary and authenticating way station on the road to faith—that the poetic question hits home. It is in this way that the poem, rather than the orator, can better persuade by interrogation. (18)

How does Hollander's discussion about the rhetoric of persuasion contribute to our understanding of Lane's riddling? One answer is that Lane's probing and complex questions persuade us that winter—the season of the land and the heart—cannot be easily defined: "The answer to the question: / *But what does it mean*? / The old Eskimo laughing at such a strange request" (20). As the "old Eskimo" knows, the best answer to Lane's riddling question is to overturn its logic; his ruling the question out of bounds removes him from the realm of its magic.

For Lane's readers, however, it is not so easy to overturn reading expectations, to *wean* themselves of their desire for meaning. Paradoxically, it is the very desire for meaning which brings Lane's readers back to his riddling text, if not to overturn the meaning, then at least to turn the pages over in an enactment of the process of continual transformation in which the riddlers—both poet and reader— are engaged.

Notes

---

[1] My thanks to Claire Rothman for this insight.

[2] John Hollander points to George Herbert's poem "Prayer" as an example of this. The poem is "all predicates, the copula verb being understood throughout, the subject being the word of the title, and the last and closing predicate, indeed, being grammatically self-descriptive for the whole poem: 'something understood'" (11).

[3] Similarly, James Thomson's "Winter" explicitly links speaker and environment: "Pleas'd, have I wander'd thro' your rough Domains; / Trod the pure, virgin, Snows, myself as pure" (ll.10-11).

[4] For a fascinating introduction to the story of Albert Johnson, as well as various accounts of it, see Rudy Wiebe's "The Death and Life of Albert Johnson."

[5]
                        the brave running
    by which he will become   poet of survival

    to our suburban pain   the silent man
    circling back   to watch them coming
    giving new tracks   to the blizzard-white trail (11-15)

the poet of our survival   his hands and feet
frozen   no name on his dead mouth
no words betraying   either love or hate (37-40)

⁶See Linda Hutcheon, *As Canadian as . . . possible*. The question is first articulated by Northrop Frye in "Conclusion to a *Literary History of Canada*" (220).

⁷A phrase used by Eli Mandel as the title of his collection of poetry, *Out of Place* (Erin, Ont.: Porcépic, 1977).

Works Cited

Bryant, Mark. *Dictionary of Riddles*. New York and London: Routledge, 1990.

Dale, Stephen. "Interview [with Patrick Lane]." *Books in Canada* 10.10 (December 1981): 31-3.

Edmunds, Susan. "The Riddle Ballad and the Riddle." *Lore and Language* 5.2 (1986): 35-46.

Frost, Robert. "Desert Places." *The Poetry of Robert Frost*. Edward Connery Lathem, ed. Barre, Mass.: Imprint Society, 1971: 296.

Frye, Northrop. "Charms and Riddles." *Spiritus Mundi*. Bloomington: Indiana Univ. Press, 1976: 123-47.

———. "Conclusion to a *Literary History of Canada*." *The Bush Garden*. Toronto: Anansi, 1971: 213-65.

Georges, Robert A. and Alan Dundes. "Toward a Structural Definition of the Riddle." *Journal of American Folklore* 76 (1963): 111-18.

Glickman, Susan. "Praising 'the form before form.'" *Event* 19.3 (1990): 119-21.

Hollander, John. "Poems that Talk to Themselves: Some Figurations of Modes of Discourse." *Shenandoah* 34.3 (1983): 3-92.

Hutcheon, Linda. *As Canadian as . . . possible . . . under the circumstances!* Toronto: ECW and York Univ., 1990.

Kroetsch, Robert. "Poem of Albert Johnson." *The Stone Hammer Poems: 1960-1975*. Lantzville, B.C.: Oolichan, 1975: 48-9.

Lane, Patrick. *Old Mother*. Toronto: Oxford, 1982.

———. *Winter*. Regina: Coteau, 1990.

McCarthy, Dermot. "The Poetry of Patrick Lane." *Essays on Canadian Writing* 39 (Fall 1989): 51-89.

Meyer, Bruce and Brian O'Riordan. "A Search through Time: An Interview with Patrick Lane." *Poetry Canada Review* 10.2 (Summer 1989): 1, 3, 29.

North, Dick. *The Mad Trapper of Rat River*. Toronto: Macmillan, 1972.

———. *Trackdown: The Search for the Mad Trapper*. Toronto: Macmillan, 1989.

Stevens, Wallace. "The Snow Man." *The Palm at the End of the Mind*. Holly Stevens, ed. New York: Vintage, 1967: 54.

Whiteman, Bruce. "White-out." *Books in Canada* 19.5 (June/July 1990): 42-3.

Wiebe, Rudy. "The Death and Life of Albert Johnson: Collected notes on a possible legend." *Figures in a Ground: Canadian Essays on Modern Literature Collected in Honour of Sheila Watson*. Diane Bessai and David Jackel, eds. Saskatoon: Western Producer Prairie Books, 1978: 219-46.

———. "The Naming of Albert Johnson." *Where Is the Voice Coming From?* Toronto: McClelland and Stewart, 1974: 145-55.

Webb, Phyllis. *Selected Poems 1954-1965*. Vancouver: Talonbooks, 1971.

Wilson, Peter. "Poet digs into psyche of winter." *Vancouver Sun* (6 March 1990): B5.

"Scanned and Scorned":
Freedom and Fame in Layton

Brian Trehearne

Irving Layton's "Whatever Else Poetry Is Freedom" has received minimal ex-
plication in the three-and-a-half decades since its first appearance in *The Canadian
Forum*, despite Layton's conviction that it "expresses better than any other poem
of [his], what [his] whole life has been about" (Thomas, 68). Such a signature
deserves thorough and various critical response, but the poem's riddling nature—
freedom from what?—and deliberate refusal of rationality and structural unity
have stymied Layton's readers, who offer only brief commentaries on the poem's
obvious dialectics of creativity and mortality. "Whatever Else Poetry Is Freedom"
begs extra-textual contexts in its deliberate echoes of other Layton masterpieces,
in its reliance on symbolism established in other poems to create present mean-
ings, in its cryptic allusions to Canute and Lear and *The Taming of the Shrew*,
and in its Heracliteanism. A perhaps less obvious context of the poem, however,
lies in its resonant relation to the history of Layton's fame. As an intuition
and projection of his imminent notoriety, "Whatever Else Poetry Is Freedom"
allowed Layton to articulate an ethics of creativity which denies the audience's
ability to fix and categorize the poet with its institutions of literary acceptance
and reward. The poem trumpets the poet's Canute-like independence from the
"twentieth century game of fame" (as Michael Ondaatje has it),[1] even as he
joins the game by assuming that his fame is not only imminent, but deserved.
Thus he avoids the sterile fixity of public "reputation" without wholly sacrificing
fame itself.

Layton's career and indeed the private life as we have it in Elspeth Cameron's
Irving Layton: A Portrait strongly suggest his urgent, perhaps unconscious, need
to adopt, critique, and then abandon fixed positions of all categories. In his
political thinking, for instance, there is a distinct pattern of fervent adherence
to doctrine followed by radical rejection of it, in his early Stalinism and later
rejection of Stalin, in his admiration and eventual denunciation of Mao Tse-
Tung, in his passionate support of Israel during the Arab-Israeli wars and his
present-day condemnation of its administration of the Palestinian West Bank.
His creative response to his Judaism is similarly rhythmic—it was not apparent
in his poetry in the first decade of his work, then gradually emerged, and was
suddenly celebrated during the 1960s and 1970s. The notoriety of his relation
to his earliest literary friend Louis Dudek depends in part on the earnestness
of its early years, the extreme bitterness of its breakdown during the 1950s,
and Layton's poetic invitations to mutual forgiveness that appeared during the
1980s. The history of his sexual and romantic life as he has himself candidly
described it—one does not need Cameron's biography in this regard—suggests
a restlessness of passion that clearly reflects these political, religious, and personal

affiliations. Layton has never been a poet to adhere to particular poetics in distinct creative periods, so such rhythms of acceptance and rejection are not remarkable in his developing style; although his very indifference to aesthetic "consistency" similarly suggests the sacred right to perpetual change that has been so central to his self-understandings.

Such a reading of Layton's progress from the Depression to the *fin-de-siècle* illuminates more in his poetry than its eclecticism of form. Seymour Mayne has argued a parallel cyclical progress in Layton's creative development, in which he regularly returned to the inspiration of earlier poems and "re-wrote" those visions into new poetic forms, in keeping with contemporary aesthetic experiment (Mayne, 3). Such a reading highlights the poet's conscious distance from an earlier self and desire to re-present himself in distinction—and so in implicit relation—to that younger artist. Emergent from Mayne's view is a dynamic poet keenly aware of the need to assert his own growth, to insist that his increasing age is well-balanced by increasing genius. Eli Mandel's treatment of Layton depends on a conviction that "the only unifying principle in Layton's work is his refusal to be categorized" (Mandel, 17), a view confirming the implications of Mayne's approach and of the above outline of Layton's intellectual history. Most rewardingly, Kurt Van Wilt has interpreted the Layton career in relation to "overcoming," a process of self-definition by dialectical growth that distinguishes the Nietzschean *übermensch*.[2]

Layton has himself encouraged such a transformative reading of his creative and personal development in a variety of self-representations, most striking among them "There Were No Signs," selected to introduce *The Collected Poems of Irving Layton* in 1971:

> By walking I found out
> Where I was going.
>
> By intensely hating, how to love.
> By loving, whom and what to love
>
>   . . .
>
> Almost now I know who I am.
> Almost I have the boldness to be that man.
>
> Another step
> And I shall be where I started from.

Despite the circularity and closure implied in its last line, the poem denies a *telos* for Layton's divagations. In the wished-for return to the point of origin he merely reaffirms the need for perpetual beginning. The poetic "self" is a continual becoming; it can never be fixed for interpretation so long as the poet retains his creative authenticity. The division of the poet's consciousness into "I" and "that [younger] man" reflects Mayne's view that Layton is always rewriting his past art and projecting it into his future. The poem suggests that authenticity is to be found in a "courageous" accommodation with one's past selves but does not admit closure once "be[ing] that man" is achieved. The past Laytons are indeed dead, though their vitality is retained.

The transformative model of selfhood is echoed in one of Layton's most striking formulations of his creative development, the "Foreword" to *A Red Carpet for the Sun*:

> The poems in this collection are all leaves from the same tree. A certain man living between 1942 and 1958 wrote them. That man is now dead, and even if he could be resurrected wouldn't be able to write them in the way they were written. Nor would he want to. They belong to a period of my life that is now behind me: a period of testing, confusion, ecstasy. Now there is only the ecstasy of an angry middle-aged man growing into courage and truth. (n.p.)

To this very dramatic statement Layton was forced to add a later ironic gloss, when his first volume of *Collected Poems* appeared in 1965:

> When I wrote my foreword for the poems in *A Red Carpet for the Sun*, some rash imp pushed me to state that "A certain man living between 1942 and 1958 wrote them. That man is now dead. . . ." I never once thought these words would be taken literally . . . the poet dies with every poem he writes, with every volume he publishes. That is, if he is *alive*, to put the matter paradoxically. (xix)

Both versions clearly reflect Layton's urge to identify, delimit, and set aside a past self which he no longer finds sufficient to his needs—the second passage geometrically affirming the pattern by implicitly correcting the first statement of the idea. He thereby implies that the present Layton is a newly invigorated and rejuvenated individual, more than equal to the day's new passions and to the denunciations he anticipates from his readership.

This strain in Layton's "self-fashioning" is essential to an understanding of his poetry's growth from the impersonal, rather cluttered Audenesque poetics of the 1940s ("Newsboy," for example) to the masterpieces of the 1950s that would earn him a Governor General's Award in 1959. One of those masterpieces, "The Cold Green Element" (1955), is remarkable for its achievement of a poetic structure that directly reflects Layton's philosophy of dynamic personal growth, the younger personae here rendered as the "murdered selves" of the poet-speaker. "The Cold Green Element" cannot be read linearly, logically, or rationally. The poem moves forward according to a transformative aesthetic parallel to the notion of selfhood the poem articulates. Each vivid or surreal image gives rise, dreamlike, to the next, which is in turn transformed into a subsequent image; between the first and the third there may be no more apparent connection than their mutual relation to the second. In effect, each image is "murdered," but incorporated at least subliminally into the next, the total effect baffling but intensely suggestive of creative vitality and liberty. This notion of poetic structure is perfectly in keeping with the self-transformations of the persona as he too proceeds through discrete stages of dismemberment, sympathy, ageing, fear of death, and an eventual rejuvenation when he is "misled by the cries of young boys." These youths might well be the "murdered selves" of the poet's past, their voices still resonating in his perpetual return to "breathless[ness]."

"The Cold Green Element" situates these aesthetic and personal transformations in two broader contexts. The first of these, the mortality symbolized by the "black-hatted undertaker," is easy enough to align with the transformative aesthetics above: the poet's consciousness of his own death makes him yearn here for a perpetual rejuvenation. The second context is evoked in a parable of bourgeois audience indifference to the corpse of a dead poet, blown by "a great squall" from the bottom of the Pacific to "hang from the city's gates." The resonance of these images with the poet's transformative selfhood is harder to perceive: it was already routine for Layton to decry the ignorance of his Canadian readership, but in what sense does that ignorance necessitate the poet's dynamic refusal of fixed and permanent self-definition?

"The Cold Green Element" does not elaborate as full a response as does "Whatever Else Poetry Is Freedom" two years later, but Layton's prose of the period once again illuminates this emerging triangulation of regenerative poet, bourgeois audience, and inevitable mortality. In the same decade that saw him develop the figure of the "murdered selves" as a response to his own earlier poetry, Layton began the assault on his Canadian readership that reverberates in his reputation to this day. One of the fascinations of the recently published correspondence with Robert Creeley is the visible emergence of the denunciatory Layton at war with his necessary audience:

> For this country the shits and pisses etc., the sex and scatology are a necessary antidote to the prevalent gentility and false idealism. Aside from the purely local and geographical I am convinced that the only protest, the only effective protest that a man can make today to the pressures seeking to annihilate him either physically or spiritually is the biological one . . . The teachings of a vaporous Christian idealism for almost two thousand years has [sic] falsified our position; to remind ourselves that men in addition to being God-seekers and truth-seekers are also farting and excreting animals is a piece of wisdom that might save us from the follies of pride and overweening ambition. (Layton to Creeley, 20/3/55; Faas, 221)

Layton contends that his radical sensuality is a self-differentiation necessary to épater le bourgeois Canadien, but one might accurately figure the process in reverse and remark that the poet's behaviour is *determined* by his audience's reaction: that he is trapped by his antinomianism in the sensualist displays that shock his readership.

Layton was aware that his extremist response to his audience made him as dependent on them for self-definition as were the more conventional artists who predicated their creativity on the audience's expectations. He began in a series of prose commentaries to conceive literary reputation—that is, wide audience approval—as a kind of death knell for true creativity, as in the "Foreword" to the *Collected Poems*: "Literature is the revenge society takes on the poet, its muted polite hosannah over the fact that it has blunted his shafts and rendered them harmless" (xx). In "Poets: the Conscience of Mankind" he suggests that totalitarian states suppress the poet's freedom because poetry's power is recognized and feared in those societies, whereas in the United States and Canada poetry is rewarded with public reputation because it is considered a harmless and irrelevant art form by which the mass sensibility cannot be stirred.[3] And in the "Preface" to *The Laughing Rooster* (1964) Layton recognizes that the poet's real enemies are those to whom he turns for encouragement:

> Yet I can't help feeling sometimes that the greater threat to the poet comes today not so much from his middle-class environment (by now this enemy has an easily recognizable face) as from those who wish to appear his friends and allies . . . They're the ones who wish to bracket the poet between Culture and Education . . . should this notion that the poet is the servant of Culture and Education gain adherents in and out of the universities you can kiss poetry a fond good-bye. The poet is doomed. (23)

The earliest formulations of this thinking emerge in the period of Layton's neglect by the literary establishment, so it is not surprising that he should find the means at such a time of devaluing fame; but the line of argument continues well after the consolidation of his fame and suggests that he was as disturbed by the implications of reputation as he was frustrated by its initial elusiveness.

In so figuring the burdens of fame, however, Layton enforces two consequent pressures on his creativity: first, he must maintain a negative view of his audience's value as readership and as culture (else their approval might indeed be requisite to his well-being), and second, he must perpetually renovate his ability to shock that audience and earn its disapproval by seeking more and more extremist matter for the poems he offers them. These pressures have forced Layton into some odd rhetorical swerves. In the "Foreword" to *Love Where the Nights Are Long* (1962), for example, he deploys a striking dual manoeuvre in defining and defying his Canadian audience:

> But Canada is not one of the great centres of civilization . . . we do not kill and mutilate and torture each other as is done in the more advanced countries of the world. The dehumanizing forces are not so irresistibly powerful here as they are in the United States or Soviet Russia or Great Britain—not yet. They will, of course, mature and ripen in time and will be as devastating to Canadians as they have been to the denizens of New York, Moscow, and London. (100)

The initial compliment to Canada is rather a slip, because in the model of fame he has initiated, any positive comment on his readership increases its right to define and entrap him with its approval of his artistry. Thus, the second corrective prophecy—that Canada will improve its powers of dehumanization—restores the negative audience relation, demands denunciatory verse, and guarantees, in effect, that his future "shafts" will not be "blunted" by its approval.

It is now possible to triangulate the imagery of "The Cold Green Element"— self-transformation, mortality, and audience-relation—in a manner that anticipates its full elaboration in "Whatever Else Poetry Is Freedom." The poet faces mortality as do we all, but to the death of his body's vitality is added the possible prior death of his creative vitality. This is especially at risk in his necessary attempt to find and relate to a readership, whether in the period of his obscurity, when the audience ignores him, or in the period of his reputation, when the audience's approval of his achievement leads to false definition, expectation, and fixity. As he is unwilling to retreat in a high modernist scorn of the marketplace, he must find the means of simultaneously winning and rejecting his audience: earning their temporary approval of short-term images of his self which he can then "murder" and transcend in new incarnations located beyond the boundary of the audience's brief applause. That new self will win its eventual praise and will then require abandonment in turn. This dialectic of mutual acceptance and rejection by poet and audience preserves the poet's radicalism without denying the crucial function of the audience relation in his self-creation.

In 1957, when Layton was working on "Whatever Else Poetry Is Freedom," this nexus of ideas was not entirely codified in his thinking, although he had articulated its various components in poetry and prose during the previous several years. The period of the poem's composition is significant in that Layton was on the edge of his public triumph with *A Red Carpet for the Sun*, then under contract with McClelland and Stewart. Of course he could not have anticipated the volume's unprecedented success, but he must certainly have felt the significance of a collection of two decades of creative industry under the imprint of Canada's most important publishing house. The years of publication at his own expense were to come to an end; a national and limited international readership was guaranteed. Moreover, he had won the approval of such major American poets as William Carlos Williams, Robert Creeley, and Charles Olson, especially for *In the Midst of My Fever*, published by Creeley's Divers Press in 1956. Such contacts left him less reliant on his Canadian literary friendships for encouragement and understanding, and perhaps gave him intimations of the striking success that awaited *A Red Carpet for the Sun*.

Elspeth Cameron relates the concerns of "Whatever Else Poetry Is Freedom" to the personal crisis of this same period that would end Layton's marriage to Betty Sutherland and eliminate his relatively stable family life (Cameron, 266). She suggests that the couple's pursuit of independent love affairs emerges in the poet's insistence on his right to perpetual freedom, and she remarks other poems of the period which, in her reading, reflect similar concerns. So little of the poem has to do with marital, sexual, or romantic relations, however, that Cameron's reading is regrettable. Its unidimensional biographical approach ignores the bulk of the poem's declarations and offers for its contextualization only a single facet of Layton's private life. A more compelling contextualization of the poem is offered by the complex of Layton's responses to the consequences of fame sketched above: an equally biographical approach, indeed, but one which will more fruitfully open up the multiple layers of imagery and meaning in the poem. Although Layton was not yet a "famous poet," he was already able to scent the first fumes of his imminent lionizing and translate them into the numerous repugnant olfactory images of the poem he sat down to write while waiting for *A Red Carpet for the Sun* to appear.

The first concern of "Whatever Else Poetry Is Freedom" is with "the rhetoric, the trick of lying / All poets pick up sooner or later" (2-3). The lines not only provide a first gloss on the poem's title (true poetry is free of rhetoric and lying) but also anticipate the theme of inevitability that concludes the first stanza: "Poplars and pines grow straight but oaks are gnarled; / Old codgers must speak of death, boys break windows, / Women lie honestly by their men at last" (5-7). If "all poets" pick up "rhetoric" and "lying" eventually, so must Layton; nothing and no one can avoid the organic processes of growth, completion, and decay. Intervening between these lines is the first image of "the mist," "Rising like the thin voice of grey castratos" (4) and thus enforcing the ambivalence that grounds the whole of the poem: rhetoric, lying, gnarled skin, and death are all, like castration, an elimination of potency, but they are as inevitable, indeed as random, as the breaking of windows by playing boys.

Rhetoric and lying in poetry are therefore like a castration of the male that "thins" the "voice"; this is the premise with which the poem opens, and it remains the implied context of all that follows. But why is such a faltering of poetic potency inevitable, and how may poetry itself offer freedom? The second stanza initiates an attempt to elaborate these paradoxes. In it, the poet, having "ma[d]e up an incredible musical scale" to the "vivid changing colours" of his wife's eye after he has struck her—a powerfully objectionable image to which I will return later—performs his music "on wooden stilts" that allow him to "sing to the loftiest casements" (9-12). Note that the image implies a surreptitious bedroom audience for the poet even as it elevates him artificially above a "lower" audience. When he cries at the end of the stanza, "Space for these stilts! More space or I fail!" (14), he implies a crowd of gawkers who are so impressed with his "dance" that they threaten its performance by their very eagerness to surround him. This invisible audience, unnamed and unportrayed, is the first indication that "Whatever Else Poetry Is Freedom" is an articulation of the disturbing relation between the falsely elevated poet and the uncomprehending crowd he addresses.

No reading of the poem has satisfactorily accounted for the presence of the Canute legend in the third stanza, but its pivotal role in the poem and its invocation for closure in the last line suggest that an interpretation of the story is crucial to a full treatment of the poem. The story is first evoked by the speaker's call for his own coronation, despite the "buffoon's head" (15) that has led him to his clownish stilt-performance in the previous lines. He then aligns himself with the Danish king of England by claiming that their folly—and implied wisdom—is equal. Canute was the "Lord of our tribe," the tribe of poets "who scanned and scorned" (17): a powerful figure that includes Canute's sweeping gaze over the sea and scorn for his courtiers as well as the poet's scansion of his rhythms and scorn for his audience. In this sense, Canute's "courtiers" are his readership. When they inflate his importance by treating him as a god, he renders himself a fool by placing his throne at the sea's edge and rebuking the approaching tide. When the "first white waves come nuzzling at his feet" (19) and so confirm his mortality, the audience's excessive adulation is punctured and Canute is restored to the free humanity that lies outside of their conception of him. Canute had been "half-deceived" (18) by the courtiers' apotheosis, as the poet may be by excessive fame; but both are restored when the misled self is murdered and the authentic poet faces the undeniable fact of his own mortality.

The mist has thus far been aligned with the false rhetoric that comes to "all poets" and with the inevitable processes of completion and decay that await all life's energy. In the fourth stanza the implications of the mist broaden as a result of the Canute legend. "It was the mist" (22) that led him to be "deceived" (18) by his courtiers, and it is now located "inside" the king and other poets, "rotting like a lung" (23), denying the inspiration and afflatus necessary to creativity. It is associated with "the scent of dead apples," the pollution of "black oily waters at evening," and "the fraternal graves of cemeteries" (26-8). But it is also "a crown" for the poet, who "wear[s] a wreath of mist" (25) even though he is "undone" and "a clown" (24). Clearly the mist is increasing in ambiguity. As a figure of death, it lies within us and leads us to be "deceived" into thinking ourselves immortal; but as a "crown," it is a symbol of circularity, completion, and royalty, indeed the basis of the poet's important identification with King Canute.

The mist takes on this dual meaning largely because of its misconception in the hands of the shadowy audiences that surround the scenes of the poem. When the courtiers of Canute, like the readers of the poet, proclaim his immortality, they render him a fixed fact and deny him further freedom to change. They also flout the patterns of mortal inevitability that underpin the poem's vision. But the poet-king cannot allow these misapprehensions of immortality to prevent him from seeking the more authentic immortality of his poet's "crown." He must continue, "half-deceived," to believe in his truer quest for a crown despite, and in the very teeth of, the false crowns held out to him by an ignorant audience. Acknowledging his own inevitable death, he will nevertheless struggle for a perpetual rejuvenation, casting aside the "murdered selves" that have won him mundane acclaim one after the other, and thus defying the audience's successive versions of his creativity. In doing so he lives his life in a way that will render his eventual death the "crowning" transformation of a dialectical process of fame and scorn that leaves his audiences powerless to contain him.

But this affirmative response to death in life does not alter the fact of our mortality, nor our fear of it, nor does it imply that the poet is ever finally free of his audiences. He must engage in a perpetual struggle with their expectations, briefly satisfying, abruptly alienating; to eschew their approval altogether is to lose the sense of false closure that fuels his desperate rejuvenation. So with death itself: living (like Canute after the legend) with the fact of death for a crown in no way reduces one's fear of the end; indeed, a loss of that fear would similarly eliminate the urgency of self-recreation that is crucial to the poet's energy. Thus, the images of the next two stanzas are bitter with mortality and recrimination; in them, death is restored to its "crazing" terror and the audience to its stifling power.

Although it has crowned him, the speaker knows that the mist of rhetoric and death will hound him to the end: "It shall drive me to beg my food and at last / Hurl me broken I know and prostrate on the road" (29-30). His continual escapes from his audience's pleasure will take away the means of his subsistence, and a more literal death will shatter him and leave him like refuse on the road side, ignored by the passing cars of his erstwhile readers, visualized in the subsequent stanza. As a major ironic undermining of his earlier crowning, he now identifies with a "huge toad" that he saw, "entire but dead, / That Time mordantly had blacked" (31-2). But the metaphoric transformation from king to toad still resonates with the earlier self-celebration; this toad, though "dead," is "entire" in death (31), only "Time" having killed it: it has presumably not been crushed under the wheels of the passing cars. And indeed, after the speaker asserts a future identity with the toad, he adopts for them both the language of another King of Britain, Lear: "for sick with mist / And crazed I smell the odour of mortality" (34-5). When, in Shakespeare, the blinded Gloucester seeks to kiss the hand of Lear and perpetuate his sovereign's lost royalty, Lear's "crazed" rejoinder is, "Let me wipe it first. It smells of mortality" (IV, vi, 128). So kingship is not lost in Layton's poem; rather it is reconciled with the poet's starvation and abandonment by the spurned audience.

The Heraclitean premises of the following lines ("And Time flames") are obviously appropriate to the poem's vision; they serve further to unfold the complex sixth stanza, which depends for some of its meaning on the reader's familiarity with other Layton poems. In this sense the stanza ironically projects Layton's reliance on his own fame. By no other means can we interpret the elaborate sun imagery than by referring it to the solar symbolism Layton had already developed in numerous poems from the 1950s. Here, the sun, Layton's favoured symbol of Dionysian exuberance, invited down to earth by those who "lift feet of fire from fire" and so "weave a red carpet" for its approach, is perverted by the uncomprehending masses into a false replica: "At certain middays I have watched the cars / Bring me from afar their windshield suns; / What lay to my hand were blue fenders, / The suns extinguished, the drivers wearing sunglasses. / And it made me think I had touched a hearse" (38-42). The cars that passed the toad "entire but dead" on the roadway are driven by those who hide from the sun behind sunglasses, afraid of intensity. With their false reflection they can "half-deceive" the poet into "believing" himself close to the true sunlight, but when he reaches for this false prize he touches the material world, and the sensation is of a contact with death. Once again, the misguiding audience offers its false coronations, and once again, the result for the poet is a brush with creative stifling.

In the first period of the poem's composition, this was as far as Layton could reach toward a fusion of the poem's ideas. He ironically asserted a quality of proof to its progress by offering the phrase "So whatever else poetry is freedom" as a seventh stanza, and it was this truncated version of the poem that appeared in *The Canadian Forum* in February 1958. According to Cameron "it took him six months to find a concluding stanza" (266), but he had done so in time for its inclusion, complete, in *A Red Carpet for the Sun* in the following year. This textual history obviously draws particular attention to the seventh stanza, which Layton had some trouble discovering and which, once written, presumably seemed to him an appropriate conclusion to an elaborate and difficult poem.

The opening "So" proclaims the poem's logicality, and although it is an ironic logic, the subsequent lines do indeed brilliantly gather up the threads of "Whatever Else Poetry Is Freedom." First the speaker calls for "the impatient cadences," "far off," to "reveal / A padding for [his] breathless stilts" (44-5). (The lines are resonant with other Layton phrasing: in "The Birth of Tragedy" "someone from afar off / blows birthday candles for the world," and in "The Cold Green Element" the poet's final transformation leaves him a "breathless swimmer.") Perhaps then his own poems, evoked intertextually here, are the "impatient cadences" that will pad his stilts and protect him from the excessive enthusiasm of his audiences, even as his reliance on our hearing these echoes suggests his confidence in our having read him well. The "cadences" may also be the rhythms of the tide that swamped Canute or the "thin voice of grey castratos" that rose with the mist from the river. In these readings, the casing for his stilts is a padding of mortality, true death protecting him from false, not unlike the "wreath of mist" that crowned him earlier. What follows is an imperative to himself and to Canute and, by extension, to all poets of "our tribe" who "scan and scorn": "Swivel, / O hero, in the fleshy groves, skin and glycerine, / And sing of lust, the sun's accompanying shadow / Like a vampire's wing, the stillness in dead feet— / Your stave brings resurrection, O aggrievèd king" (45-9). This peroration subsumes the poem's images and transliterates them into a suggestive program for the poet's ongoing self-salvation. "Swivel" suggests both the turn-and-turn-about of the poet struggling towards and away from his audience and his pivoting dance on the false elevation of "breathless stilts." The "fleshy groves" not only assert the poet's mortality but also gather up the "poplars," "pines," and "oaks" attaining their organic form. "Glycerine" echoes the artificiality of emotion "all poets pick up sooner or later," as in "glycerine tears." "The sun" here is now the true sun, not the spurious reflection from the vehicles of the readership; its "shadow"—and of course the sun can have no shadow—"accompanies" the poet even as its rise and fall sucks away his blood, "like a vampire's wing." These incorporations of the poem's imagery give the final stanza its summary and corrective impact: the poet will earn "resurrection" from creative death only by a passionate singing of his own mortality, his fleshiness, in the full light— and intense burning—of the sun. His song will not exclude but will resonate with "the stillness in dead feet," even if with that inclusion he risks occasional rhythmic flaccidity, the "dead feet" of a conventional metre.

The "stave" that "brings resurrection" has been variously glossed; its meanings include "sceptre," appropriate to the "aggrievèd king" who wields it; "stanza," the vehicle of the poet; and "phallus," the symbol of the male poet's urge both to entrap himself and to free himself from entrapment. In the latter sense the king's "resurrection" is his "res-erection," the pun suggestive of the powerful link now established between creative salvation and the poet's libido. This polysemous image thus continues, indeed triumphantly, the concluding stanza's successful concatenation of the poem's meanings. Only at this point can the audience be said to be eclipsed from the poem: the "aggrievèd king" stands alone at its conclusion, his rebirth guaranteed by his "stave" and his kingdom assured by his rejection of the false court. The "resurrection" asserted here is ambiguous: the burden of the poem emphatically insists that it is not a transfiguration of the poet in this life, wherein his fate is a perpetual dialectical struggle with his praisers and decriers. Perhaps instead, it is the "resurrection" of a truer immortality, the "loftiest" readership after his death, who will be forced to accommodate all of his "selves"—indeed his very principle of self-transformation—if they wish to read him at all. In this sense the final crowning, the "wreath of mist," is the only valued one; before death the poet is a stilt-lifted clown, "half-deceived" by his own inevitable "trick of lying."

So poetry is freedom from Poetry, from the "muted polite hosannah" of the satisfied audience. When Paul Verlaine wrote, "Et tout le reste est littérature," he was expressing a similar scorn for public institutional means of silencing the poet's radical vision. Layton was perhaps not aware of these implications of "Whatever Else Poetry Is Freedom"; his fame had not yet—not quite—been thrust upon him. But the poem powerfully prefigures the eventual dynamic relation to his audience that he would achieve and codify in the coming years, and exemplify for the balance of his career. If his poetry is now passing through a period of critical neglect, it is in part an affirmation of the vision of the poet, clown and king, worked out here; and it perhaps suggests, by inversion, the later crowning that he promised to Canute.

As a final and practical exemplification of the poem's insistence on its own freedom I wish to return briefly to what must surely be its most outrageous image: "And I who gave my Kate a blackened eye / Did to its vivid changing colours / Make up an incredible musical scale" (8-10). Layton cannot have known that he was placing in the poem an image that would become so objectionable to a later audience that the poem is now, for some, unreadable. After all he composed it in part for a popular culture that routinely minimized the presence, damage, and political nature of conjugal violence. A popular Hollywood musical of 1956, *Carousel*, would find its "happy" ending with a mother telling her daughter that a man's violence can sometimes feel to a woman like an act of love. But I suspect that, if challenged on the image, Layton would find in it the ideal exemplification of the poem's point about the nature of fame and poetic freedom. In 1992 "Whatever Else Poetry Is Freedom" aggressively asserts its own absolute liberty and defies the ethical and political codes that would question its content. As audience, we have of course the power of rejection, but we do not have the power to change the poem. We can take away the fame but not the freedom; and we will have to admit, as the poem takes for granted, that we are not the final arbiters of Layton's fame anyway.

Notes

¹The phrase summarizes the dialectic of creativity and audience expectation that energizes, paralyses, and finally destroys Buddy Bolden in Ondaatje's *Coming Through Slaughter*. Ondaatje's powerful figuration of those relations and their manifestation in Bolden's "extremist" art has necessarily inspired, without I hope distorting, my reading of Layton's relation to his own fame.

²Material that has been important to Van Wilt will also figure in my interpretation of Layton's development, and his useful Nietzschean reading of the poet's sense of selfhood stands squarely behind my inquiry into Layton's relation to his own fame. Van Wilt's interest, however, is more exactly in the self-overcoming of the Nietzschean artist. The model is effective, but it does leave out the crucial role played by Layton's audience—and by his doubled responses to it—in his self-representations.

³Pp. 46-7. Layton completes the article by a triumphant citation of "Whatever Else Poetry Is Freedom," thus supplying an explicitly political—if somewhat limiting—gloss on the poem's cryptic title.

Works Cited

Cameron, Elspeth. *Irving Layton: A Portrait*. Toronto: Stoddart, 1985.

Faas, Ekbert and Sabrina Reed, eds. *Irving Layton & Robert Creeley: The Complete Correspondence, 1953-1978*. Montreal and Kingston: McGill-Queen's Univ. Press, 1990.

Layton, Irving. *Collected Poems*. Toronto: McClelland and Stewart, 1965.

———. *The Collected Poems of Irving Layton*. Toronto: McClelland and Stewart, 1971.

———. *In the Midst of My Fever*. Mallorca: Divers Press, 1956.

———. *The Laughing Rooster*. Toronto: McClelland and Stewart, 1964.

———. "Poets: the Conscience of Mankind." *Globe Magazine*, 15 June 1963; rpt. in *Engagements: The Prose of Irving Layton*. Seymour Mayne, ed. Toronto: McClelland and Stewart, 1972: 46-50.

———. *A Red Carpet for the Sun*. Toronto: McClelland and Stewart, 1959.

———. "What Canadians Don't Know about Love." Foreword to *Love Where the Nights Are Long*. Toronto: McClelland and Stewart, 1962. Rpt. in *Engagements*, 98-103.

———. "Whatever Else Poetry Is Freedom." *The Canadian Forum* 37 (Feb. 1958): 252.

Mandel, Eli. *Irving Layton*. Toronto: Forum House, 1969.

Mayne, Seymour. "Introduction" to *Irving Layton: The Poet and His Critics*. Seymour Mayne, ed. Toronto: McGraw-Hill Ryerson, 1978: 1-22.

Ondaatje, Michael. *Coming Through Slaughter*. Toronto: Anansi, 1976.

Thomas, Clara. "A Conversation About Literature: An Interview with Margaret Laurence and Irving Layton." *Journal of Canadian Fiction* 1.1 (Winter 1972): 65-9.

Van Wilt, Kurt. "Layton, Nietzsche and Overcoming." *Essays on Canadian Writing* 10 (Spring 1978): 19-43.

Re-reading Livesay's "Call My People Home"

Dick Harrison

Dorothy Livesay has remained one of Canada's most celebrated poets over a period of sixty years primarily on the strength of her lyric verse. As Paul Denham says after his survey of critical response to her work, "the critical consensus has been that her long social poems are the most vulnerable to negative evaluation as historical curiosities rather than real poems; if defensible, they require defence" (73). Livesay, on the other hand, has attached a particular significance within her *œuvre* to the long poems, with the publication of *The Documentaries* in 1968 and in her essay "The Documentary Poem: A Canadian Genre." She argues that they are important not only to her own work but to the national literature and culture, as contributions to a distinctive Canadian form. "Call My People Home"—while critics have found it among the easiest of the long poems to dismiss—is one of two of her own poems that Livesay cites in her essay. It should therefore reward re-examination in relation to Livesay's theory and practice of the documentary genre. To re-read the poem now, however, is to engage the problems of reclaiming for the present a poem of the 1940s that is, by the author's own definition of its genre, both topical and didactic. These problems are particularly acute in a poem that crosses ethnic lines.

"Call My People Home" is arguably the most documentary in form of Livesay's long poems. It addresses a specific historical event: the expulsion of Japanese and Canadians of Japanese origin or descent from the Pacific coast after Pearl Harbor. It proceeds not by sustained narration but through the statements of witnesses, fictional participants who are allowed to speak for themselves with a minimum of interpretive commentary. The form accomplishes the presentation of evidence but also the creation of voice, especially in its intended medium of radio. The voice of the announcer/narrator which introduces the others is restrained, detached but sympathetic, doing little to textualize the testimony of the witnesses or bring under scrutiny their authenticity or their perspective on events. The effect is a polyphonic narrative in which a plurality of equally authentic voices are potentially in dialogue with each other, their narrator, and the audience or reader.

The two choruses that frame the narrative span the development of the poem's explicit theme with their contrasting definitions of the word "home." The Issei (Japanese-born) chorus initiates the problem of redefinition: "home," which once meant "where the heart is," be it the exquisite gardens of Japan or a shack on stilts over the Fraser River, now signifies "the uprooting" itself, the separation, fear, and despair, but also the self-sacrifice, resignation, and hope needed to combat them. For the older generation, "Home was in waiting: / For new roots holding / For young ones branching / For our yearning fading . . . ."[1] They introduce a progression of organic metaphors to be completed in the Nisei chorus. The resemblance of these framing voices to the chorus in Greek tragedy encourages an impression of fate compelling a people from a catastrophic disruption of their community to a condition of stability regained through tragic sacrifice.

Each of the seven intervening voices advances the historical narrative and elaborates the theme, with variations on the idea of home. A fisherman whose home is his boat narrates his personal experience of the impounding and confiscation of the Japanese-Canadian fishing fleet. For a young Nisei, home is defined by family, the security of being "*Locked in the harbour / Of father and mother.*" The child witnesses the violation of that home by the sudden incarceration of her family. Home is more ambiguous in the letter of a young woman confined to the "re-allocation centre" in Hastings Park, where women are segregated from their men and billeted in horse stalls. She is acutely sensitive to her mother's shock and humiliation, but the home she longs for is not so much the social nucleus of her past but the lost dream garden promised by her lover, Susumu, where her name "MARIKO, would be written in flowers." The next stage of the displacement, forced removal to the Interior, is narrated by a sympathetic white mayor, willing to brave the hostility of his community to integrate the displaced people: "By spring, I vowed, those people would be mine! / This village would be home." The next speaker, "The Wife," faces the dilemma of choosing either to stay in the mountain towns "with idle hands embroidering the past" or to begin again the task of building a home on the Prairies. Her choice reasserts the importance of generational differences in the voices. Because the parents regard Canada as "the children's country," and the children "chafed for independence / Scenting the air of freedom in far fields," the family is uprooted again. Their hardships, evoked in such images as "the sun's beak / Tore at our backs bending over the rows," are eventually overcome by a new feeling for the community of pioneering, specifically with a Ukrainian immigrant neighbour who shares his vision of the land as new, big, and clean. The land can be accepted as home because it is said to be good for growing—not only wheat, but children.

The last two individual voices form a separate commentary. "Nisei Voice" is paired with "The Student" to offer alternatives for the children whose country this is to be. The announcer points the contrast with his parallel introductions of "a renegade" who "wanted the world / In his two hands" and "a philosopher" who "wanted the world / For others." The renegade, Shig, refuses to be exiled from his "home town," sneaking back to Vancouver to end in a life of crime. He is condemned by both the announcer and the Nisei voice in which his is contained: "There were only a few of us such as he / But he blackened our name / Shut the gates to the sea." Clearly the Student has made the right choice: acceptance, stoicism, and "the habit of grace." He also identifies no material home other than the lost one of childhood, and the closing chorus of Nisei demonstrates that the concept of home has evolved through the narrative to something spiritual, transcending the need for any physical locus.

Despite its polyphony of voices set in a context of apparently dispassionate inquiry, "Call My People Home" is also documentary in the sense of documenting a case or adducing evidence for a particular argument. In this respect, it answers to Livesay's definition of the Canadian documentary poem:

> My premise is indeed that the Canadian longer poem is not truly a narrative at all—and certainly not a historical epic. It is, rather, a *documentary* poem, based on topical data but held together by descriptive, lyrical, and didactic elements. Our narratives, in other words, are not told for the tale's sake or for the myth's sake: the story is a frame on which to hang a theme. Furthermore, our narratives are told not from the point of view of one protagonist, but rather to illustrate the precept. ("Documentary," 269)

In the terms of this definition, finding the significance of Livesay's poem should require only uncovering the themes imbedded in the imagery of home and the precept demonstrated by the progression the voices describe from beginning to end. But the poem's documentary form, and particularly its dialogic structure, raise prior questions about how its themes can be interpreted. There is the general question of cultural appropriation of voice, but, more specifically, the declared primacy of theme over narrative raises the question of whether the voices speak for themselves or for the didactic purpose of the poem, whether Livesay liberates the voices of Japanese Canadians from the silencing they were under, only to recolonize them within an Anglo-Canadian narrative.

The demands of Livesay's theme of stoic acceptance and reconciliation with a wider community are most immediately apparent in the perspective the poem develops on the actions of the Canadian government. The voices are eloquent about their suffering and sorrow but remain virtually silent about the anger, the bitterness, and the sense of betrayal the Japanese Canadians must have felt at being robbed of their property, arrested, evacuated, and banished from their homes. There is no voice of protest or outrage comparable to the Aunt Emily figure in Joy Kogawa's *Obasan*. Hatred, mentioned rarely, is never manifest in the speakers' reflections, with one partial exception: the renegade, Shig, speaks rebelliously, but is the only principal character presented in the third person; his voice is stylized by the slang he uses and bounded by the "Nisei Voice" that narrates him and finally condemns him. Cumulatively, the tone of acceptance and the promise of reconciliation work to absolve government and society of their sins against the displaced people, and the context in which the voices are placed does little to counter that movement. The injustices done to the subject people are enumerated, but without the passion that characterizes Livesay's pre-War social poetry. The announcer rarely jeopardizes his detachment. When he once refers to "The window-breaking rabble and the politician's blackout," the line is tempered by an ambiguous parenthesis: "(Wartime panic fed / On peace-time provocations)," and his catalogue of curfews and confinements is followed immediately by the white mayor's testimony of compassion. Livesay did archival research in preparation for the poem, yet she refrains from introducing documents of the sort quoted by Kogawa, which speak bluntly of public moral culpability.

Criticism of the Canadian government and society remains oblique and muted, holding open the way to the reconciliation promised in the final chorus.

Publishing "a tribute to the endurance and tolerance of the Japanese-Canadians" (*Doc*, 32) in the 1940s was, it should be remembered, an act of moral courage in itself. The public temper was such that in 1948 (three years after the cessation of hostilities) the House of Commons could approve legislation barring Japanese Canadians from returning to the Coast for another year. It is tempting to speculate with Denham that Livesay's criticism was muted by the sensitivity of the issue at the time (85), and comparison of the various published and unpublished versions of the poem sheds a curious light on the matter. Small but significant changes from the 1949 text published in *Contemporary Verse* and *Call My People Home* to the 1968 *Documentaries* text are enough to tempt speculation. Two changes in particular suggest a modification of how the reader is to see the acceptance arrived at by the Nisei generation. The original version of the Student's last four lines reads: "So must I remember. It cannot be hid / Nor hurried from. As long as there abides / No bitterness; only the lesson learned / And the habit of grace chosen, accepted" (*CV*). In the 1968 text quoted earlier, the injunction is shifted from remembering the painful events to remembering the strategy for reconciliation, the "habit of grace." The later text also drops the reference to "the lesson learned," which recalls the announcer's reference to Pearl Harbor and carries the unpleasant suggestion that the Student must assume some moral responsibility for the actions of Japan, that his suffering has taught him something about the consequences of aggression. The *Documentaries* version, then, moves further from the possible suggestion that the mistreatment was somehow justifiable or salutary. In that edition, Livesay also changes the last two lines of the Nisei chorus from the original "A wider sea than we knew, a deeper earth, / A more enduring sun" (*CV*). Changing "wider sea" to "rougher ocean," "deeper" to "tougher" earth, and "enduring" to "magnetic" sun introduces an ambivalence to the final resolution, unsettling the impression of succeeding to an eternal and harmonious cosmos. Emphasis falls more on the hardships and less on the rewards of acceptance.

These changes, however, seem to be evidence of reflection upon the text in 1968, rather than constraints upon it in 1949. In surviving manuscripts in the University of Alberta Libraries, it is possible to trace the poem's evolution toward the first published text, beginning from earlier drafts that are, if anything, more insistent upon the virtues and rewards of accepting government mistreatment as though it were the course of fate. One hand-written draft of the ending promises "a wider sky," "a richer soil," and "a more embracing sun." It also concludes the opening "Chorus of Isseis" with four lines given the marginal notation "Envoie": "In peace of mind turning / From the family outward / From the [illegible] forward / From the dark, dayward." Here the chorus appears to counsel turning not only from bitterness but from a people's traditional reliance on family, as from a backward darkness. Overall, the manuscripts offer little encouragement to the idea of a poem compromised in publication to suit the temper of the times.

If changes to the ending in the *Documentaries* text in 1968 reflected any ambivalence or reluctance to resolve the human moral perspective into a transcendent vision of sea, earth, and sun, then it was short-lived. In *Collected Poems* (1972), Livesay returns to the first-published text—or appears to. In fact, she goes beyond it, removing at least two details from the original that draw attention to racial discrimination, government responsibility, and the bleakness of the Japanese Canadians' plight. The announcer's introduction to "The Fisherman" originally refers to white fishermen "Who hungered also, who had mouths to feed / Who pressed the government to give them licences / Before the yellow faces. So these cut his share" (*CV*). The *Collected Poems* text omits the line-and-a-half referring to the government and yellow faces. Similarly, the announcer's original introduction to "The Wife" is quite explicit about the grim choice offered to the people exiled to the interior: "What would they choose? The questioner / Paused with his pencil lifted; gave them a day / To talk together, choose. But choices loom / Two iron doors beyond which lie more doubt, more gloom" (*CV*). The *Collected Poems* text ends the passage at the word "choose," eliminating the image of iron doors and gloom and significantly softening the tone in which both the government's arbitrariness and the victims' dilemma are presented.

Among the manuscripts, one twenty-five-line typescript marked "unused section" helps to confirm Livesay's purpose in placing the emphasis where she does. It addresses the obvious and insistent questions about public responsibility and private guilt which are deferred in the published text. It questions the evil inherent in people, the culpability of the government official, the politician, the publisher: "Is he the Prince of darkness: or a tool / A massive one, men use, to let themselves be led?" The fragment ends with the lines "So do we separate the public man, his acts / From our own thinking—who should be / Our tool, our instrument, guided by sense / Stirred by the reasonableness of love?" The exclusion of this section from the final draft underlines Livesay's decision to turn from questions of the public morality of the events to concentrate entirely on the private suffering of the victims. The political implications of their suffering are not allowed to detract from the more intimate theme of acceptance and grace.

If certain areas of silence are conceded as thematic necessities, the remaining freedom of the voices depends on how Livesay develops her theme and on what underlying themes emerge. Not surprisingly, Livesay assimilates the expression of the witnesses to her own poetic idiom. The inner significance of their experience is developed around the dominating signifier "home," and its evolving denotations are directly analysed by the speakers. At the same time, its connotations depend on patterns of imagery familiar to readers of Livesay's poetry. Images of house and home have the same ambivalence in "Call My People Home" that Susan Zimmerman traces through Livesay's earlier and later work. On the one hand, and especially for the older generation, they imply security, identity, the sacred unity of family, and relation to place, as in the pastoral image, "Pastured within the Fraser's folds, the shack / Upbuilded to a cottage, now a house—." The physical home is felt as strongly by its absence, as in "Home was a blueprint only," and by mocking images of "government granted huts" or "a hen coop perched in a farmer's field." At the same time, and especially for the young, home can imply confinement. The opening lines of "A Young Nisei" bring out the ambivalence: "*We lived into ourselves | Thinking so to be free | Locked in the harbour | Of father and mother.*" The suspicion that security entails stifling limitation is heightened by the reappearance of two of these italicized lines as a refrain: "*We lived unto ourselves | Locked in the harbour.*" Similarly, Mariko associates her family home with her mother's "Embroidering blossoms on a silk kimono" and planning a traditional arranged marriage for her daughter. Mariko's letter also introduces the imagery of flight, which is consistently opposed to house and home in Livesay's poetry. The image of Mariko's lover, Susumu, flying east across the mountains is as ambivalent as the home images, signifying both freedom and loss.

Nostalgic and confining images of home are destined to be supplanted by the more expansive conception in the final chorus. They incorporate a related motif from among Livesay's staple imagery—the garden. The Japanese ancestral homes have their "copper-coloured gardens," the shacks their "small plot, raspberry laden" or "Our small plot grown to wider green | Pastured within the Fraser's folds," replete with cherry blossoms and strawberry fields. The most dream-like is the lover's promised garden where "MARIKO, would be written in flowers. . . ." This recurrent imagery, by evoking the archetypal garden, situates the narrative of the Japanese-Canadian eviction in Christian mythology, where Eden implies the Fall and expulsion. By so doing, it introduces a certain inevitability to the fate of these people, along with the Christian paradox of the fortunate fall as necessary to redemption. The presence of this mythic design as a substructure of the narrative is confirmed in "The Student" section, where the young philosopher who practises Christian virtues by wanting "the world | For others" relinquishes his Edenic home, "Under his fruit trees, canopied with apples," and is rewarded with "the habit of grace," the fulfillment of the Christian myth of redemption. At this mythic level of the poem, the public responsibility for injustices is emptied of its significance. The Canadian authorities, far from being morally culpable (except, perhaps, felix culpable), have simply acted as the hand of God. The myth serves its normal function, as described by Roland Barthes, of transforming history into nature (140). The "Chorus of Niseis" goes on more explicitly to ascribe the fate of the Japanese Canadians to nature, in a way not altogether consistent with Christian doctrine. Liberated from the "harbour" of innocence, they can rise beyond the cultural construction of family to a universal human fellowship where they labour, in the original and final versions, on a "wider sea" and a "deeper earth" beneath a "more enduring sun." "Home" remains the key signifier, but the transcendental signified is clearly "Nature," conceived as an eternal, inevitable, and beneficial order which reduces to relative insignificance the temporary injustices of humanity.

In slightly different terms, the resolution of "Call My People Home" can be said to reaffirm a pattern typical of both Livesay's poetic vision and the dominant Canadian culture. In the "Foreword" to *Collected Poems: The Two Seasons*, Livesay says of Canadians, "the unifying, regenerative principal [*sic*] is a passion with us. We make a synthesis of those two seasons, innocence and experience" (v). "Call My People Home" can certainly be seen as a reconciliation of those two states. As the term "synthesis" would imply, the structure of the narrative is not only dialogic but dialectic, as distinct from dramatic; that is, conflicts are resolved not through the triumph of one force over another but through a recognition that the contending opposites are mutually dependent, complementary parts of a larger whole. "Home," as an idyllic state of unity, is set in opposition to the alienation caused by the expulsion, and neither can be allowed to prevail. To reassert the initial, closed condition would be to "sit / With idle hands embroidering the past"; to embrace alienation is to become a Shig, a destructive outcast. Instead, the speakers achieve a synthesis in a conception of home in which both the desire for unity and the reality of alienation are subsumed in a multiracial community of labour within the transcendent order of nature.

Whether, as Livesay suggests, the Canadian passion for unity habitually expresses itself in similar patterns is a matter that has yet to be systematically explored, but Robin Mathews has argued persuasively in *Canadian Identity* for dialectic as the characteristic structure of Canadian culture, and suggestive evidence is not hard to find in the literature. A striking parallel to the pattern in Livesay's poem can be found, for example, in W.O. Mitchell's *Who Has Seen the Wind*, published about the same time. There, young Brian O'Connal also moves from a world of innocence to one of experience. His initial state of primitive unity is challenged, as he matures, by an awareness of alienation from what Mitchell calls "the living whole" ("Some Developers," 29). Once again, characters find their synthesis in community. As this comparison suggests, the terms of such dialectic oppositions in Canadian literature vary, depending on whether you are looking, for example, at the nature/culture tension in Alice Munro's stories, at Robertson Davies' Ramsay shaking hands with his devil, or at the doubleness of Sheila Watson's hooks. The common core, at least in pre-postmodern literature, lies in the fact that synthesis presupposes both a world of contradictions and the existence of a larger whole, however inscrutable, within which the opposites can find their relation. If Livesay is right, then, about the Canadian passion for synthesis, it could be argued that her Japanese-Canadian voices are further assimilated into a locally specific cultural pattern, a distinctive national variation on the symbolic system of the Western world, inscribed with Euro-Canadian values and beliefs.

"Call My People Home" is clearly open to a negative ideological critique. Livesay's imaginative identification with the Japanese Canadians could be construed as an appropriation of their voices to the articulation of myths of Western civilization and cultural codes of Anglo-Canada. It could be argued that the dialogue is overwritten with a monologue of Canadian establishment history, the voices of the witnesses liberated from their silence only insofar as they speak for the myths and cultural codes of the dominant ideology that silenced them in the first place. Such arguments advance two kinds of criticism. In part they serve the postmodernist project of exposing humanist "universals" as culturally determined and historically bounded. To that extent, they are charging "Call My People Home" with little more than being of its time. In the "Foreword" to *The Documentaries*, Livesay explains that she is leaving the poems untouched "as a record of the times," and she makes no apology for the fact that "the ideologies expressed were characteristics of that period in Canada" (v). Ideological criticism can serve to explain how the poem works in a sociopolitical context but not to discredit it as literature. Nor do we condemn Dickens' *Great Expectations* for serving the bourgeois revolution or Camus' *The Plague* for advancing existentialist philosophy, unless our agenda is political rather than literary.

The other charge laid by the previous arguments, cultural appropriation, is more difficult to deal with. It should be remembered that the issue was not publically sensitive in the 1940s. In its most general form, appropriation is also a literary judgment, driven by political concerns which would impose severe limits on the literary imagination. Unless we are willing to invite a kind of literary apartheid, we may have to accept that poems such as "Call My People Home" will connotatively signify more about the culture out of which the poet writes than about the other ethnic experience she presumes to address. They are recognizable as cross-cultural creations, like Shakespeare's Shylock. But the authority Livesay's poem claims through the choice of documentary and dialogic form justifies more specific questions about the legitimacy of cross-cultural characterizations. Ultimately, the answers must depend on how authentically Livesay's voices speak for the Japanese Canadians involved and whether her resolution to their dilemma, whatever the status of her "universals," has any validity in their culture. As far as I know, the judgment of that ethnic group has not been rendered, but comparison with Kogawa's *Obasan* suggests some tentative answers. The novel raises the same issues, along with many others, and it echoes the imagery of Livesay's poem in sometimes surprising detail, but it establishes a very different dialectic, between silence, with all its intercultural complexities, and speech, with all its moral and political implications. The voice of outrage and protest, so conspicuously silent in Livesay's poem, is clear, especially in the documentary and quasi-documentary evidence of public culpability introduced into the narrative. The narrator, Naomi, as representative of the Sansei (or third) generation, faces the necessity of achieving a synthesis between the Issei acceptance and the Nisei protest, and the terms of her resolution bear comparison with Livesay's. The larger whole in which all contradictions are to be resolved is elaborated with more philosophical complexity, but it is similarly dependent upon community, and grounded in a universalized nature. The "freeing word" which can reconcile Naomi to her fate is to be sought in primal depths suggestive of Jung's collective unconscious. It must emerge from the "amniotic deep" of a "sensate sea" that sleeps beneath consciousness (Epigraph). The imagery of Kogawa's closing scene accents the similarities. Naomi, a solitary figure seeking wholeness and community, stands in the midst of a prairie likened to the sea and reminiscent of Livesay's wider ocean, deeper earth, and more enduring sun.

Read in the 1990s, "Call My People Home" is in some ways historically curious, but hardly an "historical curiosity." While the most strictly "documentary" of

Livesay's narratives and the most prosaic, with the possible exception of "Roots," it is evidently an integral part of Livesay's poetic development and would reward closer linguistic and stylistic study than it has been given. The fact that Livesay's narrative strategies provoke questions which have acquired a new urgency in current critical debate can have the effect of reviving and expanding the poem for today's reader. Creating subjects of another ethnicity, of course, remains problematic. Their voices are constrained by Livesay's didactic purpose and by the thematic structures in which they find their meaning. Yet, in some respects, Livesay's imagined resolution to their problem in 1949 bears an uncanny resemblance to that of a Japanese-Canadian novelist some thirty-two years later. The truths on which Livesay constructs "Call My People Home" may not be universal or eternal, but they seem to have some historical validity within the culture that determined them, even for those not part of the Anglo-Canadian majority.

Notes

[1] Unless otherwise indicated, all quotations are from *The Documentaries* version of the poem.

Works Cited

Barthes, Roland. *Mythologies*. Annette Lavers, trans. London: Grafton, 1973.

Denham, Paul. "Dorothy Livesay and Her Works." *Canadian Writers and Their Works*. Poetry Series, Vol. 3. Robert Lecker, Jack David, and Ellen Quigley, eds. Toronto: ECW, 1987.

Kogawa, Joy. *Obasan*. 1981; rpt. Toronto: Penguin, 1983.

Livesay, Dorothy. "Call My People Home." *Contemporary Verse* 28 (1949): 3-19.

———. *Call My People Home*. Ryerson Poetry Chapbooks 143. Toronto: Ryerson, 1950.

———. *Collected Poems: The Two Seasons*. Toronto: McGraw-Hill Ryerson, 1972.

———. *The Documentaries*. Toronto: Ryerson, 1968.

———. "The Documentary Poem: A Canadian Genre." *Contexts of Canadian Criticism*. Eli Mandel, ed. Chicago: Chicago Univ. Press, 1971: 267-81.

———. Manuscripts of "Call My People Home." The Bruce Peel Special Collections Library, University of Alberta, Livesay Poetry Collection, Box 4.

Mathews, Robin. *Canadian Identity: Major Forces Shaping the Life of a People*. Ottawa: Steel Rail, 1988.

Mitchell, W.O. "Some of Today's Developers Have the Sensitivity of Fascist Book Burners." *Canadian Heritage* (Dec. 1980): 29. Account of an interview with Mitchell.

———. *Who Has Seen the Wind*. Toronto: Macmillan, 1947.

Zimmerman, Susan. "Livesay's Houses." *Canadian Literature* 61 (Summer 1974): 32-45.

Interim Conclusion: Reading Eli Mandel's "The Madwomen of the Plaza de Mayo"

W.H. New

"The Madwomen of the Plaza de Mayo" is the concluding poem of Eli Mandel's 1981 volume *Life Sentence*, but only an interim conclusion to the volume as a whole. The section devoted to poems constitutes the opening half of the book; the latter half records the author's journal entries, as he travelled between 1976 and 1980 to Victoria, Banff, Peru, India, Regina, and Spain. But the two halves are connected, both by their common subject—the imaginative relation between the author and his changing world—and by their common concern for what different processes of recording this relationship imply. In responding to "The Madwomen of the Plaza de Mayo," consequently, readers need to appreciate not only the poem's own internal resonances but also the significance of its placement, its "interim" position.

The poem (Mandel, 52) is set in Argentina. The Plaza de Mayo is in Buenos Aires, and the so-called "madwomen" are the mothers of the "*desaparecidos*"— people who "disappeared" after disagreeing with the political regime then current in the country. The bureaucrats and rulers tried to ignore these disappearances, and thereby maintain an illusion of an orderly society, but the mothers made their own objections clear every day, by walking silently in the public square with pictures of their children hanging round their necks. They asked inferentially for information, for a language that would declare or reclaim the presence of the absent children. Their simple persistence became politically dangerous, because their silent, daily protest constantly denied the accuracy of appearances in their society. "Madwomen" was therefore the epithet the politicians began to use to try to diminish the force of the mothers' collective protest. As history unfolded, it became clear that the language of politics and the language of silent action both had the power to effect social change. But, asks the poem, what is the effect of political context—on relationships, on the mind, on the power to conceptualize or create or imagine or act—in the interim?

Because of the poem's 1980 perspective, even the political scene in Argentina has to be seen as transitional, reinforcing the sense of flux that Mandel's book emphasizes and underlining the paradox inherent in his title: *Life* (growth, change) *Sentence* (complete thought, fixed doom). The military junta that ruled Argentina in 1980 had come to power in a coup against a civilian government in 1976. General Jorge Rafael Videla led the junta till 1981, being succeeded (when political unrest and economic uncertainty continued) by General Roberto Eduardo Viola and (later in 1981) by General Leopoldo Galtieri, who in 1982 initiated the ten-week Falkland Island (or *Islas Malvinas*) War against Britain; when the War failed (its political intent and function still in dispute), Galtieri was deposed and power transferred to retired General Reynaldo Bignone for the interim. In 1983 the civilian government of Raul Alfonsin was elected, bringing to a close this stage of military rule. Alfonsin initiated enquiries into the fate of more than 6,000 *desaparecidos*, and more than 1,000 bodies were subsequently located in unmarked graves near the capital city. The "madwomen" had their answer— or had *an* answer: one that they did not desire, but perhaps feared. Mandel's poem is poised over this uncertainty: the tension between desire and fear. It does not seek the security of historical consequences so much as it probes the way both knowledge and uncertainty prove debilitating. "Error #1," says "Hermes," an earlier poem in the book: "to think I don't mean / what I say // worse: to think I mean / what I say" (44). In choice there is danger; without choice, there is only death.

Structurally, "The Madwomen of the Plaza de Mayo" consists of seven irregular unrhymed stanzas. The first establishes a series of apparent facts, an observer's statements about reality; the second fragments reality, questioning "fact"; the third makes a simile out of the observation; the fourth extends the simile, in part through literary echoes; the fifth asks enigmatic questions; the sixth supplies a quotation as an apparent answer; the seventh generalizes (this pun hovers in- sistently behind Mandel's vocabulary here) into an ambivalent statement about recognition. Even this brief summary hints at the complexity of the relation between *form* (structure, word choice, organization) and *effect*. Throughout, the poem makes statements in order to question "statement," to call into question the efficacy of the act of stating, of constructing fixed realities in word and deed; by questioning language, however, the poem at the same time raises ques- tions about its own *métier*. The language of politics thus overlaps with the lan- guage of poetry, and the value of words, and of a life—a poet's life—lived in and through words ("sentenced" in and by them) comes under scrutiny. Buenos Aires is both physical setting and metaphor, the *site* of imaginative enquiry.

The poem opens with two complete sentences, end-stopped and apparently unexceptional: "They wear white scarves and shawls. / They carry pictures on strings about their necks." But with the next line, the speaker/persona shifts perspective, from the "they" observed to the "I" observing, and with this move, all fixity becomes illusion. The "I" begins to associate—to see "their faces else- where," in the awareness of death among the widows of Ereceira (a Portuguese fishing village) and the women of war-torn Northern Ireland. The "echoes" suggest at once the same and not the same truths about life and death—the reality of recognition confounding the apparent exactness of the specific empirical de- scriptions of the women in the Plaza de Mayo. The "guns and bombs" of disrupted lives also disrupt the language here, and neither of the next two stanzas can quite complete a sentence; the world—the world that the eye sees, that the mind constructs in words—is fragmented. Reality is reduced to isolated words, even words in other languages, and non-English constructions: "Identities / the *desaparecidos* / lost ones / the disappeared."

The speaker then tries to reclaim order by articulating a complete sentence *pattern* ("in the Plaza the Presidential Palace / reveals soldiers like fences with steel spikes"), but this statement neither opens nor closes with conventional punctuation, and along the way it steps from empirical description into revelatory simile. He tries again: "A soldier is a man who is not a man." But again his sentence stumbles away from convention: the statement is, on the surface at least, illogical, a non-statement. In both attempts, moreover, the speaker moves from statement to fragment, the resonance of the image in the fragment each time proving more apt at conveying the circumstances in which he finds himself than is the attempt at "neutral" empirical objectivity: "the rhythm of lost bodies / the rhythm of loss," "A fence, a spike / A nail in somebody's eye. / Lost man." From the women to the soldiers to himself: all have suffered loss, have lost themselves to the world around them, are lost. The poem has turned from describing the presences in the Plaza to voicing the absences, and then to locating the absences within. What then?

In the fourth stanza, as earlier in the poem, the vocabulary echoes lines by Margaret Atwood (deliberately, I think, given the poem's explicit interest in "echo"): "I am a word / in a foreign language" (Atwood, *Journals*, 11), "you fit into me / like a hook into an eye"—fish-hook and open eye (Atwood, *Power*, 1). The echoes suggest not a mere imitation but a deliberate evocation of the "power politics" (to use Atwood's title term) that tear the relations between men and women. "A soldier is a man who is not a man," says Mandel's speaker: "A fence, a spike." The *lost* hu*man*ity in this person is what makes him a *soldier*; having lost humanity, he has become mechanical, pure weapon, and this loss of manhood keeps him from connecting tenderly with others. In the juxtaposition between this stanza and the next, Mandel then extends the parameters of his working metaphor: one stanza ends "Lost man," the next begins "Why are the women weeping?" For these women, life is a question, or a series of questions, but juxtaposing them this way with the lost men establishes further that they live their lives beside but in conflict with the men, fenced apart from them, in tense opposition to them and their desire to *rule*. The politics of power separates them, whether it affects social organization, language, or (as is implied by the perceived "loss of manhood") the possibility of sexual union. They might live in a land of bossa nova rhythms—"under the orange moon / under the lemon moon of Buenos Aires"—but they "cry" here, they do not dance. Violence intervenes, robbing their world and their relationships of love; love itself becomes one of the *desaparecidos*, the victim of the military patriarchs who make up the junta and of the declarative authority they apparently prefer to embrace.

The penultimate stanza quotes the women's plea: "'If only for humanitarian reasons / tell the families of the living / where are they / tell the families of the dead / what they need / what they deserve to know.'" Even their imperative "tell" turns ("where are they") interrogative in form; and quoting—echoing— their words, the poem cannot articulate answers to their questions. Living in a world of "if only," the women seek communication: "tell . . . / tell . . . / need . . . / deserve to know"—but when the talking is all on one side, no effective communication occurs.

The last stanza, consequently, is resonant with denial: "No one speaks. / The junta says nothing. / The *desaparecidos* remain silent. / The moon has no language." But negation and refusal are merely interim answers. As the generals found in dealing with the "madwomen," apparently absolute statements sequentially prove ambivalent. If "*no one* speaks," and the junta goes on to "*say*," then in this context the junta appears to be "*no one*"—which either robs them of power and identity (paradoxically identifying the generals with their victims) or grants them more power through anonymity (the state to which they have attempted, for contrary reasons, to consign their victims). Further, even if the moon and the *desaparecidos* are without speech, it does not follow that their *silence* is not itself a language; the "madwomen," who have claimed through their silent vigil a power that the generals cannot quell through words, are testimony to this logical conundrum. Whatever has been suppressed, it seems, is waiting still to be recognized and reclaimed—a statement which comments on Argentinian politics and also bears on the several other motifs that figure in *Life Sentence*: male-female relations, selfhood, and poetic creativity.

But what has been suppressed? This is the question that is repeated throughout the book. Roughly speaking, the answer in the case of "The Madwomen of the Plaza de Mayo" is "love," but in other places the answer is jealousy, pain, suspicion, uncertainty, selfishness, violence, the urge to violence, the Holocaust, the monstrous, the punitive, the authoritarian, the "other" inside oneself that sometimes circles to destroy. One poem speaks of the allegory of guilt (26), another of the nature of betrayal (31). The capacity for betrayal (in "Fatehpur Sikri: Lost City"—reiterating the metaphor of loss) is juxtaposed with "Ventriloquists," about the loss of self that occurs in the adoption (out of love, out of fear) of another's voice. "Ventriloquists" in turn is followed by "Poem as Person as Place as Words," in which the questioning of domestic fidelity parallels the questioning of religious faith, neither resolvable in easily accessible language. Such motifs set up the tensions that "The Madwomen of the Plaza de Mayo" later reverses, but the point is that the capacity for all these competing emotions lies within the life of a single individual. Love competes with the fear of the loss of love and with the fear of the loss of the ability to love; the creative imagination competes with its own capacity to imagine the loss of creativity; the appreciation of freedom competes with the desire for control over circumstance—and all such tensions compete for precedence in the life of the individual and in the memory that helps shape that life's identity. "*Life Sentence*," says the book's careful preface. "A way of putting it. To be a writer. To serve the sentence. A life *of* words or a life *in* words. 'He's been given life,' the journalist exclaims . . . First, then, the statement of a problem in writing: how to say it? But it soon changed dimensions, became other things: something political, something resonating out of dreams—dreams of examinations, trials, streets too ominous to walk down." What the poet seeks to produce in this book is a "grammar of a life" (7), a record of the ways in which a highly personal set of experiences and observations turns into language, into the metaphors of recognition that delineate person as politics and politics as person, both in metaphors of place. All depends, consequently, on the honesty of the recognition.

Hence, when the poet speaks of the "false openings" into his own memories, which include "family history" (14), he is already aware of the ease with which attributes of self (particularly the least attractive ones) can be articulated in terms of others, and he refuses such projections. When subsequently, in the poem called "In My 57th Year," the speaker turns to reflect on his mother's stroke and his father's groin cancer—physical debilitations, and metaphors involving loss of language and "unmanning" (51)—he can no longer stand completely apart from them: "I no longer know time or age / thinking of parents, their time, their grave of names. / Telling the time fiction consumes me" (51). Consumed by the imaginative re-creation of others, he risks becoming a lost man himself, risks losing the power to evoke reality through language. Not to risk, however— to play safe instead, with emotions, experience, or words—would be to abandon in advance the life of the poet. To be a poet requires Mandel to face his own sentence; and not choosing the safe option leads him further into the thickets of self-appraisal.

In this context it is worth returning to the book's epigraph, a quotation from Clark Blaise: "When autobiography ceases to be, then I shall write from the point of view of a Brazilian General." For Blaise this remark is something of a joke, a statement that a writer can only write in an autobiographical mode, never being quite able to inhabit the mind of another. For Mandel, the statement can be read differently, as a challenge to see that the General is already within himself, waiting—whether waiting to seize control, or waiting to be recognized and so controlled, is left unsaid. Allusions to Latin America recur frequently in *Life Sentence*, the distinctions between Brazil, Argentina, Peru, and Central America being blurred in the larger metaphor of the politics of political violence. (Never far from this metaphor is yet another question for Mandel: how does a Canadian Jew—or any Jew—deal with the memory of the Holocaust? Directly, through political action, or indirectly, through the language of violence and victimization?) The murder of Salvador Allende (19), the rule of Generals Pinochet and Somoza and the secret police (23), the writings of Neruda and Vallejo and Borges (24), the temple practices of the Incas (29): these are historical realities. But what the poet calls "central-american games / about long afternoons of torture" ("The Spies," 25) are as much North American inventions as are the movie images of Herzog (22) and *Marathon Man* (27) that perpetuate stereotypes about monomaniacal madness, both artistic and fascist. Asking where such a fascination with power and violence comes from, and what it signifies, the poet goes on in "The New Man" to spell out his own connection with it, with "the killer person" who counters all the usual stereotypes: "He speaks to you softly about yourself: if you were expecting anyone, / would you expect a South American terrorist? And you say, no. It was / another. And he says, I am the other . . ." (46). Within *Life Sentence*, recognizing the "other" *in the "I"* is not merely a casual trope or a clever paradox; it is a way of locating the source of violence in the competing demands of desire. Love and authority: despite illusions to the contrary—and without implying easy harmony—they coexist, as in the Plaza de Mayo.

The process of *locating* violence is a reminder that, in this book, *place* and *poem* and *person* are equated. To find one is to glimpse the others; hence the task of naming places is part, here, of identifying the creative self. It is a task that the Journal section of *Life Sentence* will explore further. The exploration metaphor here is deliberate, for "discovery" is important to the poet, even if it leads him toward what seem to be undesired recognitions. To the degree that all experience serves the creation of the self, and therefore serves the power of creativity, all recognition has to have value. The difficulty of recognizing the violent or the monstrous or the authoritarian within oneself—of discovering that one *is* the "Brazilian" or Argentinian "General"—is that it seems to deny the values for which the poet-as-lover, or as would-be-lover, stands. Without excusing violence, the poet has to try to find a way to prevent the recognition of it from silencing him—which brings him to the positioning of "The Madwomen of the Plaza de Mayo" as his interim conclusion.

He will go on in the Journal section to record in diary format—the writer talking (silently?) to himself—his glimpses of what he has seen and why he finds that significant, and his statements about what he has done and whether he finds that of value. Returning to Regina in 1979 to write the book in which these notes and poems appear, he comes finally to accept his Jewish Saskatchewan origins. Once lost, elsewhere, he seeks to find, here; and one of the things he finds is that he empathizes with the Ukrainian Saskatchewan poet Andy Suknaski, who has also been writing of "Betrayal Beginning in Dreams." "We are writing each other's poems," Mandel notes laconically. "Dark Ukrainian boy, I know your home, your young years, lost. / We write ourselves into existence / on these plains. / Invisible. / Ukrainians. / Jews" (133). And so the book closes. Accepting "plain-ness" and invisibility, he no longer finds these attributes to be impediments to identity or existence, but rather the place and the *métier* in which existence comes to light.

At the end of "The Madwomen of the Plaza de Mayo," what had seemed to be fixed was the negation of speech, the absence of language. Because they implied an absence of person (therefore of place and poem), these negatives seemed to imply an absence of love and a fear of failure. If negation is all one can see, and silence all one can hear, runs the speaker's line of thinking at the time, then authority seems to be stronger than creativity. But as the "madwomen" themselves testify—their actions and their faithfulness belying the name that has been imposed upon them—the power of authority, despite the real violence that serves it, is another form of illusion. For the poet, then, the fear of the monstrous authoritarian "other" inside himself, the general who makes language and love disappear, can also prove temporary. He can find speech again when love is no longer suppressed. He may not find ease—honesty with oneself sometimes precludes it—but recognizing that this distinction need not be debilitating can lead him, he finds, away from what he has taken to be an "unmanning" sentence and back to creativity.

Works Cited

Atwood, Margaret. *The Journals of Susanna Moodie*. Toronto: Oxford, 1970.
———. *Power Politics*. Toronto: Anansi, 1971.
Mandel, Eli. *Life Sentence*. Toronto and Victoria: Press Porcépic, 1981.

'From Radical to Integral':
Daphne Marlatt's "Booking Passage"

Pauline Butling

I have always enjoyed Daphne Marlatt's writing for its multi-directional meanings, its participatory aesthetic, and its feminist politics. Her texts engage the ear, the eye, the mind, the body. Entering a Marlatt text is like entering a playground where many different activities take place at the same time: there are words at play; subjects in motion; images forming, dissolving, re-forming; frames shifting in kaleidoscopic motion. Sometimes, I must admit, I may feel lost or confused by the mêlée. But invariably a second or third reading brings participatory pleasures as well as a recognition of the political value of such a process. That is to say, a polyvalent, multi-directional text demands that the reader join in the process of making up meaning. This I like. As well, such texts loosen the boundaries of meaning and thus allow for interventions—by both the writer and the reader—in the symbolic order. Each of Marlatt's books, for instance, challenges the received definitions of female subjectivity and female experience. In so doing, she changes how we see and value women.

This is not the telephone-line model of communication, however, where the sender encodes a message and the receiver decodes the exact same message. Given a text that insists on multi-directional meaning, the communication model becomes one of intersecting or overlapping circles. In such a model, communication takes place by means of intersections, conjunctions, interactions—even disjunctions—as various trajectories intersect within a textual field. These trajectories are formed by such factors as gender, race, class, time, and place; by the relational networks within the discourse (whether I/you or we/they or you/me or he/she) as well as by "individual" life experiences. My discussion of Marlatt's poem "Booking Passage," the last section of her recent book *Salvage* (1991), will be based on this model of communication as intersections and interactions within a system of variables.

In the case of "Booking Passage," the title itself draws attention to the communication process. I begin reading this poem by thinking about the processes of reading and writing: of "booking passage"—*booking* as in buying a ticket to somewhere. Or, *booking* as the act of writing or reading a book; how to find the passageway into a book. How indeed. I do not just pick up my ticket at the nearest booking agent and get on board. I pick up words. I play with meanings, I construct scenes and stories. At the start of the poem, for instance, I construct a landscape:

> gazing at trees, rocks, boats, we feel the boats rock waves in our arms, these arms of land go out of focus up the pass, ça gaze? things go okay? like us, "like ones," who come and go in the watery sound a sailboat makes, no wind, engine drone, and the wake rolls to us, eyes closed to avoid our gazing (gauze of a certain hue—

nothing distinct beyond blue) we find how things are in each other's skin, undone
up close, we rock our ends in each other's surge, wake on wake of desire's passing,
shudders, shifts . . . (113)

The words bring to mind a West Coast scene of tree-lined shores with rocky
cliffs and outcroppings, a geography of trees, rocks, water. I also see the landscape
as a metaphor for the lover's body as the speaker connects the physical sensation
of being in a boat to the sensation of making love: the body rocking to the
inner surge of desire ("we rock our ends in each other's surge, wake on wake
of desire's passing, shudders, shifts . . . ").

At the same time, the rhythms, the tissue, texture, and movement of the words
foreground the physical presence of language and the erotic connections between
words. Words "call each other up," Marlatt writes in "musing with mothertongue,"
and in so doing generate "a form of thought that is not rational but erotic because
it works by attraction" (224). The sound sequence in "trees, rocks, boats" reverses
in "boats rock waves," producing a rocking motion of words, of a boat, of
two bodies making love. Some words and phrases seem detached, disconnected
from the rest. They interrupt the narrative line—"ça gaze? things go okay? like
us, 'like ones.'" Other phrases seem built more on rhyme than reason: "gauze
of a certain hue—nothing distinct beyond blue." Desire comes into language
here, as Kristeva argues, at the pre-symbolic level—in the tissue, texture, and
rhythms of language more than in the meanings—for that is where the libidinal
energy finds expression (79-83). Coming out of the closet means coming into
language. And "coming" in language is often Marlatt's way of coming out of
the closet[1]: "nothing in the book says where we might head. my tongue / in
you, your body cresting now around, around this tip's / lip-suck   surge
rush of your coming in other words" (116). Having recognized the lesbian erotic
in the poem, my reading becomes more purposeful. I look for the emergence
of the lesbian body in language. "To write in lesbian" (118), as the speaker
says further on, is one of the poem's directives. To write in a particular language
(the language of lesbian) and to write something into language (the lesbian ex-
perience). The poem enacts as well as thematizes the struggle to articulate lesbian
desire: "we haven't even begun to write . . . what keeps us going, / this rush
of wingspread, this under (nosing in), this wine- / dark blood flower. this rubbing
between the word and our / skin" (116).

IDENTITY POLITICS, FEMINIST POLITICS

But how do I, a heterosexual reader, read these poems? I am not the "i" of
these poems, yet I share the feeling of dislocation, as in "(Dis)spelling": "the
alphabet of fear, a current running just offshore, off / the edge of some clan
pier which wasn't mine, the sinking / feel of footings underwater, ankle-deep
on what remains, / afraid i'll drown, swept out (there was a broom) to sea"
(114). Not walking on water, but walking in water. Not an easy thing to do.
Walking against the resistance of the water. Will I drown, be swept out by the
tide—that pull of the symbolic order that takes you where you hadn't intended,
didn't want to go? No, the footings hold, feet on the ground. But the ground

keeps shifting. If I conflate lesbian desire with any female desire (and thereby identify with the "i" of the poem) do I then appropriate the lesbian experience? If I resist the identification, do I erase that experience? How can all women share in the process of empowerment without erasing differences?

These questions lead me to feminist theory, in particular to Nicole Brossard's essay "From Radical to Integral" where Brossard posits ways of creating the integral woman through radical action. While the forms of radical feminism may differ, Brossard suggests, depending on one's particular experience of marginalization, the process of creating a female culture has a common ground—that of re-defining woman as sign. Creating a female culture involves literally *making* sense (103)—that is to say, making up new meanings for the term "woman" within the semiotic system:

> For as soon as we speak of culture, we necessarily speak of codes, signs, exchanges, communication, and recognition. Likewise, we must speak of a system of values which, on the one hand, determines what makes sense or non-sense and which, on the other, normalizes sense so that eccentricity, marginality, and transgression can be readily identified as such, in order to control them if need be. (103)

The radical feminist literally *makes* sense out of the supposed "eccentricity, marginality, and transgression" attributed to women. That is to say, she invests the term "woman" with meanings other than the "patriarchal one-way sense" (109) by "unfurling of polyvalent and multi-directional words" (111). Such a process shatters the "one-way sense" of patriarchal meaning. It produces

> a void, a mental space which, little by little, will become invested with our subjectivities, thus constituting an imaginary territory, where our energies will begin to be able to take form. (111)

The closed circle of sense is disrupted by a spiral which loops out into the unspoken and incorporates women's subjectivities into an expanded circle of meaning—"we quit the circle in order to enter into the spiral" (111). The radical becomes integral when the "integral woman" enters the sentence:

> *When I saw you right in the middle of a sentence, it occurred to me I was naturally inclined toward you, as real as the idea I have of us, as real as the energy which speaks me emerging from our life stories.* (115)

Brossard's delight here in recognizing the emergent woman "right in the middle of a sentence" parallels my own experience of reading Marlatt's "Booking Passage." It is not a matter of identification but of recognition, even celebration, of new meanings of "woman." In such a context, the term "woman" "speaks me"—that is to say, gathers my own experience of female subjectivities into its circle of sense—and at the same time speaks a plurality of female subjectivities.

FROM RADICAL TO INTEGRAL

In Marlatt's poem, the movement from radical to integral involves, among other things, moving from a singular subject ("i") to a plural and communal subjectivity ("we"). The speaker discovers "the energy which speaks me emerging from our life stories" (Brossard, 115) through writing her particular lesbian experience into language. From there, she finds a ground for identification with, and recognition of, other lesbian writing. The expanded circle of sense extends back to Sappho and forward to the moment of writing this poem: *"She shouts aloud, Come! we know it; | thousand-eared night | repeats that cry | across the sea shining between us"* (117). Earlier in the sequence, however, in "(Dis)spelling" for instance, the speaker is singular and isolated, on the edge of the circle of sense, engaged in dispelling "the alphabet of fear, a current running just offshore" (114). The pronoun configuration here is the I/you structure of the traditional lyric, which separates "I" from "you" and demands negotiation of the distances between. In a (male) culture which valorizes individuality, such a structure works well. The form is ideally suited to the expression of male desire for the female object. It enacts the patriarchal structures of desire, what Brossard calls the "patriarchal one-way sense." "To write in lesbian," however, requires other relational networks. In "(Dis)spelling," the "i" explores her fear of erasure, of drowning, of being silenced. She returns to childhood to find footings, to "this once bombed island" (probably a reference to the island of Penang where Marlatt spent her childhood) and re-enters the "singular, body alive in the halflight morning." The speaker is a shadowy, isolated, half-formed figure—unable to speak to "you": "you call me and I am speechless. you call me and I am still" (114).

Increasingly, in the next (and final) poem of the sequence, the grammatical subject is "we," as the speaker dis-spells the language which oppresses and silences this lesbian woman, recognizes "the wall that isolates, that i so late to this," discovers connections to others, dis-covers hidden lesbian texts within the patriarchal structures of language and "his-toricity":

> one layer under the other, memory a ghost, a guide, his-
> tolytic where the pain is stored, murmur, *mer-mère*, his-
> toricity stored in the tissue, text . . . a small boat, fraught.
> trying to cross distance, trying to find that passage (se-
> cret). in libraries where whole texts, whole persons have
> been secreted away. (117)

This is not a search for female essence, as some have argued,[2] but a search for *presence*. To find a lesbian presence in language. To expand the circle of sense so that the "radical" woman (the eccentric, the transgressive) becomes integral. To find a shared subjectivity where "I" can speak "we":

> the dark swell of a sea that separates and beats against our
> joined feet, islands me in the night, fear and rage the iso-
> late talking in my head. to combat this slipping away, of
> me, of you, the steps . . . what was it we held in trust, tiny
> as a Venetian bead, fragile as words encrusted with pearl,
> *mathetriai*, not-mother, hidden mentor, lost link? (118)

MOVING "INTO AWAKE"

> this is not the distinction of looking (long and fixed the gaze) as in backward ("summer is
> over") or back at you ("i want to memorize your face forever . . .")—thoughts up the pass.
>
> it's us who move into awake, finding our calling. (113)

Moving "into awake," the closing metaphor of the first poem of the sequence, offers another way of moving from radical to integral, of "booking passage" for lesbian desire. The metaphor proposes a change in mental state (to wake up) and a change in physical position (to move into a/wake—the track left behind when a boat moves through water), and a change in the relational grid (not "my" or "mine," but "*our*" calling). Metaphorically, the "wake" is the space in language behind the patriarchal boat, a widened space where the movements can be circular or sideways or backwards (rather than the straight-ahead narrow track of patriarchy). These unconventional movements lead to "finding our calling" because they lead away from the "patriarchal one-way sense" into polyvalent meanings. Parentheses and dashes (as in the above excerpt), repetitions, incomplete or multi-directional syntactic structures—these are some of the ways that Marlatt creates lateral and circling movements in the poem.

Consider, for instance, the effect of the shifting syntax of "awake" and "calling" in the last line: "it's us who move into awake, finding our calling." How can one move into "awake"? "Awake" is an adverb, not a noun; a condition, not a place. Likewise, "calling" is an action, not an object to be found. But the syntax demands/creates nouns here. "Awake" becomes "a *wake*," which widens the circle of meaning to include the track behind the boat (an appropriate metaphor for lesbian writing) and a funeral ritual. The female awakening brings with it a "wake" for the death of the patriarchy. Likewise, "calling" becomes both noun and verb. As a noun, it signifies a "strong inner impulse toward a particular course of action" (*Webster's Collegiate*). In this context, it refers to discovering the "lesbian in us," to use Adrienne Rich's phrase. As a verb, it signifies the act of calling out—in this poem, of speaking lesbian desire. Reading further in the dictionary entry, I discover that calling also means "the characteristic cry of a female cat in heat." The multi-directional syntax creates a radiating network of meanings; it makes the reader stop, circle back, re-read. In following this growing circle of meanings, the reader joins the writer in producing the polyvalent context necessary for "finding our calling."

CHANGING THE SENTENCE / THE PROSE POEM

Marlatt resists and subverts the sentence—both the life sentence of patriarchy which defines female as secondary and the grammatical sentence which demands linearity, order, and closure. In Marlatt's writing, the period marks a break in the movement of thought, but not a "complete" thought. Look at the sentence units in the first seven stanza-graphs of the final poem in the sequence "this coming and going . . . our fear of this." The first "sentence" contains actions without agency (verbs but no subject). The second seems conventional at first, but the adverb phrase "under a cover of white" slides into a clause which turns the subject around (from "we" to "you"). The second stanza-graph begins with an infinitive phrase (again action without agency), followed by a sentence which starts out on the straight and narrow, but then veers off with a string of qualifiers which are connected paratactically rather than syntactically. The third and fourth stanza-graphs together form one "sentence" consisting of a series of phrases and clauses linked by commas and dashes. Again the structure is paratactic rather than syntactic, with words, phrases, or clauses placed one after the other without syntactic connectors.

The conventional sentence provides connection and integration. Marlatt's sentences refuse integration.[3] They de-contextualize and dis-integrate meanings; they are rhythmic units which bring words together in metonymic relationships, rather than syntactic structures which integrate all the parts. The effect is to expose the integrative processes, to expose the structures of meaning, and to redirect attention to the *thingness* of the word. Against the narrative line of discovery and exploration which propels the text toward closure, the dislocated syntax creates a counter condition, a condition that Gertrude Stein termed the "continuous present." Like the cubist painters (from whom Stein derived her concept) who refused the integrative structures of perspective and three-dimensionality and instead placed all the visual elements on the same plane, the writer resists the integrative networks of syntax and thus brings each word into focus, gives each word individual presence. Verbs, for instance, are often detached from subjects or objects, as in the above excerpt where there are actions without agency, or in the many "-ing" forms that appear throughout the sequence. Booking, gazing, looking, finding, calling, (Dis)spelling, sentencing, etc.—these words are neither verb nor noun ("verbals" or "gerunds," we call them). They refuse the linear progression from subject to verb to object. Syntactic connections are loosened and syntactic functions disrupted. Roland Barthes describes this specificity of the word as the hallmark of modern poetry: "The poetic word," he writes, is "an act without immediate past, without environment, and which holds forth only the dense shadow of reflexes from all sources which are associated with it" (47-8). And further that "Each poetic word is . . . a Pandora's box from which fly out all the potentialities of language" (48).

While the movement toward sentence and paragraph integration is constantly interrupted, suspended, or slowed, Marlatt does not, as Barthes suggests, reduce the word to a "zero degree" (48). As the *thingness* and *presence* of the word pushes against the narrative line, so also the narrative and metaphoric connections constantly pull the word into their integrative structures. This see-saw motion is the result, at least partially, of the prose-poem form, which combines narrative and poetic elements in a constructive tension. The horizontal movements of prose (enacted in sentence and paragraph) intersect the verticality of the poetic word, creating multi-directional vectors. As well, in Marlatt's texts, there is an integrative movement at the phonic, or rhythmic (emotional), level. Stanza-graphs flow out in varying lengths that enact sexual or body (breathing) rhythms. The pace quickens, climaxes, subsides. Marlatt describes the rhythms in physical terms, as "multiple orgasms" which produce rhythmic units (Interview).

To take an example: the final stanza-graph of the sequence does indeed have a story line which moves toward closure. The speaker's struggle "to write in lesbian" leads to the formation of a community of lesbian writers. As Sappho's words flow into the blood/language/desire of the present, the poem comes to a satisfying emotional conclusion. The stanza-graph also moves toward a rhythmic climax, at the word "rush," and then levels out with a closing cadence. The "incomplete" sentences, however, work against these integrative structures. Words such as "*this* page," "*this* mark," or the phrase "coming and going"—inserted between the subject and verb of the final statement "this . . . is"—interrupt, if not disrupt, the narrative and foreground the presence of the individual word:

> like her, precisely on this page, this mark: *a thin flame runs under | my skin.* twenty-five hundred years ago, this trembling then. actual as that which wets our skin her words come down to us, a rush, poured through the blood, this coming and going among islands is. (119)

Marlatt's writing continuously enacts "this coming and going" of words, sentences, lines, and stanza-graphs in vertical/horizontal tensions.

Notes

---

[1]My thanks to Susan Rudy Dorscht for suggesting this particular turn of phrase.
[2]See Frank Davey, "Words and Stones in *How Hug a Stone*" and Dennis Cooley, "Recursions Excursions and Incursions." See also Stan Dragland's response to Davey and Cooley in *The Bees of the Invisible*, p. 168.
[3]For further discussion of the function of sentences in the prose poem, see Ron Silliman, *The New Sentence*, and Lyn Hejinian, "Language and 'Paradise.'"

Works Cited

Barthes, Roland. *Writing Degree Zero*. Annette Lavers and Colin Smith, trans. New York: Hill and Wang, 1968.

Brossard, Nicole. "From Radical to Integral." *The Aerial Letter*. Marlene Wildeman, trans. Toronto: Women's Press, 1988: 103-19.

Cooley, Dennis. "Recursions Excursions and Incursions: Daphne Marlatt Wrestles with the Angel Language." *Line* 13 (Spring 1989): 66-79.

Davey, Frank. "Words and Stones in *How Hug a Stone*." *Line* 13 (Spring 1989): 40-6.

Dragland, Stan. " 'Creatures of Ecstasy': *Touch to my Tongue*." *The Bees of the Invisible: Essays in Contemporary English Canadian Writing*. Toronto: Coach House Press, 1991: 152-71.

Hejinian, Lyn. "Language and 'Paradise,'" *Line* 6 (Fall 1985): 83-99.

Kristeva, Julia. *Revolution in Poetic Language*. Margaret Waller, trans. Roudiez. New York: Columbia Univ. Press, 1984.

Marlatt, Daphne. Interview by Pauline Butling and Susan Rudy Dorscht. Calgary, November 1991. Unpublished.

———. "musing with mothertongue." *Touch to My Tongue*. Edmonton: Longspoon, 1984: 45-9; rpt. in *Gynocritics/La Gynocritiques*. Barbara Godard, ed. Toronto: ECW, 1987: 223-6.

———. *Salvage*. Red Deer: Red Deer College Press, 1991.

Silliman, Ron. *The New Sentence*. New York: Roof, 1987.

P.K. Page's "Portrait of Marina"

Geoffrey Durrant

Coleridge asserts that one of the signs of promise in a young poet is "the sense of musical delight." In the work of a mature poet this gift—rare among modern verse-writers—shows itself in the creating of intricate and aesthetically gratifying patterns of sound which serve as the web upon which the imagery and thought of the poem are embroidered. This grounding of imagery and thought in unifying verbal textures is beautifully achieved in P.K. Page's "Portrait of Marina," where the verse and the interplay of related sounds bind the separate parts of the poem in an aesthetic unity. At the same time, and with great subtlety of suggestion, the verbal harmonies are set off against the sharp particularity of the imagery and the verbal wit. These tend to disrupt the aesthetic unity of the poem, to join in a marriage of opposites, in which there is an ironic interplay between sound and vision, seafaring and beach-walking, adventure and suffering, fulfilment and abnegation, action and vision, so that the unifying force of verbal texture and the disruptive ironic particularities of the imagery are held in tension, in a delicate balance.

The opening lines invoke the dead sea-captain's nostalgia, expressed in the clumsy and frustrated artistry of an embroidery: "Far out the sea has never moved. It is / Prussian forever, rough as teazled wool, / some antique skipper worked into a frame / to bear his lost four-master." The pattern of thick fricatives emphasizes the rough texture of the "teazled wool" and—since it is after all a pattern—serves to hold together the complex and discordant ironies of the "rough" sea, fixed and diminished in the confining frame of a woollen embroidery. The motionlessness of sea and embroidered ship may be an ironic allusion to "The Ancient Mariner," with its far-ranging voyage that leads to spiritual thirst, and to his "painted ship / Upon a painted ocean"—a hint that what might look like insignificant domestic unhappiness is akin to the intolerable suffering of the Mariner. The Ulyssean search for the ultimate and absolute is pursued at the expense of the daughter, who has grown "transparent with migraines," without texture or colour.

Marina—a name evocative of *Pericles* and, as the last line of the poem suggests, of *The Tempest*—has been so called by a youthful father to fulfil his dream of her as embodying his own aspirations, to "make her a water woman, rich with bells." This romantic vision of a life transfigured by the magic of adventure is ironically commented upon by the placing of the embroidery in the domesticated interior of a "dimity" housewife whose bells are safe under clocks and who remembers the old man only in his decrepitude: "his fingers knotted with arthritis, his / old eyes grown agatey with cataracts." Even in his retirement, the old man's will deprives his daughter of her life: "Aunt Marina in grey worsted, warped / without a smack of salt, came to his call / the sole survivor of his last ship-wreck." The "salty man"'s daughter has a life of "grey worsted," not of brightly embroidered wool, an existence without savour. In these lines the alliterative pattern of initial consonants is so regular as to bring ironically to mind the formally alliterative verse of Old English heroic poetry, and in particular, in this context, *The Seafarer.*

The third section of the poem is a brilliant evocation of the broken and dazzling patterns of a migraine headache, with its attendant pain. The pin-pricking of alliterative plosives emphasizes the hypersensitivity to light and sound that a migraine brings with it; and the imagery that rides upon these sounds enacts the extreme exposure and fragility of the sufferer's nerves: "She walked forever antlered with migraines / her pain forever putting forth new shoots / until her strange unlovely head became / a kind of candelabra—delicate— / where all her tears were perilously hung." Here the legend of Diana and Actaeon is sexually inverted—to use modern jargon, "gender-inverted"—so that it is Marina who is metamorphosed into a deer and hunted by the hounds of her father's will. At the same time, the image of the antlers vividly reminds us of the deep-rooted branching pain of a violent headache. This is a wonderfully successful stroke of metaphysical poetic wit. The whole passage shows an assured command, a mature art speaking with freshness and audacity: "The needle shook / like ice between her fingers. / In her head / too many mirrors dizzied her and broke." This brilliance and intensity of light persists in the following passage, where the sea breaking on the shore—in contrast with the deep blue waters of the seafarer—signifies the life of perception in opposition to the life of "action." The act of pure vision in the vivifying glass of the wave is frightening to Marina, whose existence, caught in the doldrums between action and perception, partakes of neither: "But where the wave breaks, where it rises green / . . . / Marina never knew." The transparency of the wave, like the painter's art, reveals the evanescent details of shells and pebbles, heightens their brilliance, and transfixes the endless flux in a moment of permanence. The daring image of vision as "gelatin" with the power of revealing and preserving, making "an aspic" of experience, startles and convinces at once, like the audacities of the Metaphysical poets.

The final verse paragraph develops the dialectic of the shallows and the deeps, with a clear suggestion that the romantic love of "depth" may be misplaced, that surfaces may be more revealing and more valuable: "For her the sea was Father's Fearful Sea . . ." The deep sea of her father's enacted experience is for Marina full of terrors and temptations; she knows it only through the domineering sea-captain—a driven Ulysses, Ancient Mariner, and Captain Ahab—seeking always the ultimate. But the shallows are still more threatening, since it is on shallows and reefs that most ships are wrecked, not out at sea. The waves breaking on a familiar shore offer "a glass / simply for seeing stones through"—a transforming vision. But for Marina the shallows are a danger because, as Eliot puts it, "human kind / Cannot bear very much reality." The very vividness of a world imaginatively perceived is feared by a woman deprived of her vitality, since perception is more radically disturbing, and dangerous, than action in the world. Here there is a clear association of the shallows with vision, and of the "deep" with dreams and obsessions; so that we seem to hear an echo of T.E. Hulme's prediction of a poetry that avoids romantic "depth" and seeks instead a series of sharply focused images that do not easily blend into the poem in a harmony, but claim a separate attention as acts of mind. Yet the bright and brittle images, the lively wit, do not finally disrupt the unity of the work, which in spite of its metaphysical bravura remains a work of "musical delight," ending with the sea-music of *The Tempest* and the lyrical flight of Ariel's song.

Superficially this is a poem on the familiar theme of parental tyranny and patriarchy as, in a limited way, is *The Tempest* itself. It is tempting, pursuing the resonances of its symbols, to take the poem also as an act of resistance to the calls made on us, in the name of any Authority, to voyage in strange seas of thought, and in a world of settled purposes. These implications seem to me however to be less central than the idea of perception as the key to a lived experience. There is no rhetorical descent into the condescension of pity or the self-indulgence of bitterness, but a celebration of the vivid immediacy of the sharply imagined moment, so easily made inaccessible by commitment to a cause, an ultimate goal, a fixed human purpose of any kind. The most pervasive irony of the poem is its subversion of its own "message."

On Purdy's Galapagos

George Woodcock

Charles Darwin returned in the autumn of 1836 from the voyage of the *Beagle*, which earned him recognition as a leading British scientist even before he published his great work of evolutionary theory, *On the Origin of Species*. In a personal journal written later, he remarked that in July of 1837 he opened a notebook on "Transmutation of Species":

> Had been greatly struck from about month of previous March on character of S. American fossils—& species on Galapagos Archipelago. These facts origin (especially latter) of all my views.

Darwin was actually in the Galapagos Islands during September and October 1835 (and never returned) so that this note seems to establish, like his account in the *Journal of Researches . . . during the Voyage of the "Beagle,"* that the facts he observed in the Islands did not, as legend-making writers have often suggested, strike him with the force of immediate revelation. Darwin was in fact, as Charles Lamb once said of William Godwin, "a slow man but a sure": a man whose style of intelligence was oriented towards observation and intuition rather than ratiocination. It was only in the spring of 1836 ("about month of previous March"), on the long voyage back from the Pacific, that he began to perceive the implications of what he had observed in terms of the variation of birds and reptiles in the pre-mammalian ecology of these remote and isolated islands. The revelation, in fact, came after the perception, and was developed in the long years at Down, fiddling with earthworms, quizzing his farmer neighbours about techniques of animal breeding, and persistently picking the brain of his admiring botanist friend, Joseph Hooker.

God (rhetorically speaking) knows how long Darwin would have spent building up by ant-like accretion his vast manuscript on natural selection if he had not been prodded into action by the forces of synchronicity, having in 1858 received from the East Indies Alfred Russell Wallace's manuscript putting forward a theory of evolution by natural selection almost identical with his own. It was only then that he wrote, under great pressure, and with the help and support of Lyell and Hooker, that brilliant and concise work, *On the Origin of Species by Means of Natural Selection*, which not only changed the thinking of scientists worldwide and destroyed the authority of "Divine revelation" as an explanation of the development of the earth and its life forms, but was in itself a brilliant model of clear scientific prose.

Still, even if it was not the place of instant revelation so far as Darwin was concerned, and occupied only a relatively small space on the *Voyage of the "Beagle"* (as it quickly became known) when it was first published in 1839, the Galapagos Islands were the initial source of Darwin's intuitions regarding the causes of evolution. He had gone there primarily as a geologist, and we should not forget that geology was for long his professed science; during an unhappy period he was even Secretary of the Geological Society. At the beginning of his account in the *Voyage of the "Beagle"* it is the rocky formations of the Islands that impress him, a "strange Cyclopean scene," and it is only in a few lines at the end of his account of the first day that he mentions the even stranger inhabitants.

> As I was walking I met two large tortoises, each of which must have weighed at least two hundred pounds: one was eating a piece of cactus, and as I approached it, it stared at me and slowly stalked away; the other gave a deep hiss, and drew in its head. These huge reptiles, surrounded by the black lava, the leafless shrubs, and large cacti, seemed to my fancy like some antediluvian animals. The few dull-coloured birds cared no more for me than they did for the great tortoises.

The use of the word "antediluvian" here is significant; it suggests that Darwin has not yet shaken his mind completely free from the catastrophist school of geology which attributed changes of the earth's surface to a series of vast biblical floods. And later in the narrative, even as the extraordinary nature of the Islands' animal population becomes evident, he is still using what would soon be an outdated terminology, talking of them as aboriginal "creations," as if God had been dropping them off individually over a period of time. And even if he does not mention a Creator at this point, he seems sure that there is something special about what has happened in the Galapagos, and remarks, "we seem to be brought somewhat near to that great fact—that mystery of mysteries—the first appearance of new beings on this earth."

No more was said at the time, and thus it was in hindsight that the Galapagos opened their full meaning to Charles Darwin with such an intensity that he was forced to speak. We can trace with a degree of exactitude when that happened, for early in 1844, well over eight years after Darwin's visit to the Islands, he wrote to Hooker, in typical self-deprecation, that he was "engaged in a very presumptuous work, and I know no one individual who would not say a foolish one."

> I was so struck with the distribution of the Galapagos organisms, &c., &c., and with the character of the American fossil mammifers, &c., &c., that I determined to collect blindly every sort of fact, which could bear any way on what are species . . . At last gleams of light have come, and I am almost convinced (quite contrary to the opinion I started with) that species are not, it is like confessing a murder, immutable.

He goes on to deny any agreement with Lamarck's notions about the process of evolution, yet proceeds to admit: "But the conclusions I am led to see are not widely different from his; though the means of change are wholly so. I think I have found out (here's presumption) the simple way by which species become exquisitely adapted to various ends . . ." It was already the best part of a decade since he had first sighted the worn-down volcanic peaks of the Galapagos surging out of their ocean depth, and it would be well over another decade of painful gathering of minutiae and meticulous fitting together of facts before he would offer his conclusions to the world, so that though the slow-fused original revelation may have come from matters observed in the Galapagos, the charge that exploded the great Darwinian controversy was unwittingly prepared by Wallace when he wrote from Ternate in the Moluccas, an almost equally remote location, in the summer of 1858. Yet there are no pilgrimages to Ternate where Wallace gathered so much to support his own version of natural selection, while a hindsight even more monumental than that of Darwin reigns in the Galapagos.

The archipelago has become a well-deserved refuge for its extraordinary wild life, but also a symbolic destination where people of the late twentieth century can imagine themselves both close to the sources of the great Victorian revolutions in thought and in some way in touch with the last vestiges of an innocent earth before the mammals and human beings arrived—a kind of vestigial Eden, with Adam and Eve encased in horny armour and still innocent, if imperiled. Sophisticated quasi-scientific tours are organized and patronized partly by the intelligentsia, and it is not surprising that a number of writers have recently made their way to the Islands, including—among Canadians—Margaret Atwood and Al Purdy.

Al Purdy went in 1980 and wrote, in all, seven poems about his experience there. Four of them—"Birdwatching at the Equator," "Moses at Darwin Station," "Moonspell," and the brief "Darwin's Theology?"—appeared in 1981 in *The Stone Bird*. Three others—"Seal People," "Iguana," and "Adam and No Eve"— form part of his next collection, *Piling Blood*, published in 1984. No reason is given for the delay in publishing the last three, and one can only assume that Purdy held them back for further working. All appear reasonably close together in *The Collected Poems*, so that comparison is easy within the context of Purdy's own evolution as a poet.

Two of the seven, "Birdwatching at the Equator" and "Seal People," are not heavily stamped with the mark of the Galapagos; they could easily have emerged from other Purdy travels, for the aura of antique inexplicability does not hang over them as it does over the other five poems, which I propose to consider as a group.

Seen in this way, these five poems—two about giant tortoises, two about iguanas, and one about God's so palpable absence—seem to reflect that peculiar combination of poet, space, and time which we have come to associate with Purdy's more recent and more ambitious work. The poet is inclined to be knowingly foolish and yet cunningly Protean, taking disguises to fit the shifting theme that, as always in Purdy, is emphatically present. The scene tends to be particular, tied in by that sharpness of physical observation Purdy actually shares with Darwin himself. How else does the modern poet agree with the scientific prose writer who published the journal of his observations a full 150 years ago? In two important qualities, I suggest: a sense of wonder and sad ineptitude faced by the insoluble problems of origin and of the vast slownesses of time by which people developed from the *protozoa*; and—this is a literary link—by a plain man's clarity of speech in discussing matters heavy with philosophic content.

Purdy does not profess to be the scientific expert, yet through his vast polymathic reading he has acquired a good deal of specific knowledge and a power to create poetic generalizations about scientific matters that most of his fellow writers lack. After all, how many poets in all history have effectively projected the wonder of scientific thought and enquiry? Xenophanes in the pre-Socratic dawn, drawing from the fossils of the quarries of Syracuse verses that prefigured the theories of evolution; the Epicurean Lucretius among the Romans developing in his *De Rerum Natura* an early atomic theory; a few passages in Pope and Marvell reflecting the doings of the early Royal Society and of Prince Rupert in his laboratory; *The Botanic Garden* and *Zoonomia* of Erasmus Darwin, Charles' grandfather; some isolated modern poems philosophizing upon human fate seen through the scientific lens, like Kenneth Rexroth's splendid "Towards an Organic Philosophy" and "Lyell's Hypothesis Again," and in Canada, of course, the physicist conceits and precise observations of Christopher Dewdney.

More than anything else, what strikes one about Purdy's Galapagos poems is, apart from their rendering of personal fantasy and particular observation, a preoccupation with the implications of one sub-science, palaeontology, the study of the fossil record. This was a particular concern of his in the late 1970s and early 1980s, appearing in poem after poem in *The Stone Bird* and *Piling Blood*. "Lost in the Badlands" described comic adventures in search of dinosaur bones, "In the Early Cretaceous" dipped back to an important moment in far pre-antiquity, the blooming of the first flower, and a poem noncommittally entitled "Near Tofino, Vancouver Island" contains this verse which relates closely to the central preoccupation of the Galapagos poems:

> My poor blood relatives
> whose fossil bones are found
> in limestone strata lying prone
> or upright in earth catafalques
> as if beseeching time more time
> for reaching mammal status
> or else descending back to slime
> and praying to a lizard god.

Who were they? extends into the question *Who are we?*

Reading poems of this kind, I am reminded of the extraordinary revelation that burst upon me belatedly in the 1920s when, having been brought up on strict fundamentalist lines, I came in late adolescence on the writings of Darwin and Huxley and of the proponents of even more corrosive variants of evolutionary doctrine like Ernst Haeckel, with his *Riddle of the Universe*. My mind seemed to be pried open by rays of ferocious light, as minds must have been pried open in less rustic backgrounds sixty years before. It was to such a time of bewildered liberation that Purdy seemed to be leaping back, and using it as a springboard into his further meditations (if one can apply so restful a term to such a restless process) on what Darwin himself would call, with superb ambiguity, "The Descent of Man."

All the ambiguity is there in Purdy's Galapagos poems, and also the bewildered liberation and a great deal of the ferocious light, all expressed in the kind of straightforward English that Darwin would have appreciated. When Darwin wrote, as one of his recent biographers (Peter Brant in *Charles Darwin: A Man of Enlarged Curiosity*) remarked with seeming disapproval: "His words were the general ones of everyday use, blurring at times what should have been edged factuality." Darwin himself, advising the botanist John Scott on the eve of his departure to become Curator of the Botanical Gardens in Calcutta, said: "I never study style; all that I do is to try and get the subject clear as I can in my own head, & express it in the *commonest* language that occurs to me."

And, *pace* Brent, Darwin was right; the best way to develop a good and vital style is not to study it, but to strive to write intelligibly, and in doing precisely this Darwin and a group of scientific travellers in South America who were his contemporaries—Bates of the Amazon, Waterton of the Orinoco, Belt of Nicaragua—created a serviceable and vividly descriptive narrative and expository way of writing that professionals long admired and used as a model.

The Anglo-Spanish writers connected with Argentina—like Cunninghame-Graham and W.H. Hudson on the English side and Jorge Luis Borges on the Spanish side—were heavily influenced by the travelling naturalists, and so were a number of English writers in the early part of this century. The South American section of Herbert Read's novel, *The Green Child*, is written in early Darwinian prose, and George Orwell once remarked in a letter to me that "all nineteenth century books about S. America have a wonderful Arcadian atmosphere."

So we come to the double points where Darwin and Purdy meet. Both of them—in their own way echoing Wordsworth who had friends in the Darwin-Wedgwood clan—have striven to write the "commonest" language, for Purdy's great triumph has been the serious use of the colloquial in poetry. And both are inspired by troubling thoughts about the placing of human beings in the dwarfing context of universal process.

We can see the problem stated in "Darwin's Theology?" It is a poem that asks and even begs questions, as its querying title suggests. Did Darwin *have* a theology? My impression from reading his own writings and biographies of him is that the theological implications of his teachings were those he left for others to argue. Certainly it is extremely doubtful whether he was talking about the absence of a God during the voyage of the *Beagle*. At that time, he was still thinking of the possibility of settling down into a country parsonage, and he was also in the intimidating company of the extreme fundamentalist Captain Robert Fitzroy, who later would bitterly and in public denounce *The Origin of Species*. And we have the evidence of Edward Aveling, Marx's militantly atheist son-in-law, whom Darwin told in 1881, the year before his death, that he had abandoned Christianity when he was forty, which would mean in 1849, fourteen years after his visit to the Galapagos.

Looking more closely at the poem, we perceive its formal tentativeness. With its uncapitalized opening, preceded by a dash, its lack of punctuation, it looks like one of those surviving papyrus fragments that represent so many poets of antiquity. But it is not only a fragment, but also a palimpsest, for Purdy superimposes his thoughts on Darwin's, the over-writing being emphasized by the false echo created by the succession *absence-presence-presence* which leaves us paradoxically with an absence—the *non-existent monster*—that is more than a presence. God may be dead, but matters of cause and creation occupy our minds in this special place, the Galapagos, circumscribed, as the description of the sky as both *round* and *circling* suggests, and thus a true *omphalos* concentrating not only all our doubt but also our sense of a world that refuses to answer our questions—something near to the "benign indifference of the universe" of which Albert Camus used to write.

The questions continue as in the remaining poems we explore this *omphalos* of the primeval, this fragment—once again—of a strange prehuman and premammalian Eden, where before the white men arrived, the inhabitants lived to immense ages unthreatened by predators, and where even the largest creatures were harmless and vegetarian. In the very place where *Genesis* seemed to be discredited by scientific observation, we are back in a different kind of *Genesis* with its leading figures reappearing in a kind of burlesque miracle play in which the poet, blundering Everyman, intrudes like a bewildered Wellsian time traveller, and among the iguanas encounters the God who was absent from the great sky.

> Hunkered on hands and knees
> then collapsing sideways
> cheek on stony ground
> in order to see close-up:
> Tyrannosaurus thirty feet high
> looming over my head
> about to have me for breakfast
> My left eye sees separately
> seventy million years in the past
> but the right eye sees only
> a harmless vegetarian
> this spring day in 1980 . . . ("Iguana")

Everyman stops clowning and lapses into erratic thought about his quest for relations, and relations means, of course, the great ancestral chain that unites people with the whole natural world as it has lived in time. But the game of magnification that has turned simple iguana into Tyrannosaurus Rex is resumed, and suddenly God, the "non-existent monster" of the earlier poem, is reincarnated as the patriarchal iguana, head of a submissive harem (shades here of the primal horde of the early anthropologists that so fascinated Marx and Engels). And Everyman Purdy ventures with trepidation to touch the back of "old man God." "But God just sways his head / sways it up and down up down / irritated at this presumption." And Everyman Purdy feels "humble" and "sad" that one can understand only one's kin, understand neither the past nor the future, "understand nothing but now / balanced in the needle's eye / and the impulse to touch God / is as close as I'll ever come." What is projected is not wholly the negation of *carpe diem*. Shades of *Genesis* have already floated over when Purdy has been talking of "old Man God" observing "lizard restraint" in "the act of creation," and one seems to move now into a pantheist realm where one touches God in the most alien of creatures.

The sense of identification and remoteness coming together in the human mind on a set of barren rocks populated by archaic survivors from some kind of earthly dawn is extended in the three other poems I am reading. Two of them, "Moses at Darwin Station" and "Adam and No Eve," start off with encounters with giant tortoises, and, as their titles suggest, each looks back ironically into *Genesis*. The third, "Moonspell," is really a kind of meditation on how fragile, during such an experience, the sense of one's self and one's time can become. But the first two poems are, in their approach if not in their form, elegiac— in a special and rather ancient sense, for, as in Purdy's poetic hero from antiquity, Archilochus of Paros, the threnodic is mixed with the satirical and (in Purdy's case, benign) the outrageous.

Moses, the eponymous hero of "Moses at Darwin Station," is described as a "huge strongbox," "seven hundred pounds and 160 years" old, therefore ante-dating Darwin's arrival, which was about 145 years before Purdy's. His companions are "like small boxcars" and, in Purdyish manner, this comic and condescending joviality dominates the poem at first reading. But questions arise that nudge us towards profundity. How does Moses perceive us if he can only see us as black-and-white shadows? What awarenesses may occur in that reptilian head on its long neck, "exploring silence . . ."? Abruptly, we are in the incongruous consideration of the subject of "Darwin's Theology?" when Purdy inserts a Groucho Marx-ish side-thought of Moses in the act of speculation: "investigating the either/ / or of persistent rumours / that God exists/ or does not."

Yet, as the poem continues in its narrow annelidan form, with short lines that give a sense of hesitancy under the raucousness (perhaps because of the raucousness), Purdy is suddenly questioning, as he sees the tortoises for beings in themselves, the point of the scientific knowledge he had read upon and brought with him to the Galapagos: "and yet I think / who are they? / despite trite labels / perishable description / vanishing sound-glyphs / who are they?" But there is no avoiding triteness, and perhaps necessary triteness, in the kind of Everyman reflections into which Purdy now proceeds, of the hundred million years of respectable tortoise ancestry compared with our meagre human record, and of the evidence that persuades the poet to believe that "those distant / ancestors of old Moses / are unrecognizably / but yet indubitably / my own." His final conclusion nevertheless is that, go back though we may to the primitive one-celled beings surviving the ages of cosmic disasters, we find that all the ancestors we may have had and all the theories we may hold about how the world once was are irrelevant to the eternal now, and in another way we are back with Moses at *carpe diem*.

> Ol Granpappy Moses
> brushes off this nonsense
> of uranium clocks

> and scientific theories
> of continental drifting
> glaciation and star-birth
> remembering only
> the linchpin now
> this permanent moment
> the same as always
> its name is Moses.

But if the *leitmotif* of "Moses at Darwin Station" seems to be a statement of the centrality, even in the great continuity of being, of the individual—tortoise or human being—there is a clear statement in "Adam and No Eve" of the ultimate insufficiency of such centrality. On Abingdon Island in the Galapagos there is "a giant yellow-faced tortoise / the last of the species" ("call him Lonesome George" is Everyman Purdy's aside). Because of his uniqueness he has been "coddled and cuddled" by the local scientists who have offered to pay ten thousand dollars for a female (alive) of the same species. But no bounty man has responded, and it is clear that even a billion dollars would not restore "one nubile female." And once a species comes to the verge of extinction, there is no reversing the process of evolution (or devolution); Purdy assumes a favourite oracular tone as he pronounces:

> Not again shall mud conceive
> or the stars bear witness
> and lightning flash over chaos
> nor any deity of the flesh
> send his small amphibians
> scuttling onto land for safety
> the amino acids are dissolved
> their formulas forgotten.

Survival depends on the attraction we call love, and if there is no longer a pair to develop that attraction, then the species need only wait for death, as Lonesome George does. And it is with a threnodic resonance, lamenting love as well as tortoises, that Purdy ends:

> —and whatever love may be
> weighed and counted and measured
> in books and artistic symbols
> one female tortoise (shaped
> somewhat like an old shoe)
> has taken it with her alone
> into the darkness.

But there is of course another kind of love, the all-absorbing love that is not directed to a single being, the Buddhist or Jain mystic's love for all beings, the Pantheist's love for all that exists because he is part of it and hence part of God. It is clear that for some people these generalized loves can be as intense as those of a woman and a man for each other, of a parent for a child, or that between true friends. Many people have had at some time in their lives the experience of such a total immersion in natural beauty that they have felt their own separateness, as species and individual, dissolving into the marvellous whole, and Purdy expresses feelings of this kind when, in "Moonspell," he describes standing in a cottage doorway one moonlit night in the Galapagos. He has inquired of the animals in his own way, has sought to "find the iguana's secret / name embroidered / on his ruby brain" until "my speech is grunts / squeaks clicks stammers." And the poem follows its annelidan way, rich with tolling repetitions like bells under water ("let go—let go," "follow—follow," and "this—this—these") into a kind of self-hypnotic self-surrender in this place of incomprehensible origins or, equally, inconsequential vestiges. It seems almost as if the very self were an inconsequential vestige, fit only for merging in the great debris of biological time, as the poem ends:

> let go let go
> follow the sunken ships
> and deep sea creatures
> follow the *protozoa*
> into that far darkness
> another kind of light
> leave off this flesh
> this voice these bones
> sink down.

"Moonspell" thus forms a kind of summation of Purdy's Galapagos, and in doing so it gives emphasis to two complementary elements that recur in his mature poetry. One is the autodidacticism of a man self-taught by enormous reading, which tends to fix his point of departure in the time before academic specialization, when even *The Origin of Species* was a book of clear and simple eloquence available to any literate person. His preoccupations, even some of his opinions, seem to be set in that era. The bony and stony realities of palaeontology stir his imagination in ways that nuclear physics can never do, as one immediately realizes comparing the role of science in Purdy's poems and in Christopher Dewdney's poems, where the abstractions of physics glitter like crystal artifacts. But at the same time, there is the essentially Romantic attitude—belonging to times before and after the peak era of evolutionary controversy and biological speculation with its militantly materialist overtones—that can see human beings merging with their habitat and in ecstatic communion with the "non-existent monster," that godly absence which filled "sea and sky"—a communion the materialist evolutionists may have glimpsed but never confessed to.

Boldness, Audacity, Insolence:
A Reading of F.R. Scott's "Audacity"

Lilita Rodman

In discussing F.R. Scott's language, critics have tended to focus on the levels of sound and word. Warkentin, for example, has explored the prosody, imagery, and diction in "Lakeshore." Scott's use of the pun has been discussed by Scobie in the context of his "profoundly ambiguous outlook," and by Djwa, who explicitly mentions his linguistic audacity: "Scott is able to develop emotional resonance from the pun in much the same way as did the metaphysicals, by transforming an initially audacious comparison into a structural conceit" (*CWTW*, 207). Djwa also notes how Scott can manipulate audience response at the level of argument—what I would call ambiguity at the level of argument—when she refers to his "presentation of a series of statements, at first appearing to argue in one direction, which turn about to force the reader to an opposite conclusion" (*CWTW*, 198). F.R. Scott's experiments with language, not just at the levels of sound, diction, and argument, but also at the levels of syntax, pragmatics, and genre, can be seen in "Audacity," first published in 1964 in *Signature*. Although this poem has escaped critical attention, except for Skelton's reference to its "deftly Whitmanesque opening" (41), this poem rewards closer examination because the rich texture of echo or resonance and ambiguity that pervades all the levels of linguistic structure creates ironic tensions that repeatedly force the reader to reassess initial readings.

The first stanza has the structure and appears to have the function of a typical introduction to an academic or legal argument. The first two lines, both beginning with the parallel "They say . . . ," identify the position that the author will refute. The "But" in line 3 signals the turn in the argument, and is reinforced by the contrasting, though parallel, "I say." The final three lines, each of which is a main clause, present the thesis of the poem: we do not lack audacity, boldness, or insolence.

But who are the "they," the "we," and the "you"? To answer this in part, we need to go to the epigraph—("*Audacity is missing in Canada.*" The *Times 30/11/59*)—which directs us to *The Times* (London) of November 30, 1959. At the back of a supplement on Canada, this issue ran an article by Robert Fulford entitled "Is Adventure in Abeyance?" in which a single subheading, "Audacity Missing," is followed by this explanation:

As several distinguished visitors have told us, Canada is a middle-class country, perhaps more emphatically middle-class than any other country west of Switzerland. Few Canadians are conscious of working-class status, and almost none would recognize themselves as members of an *élite*. Thus the adventurous spirit that might arise elsewhere from the desperation of the lower classes or the tradition of the upper classes does not appear in Canadian life. This is one reason why audacity is missing in Canada.

We see, then, that this poem does not function only as an academic or legal argument, but also belongs to the particular genre of letter to the editor: the "you" of line 3 is both the reader and *The Times*. Furthermore, whereas at first one might have read "they say" in the indefinite or unspecified sense of "It is said by some people that . . ." we see now that "they" refers directly to the "several distinguished visitors" of this passage in Fulford's article. "We," of course, are Canadians.

In fact, the opening two lines rework the *Times* passage. Replacing "several distinguished visitors" with "they" removes the specific weight of number implied by "several," but retains only the sense of plurality; it removes the specific authority implied by "distinguished" and the specific foreignness of "visitors," but retains a sense of otherness that can be countered with "I." Replacing "have told us" with "say" removes the finality of the present perfect and the need for an audience (us). At the same time, "they say" introduces the diphthong sound that will be continued in "I *say*" and "you *may*" and thereby establishes a phonological cohesion that reinforces the syntactic cohesion of the grammatical parallelism ("they say" / "I say"). What is reported as being said, or told, has also been changed. The original focuses on class structure in Canada, on *why* we lack audacity, rather than on *whether* we lack audacity. Moving "we lack audacity" from the final "why"-clause to the first predicate of the main clause of the opening sentence gives it much greater prominence since it is then asserted rather than presupposed. The omission of "perhaps" and "might" also strengthens the claims. Replacing the more neutral "emphatically middle-class" with the clearly pejorative "emphatically middling" shifts the focus to mediocrity and links this line with "riddled" of line 6. The last part of line 2, "and that boldness and experiment are far from our complacent thoughts," is largely Scott's addition. In the original, "boldness" is not used anywhere; "experiment" is used only in the context of experimental theatre, and not in the wider sense of trying things out; and "complacent" is also used only once, in the final sentence: "So far, however, they [immigrants] have shown themselves all too eager to fit smoothly into the complacent atmosphere of contemporary Canada."

With the third line, the poem turns as the original newspaper article is left behind, and the response begins, signalled, as one might expect, with the "But," followed by "I say to you." The emphatic explicitness of "to you" and of the performative "say" adds considerable force to the refutation, which at this point is framed not in terms of whether we have audacity, but in terms of the knowledge and vision of the "they": "they do not know where to look, and have not the eyes to see." This line also brings together "I" and "eye," a pun Scott is fond of, and one whose importance Brewster has noted. Line 3 is answered, in a sense, by line 39: "These surely you can see . . ." The vision image is also picked up in "omniscient" in line 38, where the godlike vision is ascribed, ironically, to the great executives. Line 3 also draws on several biblical echoes: "Having eyes, see ye not? and having ears, hear ye not? and do ye not remember?" (Mark 8.18) and "Son of man, thou dwellest in the midst of a rebellious house, which have eyes to see, and see not; they have ears to hear and hear not: for they are a rebellious house" (Ezekiel 12.2). Particularly striking is the similarity of "But I say to you" to "But I say unto you," which is used in the Sermon on the Mount (Matthew 5) to counter various reported arguments: "Ye have heard that it was said . . ." or "It hath been said . . ." or "Ye have heard that it hath been said . . ." In addition to being in the letter-to-the-editor genre, then, and employing the structure of academic or legal arguments, this passage echoes a biblical argument and may even parody the Sermon on the Mount. Furthermore, if we recall "Blessed are the meek: for they shall inherit the earth" (Matthew 5.5), we see an ironic tension here between what Scott appears to be arguing (that audacity is a desirable quality that we don't lack) and what he indeed ends up arguing (that we have audacity, but it would be better if we didn't).

The marked change in line and sentence structure in lines 4-6 focuses attention on these lines and adds force to the thesis, which these lines state. Instead of the very long opening lines with multiple embeddings of clauses and phrases, we here have lines of only five or six words (nine or ten syllables), each a main clause with no embeddings. Also, in contrast to the parallelism between and within the opening lines, these three are clearly not grammatically parallel: the first contains the copula "is," the second the intransitive "sits," and the third the copula "are" with the adjectival past participle "riddled." "Riddled" is linked phonetically to "middle class" and "middling," and so serves to link line 6 to lines 1 and 2, but semantically it may also be a pun. Its emphatic position in the final clause of the thesis may underline the riddle quality of this poem; at the same time, the fact that "riddle" has negative connotations—that one can't be "riddled" with something valuable—establishes Scott's ironic intent.

The three clauses are linked by three semantically related, though not synonymous, abstractions: "audacity," "boldness," "insolence." This strategy invites a closer look at these three terms and also implies, together with the title and epigraph, that this poem concerns the *meaning* of "audacity." In other words, it appears that this is another of what Smith called Scott's "defining" poems (31). In the *Times* article, "boldness" and "insolence" do not appear, and "audacity" appears only twice, once in the passage that is the direct source of lines 1 and 2, and once in the opening sentences of the article:

> The special nature of Canada implies adventure. Impossible geography makes even the building of a railroad a gesture of quixotic majesty. An immense northland makes even the exploration of boundaries an act of audacity. The relationship of Canadians to Americans makes even the idea of national identity sound like a brave and gloriously hopeless dream. Yet Canadians, living with these facts, are not an adventurous people.

To borrow from this passage, we could say that this poem is an "exploration of [the] boundaries" of the term "audacity" and also that this exploration is itself an audacious act.

How does "audacity" differ from "boldness," "insolence," and the word that dominates the *Times* article, "adventure"? "Adventure" is the broadest of these terms, has positive connotations, can be unintended or accidental, and need not have a social context or audience. Both "boldness" and "audacity" can be used positively and negatively, with the positive senses including courage and daring, and the negative senses including impudence and shamelessness (*OED*). Both imply intent and require a social context or audience; one cannot be either bold or audacious by chance or in isolation. Scott uses the similarity between "boldness" and "audacity" as a structural component in the poem. The two words are paired in lines 1 and 2, 4 and 5, and 26 and 30, leaving only the "boldness" in line 17 unpaired. The "audacity" in line 7 is paired with the "audacity" in line 40 to provide a frame for the catalogue of examples of audacity; the examples up to line 32 illustrate that "audacity is all around us," and the example of audacity in lines 33 to 38 illustrates that "Boldness sits in the highest places." In connotation, "boldness" appears to be less negative than "audacity." Also, "boldness" subsumes "audacity," in that one can be bold without being audacious, but one can't be audacious without being bold. Finally, we come to "insolence," which is the narrowest in its meaning, being restricted to verbal boldness that intends to offend. It occurs only once in the poem, but in the position of greatest prominence—at the end of the sentence, line, and stanza. This part of the thesis is illustrated in the final three lines of the poem, in the proclamation of the "supremacy of God" in the Bill of Rights.

The stanza break at line 7 signals the second turning point in the poem, the pivotal ambiguous question, "Do you want audacity?" First, in the context of a reply to *The Times*, it can simply be a challenging question (equivalent to "So you want evidence of audacity, do you?"); the line then serves to introduce the evidence with which the "I" will prove Fulford wrong. The tone is informal and even a little cocky. However, the question also asks about the desirability of audacity; now "want" is read literally as "desire" or "wish for," the "you" is the reader, and the tone is much more neutral. There is even a third possibility, that of a formal rhetorical question with the Biblical sense of "want" as "lack": "Is it true that you lack audacity?"

The syntactically audacious 500-word final sentence—lines 8-41—answers line 7. Lines 8 and 39-41 constitute a frame within which are embedded the seven parallel main clauses of lines 9-32, each beginning with the structure "you may" plus a verb, followed in lines 33-9 by another main clause co-ordinated to these seven with the conjunction "But." Each of the embedded eight main clauses in turn has a complex internal structure characterized by parallelism and multiple embedding.

Line 8, "Let me tell you," functions as a discourse marker that introduces a new "episode," in this case the catalogue of audacities. However, like line 7, it is also pragmatically ambiguous. Corresponding to the reading of line 7 as a challenge is an equally challenging reading of line 8 that could be paraphrased as "I'm about to tell you, whether you want me to or not," or simply "Here is the evidence." Yet if line 7 is read as a question about whether or not audacity is desirable, then line 8 can be read as a more polite, more chatty introduction to the catalogue, which now serves more to illustrate what audacity is like. The shift from the "I say to you" of the first stanza to "Let me tell you" empowers the audience to control the exchange of information and to participate as listener. Throughout the long second stanza, then, a tension in tone and formality provides two major structural schemes for the poem.

At line 9 the catalogue of audacities begins with the informal "Any day in Montreal," which modifies at least the next seven main clauses (ending at line 32) and thereby constitutes one more frame, restricting the social criticism to Montreal. "Any" echoes "any country" in line 2, but more importantly, since it implies "every," it establishes the temporal universality of the clauses that follow. "Day," found also in "Day after day" in line 23, links phonetically with "say," the verb that established parallelism in the first stanza, and with "may," which is a key component of the parallelism of the second stanza. The "you may," which is the basis of the parallelism of the seven types of audacity, is again ambiguous, for "you" may be read as an equivalent of the impersonal "one," meaning "anyone," or as referring directly to the reader, or *The Times*, and "may" can indicate either permission or possibility. All of these interpretations, nevertheless, make the "you may" structure a means of adding credence to the argument or proof. Having "you" as the main subject of each clause forces the audience to become responsible for recognizing the corruption displayed in the catalogue. As each of the seven pieces of evidence is paraded, their cumulative force increases. The verbs that follow "may"—"hear," "watch," "learn," "marvel at," "follow," "stand in awe at," "be amazed at"—are verbs of perception, of cognition, of cognitive or emotional response that explicitly emphasize the audience's function as observer and experiencer. In other words, the force of saying "you may hear the guns crack," rather than just "guns crack," is that it explicitly involves the "you" as perceiver, as a kind of participant in the scene, and thereby allows the "you" to verify what is claimed to be the case.

The first three main clauses—lines 9-16—form a unit within the catalogue of audacities; here audacity or boldness is implied rather than mentioned explicitly. In lines 9 and 10 the target of the criticism appears to be deliberately obscure. Is it the police who are being criticized, or the bank-robbers, or both? This uncertainty is created in part by mentioning the sound of the guns, but not saying who the guns belong to, and by saying the police "give chase," but not saying whether or not they catch the bank-robbers. The "as"-clause emphasizes the simultaneity of the police giving chase and the guns cracking, but obscures causality. The comparison of the robbers to the *coureurs de bois* and the English fur-traders serves to extend the targets of criticism into the past. The final phrase, "rolled into one," which suggests bank-rolling, together with the verb "chase," introduces the central image-pattern of circularity. In its most local sense here, it simply relates the current corruption to past corruption and the corruption of the bank-robber to the corruption of the policemen. In the rest of the poem it will become more clearly representative of the circularity of the structure of the poem. In lines 11 and 12 the focus falls on the circle of corruption in which the police and café-owners participate. Like the "guns" of line 9, the "cars" de-personalize the police. The verb "circle," of course, makes explicit the image introduced more covertly in the previous lines, but now the purpose of circling is not to chase, or catch robbers, but to rob the café-owners, who, in turn, break the law to appease the police. The policeman's purpose, to collect pay-offs, is represented by the apparently innocuous verb "gather" (which evokes its more usual collocation with "crops" or "berries" or "rosebuds") and is buried in an infinitive phrase.

With lines 13-16, the target of criticism shifts to corruption in government and the complicity of the church. Corresponding to the policemen's cars is just the "name" of the distinguished Councillor. The image of the circle is picked up in the "coin," but more importantly, the circularity is conveyed through the chain of relative clauses—"who controls . . .," "Into which rattles . . .," "that makes possible . . .," "who tips . . ."—and through the structure of the final lines, where the pairing of the active verb "tips" and the passive "is saluted" is another syntactic means of creating circularity, in this case reinforced explicitly by the phrase "in return." These lines also introduce an important sound sequence that is developed later in the poem: "*coun*cillor," "*con*trols," "*coin*," "*con*tracts." The prefix "con-" of course suggests the "con" of "convict," which relates very directly to the corruption displayed in this catalogue of audacities. "Coin" also continues the monetary imagery of "wealth" and "pay-off" and is reinforced, somewhat obliquely, by the monetary sense of "tips," which would thereby become a pun. Similarly "return" suggests monetary returns as well as reciprocity. The very short final pair of lines, with the native diction of the first answered by the Latinate diction of the second, signal the end of the first three examples.

With the next example, the corruption of promoters, the internal structure of the main clause changes. The verb "marvel at" includes a particle ("at"), as do the verbs in lines 26 and 30. The word "boldness" is explicitly included. The subordinate clauses of the previous lines are also replaced by a parallel series of participial phrases—("getting . . .," "playing . . .," "turning . . .," "loading . . .," "demanding . . .")—all concerned in some way with acquisition, and all implying control. The series creates a sense of activity in this remarkably long clause. Since the subject of the embedded structures remains constant (promoters), the circularity of the previous sections is replaced by unidirectionality. The prefix "con-" is repeated in "concessions" and "control," but as in his poem "Conflict" ("Pro and con have single stem / Half a truth dividing them" [*CP*, 97]), it is also played off against the "pro-" prefix of "promoters," "production," and "product." These lines also introduce the motif of the victimization of women. The promoters are explicitly called "men" and mining is seen in terms of rape: "getting . . . access to underground treasures awaiting man's use in the womb of our northland." The feminine sexual passivity implied by "awaiting man's use" is reinforced by the passivity of the housewife, implied by using the full passive "is paid by." The Italian "spaghetti" links these lines to "Savonarola" in line 31. The interplay of "under" and "over" in "underground" and "overhead" suggests the pervasiveness of the domination of the promoters. The "rights" in line 18 looks ahead to the "Bill of Rights" of the final line.

The next attack, on the hypocrisy of the hucksters and admen, again uses a series of short participial phrases—"compiling . . .," "planning . . .," "setting . . .," "writing . . .," "confusing . . .," "baiting . . .," "laughing . . .," "fixing . . .," "posing . . .," "undermining . . .," "singing . . ."—to create syntactic texture and the impression of relentless activity. This impression is enhanced by the invitation for the "you" to "follow" the hucksters and admen, and the relentlessness is reinforced by the phrase "day after day," which echoes the "any day" of line 9. Various phonetic, morphological, and semantic echoes further contribute to the poem's texture. "Hucksters" relates semantically to the "peddlers" of line 17; the "admen" (again, explicitly "men") are also linked phonetically to "admirers" in line 24; "assault" echoes "man's use" in line 18; "weeklies" echoes the "weekly" pay-off of line 11; "journals" looks forward to the "journalists" of line 26; and "fixing" relates to "fixers" in line 17. "Undermining" recalls "underground" of line 18 and puns on the mining image there. The "con-" prefix is used again in "confusing," "concept," and "contracts." Perhaps the quintessential word in this clause is "relies," which could be a pun on "to lie again."

With lines 26-9 the criticism shifts to journalists and news, and the structural principle shifts slightly once more. After the activity of the previous clause, the "you" is now to "stand." As in line 17, a phrasal verb is used—"stand in awe at"—and "audacity" appears now for the first time since line 7. "Awe" is of course linked phonetically to "audacity," and "stand in awe at" might even hint at the "stand on guard" of the national anthem. The present participial phrases continue, but now there are only three—"twisting . . .," "blanking out . . .," and "laying down . . ."—as they give way to the long "while"-clause. Again, various echoes link these lines to other parts of the poem. "Twisting" pairs with "turning" in line 19, "rewrite" echoes "relies" of line 25, "paid hack-men" recalls "paid by the housewife" in line 19, "hack-men" echoes the consonants of "hucksters" in line 21, the "add" of line 29 echoes the "admen," "radio stations and TV outlets" links referentially to "CBC" in line 23, and "free opinion" relates to "free enterprise" of line 25. The "con-" prefix is again picked up in "conventional" and "unconventional." The allusively rich "gather dailies into chains run by gangs" echoes "daisy-chains" as well as "chain-gangs," which in turn relates to "convicts" and hence the prefix "con-." The verb "gather" also links this line to line 11 and the corruption of the police. Furthermore, the chaingang image relates to "escape" in line 29 and the "free" in lines 25 and 29. The chains suggest confinement but also embody the sense of circularity that has been seen both explicitly and implicitly elsewhere in the poem.

The last of the seven parallel main clauses, much shorter than the previous three, once more criticizes the church, but now much more explicitly than in lines 15 and 16. Again we have both a participial phrase—"meeting . . ."—and a relative clause—"who wax or denounce . . ."—and, as in lines 15 and 16, the much shorter line 32 signals the end of a subsection. "Amazed" suggests both "amazing grace" and "a maze," which would reinforce the covert "riddle" image of line 6. "Audacity" is now replaced with "boldness," which rhymes, of course, with "sinfulness," which in turn is linked phonetically to "synod." Once more the focus is on men ("churchmen") and once more the "con-" prefix appears in "conclave" and "conference." The reference to Savonarola calls attention to itself with its foreignness: as a fifteenth-century Italian martyr who was burned at the stake after having set up a republic in Florence, not only was Savonarola intense, but his intensity related to religious, political, and social issues, issues that Scott is pursuing in this poem.

The "But" at the beginning of line 33 signals the first contrast since line 9: "But all this is as nothing, not worthy of mention, / Beside the supreme, the breath-taking audacity / Of the great executives in their panelled boardrooms." Line 33 looks back with "all this" at the seven long parallel clauses of lines 9-32 and dismisses the audacity displayed there, but "all" also looks forward semantically to the "omni-" or "all" of line 38: "omniscient, omnipotent, omnipresent, omnivorous." Like line 3, which also began with "But," this clause is dominated by negatives: "nothing," "not worthy of mention," and at the end of the clause, "no hospital . . ., no charitable . . ., no church . . ., no university . . .," and, "not to mention." The contrast between "all" and "nothing" and the other negatives serves to emphasize both nothingness and the omnipresence. "Worthy of mention" also looks forward to "not to mention" and the "men" syllable is probably not wholly coincidental. The "supreme" of line 34 not only makes audacity a gradable quality, but it also very obviously looks forward to "supremacy" in line 40. "Breath-taking," by contrast, relates in its non-figurative sense to the hospitals that are controlled by the executives, to "omnivorous" in line 38, and perhaps even to the guns cracking in line 9. Also, "executives" in the proximity of "breath-taking" also suggests "executioners." At this point we realize that lines 9-32 demonstrate that "audacity is all around us," and lines 33-8 reiterate that "Boldness sits in the highest places."

The "great executives" are modified by two participial phrases—one beginning with the passive participle "found," and the other with the very active participle "daring to be"—and by the long relative clause beginning with "without whom" that contains within it four clauses that negatively emphasize the pervasive power of these executives. Of these clauses two are passive (with "hospital" and "charitable campaign" as recipients of the action), and two active (with "church" and "university" as subjects). The three cases of "can" in line 37 contrast with the "may" of lines 9-32, but in this context emphasize the inability of the social organizations to do anything without the support of the great executives. "Can" also looks forward to the emphatic "can see" in line 39 and to the "can" of "Canada"; its consonants recall the prefix "con-" that was emphasized earlier.

Line 38 is the climax of the proof that began with line 9. Now, we finally have a form of the verb "to dare," the verb that is a verbal synonym of the noun "audacity," for "audacity" is derived from the Latin *audare*, meaning "to dare." Also, whereas normally we expect "dare" with a more active verb, here the phrase is "daring to be" plus an adjective. However, the adjectives are "all seeing," "all powerful," "all present," and, rather unusually, "all devouring." This depicts the executives as daring to be gods. "Omniscient," placed first, relates to the visual metaphor from which Scott argues; these executives are the opposite of the "they" of the opening lines who "have not the eyes to see."

The final three lines return us to the frame started with line 8 as an answer to line 7: "These surely you can see in this Canada of ours, O London *Times* / In this country that has the audacity to proclaim the "supremacy of God" / In its Bill of Rights?" The opening "these" has no clear antecedent, for there is no explicitly stated plural noun it can refer to. However, loosely—perhaps colloquially—we can say it refers to all the examples of audacity and boldness Scott has cited. In changing the normal order of "you can surely see these," with its emphasis on "these," to "These surely you can see," Scott has placed the emphasis on "see" instead. "See" of course relates, first, to line 3—"they do not know where to look, and have not the eyes to see"—and then also to the "omniscient" of the previous line. "Surely" is another emphatic device to persuade the reader of the truth of the thesis. The "can" continues the string of "cans" of the previous lines and relates also to "Canada" in a kind of inverse of Scott's well-known phrase, "O Canada, O Canada, O can / A day . . ." in "The Canadian Authors Meet," which may also be the source of or echoed in the "day" in lines 9 and 23. "This Canada of ours, O London *Times*" echoes "O Canada, our home . . ." and in the context of *The Times* may contain a pun on "hours" and "ours." Furthermore, whereas in lines 9-38 the examples are explicitly restricted to Montreal, now the reference extends to all of Canada.

In lines 40 and 41, which should merely conclude the poem, Scott ironically introduces yet another kind of audacity, the audacity of proclaiming the supremacy of God in the Bill of Rights. The "In" which begins the final two lines continues the pattern of "in this Canada," but it also relates phonetically to the "in" of "insolence" in line 6; the final audacity, a verbal audacity, is a case of insolence. The phrase "'supremacy of God'" also recalls the "supreme audacity" and the godlike qualities of the great executives cited in line 38. Whether or not proclaiming the supremacy of God is audacious is not debatable; it is presupposed in the relative clause "that has the audacity . . ."[1]

This poem, then, is ambiguous at all levels of language, and this ambiguity creates ironic tensions that keep the reader off guard. Probably the most significant ambiguity is that which operates at the level of genre, for genre provides the schema, the largest framework within which a reader processes a text. While at first this poem appears simply to be an argument to prove that Canada does not lack audacity, it becomes a litany of social criticism. The debate between Scott and *The Times* provides the surface structure for the poem, the surface frame for the argument that is encoded syntactically by the exchange between "they say" and "I say," the statement of the thesis, and the "Let me tell you" frame. The ostensible aim of the argument—to show that we don't lack audacity—is, of course, also ironic, for in order to achieve it and to win the argument, Scott has to prove with the details in the long second stanza how morally deficient Canada is. These details force the reader to define audacity and to question its value. In other words, what appeared to be the aim of the poem becomes a means to another end, the end of defining audacity, boldness, and insolence. In this sense the poem is rather like a Möbius band, the topological space produced when one twists a rectangle before joining its ends. Within the language of the poem this structural principle is echoed in the images of circularity and reciprocity, sequences of embedded subordinate clauses, and the references to mazes and riddles. The poem reveals social criticism through definition and definition through social criticism, turning the surface argumentative structure into a frame through which Scott anatomizes the implications of argument itself.

Notes

[1]Scott was asked to revise and condense the Bill of Rights in 1978. In a letter explaining his refusal, he wrote as follows: "Did I have to accept the basic principles already agreed on? Suppose, as is highly probable, I found them inadequate or even offensive (like the present phrase about 'the Supremacy of God'?)" (Djwa, *Politics*, 434).

Works Cited

"Audacity." *The Compact Edition of the Oxford English Dictionary* (1971).

"Boldness." *The Compact Edition of the Oxford English Dictionary* (1971).

Brewster, Elizabeth. "The I of the Observer: The Poetry of F.R. Scott." *Canadian Literature* 79 (Winter 1978): 23-30.

Djwa, Sandra. "F.R. Scott." *Canadian Poetry: Studies, Documents, Reviews* 4 (Spring/Summer 1979): 1-16.

———. "F.R. Scott and His Works." *Canadian Writers and Their Works*. Poetry series, Vol. 4. Robert Lecker et al., eds. Toronto: ECW, 1990: 173-227.

———. *The Politics of the Imagination: A Life of F.R. Scott*. Toronto: McClelland and Stewart, 1987.

Fulford, Robert. "Is Adventure in Abeyance?" *The Times* (London) (30 Nov. 1959), Supplement on Canada, xx.

Scobie, Stephen A.C. "The Road Back to Eden: The Poetry of F.R. Scott." *Queen's Quarterly*, 79.3 (Autumn 1972): 314-23.

Scott, F.R. *The Collected Poems of F.R. Scott*. Toronto: McClelland and Stewart, 1981.

———. *Signature*. Vancouver: Klanak, 1964.

Skelton, Robin. "A Poet of the Middle Slopes." *Canadian Literature*, 31 (Winter 1967): 40-4.

Smith, A.J.M. "F.R. Scott and Some of His Poems." *Canadian Literature*, 31 (Winter 1967): 25-35.

Warkentin, Germaine. "Scott's 'Lakeshore' and Its Tradition (For A.J.M. Smith)." *Canadian Literature*, 87 (Winter 1980): 42-50.

Reassembling Fragments:
Susanna Moodie, Carol Shields, and Mary Swann

Clara Thomas

In a 1989 interview with Eleanor Wachtel, Carol Shields links her M.A. thesis for the University of Ottawa, *Susanna Moodie: Voice and Vision* (1975), to the writing of *Swann* (1987). "I knew I wanted to write about the disappearance of manuscripts," she says, as she responds to Wachtel's questions about the genesis of the novel. "When I was working on my thesis on Susanna Moodie, some of the material had been stolen from the archives at the University of Western Ontario. I began to wonder what would happen if someone tried to monopolize this market of Moodie papers. [*Swann*] was a very different novel at that time— it was a male poet. I wanted these two things going on at the same time: the actual theft of manuscripts and I wanted all these people to be stealing from each other" (34-5).

From the very beginning of her fiction, Shields established Susanna Moodie as an important continuing personage in her work. In her first novel, *Small Ceremonies* (1976), Judith Gill, the heroine, is in the process of writing a biography of Moodie, and in some half-dozen passages scattered through the book, Moodie is portrayed with shrewd insight. First comes Judith's overview of her subject:

> Decency shimmers beneath her prose, and one senses that here is a woman who hesitates to bore her reader with the idle slopover of her soul . . .
> Instead she presents a stout and rubbery persona, that of a generous, humorous woman who feeds on anecdotes and random philosophical devotions, sucking what she can out of daily events, the whole of her life glazed over with a neat edge-to-edge surface. It is the cracks in the surface I look for; for if her reticence is attractive, it also makes her a difficult subject to possess. (6-7)

Some ten years later, when *Swann* finally came together, Shields devised a whole cluster of characters, all trying to "possess" the dead poet, Mary Swann.

The word "poet" provides another important link between Susanna Moodie and Mary Swann. For all the readings of *Roughing It in the Bush*, remarkably little notice has been taken of the poetry throughout the text, though obviously Susanna spent a good deal of time on it. Her sister, Catharine Parr Traill, commonly affixed epigraphs from a whole range of poets to her chapters; but Susanna composed her own poetic epigraphs. She also interrupted her prose for some pertinent lines of poetry whenever the mood took her, and sometimes included an entire, fairly lengthy poem in her text, her effusion on the Otonabee River, for instance, or her patriotic ballad, "The Oath of the Canadian Volunteers."

In fact, because the book has so often been printed in a condensed form, it comes as something of a surprise to realize just how much original poetry Susanna did include in her early text. In the second Bentley edition of 1852, which she supervised, just recently available in an unabridged New Canadian Library edition, there are sixty passages of poetry altogether, both complete poems and fragments, forty-eight by Susanna, eleven by her husband, J.W.D. Moodie, and one ballad sung by John Monaghan, the irrepressible Irish boy who for a time was the Moodies' servant. This is more than twice the number included in the edition of 1962 edited by Carl Klinck, the radically truncated edition that for more than two decades most of us read and taught. Klinck's perception of *Roughing It* as an "apprenticeship novel," and his approval of the early editor who called Mrs. Moodie a "true heroine" and her work a "genuine romance," have been fruitful and lastingly influential, but they governed his own editing and resulted in an edition that does not do justice to Susanna's poetic propensities or to the diversity of her sketches.

Her verses range in mood and tone from an awestruck fear of a vast, alien land to which she is an unwilling immigrant, through weary resignation, to a lively fascination with her strange, eccentric companions-in-misery, and finally to a sometimes grudging, but just as often hopeful, faith in the future, for her family and for a great and growing Canada. The poems Klinck does include lean heavily toward the hopelessly fractured outlook that gave rise to the bleak Susanna of Margaret Atwood's *Journals of Susanna Moodie*. An early poem, an integral part of the chapter called "A Visit to Grosse Isle," for example, speaks of an "awful silence" that "broods profoundly o'er these solitudes" and of "desolation" that "reigns o'er these unpeopled forest plains" where "man finds himself with God—alone" (24). As they leave the cholera-stricken Montreal for "Our Journey up the Country" even Nature is seen as terrorized: "Nature holds her breath / In abject fear, and feels at her strong heart / The deadly pangs of death" (38).

Only when she embarks on her tale of Tom Wilson does Susanna's lively sense of the ridiculous break out in a happy-hearted little ditty, pleasantly introducing the good-hearted wanderer who witnessed her first disastrous attempt at bread-making: "A nose, kind sir! Sure mother Nature, / With all her freaks, ne'er formed this feature. / If such were mine, I'd try and trade it, / And swear the gods had never made it" (84). Such light-heartedness is by no means usual: the tale of John Monaghan, the feckless Irish lad, is preceded by an invocation to "Dear Mother Nature," obviously one of Susanna's most useful poetic conventions. Just as obviously, the invocation bore only a limited connection to experience, for after some months of hardship in the woods, any deep belief she might have had in the benign, care-giving powers of "Mother Nature" dwindled or disappeared.

The two stanzas that introduce "The Charivari" offer a more persuasive glimpse of her real perspective. The first of these counsels a weary resignation to counter despair; the second rises to hope and even gratitude. In sum, Klinck's editing of Moodie resulted in a nicely shaped "novel," its finish the climactic "Adieu to the Woods," and its final verse the sentimental epigraph to that chapter. In contrast, the Bentley edition is much more diverse in mood and subject matter, much more the product of Dunbar Moodie as well as of his wife, and much more characterized by insertions of humour from the pens of both of them. In its total effect it is an upbeat, if not exactly rollicking, account of the vicissitudes of settling in Upper Canada. Far from serving as a sad refrain, its poetry is often used to balance the tales of difficult times with glimpses of contentment and hope for the future. The chapter "Our First Settlement," for instance, ends with a four-stanza ballad, "Oh Canada! Thy Gloomy Woods," whose final lines belie its title:

> I see my children around me play,
>   My husband's smiles approve;
> I dash regretful tears away,
>   And lift my thoughts above:
> In humble gratitude to bless
>   The Almighty hand that spread
> Our table in the wilderness,
>   And gave my infants bread. (112)

The dire and often-quoted warning at the end of "Adieu to the Woods," "If these sketches should prove the means of deterring one family from sinking their property, and shipwrecking all their hopes, by going to reside in the backwoods of Canada, etc., etc.," is, in the Bentley edition, massively undercut by a six-stanza poem, "The Maple-Tree," a paean to the beauty of the tree and the land it graces. And the poetry written to accompany her account of the uprising of 1837, and Dunbar Moodie's patriotic part in it, curiously but definitely voices Susanna's conviction that only now, in turmoil and adversity, can this new land take its place in the glorious sum total of British history.

■ ■ ■

Begun just after the publication of *Happenstance* (1980), Carol Shields' third novel, *Swann: A Mystery*, was, in the author's words, a stubbornly hard novel to write: "a large labour" (Wachtel, 44). After two false starts she gradually "realized . . . that I could get a little bit off the ground and let the story find its own way. I decided to let that happen, let it go where it seemed to go, even if it didn't make any naturalistic sense" (41). Shields is a cautious advocate of postmodernist ideas, but they "do allow you to do things that you can't do as a naturalist . . . it [postmodernism] gets you off the ground. It can take you around some sharper corners that you didn't even know existed. It gives you permission to let the story go in curious angles. To imagine unimaginable possibilities" (45).

The novel that she finally liberated is a wonderfully knowing, playful compound of techniques and echoes, from its Proustian title to its David Lodge-like academic farce and parody elements. *Swann: A Mystery* predated A.S. Byatt's *Possession* by some three years, but it neatly anticipated Byatt's plot, the academics' search for long-dead authors, while even more neatly sparing readers the *longueurs* of Byatt's insertions of windy, pseudo-Victorian poetry and tales. *Swann: A Mystery* also reveals Shields' strong current of benign wisdom, her acceptance of the mysteries of individuals and the strange synchronicities of real lives.

The 125 poems of the murdered Mary Swann are the very *raison d'être* of the novel's text, and the seventeen examples of her work that actually occur in the text keep this fact before the reader at all times. As well, each poem (or poetic fragment, as most of them are) is contextualized to the character whose concerns call it to mind. Whereas Moodie's prose can stand by itself, though diminished without the accompanying poetry, *Swann: A Mystery* is unthinkable without the poems. Its climactic, wonderfully wise, and funny finale would be pointless without "Lost Things," the poem that ends the text, whose reassembly from shaky memories temporarily forges warring factions into a purposeful community and casts its significance back over the entire work. To understand this poem it is necessary to rehearse briefly the plot, which shifts rapidly from Gothic beginnings to pungent satire.

Mary Swann lived on a decrepit farm outside Nadeau, Ontario. On a December day in 1965 she visited Frederic Cruzzi, eccentric man-of-the-world, journalist, editor, and publisher, resident of Kingston. She left with him a paper bag containing her poems. That very night, her husband, Amos Swann, shot and dismembered her, put the pieces of her body in his silo, and then shot himself. Cruzzi and his wife assembled a manuscript of 125 poems that he called *Swann's Songs*, a title that he has since had the grace to regret: "An inexplicable lapse of sensibility. A miscalculation, an embarrassment" (203). In 1966 he published 250 copies, but as the novel begins, in the 1980s, only about twenty copies are known to have survived.

A Mary Swann industry is burgeoning among academics and is about to be dignified by a Christmas-time symposium in Toronto. Sarah Maloney, a young Chicago professor, whose Ph.D. thesis, *The Female Prism*, had, astonishingly, become a bestseller, was Swann's discoverer: she found a copy of *Swann's Songs* among the predictable fly-specked discards in a run-down cottage on a lake in Wisconsin where she was recuperating from a brief and unhappy marriage. Her subsequent article on Swann and her poetry began an academic industry; her own moderate, rational attitude, "My own responsibility toward Mary Swann as I see it, is custodial" (31), is belied by her passionate resentment of those who have also staked their claims to Swann territory. Sarah is anything but a disinterested sponsor. Her appreciation of Swann's achievement borders on religious awe: "Reading Mary Swann's poetry for the first time . . . I found myself suddenly grabbed by an elemental seizure of the first order. I was instantly alert, attenuated, running my fingers under the words, writing furiously in the margin . . . I read *Swann's Songs* at one sitting. Then I sat perfectly still for a few minutes, and then I read it again" (40).

In Part I of *Swann: A Mystery* Sarah Maloney tells us a great deal about herself and an intriguing amount about the dead poet whose haunting work emerged from a background of almost total deprivation:

> Mary Swann discovered herself, and therein, suspended on tissues of implausibility, like a hammock without strings, hangs the central mystery: how did she do it? Where in those bleak Ontario acres, that littered farmyard, did she find the sparks that converted emblematic substance into rolling poetry? Chickens, outhouses, wash-day, woodpiles, porch, husband, work-boots, overalls, bedstead, filth. That's the stuff this woman had to work with. (31)

The spare and gnomic verses that Sarah treasures so much and that have excited a whole clutch of scholars resonate with sadness and loss, but sometimes they also celebrate dailiness, the ordinary round that "has its hard deposits of ennui, but it is also, as Mary Swann suggests, redemptive" (22): "A morning and an afternoon and / Night's queer knuckled hand / Hold me separate and whole / Stitching tight my daily soul" (21).

Of the six of Swann's poems quoted in Sarah's section, four are quoted by Sarah herself, one by her elusive lover, Sam Brown [Brownie], and one by Morton Jimroy, Mary Swann's biographer, who writes to Sarah begging for a look at the poet's notebook, which Sarah possesses. They are all brief snatches—"The rivers in this country / Shrink and crack and kill / And the waters of my body / Grow invisible" (63). They resist easy understanding and readily persuade the reader that a collection of such verse would indeed titillate the jaded tastes of scholars. Taken together, they are no mean achievement on Shields' part— a reminder that she had published two books of poetry before any of her novels. The fragments are tantalizing enough to pull readers into the mystery and hold them there, willing fellow-travellers among the odd assortment of characters who are all, in their own ways, striving to possess Mary Swann.

Immediately after her discovery of *Swann's Songs* Sarah drives post-haste to Nadeau to find out whatever she can about Mary Swann. There she meets Rose Hindmarch, town clerk, librarian, and emphatically Mary Swann's protector and local custodian. Frightened of her city visitor at first, Rose gradually relaxes, and after two days of talking and visiting, Sarah is taken into Rose's confidence. As a parting gift she is given Mary Swann's rhyming dictionary and her notebook, both of which had been left in Rose's keeping by the real estate agent for the Swann farm. Driving toward the border, she is tantalized by the books beside her and progressively more and more distressed by the presence of the rhyming dictionary that threatens her own cherished view of Mary Swann as a natural, untutored poetic genius. Finally she stops and throws it into a roadside litter box. This is a landmark action, her first—but not her last—manipulative and culpable gesture toward making Mary Swann hers and hers alone, an extension of Sarah Maloney and not the always mysterious, ultimately unknowable, un-possessable individual she must, if truth be told, remain.

The notebook, however, Sarah keeps; though it is a total disappointment, yielding nothing but commonplace grocery listings and weather jottings, she refuses to release it to any of the avid Swann scholars. Partly she keeps it hoping that it will someday yield a clue—this is the reason she gives herself. At least as important is her wish to keep it away from Jimroy and the others, the same possessive impulse that impelled her earlier to discard the dictionary. *She* discovered Mary Swann; *she* began the process of canonizing her in the literary world; and *she* claims the right both to reveal and to conceal Swann's mysterious being. Ironically for Sarah, the forces of opposition are already at work. By the end of the first section of *Swann: A Mystery* the notebook has disappeared from Sarah's house; its copy, deposited in the university library, has, seemingly, been lost; and Brownie has not returned her only copy of *Swann's Songs*.

Part II is Morton Jimroy's section. He is in California on sabbatical, ostensibly to write his biography of Mary Swann, but in fact to nurse his badly-damaged ego. To make a thoroughly unlikeable character understandable, even sympathetic, is Carol Shields' challenge and, by the end of the section, her success. A well-known, even famous, biographer, Jimroy is both personally and professionally pathetic. His attempts to possess his subject range from largely useless interviews in and around Nadeau and pretentious linkages of Swann to Emily Dickinson and Jane Austen, to petty thievery. When he visited the Mary Swann Memorial Room in the Nadeau Museum, he stole one of the only two existing photographs of the poet, and on one of his weekly visits to Frances Moore, Mary's daughter, he also stole Mary Swann's Parker 51 pen.

Jimroy is forlorn and unhappy, well in tune with the bleak fragments of poetry that dot this section: "A green light drops from a blue sky / And waits like winter in its jar of glass / Tells a weather-rotted lie / Or stories of damage and loss" (108). Unable to hide from himself the failure of his research, and tormented by the inexplicable disappearance of the stolen photograph of Mary Swann, he takes refuge in erotic fantasies about Sarah Maloney, with whom he corresponds. Then, inexplicably, on Christmas morning, working over his notes outside in the California sunshine, writing the hopelessly pedantic and ludicrously unlikely line, "It is highly probable that Swann read Jane Austen during this period" (119), Jimroy's spirits soar. Transfigured, "in the embrace of happiness," Jimroy finally commands our sympathy.

Part III of *Swann: A Mystery* is Rose Hindmarch's story. Besides being town clerk and librarian of Nadeau, Rose is curator of its Local History Museum and sole creator of its Mary Swann Memorial Room. She describes herself as "wearing many hats," and indeed she is always busy at one or another of her jobs, but in essence she is a lonely spinster, sometimes experiencing "an appalling sensation of loss, the naggy suspicion that beneath the hats is nothing but chilly space or the small scratching sounds of someone who wants only to please others" (126). Of all of those seeking to "possess" Mary Swann, Rose is both the most culpable and the most innocent. Dazzled by Morton Jimroy's visit to Nadeau and his attentions to her, she fabricates a close and friendly relationship with Mary, when in fact they had hardly done more than pass the time of day: "The two of them had not gone for long walks together. They had *not* discussed—not even once—the books Mary Swann borrowed from the library. Mary Swann had not given Rose Hindmarch copies of her poems to read and comment upon. They had not—not ever—discussed their deeply shared feelings about literature or about families or about nature" (152). Rose had, indeed, suggested to Mary that she show some of her poems to Frederic Cruzzi, the Kingston publisher of Peregrine Press, but that authentic bit of lore she has never admitted to anyone. Furthermore, if anyone were to suggest to Rose that the Memorial Room had been "wrenched into being through duplicity, through countless small acts of deception, she will be sure to look injured and offer up a pained denial" (163).

Her response to Mary Swann's poems is unswervingly literal: "Blood pronounces my name / Blisters the day with shame / Spends what little I own, / Robbing the hour, rubbing the bone" (148). To Jimroy, pretentiously pedantic, the lines are "a pretty direct reference to the sacrament of holy communion. Or perhaps, and this is my point, perhaps to a more elemental sort of blood covenant, the eating of the Godhead, that sort of thing" (148). To Rose they are, quite obviously, a reference to menstruation, though she cannot bring herself to say that word out loud. Though she feels twinges of guilt for her claiming of closeness with Mary Swann, these speedily vanish after Jimroy's visit when she finds that one of the two photographs of Mary has disappeared from the Museum. Jimroy certainly stole it—he is equally culpable. "Their imperfections, colliding in a blue sky somewhere between Ontario and Manitoba, merged and cancelled each other out" (152). The arrival of an invitation to the Swann Symposium in Toronto dazzles her with joy; despite the anxiety and exhaustion occasioned by her persistent bleeding, and the puzzling disappearance of her only copy of *Swann's Songs*, her Christmas Day eggnog party ends for her with a flash of happiness: "out of the blue, she remembers a line from one of Mary Swann's poems. It just swims into her head like a little fish. 'A pound of joy weighs more / When grief had gone before'" (171).

Frederic Cruzzi's section contains the most stunning, surprising revelation in the book. Cruzzi, elderly, cosmopolitan, a scholar, publisher, and bon vivant, replete with friends and resources of mind and soul, in many ways the antithesis of Rose Hindmarch *and* Mary Swann, with his wife Hildë, now dead, undertook a complete pre-emption of Swann's words and virtually "made" the text of *Swann's Songs*. The very night that Mary Swann was murdered, he and Hildë laboriously assembled a manuscript out of the bag of poems she had left with him. Hildë had inadvertently thrown the heads and entrails of the fish she was cleaning into the bag. Appalled, and equally appalled by his momentary rage and violence against Hildë, Cruzzi began to try to decipher the blurred, slimy pages. Very shortly, he and Hildë were both completely caught up in their reconstruction:

> By midnight . . . they were referring to Hildë's transcribed notes, and not the drying, curling, poems on the table, as "the manuscript" . . .
> By now—it was morning—a curious conspiracy had overtaken them. Guilt, or perhaps a wish to make amends, convinced them that they owed Mrs. Swann an interpretation that would reinforce her strengths as a poet. They wanted to offer her help and protection, what she seemed never to have had. (222-3)

Cruzzi, though now old and alone, usually manages to enjoy his daily round, the many contacts he has with friends, and the books and music so precious to him. Rather reluctantly, he has promised to go to the symposium that will bring all of the Swann enthusiasts together, and even to give a short speech;

but when he comes home on Christmas Eve to find that his house has been rifled and his four copies of *Swann's Songs* are gone, he is close to despair.

For four-fifths of the novel Carol Shields has developed her characters away from caricature or stereotype to powerful illusions of "real people." Now, in her culminating section, called "The Swann Symposium," she switches gears dramatically, breaking up her illusory "realism" and moving to blatant artifice and artificiality. This is a filmscript, we are told. The "Set Up Scenes" follow the various major characters as they travel to Toronto: Sarah, pregnant, happy, and almost reluctant to leave Stephen, her new husband; Jimroy, insecure and vulnerable to that worst of all travellers' hazards, the falsely hearty, insensitive, and nosy seat-partner; and Rose with Cruzzi, incongruous but on the whole companionable fellow-travellers. As the script unfolds, we are treated to many of the hoariest conventions of the genre, particularly scenes of farce, with much hide-and-seek among the characters, sudden dousing of lights, locked doors, hiding in closets and behind curtains, and, finally, a pillow-case stuffed with Mary Swann's poems pitched out of a twenty-fourth-floor hotel window into falling snow. The various symposium sessions hilariously parody every academic conference in the world. In fact, in one of her final Director's Notes, Shields suggests that the scene "may be played with a very slight parodic edge" (297)—as if we hadn't already caught on! We finally learn what we have long suspected, that the villain obsessed with possessing all the relics of Mary Swann is Brownie, Sarah's old lover, the book collector who never reads books. Like all the rest of the would-be possessors, he is finally foiled.

It is far from a nonsensical denouement. Superficial mysteries are solved, but the major mystery, the universal mystery, of unique individuality and inexplicable achievement, remains: at the end, Mary Swann and the poems she alone wrote are still untouched and untouchable. There is even one more mystery, the greatest one of all; and this too remains inviolable. In the filmscript's final scene, a group of the most disparate individuals imaginable join in a voluntary act of community, even of grace, to restore from memory as far as possible the text they know as Mary Swann's:

> Director's Final Note: The faces of the actors have been subtly transformed. They are seen joined in a ceremonial act of reconstruction, perhaps even an act of creation. There need be no suggestion that any one of them will become less selfish in the future, less cranky, less consumed with thoughts of tenure and academic glory, but each of them has, for the moment at least, transcended personal concerns. (311)

The poem they are reassembling is "Lost Things," presented, as they recall and refashion it, on the last page of the novel, its lines resonant with meaning for the lives of Sarah, Jimroy, Rose, and Cruzzi as well as for the lost Mary Swann. All the participants—and all the readers—know the meaning of loss and sadness. In its context here, however, the poem represents a triumph and a celebration. Its theme is haunting, resonating back to all the other Mary Swann fragments that, far from being simply ornamental, have provided—each in its context—the strong skeleton for this remarkable, wise, and witty novel.

Works Cited

Atwood, Margaret. *The Journals of Susanna Moodie.* Toronto: Oxford, 1970.

Milburn, Thomas. *Roughing It in the Bush: A Literary History.* Unpublished M.A. thesis, Trent University: 1991.

Moodie, Susanna. *Roughing It in the Bush: or Forest Life in Canada.* New Canadian Library no. 31. Toronto: McClelland and Stewart, 1962.

———. *Roughing It in the Bush; or, Life in Canada.* Afterword by Susan Glickman. New Canadian Library. Toronto: McClelland and Stewart, 1989.

Shields, Carol. *Small Ceremonies.* Toronto: McGraw-Hill Ryerson, 1976.

———. *Susanna Moodie: Voice and Vision.* Ottawa: Borealis Press, 1977.

———. *Swann: A Mystery.* Toronto: Stoddart, 1987.

Thomas, Clara. "'A Slight Parodic Edge': *Swann: A Mystery.*" *Room of One's Own,* The Carol Shields Issue 13: 1 & 2 (July 1989): 109-22.

Wachtel, Eleanor. "Interview with Carol Shields." *Room of One's Own,* The Carol Shields Issue 13: 1 & 2 (July 1989): 5-45.

"Who Is This Man Smith?": Second and Third Thoughts on Canadian Modernism

Sandra Djwa

"Who is this man Smith?" said E.J. Pratt to F.R. Scott[1] when he heard A.J.M. Smith's injunctions regarding the kind of verse which ought to be published in *New Provinces*, a proposed anthology of modern poetry to which all three poets had agreed to contribute. The implicit conclusion to his sentence was "And who does he think he is?" On what grounds was Smith setting himself up as the arbiter of what was modern in Canadian poetry? Pratt's question, as Smith promptly admitted, was both "justifiable" and "unanswerable."[2] This response reminds us that in 1934 the notion that there were two schools of Canadian modernism, one at Toronto and another at Montreal, had not yet emerged. This was to be a critical pronouncement of W.E. Collin in *The White Savannahs*, a book which was not to be published until 1936, the same year as *New Provinces*. Fifty years later, Pratt's question still remains an intriguing one, particularly in relation to the way in which Smith's modernism developed and was seen to have authority by successive poets and critics.

His contemporaries, F.R. Scott and Leon Edel, fellow editors of *The McGill Fortnightly Review*, saw Smith as "the real leader of the young movement"[3] who had discovered modernism independently. As Scott summarized to Edel following the Smith Symposium in East Lansing, Michigan, in 1976, "I think you and I . . . both looked upon Arthur as the man who most surely understood the new movements stirring in the literary world around us" (Djwa, *Politics*, 93). Smith's own chronology of his development as a modernist is best summarized in "The Confessions of a Compulsive Anthologist," a paper which he wrote for a conference at Trent University and published in the *Journal of Canadian Studies* in 1976. He states that as a young man he read the poems of the Romantic revival, in particular Masefield's *Ballads and Poems* (1910), Carman's *The Pipes of Pan* (1906) and *Sappho: One Hundred Lyrics* (1904), Wilfred Campbell's *The Oxford Book of Canadian Verse* (1913), and Garvin's *Canadian Poets and Poetry* (1916, 1926). He also tells us that he came across the first edition of *The New Poetry* (1917) edited by Harriet Monroe and Alice Corbin Henderson in the Westmount Public Library, circa 1920-21, when he was still in high school. In response to some of my questions in 1974 he wrote:

I read [H.L. Mencken's] *The American Mercury* (but not *The Smart Set*) as an undergraduate and also the novels of H.G. Wells, Sinclair Lewis, Scott Fitzgerald, and the early Hemingway. Also Sherwood Anderson . . . The books we read in the twenties and early thirties with most excitement were Eliot's *The Sacred Wood* and Edmund Wilson's *Axel's Castle*. And of course, Yeats' essays and autobiographies. Also Joyce's *Portrait of the Artist* and Stuart Gilbert's study of *Ulysses*. Also the one-volume abridgment of *The Golden Bough*.

He adds that he read Irving Babbit and George Santayana after he went to Michigan State as an instructor in the early 1930s.[4]

Smith has said little about his Canadian influences, but scattered biographical comments and the internal evidence of his poetry indicate that the revisionist temper of the 1920s, particularly as shown in the pages of *The Canadian Forum* from 1920 to 1927, had a shaping influence on his poetry and thought. Because the question of the modern and the Canadian were closely connected in the minds of the 1920s poets—could one be modern *and* Canadian?—I propose to discuss Smith's developing modernism in connection with his changing attitude to Canadian literature. My principal text will be three versions of "The Lonely Land" published between 1926 and 1929, the vital years in which Smith consolidated his modernism, but I will also draw upon Smith's own criticism and some biographical inquiries made in the late 1970s. This is a useful poem for exploring Smith's modernism because in its various permutations it shows the influence of the old Romanticism, the Georgians, and the new Imagists, in particular H.D. and Ezra Pound. We can also follow the development of a specifically modern idiom as Smith, in successive versions, learns to break down the lines of the poem into free verse. Finally, the poem is important as a period piece because it shows that Smith responded briefly to the prevailing cultural myth of the period, the vision of Canada promulgated by the Group of Seven and its expression, advocated by the Canadian Authors' Association, in the "Canadian" poem.

I

The first version of "The Lonely Land" was published in *The McGill Fortnightly Review* on 9 January 1926. It is subtitled "Group of Seven" and it is clear that this is meant to be the framing concept; however, the elements of the poem, and Smith's modernism itself, have somewhat broader components. These include Yeats, the later modernists, and the then current debate on a Canadian art as reflected both in *The Canadian Forum* and *The McGill Fortnightly Review*.

THE LONELY LAND

Group of Seven

Cedar and jagged fir uplift
Accusing barbs against the grey
And cloud-piled sky;
And in the bay
Blown spume and windrift
And thin, bitter spray
Snap at the whirling sky;
And the pine trees lean one way.

Hark to the wild ducks' cry
And the lapping of water on stones
Pushing some monstrous plaint against the sky
While a tree creaks and groans
When the wind sweeps high.

It is good to come to this land
Of desolate splendour and grey grief,
And on a loud, stony strand
Find for a tired heart relief
In a wild duck's bitter cry,
In grey rock, black pine, shrill wind
And cloud-piled sky. (MFR, 30)

What is most striking about this first version of the poem is that it divides naturally into two parts. The first stanza is Imagist while the second and third stanzas are Georgian, expressing typically Yeatsian sentiment, language, and form. Firs are personified, and water and ducks "cry." The use of "monstrous plaint" (archaic for complaint) in stanza two indicates that Smith still preferred a poeticism to the language of real life which he was to advocate in his essay on "Contemporary Poetry" (*MFR*, 31-2). Most importantly, the narrator is turning to nature for the same reason as do the Romantics and their descendants, the Georgians: "[to] Find for a tired heart relief."

There is a decidedly Yeatsian ring to this phrase. In fact, to navigate the rhetorical "Hark," the exaggerations of "monstrous plaint," and the inversions of "Find for a tired heart relief" invite an equally fine Irish brogue. That the references to "desolate splendour" and "grey grief" are particularly associated with W.B. Yeats, on whose poetry Smith was then writing his master's thesis "The Poetry of W.B. Yeats," may be shown by turning to the first two pages of the thesis, where Smith describes "the desolate beauty and grey splendour" of Sligo where the Irish poet spent his youth. This landscape is characterized by "the indefinite greys . . . and the sound of the wind that was like the cry of the banshee" (2-3). Further in the text Smith describes the wild ducks at the Lake of the Three Narrows whose "cackling" so impressed the Irish hero Finn (15).

However, Smith's initial emotional response to Yeats' Irish landscape appears to have been overlaid by the Imagists and by the discussion of the Group of Seven in *The Canadian Forum*. Images in the first stanza are derived from H.D.'s "Oread," published in the 1923 edition of Monroe and Henderson's *The New Poetry*:

OREAD

Whirl up, sea—
Whirl your pointed pines.
Splash your great pines

> On our rocks.
> Hurl your green over us—
> Cover us with your pools of fir.

This later modernism is grafted onto the earlier Georgians, in particular John Masefield's "Sea Fever": "And all I ask is a windy day with the white clouds flying, / And the flung spray and the blown spume, and the sea-gulls crying." In 1974, when I was attempting to show the influence of the Group of Seven on the poets of the 1920s, I asked Smith how he had come across the Group. He replied that to this point he had not attended any exhibitions of the Group but that he was reading *The Canadian Forum* regularly and he had seen the portfolio of coloured prints which *Forum* subscribers had received. In a letter to me of 27 November 1974 he wrote,

> I had forgotten Tom Thomson and I'm glad Frank Scott remembered. Of course it *was* Thomson's great painting "The Jack Pine" (seen only in a colour reproduction) that helped me get started on "The Lonely Land." Collin I see mentions Tom Thomson too. There was also a fine print of J.E.H. MacDonald's Georgian Bay painting that, perhaps between the first draft and the last helped too . . . The literary influence behind "The Lonely Land" is as you saw H.D.

Smith may be conflating Fred Varley's *Stormy Weather, Georgian Bay* with MacDonald's *A Breezy Shore*, which was reproduced in the *Forum* in July 1922. However it is clear that the Georgians (through Yeats and Masefield), the Imagists (through H.D.), and the Group of Seven combine in the first version of "The Lonely Land."

We might speculate that it is not only the Group but ideas of Canadian identity that the Group symbolizes and the poem embodies. I suspect the poem is also a response to a continuing debate between national and international conceptions of art that had been current in *The Canadian Forum* since the early 1920s.[5] Could there be a Canadian poetry based on a nationalist tradition or must art be international and judged by international standards? *The Canadian Forum* debate is vigorous, with stalwarts like E.K. Broadus, Huntley K. Gordon, B.K. Sandwell, and Douglas Bush arguing pro and con, and is reflected in the 5 December 1925 edition of *The McGill Fortnightly Review*, where Smith takes the international position and Scott the national. Smith comments disparagingly about Canadian Book Week in an unsigned editorial: "After all, it is not so much Canadian books that we should like to see the public buy, as *good* Canadian books; and as there are not very many of these latter yet, we should be very well content with a public that would buy merely good books regardless whether their writers are English, American, German or Japanese" (*MFR*, 1). In this edition he also publishes an excellent essay on "Symbolism in Poetry," showing that he had absorbed the international modernism of Arthur Symons, and two poems exemplifying his own practice of symbolism: the first, "The Woman in the Samovar," suggestive of Eliot, and the second, "The Cry of A Wandering Gull," suggestive of W.B. Yeats.[6] Both echo poems which had appeared in *The New Poetry* (1923).

In the same issue of the *Fortnightly*, Scott, in "The Royal Canadian Academy," reports on a recent exhibition, reflecting "just why painting alone of all the Arts should have deigned to take a firm root in our native Canadian soil it would be difficult to determine." Nonetheless, he recognizes that there are paintings which do stir the imagination, particularly a mountain canvas: "All the loneliness and brooding silence of the northern hills are here" (*MFR*, 14). Scott recalls that he and Smith debated the possibility of a national art. Subsequently, in the next edition of the *Fortnightly*—"just to show that he could do it"[7]—Smith produced a Canadian landscape poem, "The Lonely Land." It is one of the ironies of literary history that this poem was to become the representative poem of the nationalist 1920s.

II

The second version of "The Lonely Land" appeared in *The Canadian Forum* a little over a year later in July 1927. What is most impressive is the difference in form. The lines in stanza one now move with vigour. The pivotal "Snap" gives life to the images. How, we might ask, did Smith learn so much about modern poetry so quickly? The answer, perhaps: Marianne Moore, *The Dial*, and various anthologized sources of the new poetry.

In 1925-26 Smith was subscribing to *The Dial*.[8] He submitted his *McGill Fortnightly* version of "The Lonely Land" to the journal, where it reached Marianne Moore who (by mid-1925) was *The Dial*'s acting editor. She did not accept "The Lonely Land," but she sent it back to Smith with some encouraging suggestions as to how he could break down the poetic line for a more modern effect. Apparently Smith accepted them and began to learn how to change the Georgian into the modern.

In this second version, the broken lines make the verse much more active; here Smith is really describing the subject itself, cutting out redundancies and starting to compose (as Pound put it in his essay "A Retrospect") "in the sequence of the musical phrase." Smith develops the second stanza so that we see and hear the duck within the context of the natural landscape—we are no longer just told about it. The second stanza becomes an observation of natural process, through the active representation of the wild duck's cry and the sound of the water. This is no longer a romantic complaint flung against the sky, but rather the absorption of natural sounds into the continuum of nature. In the last stanza the whole rationale of the experience is changed to affirmation, the affirmation of a new modern beauty of "dissonance," a beauty suggestive of H.D.'s "Sheltered Garden" and her desire for "a new beauty / in some terrible / wind-tortured place" (Untermeyer 298-9).

The poem is also less derivative of Yeats: the "wild ducks" are nationalized and the Irish "stony strand" has been integrated into a Group-of-Seven landscape, not unlike Varley's *Stormy Weather*. Smith underlines the point with nationalist statement—"These are the poems of Canada"—emphasizing the idea of an indigenous art. A similar view can be found in *Forum* in A.Y. Jackson's "Art in Toronto," where the painter speaks of the *West Wind* as reflecting Canada: "a younger more vigorous people, a harsher climate, a less patient age, and we have a pine tree bending under a boisterous wind, with a stretch of grey broken water beyond" (*CF*, 180). Jackson's commentary is a synthesis of prior art criticism in the *Forum*.

However, the image which precedes this statement ("This smoky cry curled over a black pine") and its revision in the final version of the poem ("this smoky cry / curled over a black pine / like a broken / and wind-battered branch") owes something to Ezra Pound's "In a Station of the Metro." I suspect that Smith was now drawing upon two of the major American texts of the 1920s: the 1923 edition of Monroe and Henderson's *The New Poetry* and Louis Untermeyer's *The New Era in American Poetry* (1919). Untermeyer quotes from H.D.'s "Oread" and also from her "Sheltered Garden" and from Pound's "In a Station of the Metro." In my judgment Smith had the Monroe and Henderson text by 1925 but may not have had the Untermeyer text until 1926. We can date his contact with *The New Poetry* to 1925 because he published a number of early poems in *The McGill Fortnightly* in December 1925 which are clearly variations on poems by H.D. and T.S. Eliot that had been collected in the 1923 anthology. Furthermore, Smith's master's thesis, "The Poetry of W.B. Yeats" (1926), cites this edition of *The New Poetry*.

In 1975, when developing a bibliography of Smith's poems, I found it difficult to understand how a young man who, as he said, had encountered the new poetry about 1920-21, could have continued to write Romantic verse up to and beyond 1925. I expressed my doubts to F.R. Scott. Shortly after, Scott inquired at the Westmount Public Library and came to the conclusion that the library had never possessed *The New Poetry* (1917). Later I had an opportunity to tell Smith of my doubts and of Scott's conclusions. He agreed that he might have been mistaken about the date of the anthology. He and his family had been in England during the later years of the War and there he had occasionally visited Harold Monro's Poetry Bookshop and discovered "the Georgians and Yeats." Smith was subsequently to provide this new biographical information to Leon Edel, who recorded it in his entry on Smith for *The Oxford Companion to Canadian Literature* (1983).

In 1975, however, it was still not clear how Smith came across *The New Poetry* nor how he moved from Yeats and the Georgians to the modernism of H.D. and T.S. Eliot. I wrote to Harold Files, who supervised Smith's graduate work, and consulted further with Scott and Leon Edel. Files wrote on 7 January 1976 that when he came to McGill from Harvard in 1923

I joined a small group of teachers trying to interpret a long tradition of literature, ranging from Caedmon or *Beowulf* down to (but not far *into*) the present century. By taste and temperament the English Department was divided between authoritarian conservative and liberal or undogmatic members . . . The "liberal" teachers were George Latham, Algy Noad, and I . . . Prof. Latham made no claim to special expertness in poetry and its techniques, but he read it often with relish; and as a Harvard undergraduate he was among the few friends of E.A. Robinson . . . Latham cannot be said . . . to have "introduced" the young writers to "the modern movement"; but I cannot doubt that he opened their minds in various ways, and helped to deepen them.[9]

As there was a substantial selection from Robinson in *The New Poetry* (1923) and as Latham's son Allan (a friend of Smith's) became associate editor of *The McGill Daily Literary Supplement* in January 1925, Files' letter raises the possibility that it was through the Lathams in 1924-25 or through Files himself that Smith first came across the 1923 Monroe and Henderson. As Edel recalled in discussion with me in the late 1970s:

Smith was always there talking and reading poetry, reading T.S. Eliot and Sitwell and all the others but after all, Files was the one who sent me to the library . . . saying "You know, there's an interesting book on German Expressionism" and I would say, "What is German Expressionism?" And he'd said, "You'll find a book there that's just come into the library by the name of so-and-so . . ." Files was also feeding us the contemporary movement, the modern movement.

In the meantime Scott had come up with the name of Lancelot Hogben, another friend of Smith's, a young Englishman who wrote verse and lectured in Science at McGill. Edel provided chapter and verse. He remembered a brown paper-wrapped copy of Eliot's *Prufrock and Other Observations* (1917), that Smith had borrowed from Hogben, being passed around in a Shakespeare class and, with the help of Virginia Woolf's diaries, identified Hogben as a pipeline to Bloomsbury (*On F.R. Scott*, 11). But although Scott and Edel agreed that Hogben was a possible source, they disagreed on the volume of Eliot. Scott thought it was not only *Prufrock* but also *The Waste Land* that had been handed around. And Smith, who was now very ill and would soon die, told Scott from his hospital bed to tell Sandra that it was not Hogben that he got *The New Poetry* from.

I now think that a combination of the Lathams, Files, and the Redpath Library at McGill are the most probable sources of *The New Poetry* circa 1924-25; that Smith may have purchased a copy of the 1917 edition of *The New Poetry* at a later date and/or conflated it with *An Anthology of the New Verse* published in 1916. It seems probable that Hogben, during 1925 or shortly after, loaned Smith his copy of T.S. Eliot's *Poems: 1919-1925* (1925) which contained "Prufrock," "The Waste Land," and "The Hollow Men," all of which are cited in Smith's essay on Eliot, "Hamlet in Modern Dress," in November 1926 (*MFR*, 2-4). This chronology, together with the new biographical information regarding Harold Monro's Poetry Bookshop, suggests that Smith had some help in finding his way towards modernism.

Finally, an additional and important source of Smith's modernism was *The Dial*. In *The Dial*, during 1925, Smith would have come across references to Eliot and Pound and read Marianne Moore's reviews of H.D. and Edith Sitwell. The 1922 volume of *The Dial*—which he also consulted in 1925-26 for Yeats' autobiographical reminiscences (for his M.A. thesis)—also included "The Waste Land" and a selection of poems from Wallace Stevens. As *The Dial* was an infallible guide to American and British modernism, and as Smith was reading *The Dial* when he first met Scott and Edel, it is not surprising that they credited him with discovering modernism on his own. There was a sense in which he had. And, between 1926 and 1929, he demonstrated his command of the modern idiom by having five of his poems published in *The Dial*.

III

By early 1927 Smith was meeting regularly with *Fortnightly* staffers Scott and Edel. Excerpts from Scott's diaries give a clear sense of Smith's poetic taste and practice. "Last night I went out to A.J.M.S.'s. We meant to write something for the *Fortnightly*, but instead I lay on the sofa and he read me his favourite poems from de la Mare ("The Voyager," I think) and H.D., whom he admires greatly."[10] Another entry reads:

> Spent the evening with A.J.M. Room littered with literary magazines, half-finished MSS of poems, and books. Coloured prints from the *Dial* on the wall. A.J. himself in his checked jacket. Discussed the projected *Quarterly* "Revision:" scratched our heads for a milch cow. Leo Edel opened *The Golden Bough* at random, placed his finger on a line, and achieved "They tread on boards" as a title for a short story: I hailed it as the name of a poem, and A.J. at once dashed to his typewriter and produced some eight lines upon it.
>
> He is like that—from inner image to typed word, without hesitation. Revision comes by futher typing and retyping. He will go far, for he is genuine, and gifted.[11]

During early 1927, while teaching high school in Montreal, Smith kept his hand in at the *Fortnightly* and began to revise some of his early poems. He recalls that he sent two of them to a competition sponsored by the Canadian Authors' Association. When Smith won a prize, Scott sat at the back of the room at the Ritz-Carlton Hotel writing "The Canadian Authors Meet," which parodied what both young poets saw as the Victorianism and boosterism of the Canadian Authors' Association: "O Canada, O Canada, O can / A day go by without new authors springing / To paint the native maple . . .?" It was this attitude of mind which led Smith to write "Wanted—Canadian Criticism" and led him, the following year, to expunge the overt references to Canada from "The Lonely Land."

Smith had now arrived at a number of related conclusions. The first, derived from his work on Yeats and suggested in his critical essay, "Symbolism in Poetry," is that the poet can no longer invoke nature for nature's sake. The second conclusion, also derived from Yeats, is that the progress of the developing artist is from a youthful romanticism to a mature realism; the latter quality he associated with the "classicism" of a T.E. Hulme. Finally, he came to believe, largely through his experience with the boosterism of the Canadian 1920s, that good art is international rather than national. These conclusions fuse with some of the pronouncements of T.S. Eliot in *The Sacred Wood* (1920), particularly with reference to the ideas of literary tradition and poetic impersonality.

Some of these ideas found expression in his important critical essay "Wanted— Canadian Criticism" (1928). There he firmly rejects the existing Canadian romantic landscape tradition, arguing that the made-in-Canada character of a poem was too often a substitute for aesthetic considerations. He asserts that a modern poetry cannot develop in Canada without "that critical enquiry into first principles which directs a new literature as tradition guides an old one." Offended by the excesses of the new literary nationalism of the 1920s—which tended to judge a poem's aesthetic value by its demonstrable Canadian content (the far north, Canada goose, maple leaves)—he outlines the need for a "critic contemplative" to enquire into the position of the artist in a new community. What Smith finds lacking in Canadian poetry is the historical sense, especially that awareness of the present which Eliot had advocated in "Tradition and the Individual Talent." Complaining that Canadian poetry is "altogether too self-conscious of its environment, of its position in space," he argues that "to be aware of our temporal setting as well as our environment . . . is the nearest we can come to being traditional." His target is clearly the prevailing sentimental nature poetry of Charles G.D. Roberts and Wilson MacDonald. "Modernity and tradition alike demand that the contemporary artist who survives adolescence shall be an intellectual. Sensibility is no longer enough, intelligence is also required. Even in Canada." (*CF*, 600-1).

Smith's subsequent rejection of the "Canadian" subject (he wrote few nature poems after the 1920s), his rejection of Romanticism (deepened after he came into contact with Irving Babbitt's *Rousseau and Romanticism* in the early 1930s), and his insistence upon intelligence as a controlling agent whether in criticism or in poetry were all related to his repudiation of what he considered the prevailing weaknesses of Canadian poetry. Spurred by the literary chauvinism of the 1920s ("my mother drunk—or sober") into a rejection of the existing Canadian tradition, he was perhaps forced into a position of doctrinaire opposition where classic was opposed to romantic, intelligence was preferred to emotion, and, more importantly, the world of art—the literary "tradition"—was substituted for nature. This movement towards a new classicism based on the literary tradition was further encouraged by studies in the Metaphysical poets begun at the University of Edinburgh in 1927, under the direction of Sir Herbert Grierson.

In his final version of "The Lonely Land," published in *The Dial* in June 1929, Smith bids adieu to the native poem *per se* and puts some of his critical principles into poetic practice. The cedars and firs of the first stanza can no longer be assigned to the old Romanticism, as they are no longer personified but rather an animate part of nature. In this version free verse has become organic form, especially in stanza two, where sound resounds and then is lost in nature. Finally, the poeticisms and capitals have disappeared other than for the first word of each stanza, and Smith removes all of the references to Canada other than the ubiquitous "north." A coda is added, recapitulating *Forum* criticism on the strength of the Group of Seven's portrayal of the typically rugged Canadian landscape.[12] "This is the beauty / of strength / broken by strength, / and still strong." Ironically, in its final version, "The Lonely Land" is at once a recognizably modernist and a Canadian poem.

Notes

[1]F.R. Scott to A.J.M. Smith, 17 February 1934. F.R. Scott papers. National Archives of Canada (NAC).
[2]A.J.M. Smith to F.R. Scott, 19 February 1934. NAC.
[3]F.R. Scott to A.J.M. Smith, 17 February 1934. NAC.
[4]A.J.M. Smith to Sandra Djwa, 5 December 1974. NAC.
[5]See Sandra Djwa, "The *Canadian Forum*: Literary Catalyst."
[6]The first poem is signed Michael Gard; the second, Vincent Starr.
[7]F.R. Scott in conversation with Sandra Djwa, circa 1978.
[8]Discussions, Jeannie Smith and Sandra Djwa, circa 1975.
[9]Letter, Harold Files to Sandra Djwa, 7 January 1976.
[10]Unpublished diaries of F.R. Scott, 21 January 1927.
[11]Unpublished diaries of F.R. Scott, 21 February 1927.
[12]See also John Ferns, "The Poetry and Criticism of A.J.M. Smith, *Bulletin of Canadian Studies*, 2:1 (1978) 16-32.

Works Cited

Djwa, Sandra. "The *Canadian Forum*: Literary Catalyst." *Studies in Canadian Literature*, 1 (Winter 1976): 7-25.
————. *The Politics of the Imagination*. Toronto: McClelland & Stewart, 1987.
———— and R. St. J. Macdonald, eds. *On F.R. Scott: Essays on His Contributions to Law, Literature, and Politics*. Montreal: McGill-Queen's Univ. Press, 1983.
D[oolittle], H. "Oread." *The New Poetry*. Harriet Monroe and Alice Corbin Henderson, eds. New York: Macmillan, 1923: 97.
Jackson, A.Y. "Art in Toronto." *The Canadian Forum* 6.66 (March 1926): 180-2.
Scott, F.R. "The Royal Canadian Academy." *The McGill Fortnightly Review* 1.2 (5 December 1925): 14.
Smith, A.J.M. "The Confessions of a Compulsive Anthologist." *Journal of Canadian Studies* 11.2 (May 1976): 4-14.

————. "Contemporary Poetry." *The McGill Fortnightly Review* 2.4 (15 December 1926): 31-2.

[————]. "Editorial." *The McGill Fortnightly Review* 1.2 (5 December 1925): 1.

————. "The Lonely Land." *The McGill Fortnightly Review* 1.4 (9 January 1926): 30.

————. "The Lonely Land." *The Canadian Forum* 7.82 (July 1927): 309.

————. "The Lonely Land." *The Dial* 86.6 (June 1929): 495-6.

————. "The Poetry of W.B. Yeats." Unpublished M.A. thesis, McGill University: 1926.

————. "Symbolism in Poetry." *The McGill Fortnightly Review* 1.2 (5 December 1925): 11-12, 16.

————. "Wanted—Canadian Criticism." *The Canadian Forum* 8.91 (April 1928): 600-1.

Untermeyer, Louis. *The New Era in American Poetry.* New York: Henry Holt, 1919.

"mother/father things I am also":
Fred(,) Wah, Breathin' His Name with
a Sigh

Susan Rudy Dorscht

Like Nicole Brossard, Fred Wah sees "writing as a way of using the body" (Brossard, *Aerial Letter*, 91). Even those unfamiliar with all of Fred's[1] writing will recognize, in the title of an early book, *Breathin' My Name with a Sigh*, a reciprocity between physicality ("Breathin'"), language ("Name"), and identity ("My Name"). How these categories come together "with a sigh" depends on one's reading of the sigh. Is it a sigh of relief? Of resignation? Of passion?

The three poems from *Breathin' My Name with a Sigh* excerpted for this book associate mother, father, and the name "Wah" with very different kinds of sighs. The poems beginning "mother / somewhere" and "mmmmmm / hm" both insist that readers engage the literal sighs of the physical body—breath coming out of the lungs—to make them sensible. Reading these two poems means giving breath to the words, putting, for example, the letters "mmmmmm" and "w_____h" into the mouth and pushing them out. But reading this writing is an intellectual as well as a physical pleasure. For example, the repetition of the sound of the word "her" in the "mother" poem makes connections between the body speaking, the words written, and a woman desired.

Watch what happens when I add the letter *h*—which, in its absence from many of the words, signifies the breath it takes to say them—to make explicit the tonal and semantic connections: "mot[h]er / somew[h]ere / rememb[h]er / whoev[h]er / forev[h]er / to fly ov[h]er / love her / pleases her / . . . / remove her / mutt[h]er / . . . / cleav[h]er / . . . / because of her / rememb[h]er / her." Why then did *Breathin'* generate, for Fred, the content signified by the first, much less physically demanding, much more conventionally lyric poem beginning "my father hurt-"?[2]

Asked in a 1987 interview with Lola Lemire Tostevin why he is preoccupied with "finding the father" when so many "women writers have tried to displace the authority of the father and restore the influence of their mothers," Fred Wah said he "really doesn't know except . . . my father died and my mother is still alive" (3). In an essay which confronts questions of father, origin, and language—"Which at first seems to be a going back for origins"—Fred Wah argues that while the "notion of 'origins'" may be the "imposition of a male point of view," he is really more interested in "the actualization of the writing than in the reasons for it" (379). Further, he argues, the "break-up of a dictionary definition into alternatives," the dissonance and fracture of so much women's writing, "may be indicative of strong need for alternatives . . . Men are at some of these same frontiers in writing, perhaps for different reasons" (379).

The "actualization of writing," the necessary connection between the body writing and the body of writing, is a connection Fred has insisted on since he learned it from his teacher and literary father, Charles Olson, who said, as early as 1950, that verse must "put into itself certain laws and possibilities of the breath, of the breathing of the man who writes as well as of his listenings" (526). Daphne Marlatt, also a student of Olson's, extends his metaphors to include the bodies of women who write: "like the mother's body, language is larger than us and carries us along with it. if we are poets we spend our lives discovering not just what *we* have to say but what language is saying as it carries us with it. in etymology we discover a history of verbal relations (a family tree, if you will) that has preceded us and given us the world we live in. the given, the immediately presented, as a birth—a given name a given world" ("musing with mothertongue," *Touch to My Tongue*: 46-7).[3]

Wah's *Breathin' My Name with a Sigh* offers its readers a "given name a given world," as perceived by a lost child seeking mother and father:

> for
> I forgot
> memory
> remembered
> signs/words
> a genetics
> carrying the deer
> dance carrying
> the tree
> & other forms around
> something else thinking too
> from somewhere in my body
> carrying
> the other for
> ever and ever.

But the world in which the child, this "left over thing," tells a life story, a body story, a bio-graph, is one in which the father, the man who breathes, dies; while the mother, the body of language, is always alive: "languaging a feeling inside the surface feeling out the breadth of my mother/father things I am also left over thing put together calendar's event world the children's things and wind last night/biography."

Breathin' My Name with a Sigh offers a family romance involving the child and both father and mother, which recent thinking in feminist psychoanalysis can give us a way to understand. Jessica Benjamin argues that "psychoanalysis has shifted its focus since Freud, aiming its sights toward ever earlier phases of development in childhood and infancy" (11). The effect of this reorientation, she says, is to give the mother-child relationship an importance in psychic development "rivaling the oedipal triangle," causing a shift from "oedipal to preoedipal—that is, from father to mother" (11). Attention to the mother-child bond leads to a theory of self constructed on the basis of shared recognition between (m)other and child: "to experience recognition in the fullest, most joyful way, entails the paradox that 'you' who are 'mine' are also different, new, outside of me" (15). Compare, for example, the son's complete identification with his father in the "my father hurt-" poem ("that look on his face / appears now on mine") and the joyful, sensual difference his relation with his mother makes in "mother / somewhere" ("remember you flying over me mommy / outside a moist loss").

To identify with the mother is to "touch & float," to be both next to and out of her body. As a result, "mother" is not a "content" in the same way "father" is at all. The oedipal son, "who cannot bear his wish to unseat his father, because its fulfillment would deprive him of the authority who protects him, the ideal that gives him life" (Benjamin, 142), is more often and more recognizably figured in *Breathin'* because the son's wish has been fulfilled, his father is dead: "Father, when you died you left me / with my own death . . . I know now / I'd better find that double edge between you / and your father so that the synchronous axe / keeps splitting whatever this is the weight of / I'm left holding." The poems in *Breathin'* try to hold, in language, "whatever this is," to participate in both the oedipal and the pre-oedipal struggles, move toward both father and mother, knowing we carry "the other for / ever / and ever." In so doing they come to a new knowledge—very much like that identified by Benjamin—that identification can be accomplished in relation to both father and mother:

> my breathing as I look at your picture of a line which gives way at the centre and falls into the valley breathless then below the surface you've worked on I hold the cool silence and fullness there especially the emptiness the motion of falling into the middle outside it is the gulley that runs from the orchard down past the house in your picture my breath then my mind finds solace.

The words "Father, when you died you left me / with my own death" can be read to suggest that when "fatherness" becomes ambiguous—the "sister" is figured as having "'got' his eyes . . . you [sister] are left / with your own fatherness"— the child's process of identification involves more than the oedipal threat of castration.

In the following poem, the child moves to a place of water—the mother's place, of wa(h)t(h)er—to celebrate his difference, his fatherness, without fear:

> breathing in the water so much a breath
> to make a time times so simple rhythm
> early snow mountain peaks body hair finger-
> nails the death past 54 measure know
> nothing rotten smell histories it like
> layers of froth the scarlet letters parts
> of our genitals my breathing in the pool
> lengths stretched father's parts out.

These poems seek a way to breathe, and so to live in language, otherwise. As Jeff Derksen says of Wah's poetry in a quite different context, his is "A projective verse that has reciprocity—what is projected from the subject is also projected back. That is the value of movement" (164).

For example, the "Sigh" of the title signifies a reciprocal and paradoxical naming of oneself in recognition of both the burden of one's given name and the relief of knowing who one is, knowing what—and that—one is called something by someone. This ambivalent "sigh" signifies both resignation and re-signing, even re-signature. Wah both signs and resigns his name, on both the cover and the third last page of the book, by giving us a new mark, the upside-down "e," the "schwa," the "uh" sound which is "the phonetic symbol for the unstressed mid-central vowel . . . the vowel of Fred Wah's name" (Scobie, 151). The voice breathing his name with a sigh, figured as "the cry of a newborn baby: wahhhhh!" (Scobie, 151), finds a way to breathe by assuming and yet resisting the name of the father, the burden of his name, "him / thinking me / ahead of him/ myself." As a result, the voices constructed in these poems do not invoke the singular authority of a man speaking to you; these poems breathe with you.

Listen to the tentative, questioning, uncertain voice of the speaker constructed in these lines: "It's April and I feel the water running / but I don't know how to count on it / or where." Or, in another poem, "What else was there outside in the dark but night / which has always been and is an answer / trick presence to the daylight you've seen / every day you'd think, eh?, and not / simply everything over and over again forever and ever, right?" In the absence of the father, binary oppositions like outside and inside, dark and light, day and night are, like language, like mother, "trick presences(s)." What "you've seen / every day" is not "what you'd think, eh?" In the absence of the father, the son tries to assert, in a poem whose typography suggests both a chant and a scream, his lineage: "IN THE ARMS OF MY FATHER / SKY / IN THE ARMS / MOTHER NIGHT / IN THE ARMS OF US ALL / OF US OUR HOLDING / IN THE ARMS / SHE WALKS / HE HOLDS / MY FAMILY."

Consider again the "my father hurt-" and "mother / somewhere" poems. The father is "hurt- / ing at the table / sitting hurting," the mother is "somewhere . . . flying over me." The poem addressed to the father is written from the position of a child who is also an adult, who watches and also remembers watching his father hurting "deep inside," who finds on his face the "look on his [father's] face." In the poem addressed to the mother, a much younger, less articulate child speaks and questions: "[do you] remember you flying over me mommy [?]" But she is "flying over" a "me" who remains part of her, in the "heart / core," "corrine," inside her core so fully, that "outside" is "a moist loss." The linguistic slippages—from "caress" to "close" to "careless"; from "remember" to "remove her" to "because of her"—also suggest the pre-oedipal, semiotic space of the mother. The poem moves from the word "mother" to the words "mutter / mummy / maybe" suggesting, both semantically and linguistically, what Benjamin calls an "open space": "in these moments . . . the infant can explore himself and his surroundings, can experience his own initiative and distinguish it from the other's action" (41). This poem, which repeats obsessively the word "her"— a word both signifying and included in the word "mother"—suggests the child playing with words can explore himself and his place while he is in her place, or rather "our place": "Can't get it / or at least it's hard to hold on / until I think of her return, look / up behind our place into the field." In the columnal movement of the poem and the river-like, even vaginal, space it occupies on the page, the reader too seeks meaning in a process which is very much "touch & float."

Writing is a way of using the body—the mother's body, language—in *Breathin' My Name with a Sigh*: "love her / pleases her / caress / close." The world constructed here can be known only through thinking, writing, and touching "it": "I still have a name 'breathin' / it with a sigh.'" The body reading—Fred's, yours, mine—embodies the breath assumed both because of and without the father. In reading, we participate in this mothering, we reciprocate, we breathe the poems with sighs of pleasure and angst. In reading we say and sigh "wahh, wahh," participate in the family/name and the threat of silence, of both breathing out and being out of breath. The others against and for whom the poems speak and are spoken also breathe the name of the poet—Wah—with sighs (and signs) of relief, resignation, passion because, for this tentative male voice, "I" can speak only when "you" breathe my name: "thru the mist of a memory, you wander back to me, breathing my name with a sigh" (from the 1930s pop song "Deep Purple").

As Nicole Brossard's *These Our Mothers* did for the notion of the patriarchal mother, *Breathin' My Name with a Sigh* does for "the [patriarchal] father"; it exposes the oppressive limitations of that role. The poet obsessed with thinking of and through his father's death is nonetheless restless with the limits of his position as father: "that look on his face / appears now on mine / my children / my food / their food / my father / their father / me mine / *the* father." Figured as hurt, inaccessible and silent, the father is both who he is and who he is against: a fatherness ahead of, behind, and in him. The father is (in) breath, speaks the speaker, and yet the son inevitably breathes his father's name as he breathes his own name with a sigh. If the father is the breath in the name he may indeed be "nothing": "catch up to the breath / breathing somewhere / the air // as it comes out ahead of me / wah^h, wah^h." The one speaking is radically othered in and by a sigh/sign which is also a cry—wahh wahh. Yet "Wah" is, these poems insist, only a word, dependent on and made aural by breath. Like all language, it is apart from the one who speaks it. As the poet breathes his name with a sigh he acknowledges the limits of the concept of the father which he desires, resists, and finally celebrates his failure to appropriate: "I would just breathe / but away from me. Out. Give it all / back."

In an article on men as comrades in the feminist movement, bell hooks speaks of the anger, pain, and uncertainty many men feel in patriarchy: "Men are not exploited or oppressed by sexism, but there are ways in which they suffer as a result of it. This suffering should not be ignored" (72).[4] More importantly, "we need to hear" from men who are "striving to create different and oppositional visions of masculinity. Their experience is the concrete practice that may influence others" (*Yearning*, 77). Wah's long poem *Breathin' My Name with a Sigh* documents and asks its readers to participate in such an experience of otherness within and against conventional masculinity. The 32 lines that begin

> Breathe dust like you breathe wind so strong in your face little grains of dirt which pock around the cheeks peddling against a dust-storm coming down a street to the edge of town in Swift Current Saskatchewan or the air walked out into the fields across from Granny Erickson's house . . .

and end (without a syntactic pause)

> later in the summer play anywhere someone's coal bin settled into my nose and the oilyness of it on the skin I rode down the hill outside the house on Victoria on a coal shovel I hit a rock and had the wind knocked out of me I was dying and couldn't even tell anyone as they walked by but stood and waved my arms and flailed the message without air.

enact the male child's experience of breathlessness, of being out of breath, of wanting and being unable to breathe and so to speak. The reader who performs this text experiences the difficulty breathing that the poem speaks of. "The father" may be so far inside that the one speaking flails "the message without air" (and, as Stephen Scobie points out, without *heir* [150]). But by breathing him out, breathing his name with a sigh, writing and reading the poem, entering into a relation of reciprocity, the father can be renewed, reconfigured, regrown, may even become his own mother: "next spring / I'll go out to the garden / and with a stick / plant myself / and eat me in the fall." This book constructs poems which are easier to breathe in: "Poem lightens the lungs Diana says meaning / birds which fly away into the air disappear / words end up relief of carrier message also."

This relationship, based on reciprocity between child and parent, body and language, text and reader, is particularly evident in Wah's love poems, included in his latest book, *So Far* (1991). At its Calgary launch, Fred said that his love poems are for his family, Pauline Butling, Jenefer and Erika Wah, all of whom have been so often textualized in his work that Fred considers them "a unit of composition."[5] By constructing a love poem that addresses a group, Wah's family romance offers a complex notion of the bonds of love. In "Five Ones for P.," the loved one is, like breath, like the desired but absent mother/father, like the name "Wah," "out there." But the "you" is also right there, "More the body, everything / you've touched / tongue and shoulder / shoulders / dancing too." The "I" can "keep watching" her "out there" and be "out there with you." "You" are both what "I know," and what "I keep watching." Out there is here. The breath is breathed. You are mine but also different, new, outside of me (Benjamin, 15).

Near the end of the launch, Fred warned that the poems he had read so far were "uncommonly sensical" ("or did I say sensitive," he said when I asked his permission to cite those words), and launched into some of the less accessible, less lyrical, more opaque pieces for which, since *Music at the Heart of Thinking*, he has become notorious. More like *So Far* than like *Music at the Heart of Thinking*, *Breathin' My Name with a Sigh* is an uncommonly sensical book in that it challenges common sense in its refiguring of the father's name. Like Brossard, Fred makes "use of writing in order to rediscover the obvious" (149). In doing so, the poems investigate the problem of configuring identity on the basis of the oedipal relation alone. Instead, the book positions the male speaker between two marks of signature which both are and are not the father's, which may, in fact, be signs of the mother's comfort which he has made his own. The schwa on the cover and the schwa on the third last page of the book can be read as soothing words from the writing, embodied poet—Fred—to himself as text: shh-wah, shh-wah.[6] No longer signified simply as disembodied language, mother is part of the one who speaks. No longer dead, father is named by and signified through the breath it takes to say "Wah." In the comfort found in the "mother/father things I am also" is the breath, the music, the son(g), of the last poem, which follows the last schwa of the book:

> I swing
> and talk back
> sound that's right
>
> I take the breath
> through throat
> and hold it
> in the stomach
> hit the fingers
> on the horn
>
> blow the jazz
> that's where it goes.

Notes

[1] For the sake of my argument, I am deliberately attaching different signifieds to the signifiers "Fred Wah," "Fred," and "Wah" in order to identify the differences within Fred Wah, including, but not limited to, the following: the words "Fred Wah" which appear on book covers and in interviews with and in articles by and about him; the word "Fred" which signifies my friend and colleague at the University of Calgary; and the word "Wah" which figures in *Breathin'*. It is interesting that although Fred's father's name was also Fred Wah, he does not play at all with the name "Fred." He laughed when I suggested he try some kind of feminizing of Fred as text in the word "(f.)read."

[2] Fred Wah speaks of the relation between *Breathin' My Name with a Sigh* and *Waiting for Saskatchewan* in "A Prefatory Note" to *Waiting for Saskatchewan*: "Some of the poems from *Breathin' My Name with a Sigh* . . . are included in this book to give some shape to the range of forms a particular content ("father") from that long poem has generated." A shorter, continuing version of *Breathin'*—with some of the same poems,

some new ones, some revised ones—is Part 1 of *Waiting for Saskatchewan*. *Breathin'*
My Name with a Sigh also appeared in two Coach House Press Manuscript Editions
(1978, 1979). The Talonbooks edition, 1981, is referred to as a "third draft." All references
to *Breathin' My Name with a Sigh* in this paper are to the (frustratingly) unpaginated
Talonbooks edition.

³Fred Wah's admiration for Marlatt is well known. See, for example, his introduction
to Marlatt's selected writing, *Net Work*, in which he describes her as "one of the most
acute writing intelligences of her generation" (7).

⁴hooks is speaking particularly of Black men but analyzing the place of men of other
racial origins, including White men and men, like Fred Wah, of mixed racial origin,
can also be useful to feminist thinking.

⁵Conversation with Fred, 18 Nov. 1991. Used with permission. I thank both Fred and
Pauline Butling for many useful conversations about the issues *Breathin'* raises.

⁶Stephen Scobie agrees with Ann Mandel when she writes, in a review, that "fortunately
for readers, the poet has not taken this (shh-wah) as a sign for silence" (Scobie, 151;
Mandel, 152). Although I read the signifier "schwa" differently, it was Scobie's work
that drew the shh-wah of schwa to my attention.

Works Cited

Banting, Pamela. "Fred Wah: poet as theor(h)et(or)ician." *Open Letter*, 6th Series, 7
(Spring 1987): 5-20.

Benjamin, Jessica. *The Bonds of Love: Psychoanalysis, Feminism, and the Problem of
Domination.* New York: Pantheon Books, 1988.

Brossard, Nicole. *The Aerial Letter.* Marlene Wildeman, trans. Toronto: Women's Press,
1988.

Derksen, Jeff. "Torquing Time [Fred Wah]." *West Coast Line* 25.1 (Spring 1991): 161-
5.

Goddard, John. "Interview: Fred Wah." *Books in Canada* 15.7 (Oct. 1986): 40-1.

hooks, bell. *Feminist Theory: from margin to center.* Boston: South End Press, 1984.

———. *Yearning: Race, Gender, and Cultural Politics.* Toronto: Between the Lines, 1990.

Mandel, Ann. "Free Subject." *Canadian Literature*, 101 (Summer 1984): 149-53.

Marlatt, Daphne. *Net Work: Selected Writing.* Fred Wah, ed. Vancouver: Talonbooks,
1980.

———. *Touch to My Tongue.* Edmonton: Longspoon, 1984.

Olson, Charles. "Projective Verse." In *20th-Century Poetry & Poetics*, 2nd edn. Gary
Geddes, ed. Toronto: Oxford, 1973: 526-38.

Scobie, Stephen. *Signature Event Cantext.* Edmonton: NeWest, 1989.

Thesen, Sharon, ed. *The New Long Poem Anthology.* Toronto: Coach House Press,
1991.

Tostevin, Lola Lemire. "Don't Sit Around Language: An Interview with Fred Wah."
Poetry Canada Review 9.1 (1987): 3-5.

Wah, Fred. *Breathin' My Name with a Sigh.* Vancouver: Talonbooks, 1981. Unpaginated.

———. "Introduction." Marlatt, *Net Work*, 7-21.

————. "Making Strange Poetics." *Open Letter* 6th Series, 2-3 (Summer-Fall 1985): 213-30.

————. "Making Stranger Poetics: A Canadian Poetics (Plural) Inventory." Unpublished typescript. 18 pages.

————. *Music at the Heart of Thinking.* Red Deer: Red Deer College Press, 1987.

————. *So Far.* Vancouver: Talonbooks, 1991.

————. *Waiting for Saskatchewan.* Winnipeg: Turnstone, 1985.

————. "Which at first seems to be a going back for origins: Notes on a reading of some American women writers." *A Mazing Space: Writing Canadian Women Writing.* Shirley Neuman and Smaro Kamboureli, eds. Edmonton: Longspoon/NeWest, 1986: 374-9.

Meaning in Numbers: Wilfred Watson's *Gramsci x 3*

Lorraine Weir

"Number grid poetry" Wilfred Watson labels his verse form, describing it on the flyleaf to *I begin with counting* in comparison with "traditional metrical verse" which

> counts syllables. Number grid verse counts words. The structural unit of traditional metrical verse is the "line." The structural unit of number grid verse is the "number grid." The number grid, like the line of traditional verse, can be varied endlessly.[1]

To take from that book an example of the basic form, the first nine lines of "after the snow fell" are as follows:

november	1	twenty-sixth			
nineteenth	2	seventy-seven			
at	3	0937			
			hours	4	after
the	5	night's			
			snow	6	absalom
trapped	7	in			
			the	8	choke

9   cherry

Here syntax is regular and the single grid is constructed for one voice, a lyrical haiku with a rather Cubist appearance. The grid arranges seventeen words on a framework which uses the numbers one to nine and invokes Watson's compositional rules stipulating the basic grid function, the attribution of two "slots" to each numeral except nine, which has only one "slot," and the positioning of a word in each "slot." In addition, Watson specifies the repetition of as many grids as desired to compose a poem, and includes the possibility of constructing poems for up to five voices by using grids in corresponding numbers.

Several years later, in *Gramsci x 3*, Watson experiments with more complex grids, raising more interesting possibilities. For example, in the Epilogue to "Gramsci 1," Tatiana Schucht, Gramsci's sister-in-law, reads a letter which she has written to his nieces, Edmea and Teresina:

Tatiana,	1	to
and	2	Teresina
Edmea,	3	sad
Your	4	greetings.
uncle	5	Nino
died	6	Gramsci
a	7	month
today,	8	ago

9   May   (73)

Syntax has opened here and a verbal/visual counterpoint has been introduced, producing clusters of alternating three- and two-line groups on either side of the numbers as the vertical grid pattern of "after the snow fell" mutates into the threefold horizontal cluster

>   Tatiana
>   and
>   Edmea

set contrapuntally against the twofold clusters

>   Your
>   uncle

and

>   to
>   Teresina

and

>   sad
>   greetings

and

>   Nino
>   Gramsci

with a new variation

	a	7	month
today	8	ago

as the eye is directed to contend with differently disposed information.

In the next nine-line grid of the Epilogue, Watson shifts into another grid form in which regular syntax is split in alternating lines into a kind of forward and reverse formation:

	the	1	twenty-seventh.
	release	2	His
	from	3	prison
	a	4	came
	few	5	days
	he	6	before
	died,	7	but
	authorities	8	the
9	hadn't		(73)

Several grids later, this formation permits a principle of diagonal opposition to be introduced:

	In	1	January
	he	2	1927
	was	3	transferred (74)

However, not until the last act, "Gramsci 3," will we encounter another version of this visual counterpoint, this time a more emphatically aural variation. For example:

At
station
eleven
we
turn
back
to   the
station   stripping
ten   off
of
the
clothes
they   of
parted
his
garments
among
themselves   (153)

and so on, configuring the death of Gramsci in terms of the Stations of the Cross, emblem in Roman Catholic ritual of the stages of the death of Christ. Set against the theme from Bach's Goldberg Variations, transcribed for solo violin, this contrapuntal recitativo begs forgiveness for the cruelties of Gramsci's torture and continues the movement back from the Crucifixion to the beginning of Christ's Passion, Gramsci's agony, which concludes the play:

Crucifixus
sub
pontio
pilato
pilato   (178)

What construction might we put on this device of "counting," on this "returning to square one" or "analog methodology"?[2] In Watson's Catholic terms, the root meaning of "square one" is Christ's condemnation by Pontius Pilate, the founding trope of the Christian deconstruction of meaning in the world. For Watson, as for the essentially Scholastic tradition out of which he writes, the "harmonic forms" of the world—imaged in "re spences bridge" (*I begin with counting*) in terms of the meeting of two rivers—echo the divine harmonics of absolute unity. But "words are / the names / of things / and things / are items / of the / meaninglessness everywhere."[3] How, then, may "analog methodology" construct verbal meaning in the face of the world's chaos? In the words of Watson's beautiful "Canticle of Darkness," how may one see "the things of the world drop their skins" (Watson, *Friday's Child*, 3). In Kwakiutl legend, this is the moment when the animals reveal their human shape, proclaiming their oneness with all life forms. Square one is (in Barthes' phrase) the "writing degree zero" of absolute meaning, constructed not out of material substance but, rather, out of the transcendental signified represented by that first analog.

Why numbers? Why the use of recitativo, canticle, improvisation—the repeated invocation of the performative, of number grids as performance structures? Like Louis Zukofsky, like John Cage, Watson takes musical form as an icon of the order of the world, but where, for Zukofsky, it seems possible to use words to speak the world's order, for Watson, only numbers will finally do, and numbers resonant, spoken by actors whose task is to sing the world's possible order out of its pain and chaos, and thereby make that order manifest. Number grids are structures of "musemathematical"[4] meaning, and Watson's number grid poems—like the medieval Abbot Suger's architectural plans[5]—are numerical expressions of God's mathematics, the structures of things without their skins. In manipulating the complex grids and verse forms of *Gramsci x 3*, Watson seeks to strip words of their skins, to find in a system of "musemathematics" an analog to the paradigm of Gramsci's suffering construed in terms of the Stations of the Cross, the Christian trope of the word in the world, of meaning in pain.

Notes

[1] On Watson's number grids, see also Scobie.
[2] All quotations from the unpaginated *I begin with counting*.
[3] From "the theatre of the absurd of adrienne clarkson," in *I begin with counting*.
[4] James Joyce's term, "Musemathematics," in *Ulysses* (228).
[5] See Gellrich. See also Weir on the medieval notion of *musica speculativa* and its relation to Joyce and Zukofsky. Watson is working explicitly within this medieval/Modern mode, an important aspect of his collaboration with Scholastic Joycean Marshall McLuhan. For a brilliant example of Watson's *musica speculativa*, see the poem from *Mass on cowback* entitled "re mario prizek and glenn gould's examination of the music of the 1930s," reprinted in Watson's *Poems: collected / unpublished / new* (301-2).

Works Cited

Barthes, Roland. *Writing Degree Zero*. Annette Lavers and Colin Smith, trans. London: Cape, 1967.
Gellrich, Jesse. *The Idea of the Book in the Middle Ages*. Ithaca: Cornell Univ. Press, 1985.
Joyce, James. *Ulysses*. Hans Walter Gabler, Wolfhard Steppe, Claus Melchior, eds. Harmondsworth: Penguin, 1986.
Scobie, Stephen. "Love in the Burning City: The Poetry of Wilfred Watson," *Essays*

on Canadian Writing 18/19 (Summer/Fall 1980): 293-5.

Watson, Wilfred. *Friday's Child.* London: Faber, 1955.

———. *I begin with counting.* Edmonton: NeWest, 1978.

———. *Gramsci x 3.* Edmonton: Longspoon, 1983. Unpaginated.

———. *Poems: Collected / Unpublished / New.* Edmonton: Longspoon/NeWest, 1986.

Weir, Lorraine. *Writing Joyce—A Semiotics of the Joyce System.* Bloomington: Indiana Univ. Press, 1989.

Webb's Book of Revelation:
Lifting the Lid Off "'Krakatoa' and 'Spiritual Storm'"

John F. Hulcoop

"The proper response to a poem is another poem." (Webb, *Hanging Fire*)

"Someday I will explode and you will explode in another damned Apocalypse": Phyllis Webb's own prophetic words, first published in 1973 (72). "I cannot surprise you. Not with the blue jay's / return. Not with the velvet yellow of pansyface, / not with my held-back fire. Apocalypse. Every- / thing predictable in the book" (*HF*, 15). Fulfilling the prophecy or prediction of seventeen years earlier, these lines come from the second and, I think, key poem—"'Krakatoa' and 'Spiritual Storm'"—in Webb's latest volume of poetry. Its title, *Hanging Fire*, has as one of its meanings "held-back fire": originally used in relation to fire-arms, "to hang fire" meant "to delay communicating fire through the vent to the gunpowder"; figuratively, it means "to hesitate or be slow to act." In a poem dedicated to Sharon Thesen, the poet speaks of her sister-poet's attending to "possible poems / feared and held off for a moment" (*HF*, 56). But, taken even more literally, hanging fire presents itself as an activity parallel to hanging wallpaper or curtains. After invoking a "crisis of lambency" and the terrible fire-bombing of Dresden (in World War II), the poet describes a "curtain of fire" leaping and hanging in the air (*HF*, 35); and "'Krakatoa' . . .", in which "Apocalypse" follows the poet's "held-back fire," ends in a concatenation of images which not only structures this poem but also sets the scene for the entire volume, announcing the apocalyptic nature of both poem and volume: "The spring of the mouse- / trap sprung, we are caught—thus and so—in / this pose, shadowed beyond doubt. Fire hanging / back for a more effective, filmic test-site, / for desert bloom" (16).

Bikini, a western Pacific atoll, and the 1954 test-site for the first American hydrogen bomb, was perhaps more "filmic" than either Nagasaki or Hiroshima, where victims close to the explosion's hypocenter were "caught . . . in / this pose, shadowed beyond doubt," their images burned into stone at the moment of revelation. In its geophysical configuration, the Pacific atoll certainly resembles the prehistoric crater ring out of which rose the volcanic island of Krakatoa before it blew itself apart in 1883. Most filmed of all atomic test-sites, however, is that in Nevada where, throughout the fifties and sixties, the desert "bloomed" with the radiant, multi-coloured fire-ball and mushroom cloud, two symbols that spring immediately into the mind of anyone in the second half of the twentieth century who envisions apocalypse. Though Webb's first apocalyptic poem, "Rhetoric for New Years" (*EYRE*, 48), contains no allusion to the bomb, it ends with the image of the world-as-stage "that shifts like an island in the sea, uneasily, / like the age." *The Sea Is Also a Garden* contains two poems that clearly confront the eschatological consequences of the nuclear holocaust: "Countered" ("our participating marrow / clicks with destroying dust" as the "dustbowl earth completes its nothingness") and "Bomb Shelter" ("saint and man and god are done"). Another poem, "Galaxy," centres on a "curious bright tragedy" that "suddenly burst[s] . . . / taking the night into a system total, luminous, / oracular": "a crystal fire flung from . . . / sun, universe, shaking there, shining" (11)— images that might be said to reflect the advent of the atomic age. Until the publication of *Wilson's Bowl* (1980), critics tended to think of Webb as Sibylline (perhaps Cassandra-like), inscribing messages of doom in enigmatic fashion on small, lyric leaves. In the retrospective light of *Hanging Fire*, however, perhaps we should reconsider her minimalist *Naked Poems* as an attempt to shield herself against various kinds of fall-out: "doubled up I feel / small like these poems / the area of attack / is diminished" (n.p.). The movement, in *Wilson's Bowl*, is through "Poems of Failure," "Portraits," with its "dominance of male figures" (figures of power), "Wars and Crimes of War," to the dark sounds of "*Duende*" which ends with the apocalyptic "*Tremendum*," a word that rocks even the final section of the Requiem Mass: "*Libera me, Domine, de morte aeterna, in die illa tremenda . . . Dies irae, dies illa, calamitatis et miseriae.*" In *Water and Light* Webb begins by quoting Ghalib, "*the violence of the world is all around me*"; she ends with the ominous Tower of Pisa, a symbol for "the whole culture leaning" ([5], 58).

In a monograph written in 1986 (but not published until 1990), I suggested that, if Webb were indeed to "explode . . . in another damned Apocalypse," it would be one that counterbalanced "Francis Ford Coppola's Conrad-inspired, Wagner-coloured 1979 movie-monument to the machismo mystique" (*Phyllis Webb*, 47). And such, of course, is the nature of Webb's *Hanging Fire*. But before explaining how and why it is, and what part the Krakatoa poem plays in it, the inevitable question poses itself: What is apocalypse? The most useful answer to this huge and rather intimidating question is to be found, not by beginning at the beginning, with a list of authentic texts which exhibit all and only those characteristics specified by the great host of theological scholars and scriptural exegetes who have surveyed the field from China to Peru; or with a summary of all the debates on what does and does not constitute the genuinely apocalyptic. Because apocalypse and eschatology generally go hand in bony hand, the most appropriate place to look is, obviously, *the end*, i.e., the point closest to us in time and space: in this case, with the work of a Canadian literary critic who also made the Bible subject of a life-long study.

"The Greek word for revelation, *apocalypsis*, has the metaphorical sense of uncovering or taking the lid off" (*Code*, 135). So says Northrop Frye, whose metaphor not only provides the title of this essay but also points directly to its subject, "'Krakatoa' . . .," in which the cataclysmic volcanic eruption is identified with an "all-paroxysmal / sexual storm, lid blown off" (14). Like *apocalypsis*, *aletheia*, the Greek word for truth, begins (as Frye notes) with "a negative particle which suggests that truth was originally thought of as also a kind of unveiling, a removal of the curtain of forgetfulness"—another metaphor that reconnects us to Webb's "curtain of fire" which "drops over the overview, / glass-like substances, 'fragments of quartz'. // They leap and hang in the air" (*HF*, 35). "In more modern times," Frye continues, "what blocks truth and the emerging revelation is not forgetting but repression. . . . Man creates what he calls history as a screen to conceal the workings of the apocalypse from himself" (135-6).

Since apocalypse envisions an end to time, transforming *chronos* into *kairos* (Kermode, 46-9), history—the succession of human lives and events through time—figures largely in most apocalyptic texts, in most studies of such texts, and in scholars' attempts to define the term, whether it be apocalypse as a particular kind of religious phenomenon (Schmitals, 30), as a literary genre, or as an attitude to history (see Collins, 88; Frye 1982, 135-6; Kermode, 9-15 and passim; Koch, 28-32; Kreuziger, 144-8; Rowland, 13). Daniel, eponymous and probably pseudonymous hero of one of the three or four texts accepted by the majority of critics as genuinely apocalyptic (the others being Revelation, the Ethiopic Enoch, and IV Esdras: see McGinn, 6; Rowland, 11-17), "is fascinated with contemporary politics and the course of history in the post Hellenistic period" (McGinn, 9). Phyllis Webb's Daniel (*WL*, 33-42) lives "now and in time past" (history); is "Haunted by numbers" (which Daniel and his commentators interpret in terms of historical days, weeks, months, and years; see McGinn, 9); and even his dreams are of "politics, wars and rumours." *Hanging Fire* also reveals an apocalyptic preoccupation with history in all its forms: the life of an individual ("'Anaximander' 610-546? BC"); the eons of geological time ("'Seeking Shape. Seeking Meaning'"); ancient history ("Messages") and modern ("Darwin's tangled bank" and Freud's "Civilisation and its discontents" in "'There *Are* the Poems'"); social revolutions that have become historical landmarks—in Russia ("'Lenin Skating,'" "'Mother Russia,'" "'To the Finland Station'"), in India ("'The Salt Tax'" and "The end of the Raj" in "'Cornflowers & Saffron Robes . . .'"), in China ("Flashes of Tienanmen" in "'To the Finland Station'"); and, of course, the natural catastrophe, Krakatoa: "So be it. So it was: May 20, 1883, 'paroxysmal' / blast August 26, 'climax' eruption August 27, / 10 a.m" (15).

Natural disturbances (earthquakes, volcanic eruptions, etc.) constitute the first of ten phases distinguished in R.W.B. Lewis' outline of the apocalyptic process (196-7). Such disturbances symbolize the "spiritual turmoil" (Webb's "sexual storm" which is "*spiritual* for him" [14]) listed second in Koch's survey of the primary indicators of apocalyptic texts (28). Physical, psychological, or spiritual in nature, the storm clearly marks a crisis, internal and/or external (Kreuziger, 140, 144); and almost all commentators see crisis of some sort as precipitating apocalypse. Early historians may have exaggerated "the 'Terrors'" of the year 1000 A.D., "most famous of all predicted Ends," but it undoubtedly "produced a characteristic apocalypse-crisis," according to Kermode, who calls "crisis, decadence, and empire" apocalyptic "doctrines" and "types" (9, 14, 29). John May's three-part paradigm of "traditional or classical apocalypse"—"judgment, catastrophe, and renewal" (24)—parallels, formally at least, "the divinely predetermined pattern of crisis-judgement-vindication" which, for McGinn, is the "second indispensable characteristic of apocalyptic eschatology" (the first being "a deterministic view of history" [10]).

Turning from cosmically proportioned apocalypse back to the second poem in *Hanging Fire*, the tenth volume in Webb's forty-year career as a poet, we may observe that what has been said of the former is also true of the latter: apocalypse recapitulates, resumes "the whole structure" of what has gone before, making the End consonant with beginnings and middles, enabling humanity to see "history in a totally new light" (Ketterer, 7; Kermode, 6-7; Rowland, 13. See also Frye 1982, 79, 135). As I have tried to show elsewhere (*Phyllis Webb*, 30-50), Webb's history as creator falls into several distinct phases. In her first three volumes she is learning her craft, absorbing traditions and, at the same time, struggling to resist and break free from what to her was bound to appear a decadent male influence. *Naked Poems* represents the first (and perhaps major) crisis in Webb's career. Bloom believes that poets win through "the crisis of adolescence without totally decentering" and manage to confront "the Primal Scene of Instruction" with "a curious detachment towards crisis" (*Map*, 47-53); Bloom's belief Webb seemingly confirms by confessing, "I admire [*Naked Poems*] as if someone else had written them. Somehow they are apart from me" (*How Do I*, 70). Ironically, though no volume of new poems appeared until 1980, the phase following *Naked Poems*, which begins with the first *Selected Poems*, climaxes with *Wilson's Bowl*, and ends with the second selected poems (*The Vision Tree*, 1982), is in a sense Webb's empire period, the millennium in which her poetic identity is indelibly established, her "presence as a touchstone of true, good writing in Canada" is acknowledged by the community of Canadian poets (Hulcoop 1990, 9, 54); thus, she herself becomes a precursor, an instructor in the primal scenes of younger poets. Such prominence (particularly for a poet of her temperament) almost inevitably precipitated another crisis, substantive and formal. Late in 1981, she began writing ghazals—really anti-ghazals—which are, as she says, "disobedient to the inherent conventionality of the form" (quoted in Hulcoop 1986, 157). The first crisis volume marks a shift from past, represented by publicly established tradition, to present, a time of private experimentation; a contraction of larger outer to minimalist inner. The pendulum swings back in *Wilson's Bowl* from the subjective experience of *Naked Poems* to the social world of "the common good." *Water and Light*, the second crisis volume, repeats the shift from outer to inner, though this swing is neither so extreme nor so unqualified as the first.

At the centre of *Water and Light* stands "I Daniel," a poem dedicated to Timothy Findley (whose own version of apocalypse, *Famous Last Words*, was published in 1981), and directly inspired by one of the great apocalyptic texts in the Bible. Looking ahead to *Hanging Fire*, "I Daniel" illustrates quite splendidly a point made by Bernard McGinn:

Another important characteristic of apocalypses is the "bookish" nature of the re-
vealed message. In several cases the revelation was originally contained in written
tablets or books; in others the seer's obligation to write the message down is noted
[see "I Daniel," #3]. Apocalypticism, in J.Z. Smith's apt phrase, is a "scribal phe-
nomenon" insofar as the message revealed is to be communicated to its potential
audience primarily through the written rather than the spoken word. (5; Smith, 154)

Here McGinn echoes Collins who "argues that a whole new understanding of
revelation (as interpretation) is signified by the literary nature of apocalyptic,
especially insofar as revelation is given in cryptic forms: dreams, visions, mys-
terious writings. 'The reception of revelation calls not for the obedience of the
prophet, but for the wisdom of an interpreter'" (Collins, 75, quoted in Kreuziger,
138. See also Hulcoop 1985, 367).

Certainly Webb's *Hanging Fire* is "bookish" in its intertextuality. A baker's
dozen of Canadian poets are quoted or alluded to in one way or another; ref-
erences to eighteen other poets— from Homer, Sophocles, and Shakespeare
(*Hamlet, King Lear, Othello*, and *The Tempest*) to Edith Sitwell, Odysseas Elytis,
and Wallace Stevens, an important presence in "'Krakatoa' . . ."—imbricate
poem after poem. Fourteen prose writers (from Cervantes and Bunyan to Kenneth
Graham and Kundera), plus playwrights (Beckett, Max Frisch), philosophers
(Anaximander, Descartes, Sartre), politicians (Gandhi, Lenin, Mao Tse Tung),
psychologists (Freud, Jung), physicists, anthropologists, and literary critics all
make appearances in sundry guises; so do composers as different as Verdi and
Philip Glass, Stravinsky and Johann Strauss, Leoncavallo and Paul Horn; and
visual artists Van Gogh, Matisse, Picasso, Douanier Rousseau, and Harunobu.
Egyptian, Greek, and North American Indian mythology, the Bible, fairy-tale
and folk-lore (including soap-opera and other TV-lore), encyclopaedia, and dic-
tionary—"How the mind doth know / its own dictionary" (*HF*, 17)—all provide
grist for Webb's creative mill, which tends to grind much faster than God's
mills in Longfellow's view (*HF*, 29).

Webb's note on her poem-titles—mostly "'given' words, phrases, or sentences
that arrive unbidden in my head"—re-enforces the epigraph, taken from Daphne
Marlatt's "musing with mothertongue," which focuses attention on language even
before the reader reaches the table of "Contents": "in poetry . . . sound will
initiate thought by a process of association. words call each other up, evoke
each other, provoke each other, nudge each other into utterance" (*HF*, [6-7])—
poetic utterance, that is, which may or may not be spoken aloud but is, in
our own day and in the case of both Marlatt and Webb, written down, inscribed.
This literary act of writing down words as poem, prophecy, apocalypse, is what
compels the new understanding Collins refers to, of "revelation as interpretation."
"Apocalypse means revelation, and when art becomes apocalyptic, it reveals"
(Frye 1957, 125). But what? Frye offers a provocative half-answer: "it reveals
only on its own terms, and in its own forms; it does not describe or represent
a separate content of revelation." In other words, the poems are both form and
content in literary apocalypse. What they reveal is themselves—as a form of
revelation. The reader, in reading, in giving "voice" to the written word,

unconsciously assumes the multiple roles of Daniel. A "servant to powers /
that pass all understanding," he proclaims "I dream the dream, / I deliver its
coded message" (i.e., interpret); "The hand moved along the wall. / I was able
to read, that's all"; "I become the messenger" (*WL*, 35, 37, 39, 37).

Looked at as a whole, *Hanging Fire* has about it the familiarity of Freud's
uncanny, frightening because it is both strange (unknown) *and* familiar: "for
this uncanny is in reality nothing new or alien, but something which is familiar
and old-established in the mind and which has become alienated from it through
the process of repression" (340-1, 363-4), an explanation which returns us to
Frye's point that repression, rather than forgetfulness, is what "blocks truth and
the emerging revelation." The concept of *repression* (from Latin *re-primo*, *re-
pressum*, to keep back, curb, restrain, prevent from overflowing) also accounts
for Webb's richly suggestive volume-title. George Woodcock, reviewing *Hanging
Fire*, thinks "the title is not meant to be read in the sense of 'holding fire' (for
nothing of that kind goes on)" (35). That Woodcock is mistaken I shall later
suggest; but, even if he were right about this volume, it would still be true
to say that Webb has been hanging fire, holding back, repressing a great deal
(especially her anger) for a long time, a fact the Foreword to *Wilson's Bowl*
renders irrefutable. Speaking of the predominance of male figures in her "Por-
traits," she asserts that it signifies "the domination of a male power culture in
my educational and emotional formation so overpowering that I have . . . been
denied access to inspiration from the female figures of my intellectual life, my
heart, my imagination . . . the unwritten poems—are the real 'poems of failure'"
([9]).

Hanging Fire explodes with, gives vent to, these unwritten poems and, in
the last stanza of the last poem in the book, the real revelation occurs (the
pronoun "his" referring directly to Harunobu, the Japanese print-maker whose
entire *œuvre* has been called "a hymn consecrated exclusively to the beauty of
woman" [Winzinger, 5]; but indirectly "his" refers to the whole history of male-
dominated traditions, including the artistic, which have veiled, concealed, curbed,
repressed the honest image, the real person, the truth, *aletheia*, of which Frye
speaks):

> A woman emerges at last
> on the finest paper, cursing
> his quest for the line
> and this damned delicate fan
> carved in her hand
> to keep her forever cool
> factitious, apparently pleasing. (78)

Cool as in "on ice"; *factitious* in the sense of "designedly got up," artificial,
not natural; and only *apparently* pleasing. No wonder Webb excised (in *The
Vision Tree* version, 21-2) the parentheses that originally followed each stanza
in "The Colour of the Light" (*Trio*, n.p.): "(Oh who can tell the apparent from
the real?)"; "(And when is the apparent not real? / The public and the person
are inevitably / one and the same self)"; "(And who would cleave the apparent

from the real?)" Who, indeed, but the author of *Hanging Fire*? Part of what *Hanging Fire* reveals is precisely the difference between apparent and real.

In its own uncanny way, *Hanging Fire* repeats the three-part structures scholars have identified as characteristic of apocalypse. Section One, "Tour de Force," begins, and surely not by chance, with "'A Model of the Universe'"—decadent and hideously polluted (literally and metaphorically), a universe brought to the point of crisis "as transgenetic / engineering steers us to the / unity of all things" (13): the condition of mediocrity to which society is pressured to conform, as George Eliot foresees in *Middlemarch*, by the ever-expanding middle class (Hulcoop 1982); "the enormous mass of the undifferentiated" towards which Barthes' ex-nominating "*bourgeoisie as a joint-stock company*" gravitates (137-40). This model is shattered by the eruption of Krakatoa, literally "a tower of force," in the second poem of Section One. The poet's "held-back fire" explodes into "Apocalypse" (15). "'The Mind of the Poet'" is a microcosm in which the revelatory events of the larger world are made manifest as poems, the poet's mind revealing, as it must, "on its own terms and in its own forms" (see Frye, above):

> Slippages, repeat performance, soundings profounder as down we go for the third time through green waters, pearl diving, operatic; or dead poets brought back on their knees second time around, gartersnakes splitting through mind-burn, matter-disorders. . . . What a parade of fancy-frees, scared shitless half the time, sorrowing saints, dumb pets waiting for the can to open. (19)

Waiting for the lid to be blown off. Waiting, like "Irish clowns" (Didi and Gogo in Beckett's play?), like "Irish poets mad, like me" (Yeats, in "The Second Coming," Webb in *Hanging Fire*? [20]), to contemplate last things, to confront the End ("Ssh, sigh, silence is coming. . . . The end of the Raj" [23]), to open up "occluded / rage" (25):

> Writhings, rage clenches
> my fist. Frozen pea-bag
> smashes against the hearth.
>
>   • • •
>   Housebound.
> Inwardbound. Pacing.
> The wall-to-wall carpet
> raises its ugly head
> accosts my dead languages.
> Wait for the pills to take. (26)

Wait for the crushing "weight of the world" (27) which, in Section Two, will metamorphose before us: "Heavyweight a / heavy wait for / that unbearable that / moment of being" (37). Or of non-being, when we go "'The Way of All Flesh,'" the last poem of the first section.

Section Two, "Hanging Fire," combines both the meanings caught in the phrase "Fire hanging / back" ("'Krakatoa' . . ."). After years of being "Housebound. / Inwardbound," after years of holding back, the "lights go out" precipitating a "crisis of lambency" (35). During the hugely ironic "*Musical Interlude*" between

"Tour de Force" and "Scattered Effects" (Section Three), the poet hangs her curtain of fire:

> hanging f   hanging f   hanging f   hanging f
>
>   ire   ire   ire   ire

and "hanging f / ear" (39-40). This is the section of revolutions and the de-construction of revolutions (Hulcoop 1991); this is the section that announces, in a three-day slice of the poet's personal history in prose, the end of the age of lyricism: "'I think, the poetry is/not the words.' Barry McKinnon. He meant, I think, the melody lingers on. In *The Death of a Lyric Poet*. I turn back, it's too late" (43). The End/Death is wryly repeated in the lyrical "'Passacaglia'" (a musical composition consisting of continuous variations on a ground bass): "The poet dives off the deep end / of the lyric poem . . . / . . . / the / death of the lyric poem / the death—" (46). As the angry, ironic and sometimes hu-morous musical interlude ends in "'Long Suffering,'" "The little fish jump up, nevertheless, scales shining" (see her two crisis volumes for Webb's self-identification as "*star fish*" and "*Fishstar*"), and "Stravinsky's firebird sings in the heavenly shade-tree, *con fuoco*" (48). The reader is left with "Scattered Effects" (Section Three).

Isaac Luria, the Jewish mystic (1534-1572) whose "story of creation" (a re-visionist version of Moses Cordovero's systematic reflections on the *Zohar*, them-selves a commentary on the Pentateuch) provides Harold Bloom with his theory of poetry-as-revisionism, conceived creation as "a startlingly regressive pro-cess . . . in which catastrophe is always a central event" (*Kabbalah*, 39). Bloom acknowledges Gershom Scholem's work in tracing Kabbalah's "direct descent" from the apocalyptic writings of earliest Jewish esotericism (*ibid.*, 21-2). For Luria, the reality of creation "is always a triple rhythm of contraction, breaking apart and mending." The three parts he names *zimzum* ("the Creator's withdrawal or contraction so as to make possible a creation not himself"); *shevirath ha-kelim* ("the breaking-apart of the vessels, a vision of creation as catastrophe"); and *tikkun* ("restitution or restoration" [*Kabbalah*, 39-43; *Map*, 3-6]). The parallel between Bloom's Lurianic theory and Webb's three-part apocalypse is suggestive. If creation is, in reality, a "regressive process," the apparently negative implications of "Scattered Effects" may be transformed into the positive prelude to restoration or (the more apocalyptic term) renovation. As Kermode observes, Terrors, as-sociated with catastrophe, and Decadence are "two of the recurring elements in the apocalyptic pattern," and "Decadence is usually associated with the hope of renovation" (9; see also McGinn, 10-11). Webb's book of revelation begins with catastrophe behind which reaches a long period of repression, i.e., a con-traction or "holding-in-of-the-breath," which is what *zimzum* originally meant (*Kabbalah*, 39). This is followed by a breaking-apart of the vessels which, says Bloom, is the "replacing of one form by another" (*Map*, 6): of poetry by music, of verse (lyric) by prose in Webb's literary apocalypse. What should follow, however, *tikkun*, or renovation, appears to have been displaced by the regressive scattering of effects which sounds like a repetition of *shevirath hakelim*.

But truth, so long veiled, "is rarely pure and never simple" (Wilde, 8). Though we may think of the dead poets (Gwendolyn MacEwen, bpNichol, Bronwen Wallace, to whom this volume is dedicated) as "scattered effects," and though this section, which includes poems for MacEwen and Wallace, opens with another on the death of Gerard Manley Hopkins, the act of scattering, ashes or seeds, shot or light, is never simply a negative act. Obscure in origin (according to the *OED*), *to scatter* (and *to shatter*, a southern dialectal variation) is probably related etymologically to MLG. *schateren*, "to be shattered by an explosion, to resound," or, most interesting of all, "to laugh uproariously." Thus, "Scattered Effects" might be interpreted not only as the destructive consequence of a Krakatoan explosion (and a repetition of the breaking-apart of vessels), but also as the liberating (therefore positive) consequence of breaking out of that which binds—as in, to burst (out of bounds) into laughter. And one of the effects of scattering may be fertilization (just as well as infection). Webb's footnote to "To A Zen Buddhist Who Laughs Daily" (*Trio*, n.p.) states that "'Zen roars with laughter at reasoning, logic and the laws of thought.'" "Laugh out this question," runs the text of the poem: "the goose is tight / in a bottle, // How to release without injury?" ("Messages," the great cat-poem in Section Three of *Hanging Fire*, poses precisely the same question: "How to get out of the poem without a scratch?" [60]) "The answer is plain," to the Zen Buddhist: "'There, it's out! / Oh shout, scream, volley / the soul with laughing dreams of light." Shaken as it is with outbursts of anger and violence that inspire Terrors ("*Terrorist directives*" [31]), *Hanging Fire*, like much of Webb's mature work, echoes with "cackles of Zennish laughter / riming ecstatic puns" (*WB*, 78), thus unveiling the truth of an eighteenth-century poet's insight: "Truth's fort the exploded laugh shall win" (Brown, l. 223).

"Every- / thing predictable in the book" ("'Krakatoa' . . ."). *Hanging Fire* ultimately offers, as all apocalypse must, a comic vision: the overthrow of tyranny—"The Romance of Revolution? The last agony of the Oedipus complex? The anxiety of (patriarchal) influence? The poem's pure, peculiar means and ends" (43); the cleansing of corruption—"Paul Horn is in the Temple of Heaven playing flute. . . . *Look*. I hand you a golden jonquil. *Here. Now. Always*. On the outgoing breath of the whales" (68); the coming of a new age—"beatitudes, 1889, heard / here, February, leapings of '88" (51); revelation of "a new heaven and a new earth" (Revelation 21:1), or, in Webb's case, a brave new world in which woman emerges from male veiling-fictions into her own reality: "Homo ludens at play among the killing fields of dry grasses. Playful woman making a space to breathe. 'There *are* the poems,' Sharon says, she means, between the critical flash. There *are* the poems, like fists wearing birthstones and bracelets . . . or like legs running, bounding over the fields of force" (57). Running, of course, in diverse directions ("scattered effects"), bounding over the force-fields (poems), breaking bounds after the making of a space in which to breathe (*zimzum*). We suffer a sea-change, what the poet calls a "*Time lapse backwards*" ("'Krakatoa' . . .") to the moment of creation (Luria's "regressive process") which is, in the words of Bloom's beautiful epigraph to *Kabbalah and Criticism*, a breaking-apart, a shattering/scattering: "A song means filling the jug, and even more so breaking the jug. Breaking it apart. In the language of the Kabbalah we might perhaps call it: Broken Vessels" (*Kabbalah*, [7]). Or "Scattered Effects," revealing themselves on their own terms, in their own forms; reflecting and de-fracting the light of Coleridge's Imagination which "dissolves, diffuses and dis-sipates in order to recreate" (246). Deconstruction which might be called creative destruction is not only an on-going regressive process (like the taped-backwards sound of writers and musicians de-composing in their graves) but also an in-dispensable stage in the creative process, as Browning tried to explain more than a century before Derrida:

> . . . perceptions whole, like that he [the poet] sought
> To clothe, reject so pure a work of thought
> As language: thought may take perception's place
> But hardly co-exist in any case,
> Being its mere presentment—of the whole
> By parts, the simultaneous and the sole
> By the successive and the many. Lacks
> The crowd perception? Painfully it tacks
> Thought to thought, which Sordello, needing such,
> Has rent perception into: its to clutch
> And reconstruct—his office to diffuse,
> Destroy. (II. ll. 589-600)

Sordello, 13th-century troubadour, struggling (as Browning saw him) to forge a new poetic language out of the vernacular (which effort was acknowledged by Dante in *De Vulgari Eloquentia*), is the prototype of all "modern" poets. He rends perception in pieces, the preliminary act of *re-construction* (Coleridge's *re-creation*, Lurianic Bloom's *re-novation*). In words that invoke the uncanny spirit of one of her major precursors—"A sixty-year old smiling man" stared at in "momentary wonder" by the school children he wanders among (cf. "'The Salt Tax'": "the sliding doors opened to let me (age 61) see him (age 61) again as a vision" [30])—Webb, belated poet, briefly presents her "'Model of the Uni-verse'" before blowing it to pieces in "'Krakatoa' and 'Spiritual Storm.'" The last sentence of her initiating poem is significantly a *protasis*, incomplete without its *apodosis* (literally, a giving back, restitution); but *protasis* is also the first part of an ancient drama in which the characters are introduced and the subject proposed. Apart from Yeats' ghostly presence, and the late appearance of the first-person singular, the *dramatis personae* in Webb's protatic poem consist of "little holy ghosts fiddling / while the planets burn," thus calling up another, unholy ghost (or holy terror), Nero; also the Ovidian figure of Queen Anne (herself *the end*—of a dynasty), metamorphosed into *Daucus Carota* (the com-mon, weedy form of the uncultivated carrot, bearing large, lacy umbels of minute white flowers, ghostly in appearance); and the wretched "hand-made mouse with cancer / for generations," one of the "shady dealings in the lab." Its "animal suffering" ("Experimental pain" in "'Gate Crashing'" [28]) is proleptic: "we are caught—thus and so—" at the end of "'Krakatoa' . . ." like Claudius, Hamlet's uncle, at the end of the play-within-the-play scene: "The spring of the mouse-trap sprung" (16). *Of Mice and Men* suggests itself as a possible title for the ancient drama proposed in Webb's *protasis*, which is not curtailed by the knife-wielding farmer's wife but silenced by the big bang of Krakatoa: "creator creating, a whim, / wham of blowup on shores— / Java, Sumatra, Hawaii— / blasting away 2200 miles heard" (14).

Thus, poet as volcano: *creator creating*, rending her world apart before she can imagine its rebuilding. Catastrophe, terrors, "Vasty undertakings" ("'Sliding Doors,'" 18); "Crash course in Chaos science; likewise Particle Physics" ("'You Have My Approval,'" 31); but, almost in spite of herself or precisely because she is what she is, "'Seeking Shape. Seeking Meaning'": "'Mind is shapely, Art is shapely.' Ginsbergian insight, / Allen afloat on his untidy chaos, his good humours. Ahoy!" (21). In poetry, says Marlatt in the epigraph to *Hanging Fire*, "sound will initiate thought by a process of association, words call each other up, evoke each other, provoke each other." In "'The Salt Tax,'" for example, a photo of Gandhi becomes "a pho-oh-*toe of Gandhi*" (30, italics added). In "'Eidetic Image,'" we witness "a big toe pronged, little one cracked on a hub" (20). Webb once quoted Loren Eiseley on the subject: "'The little toe is attractive / to the student of rudimentary / and vanishing organs'" (*SIAG*, 7). Even earlier, in a poem first published in 1953, she projected her persona as "Pining," "wilting," "something less than / tragic," "a mimic of the great, / the giant crack / in the spine, / the central agony" (*Trio*, n.p.). "What I need / is a cosmic break"—which is what she gets, or makes for herself, in "'Krakatoa' . . ." The "something less than / tragic" is transformed into something more than co(s)mic, i.e., apoc-alyptic; yet the "creator creating" compels us to attend carefully to the "small gods" (presumably related to those "little holy ghosts fiddling") who gather for the countdown, to listen amid the catastrophe for humanly proportioned sounds ("The cries of the animals for 'human interest'" in "'Gate Crashing'" [28]), and to hear in the heart of cosmically proportioned chaos what it means to crack a toe, a little toe.

Such phonic fun, anticipated in the Marlatt epigraph, confirmed in "'Miasma'" ("putrid / matter and such a lovely / sound/ word I hear 'mimosa' / hidden there" [17]), "'The Mind of the Poet,'" and almost every other poem in the book, owes an obvious debt to the most distinguished of Canada's sound poets, bill bissett (see also "Performance" [67]). To bissett and to Dorothy Livesay, "'Krakatoa' . . ." is dedicated. Wallace Stevens (another of Webb's precursors) also makes his presence known through the bissett-sounding French phrase, "Le monocle de mon / oncle," the title of what Bloom calls a "crisis-poem" in which Stevens captures with "ferocious ironies" a "lost vision of erotic fulfilment" (*Stevens*, 37-8). The vision may be (re-)captured, but "erotic fulfilment" remains on the loose. In Stevens' poem, the speaker's wish, "that I might be a thinking stone," is not all that distant from my image of poet-as-volcano (though the difference between a thinking stone and an erupting rock turns out to be significant). After a "sea of spuming thought" has tossed up the "radiant bubble" of female beauty that his mistress-muse once was—images that whisper hints of Aphrodite's birth (Bloom sees the "furious star" that burns in Section Five as Venus)—"A deep up-pouring from some saltier well / Within me, bursts its watery syllable" (Stevens, 13: i.7-11). In Webb's poem, "wild yelps / of pure physics / crack open deep sea / buttocks thrust up love lava / world heart" (14); and later in view is "Venus swinging below the moon" (15). The speaker's metaphor for the "paroxysmal" eruption is a "sexual storm," lit up by "Radiant / marvellous sunsets for years" (14). Quite a "Spectacle," which is just the word to provoke others like "le monocle de mon / oncle" (which follow). My uncle's eye-piece (ego-piece?) is "sent flying into the eye / of the storm"—rather as it might be by Monsieur Hulot in Jacques Tati's masterpiece, *Mon Oncle*; however, the storm is not "sexual" but "*spiritual* for him, / *timbre* just right, *pinhead*" (the expression *il a le timbre fêlé* means "he's a bit cracked").

"*Pinhead*" sounds a note of contempt; and the shift (ironically in parenthesis, like the major *events* in *To the Lighthouse*) from sexual for the speaker to "*spiritual* for him, / . . . pinhead," signals a crux in terms of the poem, a *prolepsis* in terms of the volume. If the storm is spiritual for him, but sexual for the speaker, the latter is probably female: i.e., sexual for *her*, spiritual for *him*. "God how I suffer to get this down / . . . / Always this me / . . . / my held-back fire . . . Every- / thing predictable in the book"—from all these clues, plus what she says in "Performance" ("Who is this *I* infecting my poems? . . . Or with me here standing before you wondering if the mike is on, if my mask is on, *persona*" [67-8]), I infer that the speaker is one of Webb's *personae* (see Hulcoop 1991). Mon oncle's attempt to spiritualize (or intellectualize, like the speaker in Stevens' poem) what is, at rock-bottom ("Hot Magma / . . . / buttocks thrust up love lava"), a question of "pure physics," pure sexuality, is as mistaken, as dishonest, and, finally, as enraging (hence the eruption) as Harunobu's idealization of female beauty, his attempt to put woman "on ice," his evasion of the truth: "What you see best / is the ivory kimono / coming towards you. / It will stay in the same place / always, Harunobu, brocading / the threat of advance" (74). Art, like religions and cultures (not *only* Christianity, not *only* the Western world) *brocades* (rhymes with "barricades") the advance woman threatens to make, out of fiction into fact.

> Indeed, if woman had no existence save in the fiction written by men, one would imagine her a person of the utmost importance. . . . Imaginatively she is of the highest importance; practically she is completely insignificant. She pervades poetry from cover to cover; she is all but absent from history. . . . Some of the most profound thoughts in literature fall from her lips; in real life she could hardly read, could scarcely spell, and was the property of her husband. (Woolf, 44-5)

Webb's dedication of "'Krakatoa' . . ." to Dorothy Livesay (as well as to bissett) can be seen as the acknowledgment of another precursor-poet. As Woodcock points out, after explaining the impact of Auden and Spender on the Marxist

Livesay of the 1930s, her subsequent work demonstrates "that lyricism and a social conscience [are] compatible"; and her "intense feminism" is "a feminism less political than concerned with the personal intensities and ambiguities of the passional life" (*Northern*, 189). In another sentence as relevant to Webb's work as it is to Livesay's, Woodcock states that she is a poet "intensely sensitive to issues and relationships which, even when she presents them in highly personal ways, are at basis social" (237).

"The shape of history implied by Revelation is a circular one which constitutes, as Karl Löwith has put it, 'one great detour to reach the end in the beginning" (Abrams, 346). Freud's *Beyond the Pleasure Principle* thus confirms the psychological truth of Revelation. And so, in its own way, does the Romantic ideal of returning to nature which is, in literary fact, a reworking of the classical epic's odyssey: the journey back from the alien city (of Troy) and from war (in which it would be foolish not to recognize that women, both Greek and Trojan, human and divine, played a major part) to peaceful homeland, from predominantly male battlefield to Penelope who, in her biological and artistic roles, is Maker. "Mythology's identification of woman with nature is correct" (Paglia, 12). Confronted, from womb to tomb (in Mother Earth), by woman's terrible power, "her archetypal confederacy with chthonian nature," the male defends himself offensively by establishing a patriarchy. Radical feminism announces a new apocalypse, the terror-inspiring end of a patriarchal era, the building of a new Atlantis in which "the institutional and moral evils of the present world will, by an inner necessity, be abolished once and for all by a sudden, violent, and all-inclusive political and social revolution" (Abrams, 351). Millenarianism provides what Ernest Tuveson calls "a scenario of revolution" (323); and, as Abrams observes, "the Book of Revelation, together with the apocalypse in Daniel, has inspired revolutionary uprisings against the institutional powers of evil" (351).

Hanging Fire—and here, after our great detour, we reach "the end in the beginning"—is Webb's Book of Revelation, a volume full of revolutionary violence. "'Krakatoa' and 'Spiritual Storm'" annunciates, in predictable (because they are part of a long-established literary convention) images, the onset of revolution/revelation. Because Webb *is* hanging fire throughout the first forty poems in the book, the true nature of the revelation becomes explicit only in "*The Making of a Japanese Print*" (the four final poems about Harunobu). Of Reiko Chiba's *The Making of a Japanese Print* (published in Tokyo in 1959), Webb has said: "I found this little book in the Art Gallery of Ontario and knew it would turn into a poem; it took a few years to turn" (typescript of *Hanging Fire*). A wickedly witty example of *meiosis*, "it took a few years to turn," prompts the response: "Like the worm, who is also the serpent, sexual symbol associated with female Eve whose sons and daughters (Mrs. Grundy as well as Mr. Bowdler) have ironically trodden underfoot the head which has thus bruised their own heels." But the wily old Teiresian serpent, "having seen it all before" ("'Eidetic Image,'" 20), will eventually turn, return, revolve. From Latin, *re-volvo*, to unroll—and so reveal; to return—as in an odyssey; to revolve—as in a revolution.

Frye sees the Bible as "a gigantic cycle [another form of revolution] from creation to apocalypse" (*Anatomy*, 316): from Genesis, in which Eve's turning precipitates a sexual storm which is spiritual for "him" (Him?), to Revelation. Revolution as Revelation. Webb turns to and transforms a book on Japanese print-making into a poem which completes (or perhaps unconsciously initiated, somewhere in the past) the revolution symbolized by the violent eruption ("natural disturb-ance") in "'Krakatoa' and 'Spiritual Storm.'" It does so by unveiling or lifting the lid off the true nature of itself. Revelation as Revolution.

Having distinguished between "the panoramic apocalypse"—a "vision of stag-gering marvels placed in a near future, and just before the end of time"—and "a participating apocalypse," Frye goes on to say that the first gives way to the second which, "ideally, begins in the reader's mind as soon as he has finished reading." After passing through "the legalized vision of ordeals and trials and judgments," the second apocalypse reveals "a second life" in which "the creator-creature, divine-human antithetical tension has ceased to exist, and the sense of the transcendent person and the split of subject and object no longer limit our vision" (*Code*, 136-7). The desert blooms anew, but not with flowers or even with Wagnerian flower-maidens. What blooms there is a "'Pepper Tree,'" hot, like the "magma" or molten material that boils up and bursts through the earth's binding crust. It "opens its arms": "It believes in its own genius, / suddenly, after winter. / It shines with land claims. / It turns with the hidden sun." "It finds ecstatic form by changing places. / It changes places" (58). And so does the reader, engaged in the participating apocalypse. But with whom does he change places? With her. With the woman who emerges "at last," at *The End*:

> What does she think
> as she sits on the verge
> this side of anonymous water?
> She uncoils her hair
> slips off her rings
> imagines a different future. (77)

Works Cited

Abrams, M.H. "Apocalypse: theme and variations." Patrides, 342-68.

Alexander, Paul J. *The Byzantine Apocalyptic Tradition.* D. deF. Abrahamse, ed. Berkeley: Univ. of California Press, 1985.

Barthes, Roland. *Mythologies.* Annette Lavers, trans. New York: Hill & Wang, 1972.

Bloom, Harold. *Kabbalah and Criticism.* New York: Seabury Press, 1975.

———. *A Map of Misreading.* New York: Oxford, 1975.

———. *Wallace Stevens: The Poems of Our Climate.* Ithaca: Cornell Univ. Press, 1977.

Brown, John. *An Essay on Satire: Occasion'd by the Death of Mr. Pope*, 2nd ed. corrected and enlarged. London: R. Dodsley and M. Cooper, 1749.

Browning, Robert. *Sordello*. London: Moxon, 1840.

Coleridge, S.T. *Coleridge: Complete Verse, Select Prose and Letters*. Stephen Potter, ed. London: Nonesuch, 1950.

Collins, J.J. *The Apocalyptic Vision of the Book of Daniel*. Missoula: Scholars Press, 1974.

Freud, S. "The Uncanny." *Art and Literature, The Pelican Library Freud*. Vol. 14. Albert Dickson, ed. Harmondsworth: Penguin, 1985.

Frye, Northrop. *Anatomy of Criticism: Four Essays*. Princeton: Princeton Univ. Press, 1957.

———. *The Great Code: The Bible and Literature*. Toronto: Academic Press, 1982.

Hulcoop, John F. "'Bird song in the apparatus': Webb's New Selected Poems." *Essays on Canadian Writing*, 30 (Winter 1984-85): 359-70.

———. "'Min(e)d Fire." A Review of *Hanging Fire*. *Canadian Literature* 134 (Autumn 1992).

———. *Phyllis Webb and Her Works*. Toronto: ECW, 1990.

———. "'This Petty Medium': In the Middle of *Middlemarch*." *George Eliot: A Centenary Tribute*. Gordon S. Haight and Rosemary T. Vanarsdel, eds. London: Macmillan, 1982.

———. "Webb's 'Water and Light.'" *Canadian Literature* 109 (Summer 1986): 151-9.

Kermode, Frank. *The Sense of an Ending: Studies in the Theory of Fiction*. London: Oxford, 1968.

Ketterer, *New Worlds for Old: The Apocalyptic Imagination, Science Fiction, and American Literature*. Garden City: Anchor, 1974.

Koch, Klaus. *The Rediscovery of Apocalyptic*. Naperville: Allenson, 1964.

Kreuziger, F.A. *Apocalypse and Science Fiction: A Dialectic of Religious and Secular Soteriologies*. Chico: Scholars Press, 1982.

Lewis, R.W.B. *Trials of the World*. New Haven: Yale Univ. Press, 1965.

May, John R. *Towards a New Earth: Apocalypse in the American Novel*. Indiana: Notre Dame Univ. Press, 1972.

McGinn, Bernard "Early Apocalypticism: the ongoing debate." *Patrides*, 2-39.

Paglia, Camille. *Sexual Personae: Art and Decadence from Nefertiti to Emily Dickinson*. New Haven: Yale Univ. Press, 1990.

Patrides, C.A. and Joseph Wittreich, ed. *The Apocalypse in English Renaissance Thought and Literature: Patterns, Antecedents and Repercussions*. Manchester: Manchester Univ. Press, 1984.

Rowland, C. *The Open Heaven: A Study of Apocalyptic in Judaism and Early Christianity*. London: SPCK, 1982.

Russell, D.S. *The Method and Message of Jewish Apocalyptic*. London: SCM Press, 1969.

Schmitals, Walter. *The Apocalyptic Movement: Introduction and Interpretation*. Nashville: Abingdon, 1975.

Smith, J.Z. "Wisdom and Apocalyptic." *Religious Syncretisms in Antiquity*. Birgir A. Pearson, ed. Missoula: Scholars Press, 1975.

Stevens, Wallace. *The Collected Poems*. London: Faber, 1955.

Tuveson, Ernest L. "The millenarian structure of *The Communist Manifesto*." *Patrides*, 323-41.

Webb, Phyllis. *Even Your Right Eye*. Toronto: McClelland and Stewart, 1956.

———. *Hanging Fire*. Toronto: Coach House Press, 1990.

———. *How Do I Love Thee: Sixty Poets of Canada.* John Robert Colombo, ed. Edmonton: Hurtig, 1970.

———. "Letters to Margaret Atwood." *Open Letter* 2nd Series, 5 (Summer 1973): 71-3.

———. *Naked Poems.* Vancouver: Periwinkle Press, 1965.

———. *The Sea Is Also a Garden.* Toronto: Ryerson, 1962.

———. *Selected Poems 1954-1965.* John F. Hulcoop, ed. Vancouver: Talonbooks, 1971.

———. *Trio.* Toronto: Contact, 1954.

———. *The Vision Tree: Selected Poems.* Sharon Thesen, ed. Vancouver: Talonbooks, 1982.

———. *Water and Light: Ghazals and Anti Ghazals.* Toronto: Coach House Press, 1984.

———. *Wilson's Bowl.* Toronto: Coach House Press, 1980.

Wilde, Oscar. *The Importance of Being Earnest.* Intro. Adeline Hartcup. 1899; London: Methuen, 1966.

Winzinger, Franz. Intro. to Souzouki Harounobu, *Jeunes Filles Et Femmes, Gravures Sur Bois en Couleurs.* Eugène Bestaux, trad. Paris: Arts et Métiers Graphiques, 1956.

Woodcock, George. "A lambent light on Saltspring." Review of *Hanging Fire. BC Bookworld* 4.3 (Winter 1990): 35.

———. *Northern Spring: The Flowering of Canadian Literature.* Vancouver: Douglas & McIntyre, 1987.

Woolf, Virginia. *A Room of One's Own.* 1929; Harmondsworth: Penguin, 1945.

The Poet of the Mind

Stephen Scobie

(1)

The *mind* of the poet: not her emotions, or her intuition, or even her imagination. Poetry, this title declares, is an act of the intelligence; poetry can *think*. (And so immediately it distinguishes itself from any view which sees poetry primarily as "self-expression," or which distrusts any display of intellect as "élitist," or somehow foreign to the purity of the feelings.)

The *mind* of the poet: not her logic, not the linear sequence of cause and effect, not an argument. Rather, as the first word will say, "slippages": quick sidesteps of association, connections made in the play of the mind at work. The dance of the intellect in synchronicity.

In the words of Daphne Marlatt in the epigraph to *Hanging Fire*: "sound will initiate thought by a process of association. words call each other up, evoke each other, provoke each other, nudge each other into utterance . . . a form of thought that is not rational but erotic . . ."

(I like to think that words "call each other up" as if on the phone, to have a conversation. Hullo. How are you. Nice to talk to you again.)

(2)

slippage. Not a purposeful movement, but not an arbitrary one either. The site you are in determines where you slip from, where you slip to. The ground gives way under your feet. But a slip is not necessarily a fall: you recover your balance. You take a new stand. It was only a (Freudian) slip.

Slippage is perhaps the most characteristic movement of poetry (or at least of Phyllis Webb's poetry). It does not proceed in a straight line, but rather by indirections, by devious sideways movements, by sudden shifts of ground and stance. (It's the movement of thought that I see also in Derrida, the way his "différence" slips and sidesteps past the traps of binary oppositions, the way his own performative voice shifts and evades definition, as in the "Envois" section of *La carte postale*.) Slippage is a movement you can trace but not predict. It risks collapse: it risks silence. But if you're lucky, the slip- ends up on the -page.

(3)

repeat performance. Or in Webb's case: Repeat "Performance." The poem "Performance" appears later in *Hanging Fire* (67), but was written earlier. (It appears in the anniversary issue of *Canadian Literature*, number 100.) "Who is this

I infesting my poems?" the poem demands. In "The Mind of the Poet," the word "I" does not appear at all.

Performance demands repetition.[1] (Indeed, in French, "répétition" means "rehearsal.") So the moment of performance — "live," "spontaneous," full of the "presence" of the artist — is always a repeated one, a rehearsed one. Slippage*s* — plural. Each slippage a performance, unique, and each performance a repeat, the same. Phyllis Webb is famous for the quality of her reading voice. She could, they say, make the telephone book sound interesting. "Or am I reading, as they say, 'in person'?" ("Performance"). No one ever reads "in person," only in persona. Impersonating.

The mind of the poet is the stage of repetition. In the words of Leonard Cohen, a dress re-hearse-al rag.

(4)

soundings profounder. The voice, in performance, sounds. The live voice, speaking voice, guarantee of presence (the tradition of logocentrism, writes Derrida, from Plato's *Phaedrus* onwards. "S'entendre parler." I can't hear myself think.) But what then is the "repeat performance" of "sounding"? (*Re*-sounding?) The recorded voice: of Phyllis Webb, perhaps, or (in "Performance") of bill bissett. The recorded voice is a trace, no longer speech but writing. Re: writing.

The voice, in performance, sounds: sounds the depth. Always the metaphor of depth, going down, under the surface. ("In Canadian literature they are in the water or underwater . . . Canadian literature is under the ground not underground but under the ground, under the ground or under the snow or under the ice" — George Bowering, *A Short Sad Book* [110-11].) In *Wilson's Bowl*, the one who sounds the depths is Lilo Berliner, Webb's friend, who drowns herself in the ocean: "She goes out on the water / hearing" (66). Hearing the sounds. Profound, profounder, profoundest. But what is the "sounding" of "profounder"? Pro-founder. "Pro": in favour of. "Founder" (noun): an originating source, an author, a poet. "Founder" (verb): to collapse, to sink, to be shipwrecked.

(5)

as down we go for the third time.
    Repeat performance.

(6)

as down we go for the third time . . . pearl-diving, operatic. To go down for the "third time" is, idiomatically, to drown (to founder). It is not a deliberate "dive" but an involuntary descent. Christ ascends on the third day, but for those who go down for the third time, there is no resurrection. (Not from the ocean, not from the Seine.) "Those are pearls that were his eyes . . ."

As for the pearl, it hides in the oyster, irritant. "Inside this skull an oyster brain. / Pearl/ plain" (*Water and Light*, 50). Inside the oyster, inside the skull, what we are diving for is the brain: "the mind of the poet" searching for beauty. "*What are you sad about?*" demands the interrogative voice of "Some Final Questions," and Phyllis Webb responds: "that all my desire goes / out to the impossibly / beautiful." And here the intertextual dialogue is with Christopher Smart, "Jubilate Agno": "For in my nature I quested for beauty, but God, God hath sent me to sea for pearls."[2]

"Operatic" implies a performance that is formal, extravagant, staged: too much so, even. Artificial, overstated, false. But what opera does the poet have in mind?

Georges Bizet, *Les Pêcheurs de Perles*, first performance September 30, 1863. Not often performed since: famous mainly for a duet of two male voices. The plot, however, features a "priestess of Brahma," whose purity defends the pearl fishers against the perils of the ocean. ("Hieratic sounds emerge / from the Priestess of / Motion" [Webb, *Naked Poems*].) The name of the priestess is Leila. Lilo Berliner "goes out on the water / hearing." The final trio of the opera addresses "O lumière sainte." Water and light.

(7)

dead poets brought back on their knees . . .

(Too many dead poets to wonder about. Gwen MacEwen. Frank Scott. bpNichol. Bronwen Wallace. A "live" performance is always a performance of death; all poems are self-composed epitaphs. We write "in memory of," because all writing is, as Derrida says, "toilette of the dead, institution of death, wake, monumentalization, archive, heritage, genealogy, classification of proper names, engraving on tombs, burying, shrouding . . . funeral song" [*Glas*, 143a].)

"On their knees" is the position of prayer, of supplication, and of execution. On the first page of *Water and Light*: "A knocked off head of somebody on her broken knees."

. . . *second time around*. Repeat performance. But also a count-down: "down for the third time"; "second time around"; and later "half the time." Count-down towards a zero which does not, in this poem, directly appear (unless it is in the word "forgetfulness," or in the colour "white," or simply in the ending of the poem).

(8)

gartersnakes splitting . . . *Jumping bugs*. Consider, as intertext, Irving Layton's "A Tall Man Executes a Jig."[3] The "jumping bugs" of that poem, the gnats, "ephemerides," resist the attempts of the Tall Man to impose upon them a formal order of his mind's devising. Denying Euclid, Donatello, and Plato, they remain "Motion without meaning, disquietude / Without sense or purpose." "Revelation" comes to the Tall Man only when he lays aside his human pride and sees himself in the "violated grass snake" which "lugged / Its intestine like a small red valise" down under the ground to death. Layton's poem is a text-book example for the mythopoeic motif of going underground, death and resurrection (going down for the second time, coming up on the third): the gospel according to Northrop Frye. Webb's dead poets (going down for the third time, on their knees for the second) aren't so sure. Instead, they are about to be subjected to a string of amused but withering invective: *What a parade of fancy-frees, scared shitless half the time . . . dumb pets waiting for the can to open . . .* Tall Men they aren't. The intertext is slipping.

(9)

mind-burn, matter-disorders. "Mind-burn" is an interesting-sounding complaint: formed, I take it, by analogy from "heartburn." An indigestion of the intellect. Or else, perhaps, rope-burn: as the slippage of ideas moves through the mind, it burns whatever tries to hold it down. The mind on fire, burning like Carthage. And *through* this fire, sp(l)itting like snakes (speaking with forked tongues?), come the dead poets, burning their way into the mind of this poet, producing "matter-disorders."

(Or is that a noun-verb formation? Matter disorders: that is, what "matter" does is not to "order" but to "disorder." Entropy: the very existence of matter moves towards chaos, second time around.)

And in *Wilson's Bowl*, "Metaphysics of Spring": "ah, gross / matter (great / matter), it does / not, even / matter / burning . . ." (81). Ho Hum.

(10)

Ho Hum.

Pivot of the poem. Exclamation of boredom, of self-deprecation, of mild surprise. ("Matter-disorders": ho hum, here we are again.) Or a mandala, a chant. Hoooooooooooooooo. HummmmmMMMMMMmmmmm. An exercise in tonal breath control, in the "Sitting" position.

The "Ho" reminds me of that "Oh" (which it reverses) on the final page of *Naked Poems*. Or more accurately "Oh?"—the Oh? Pen? Ended? question which pitched into silence. And the "Hum" goes back once more to the mind of the poet, the oyster brain, the write brain, in *Water and Light*: "*Why Poetry?* And why not, I asked, / my right brain humming sedition" (55).

(11)

What a parade . . . What a strange parade. The Dead Poets Society marching past. I described it above as "amused but withering invective": but that was a response to the *tone* of the whole passage rather than to the implications of the individual items on this list, most of which are (typically) ambiguous. *fancy-frees*, for instance, connotes both light-hearted liberty and feckless irresponsibility.

(And is the "dead poet" here Coleridge?) If they are *scared shitless half the time*, then (is the bottle half-full or half-empty?) presumably there is another half of the time in which they are courageous (or constipated). Is a *saint* more or less venerable, more or less saintly, when she is *sorrowing*? And these *dumb pets waiting for the can to open*, are they any less helpless than dumb p(o)ets waiting for their Muse?

Bird brains, eagle eyes, sad sacks . . . this list seems to be generated mainly by alliteration. (It's easy to see how "bird" leads to "eagle," but where does "sad sacks" come from? And why is this passage italicized?) The "birds of a feather" echo, again, from *Water and Light*: the "Four swans in Fulford Harbour" (32), the "Peacock blue" of "the first morning // of creation" (30), the eagle who looks down from his "nifty height." A "bird brain," for Webb, is not necessarily a limited capacity. Rather, the bird brain flies, fancy-free, from one association to another; its movemement is slippage, spilling down currents of air. From its nifty but imperial height, the eagle eye (the ego I) sees clearly, with a poet's vision . . . But collapses, ignominiously, into "sad sacks." Inertia.

(12)

whose minds float on forgetfulness. The "mind" of the poet again—but this time it does not dive, or founder: it floats. It survives on the surface. To "float" may be a vague and purposeless motion ("People don't live or die, people just float"—Bob Dylan, 1989), but in some ways it is certainly better than sinking. As Alan Breck says to David Balfour in Robert Louis Stevenson's *Kidnapped*, "I've a grand memory for forgetting."

(13)

Quartz, sapphire, topaz, emerald . . . The names of forgetfulness? Where the mind floats, into the exotic sounds of exotic stones, "quartz" doesn't quite fit, though obviously its *z* links to topaz. Quartz is not really a precious stone ("a widely distributed mineral species" says the *Encyclopaedia Britannica*), though in some forms it is a gem: agate, amethyst, bloodstone, cairngorm, tigereye. In the various languages of gems, amethyst stands for sincerity; emerald for success in love; topaz for fidelity. In the Zodiac, topaz is the stone of Taurus; emerald of Cancer; sapphire of Leo; amethyst of Sagittarius. In heraldry, topaz represents gold and the sun; pearl represents silver and the moon; sapphire represents azure and the planet Jupiter; emerald represents green and the planet Venus; amethyst represents purple and the planet Mercury. Theophrastus, according to *Brewer's Dictionary of Phrase and Fable*, "divided precious stones into male and female, the darker being the males and the light ones the females. Male sapphires approach indigo in colour, but the females are sky-blue." "but I tell you, / *Fishstar*, the colour of chaos was not // Peacock blue" (*Water and Light*, 30). Bird brain.

(14)

forgetfulness . . . emerald-hard memory shards. There are few places in the poem
which more clearly illustrate how "sound will initiate thought . . . words call
each other up." Emerald (rather than diamond, the more classical image of a
hard stone [see "The Glass Castle," *The Sea Is also a Garden*]) follows the sound-
pattern of the *a* and *r* in quartz, sapphire, topaz; it in turn generates "hard,"
and then "shard"—a nice paradox here, since *hard* is itself a shard of *shard*.
What cannot be broken is broken off from what is already broken.

The minds of the poets float *on* forgetfulness *to* memory; forgetting becomes
the medium by which they arrive at memory, or at least at the fragments of
memory. In "The Glass Castle" ("my image for the mind"), the poet has "scratched
with diamond and gathered diamond dust": the mind, that is, is harder than
any cutting stone. It is the stone itself that disintegrates. Memory tries to inscribe
itself upon forgetfulness, but succeeds only in crumbling itself, into shards.

(15)

spooky auditions. Before you get to a performance, repeat or otherwise, you
must first go through the audition: literally, a listening. Hearing the sounding.
Hearing the voices of dead poets, as they float upon forgetfulness: their ghosts,
their spooks. Spooky, isn't it? It scares me shitless (half the time).

(16)

*Toad of Toad Hall greeting his guests at the door with his white butler's gloves
on.*
"Toad," first of all, as a sounding from "topaz." Then as the emerald-green
animal which "ugly and venomous, / Wears yet a precious jewel in his head"
(*As You Like It*). The toadstone was a cure for "any part envenomed, hurt,
or stung with rat, spider, wasp, or any other venomous beast" (says Thomas
Lupton, 1579). The toad, that is, itself poisonous, carried in its head, as a precious
stone, the cure for poison (what Derrida would call a *pharmakon*).

And then there's Kenneth Grahame. In *The Wind in the Willows*, Toad is
one of those apparently disreputable characters (not unlike— to stretch a point—
Milton's Satan) who tends to run away with the show, at the expense of the
good but dull characters like God or Badger. Toad is very *loud*: he likes singing
boisterous songs about himself, and he loves motor cars, horns, and speed. (He's
a living incarnation of Marinetti's Futurist manifestos). Above all, Toad is a
performer. He loves to project a heroic image of himself for an audience—an
audience which remains, in Grahame's highly moral books, largely unconvinced.

Toad does not (as Phyllis Webb freely admits) wear "white butler's gloves."
He does wear driving gauntlets, as part of "those singularly hideous habiliments
so dear to him, which transform him from a (comparatively) good-looking Toad
into an Object which throws any decent-minded animal that comes across it

into a violent fit" (106) (but that is Badger talking). A *butler's* gloves would be a show of false humility from Toad, toadying favour: another performance. But he does love to greet guests: like poets, he needs an audience.

There is about Toad an element of pathetic bravado: he's a jumping bug, a fancy-free, a sorrowing saint, a sad sack. But he's not a dumb pet waiting for the can to open: Toad will try to open the can for himself, even if he can't, even if the only result is to wreck his car in the process, to founder. When Grahame came to write a second book about the animals of the river bank, he didn't call it Mole, or Rat, or Badger—he called it *Toad of Toad Hall.*

(17)

"The Mind of the Poet" is a self-reflexive poem, or what speech-act theory would call a *performative utterance.* The classic instance of the performative is the promise, where the statement does not merely describe but actually accomplishes what it says. The title "The Mind of the Poet" promises a statement *about* poetic thinking, and the poem performs that promise, demonstrating the poet's mind at work (and at play, which for a poet is the same thing). There is no *argument*, no theme that can be neatly summarized in 25 words or less. There are only slippages, quick sneaky movements from one word to the next. (There is a "theme" of death, true, but there is always death in language.) The reader must fall and follow it through, slipping as if on banana peels, repeating the performative.

(18)

> Dear Phyllis,
>   Look what I've done to your poem.
>   Do you mind?
>   Stephen.

Notes

[1] As I also am repeating myself: for the essay I completed immediately before writing this one is, precisely, on "performance." ("Racing the Midnight Train: Leonard Cohen in Performance," to appear in *Canadian Culture in the 1960s*, ed. Eva-Marie Kröller, University of Toronto Press.) And before that an essay on Phyllis Webb. And before that an essay on Phyllis Webb and Leonard Cohen. This essay is my absolutely final "repeat performance."

[2] My thanks to Phyllis Webb, who sent me to see this 18th century reference.

[3] In honour of Donald Stephens, who first taught me this poem, 1966.

Works Cited

Bowering, George. *A Short Sad Book*. Vancouver: Talonbooks, 1977.

Derrida, Jacques. *Glas*. John P. Leavey, Jr., and Richard Rand, trans. Lincoln: University of Nebraska, 1986.

Grahame, Kenneth. *The Wind in the Willows*. New York: Charles Scribner's Sons, 1954.

Layton, Irving. *The Collected Poems of Irving Layton*. Toronto: McClelland and Stewart, 1971.

Webb, Phyllis. *Hanging Fire*. Toronto: Coach House Press, 1990.

———. *Naked Poems*. Vancouver: Periwinkle Press, 1965.

———. "Performance." *Canadian Literature* 100 (Spring 1984): 352-3.

———. *The Sea Is Also a Garden*. Toronto: Ryerson, 1962.

———. *Water and Light: Ghazals and Anti Ghazals*. Toronto: Coach House Press, 1984.

———. *Wilson's Bowl*. Toronto: Coach House Press, 1980.

PART THREE

New Poems

bill bissett

---

th inevitabilitee uv tossd salads dictating
plesur

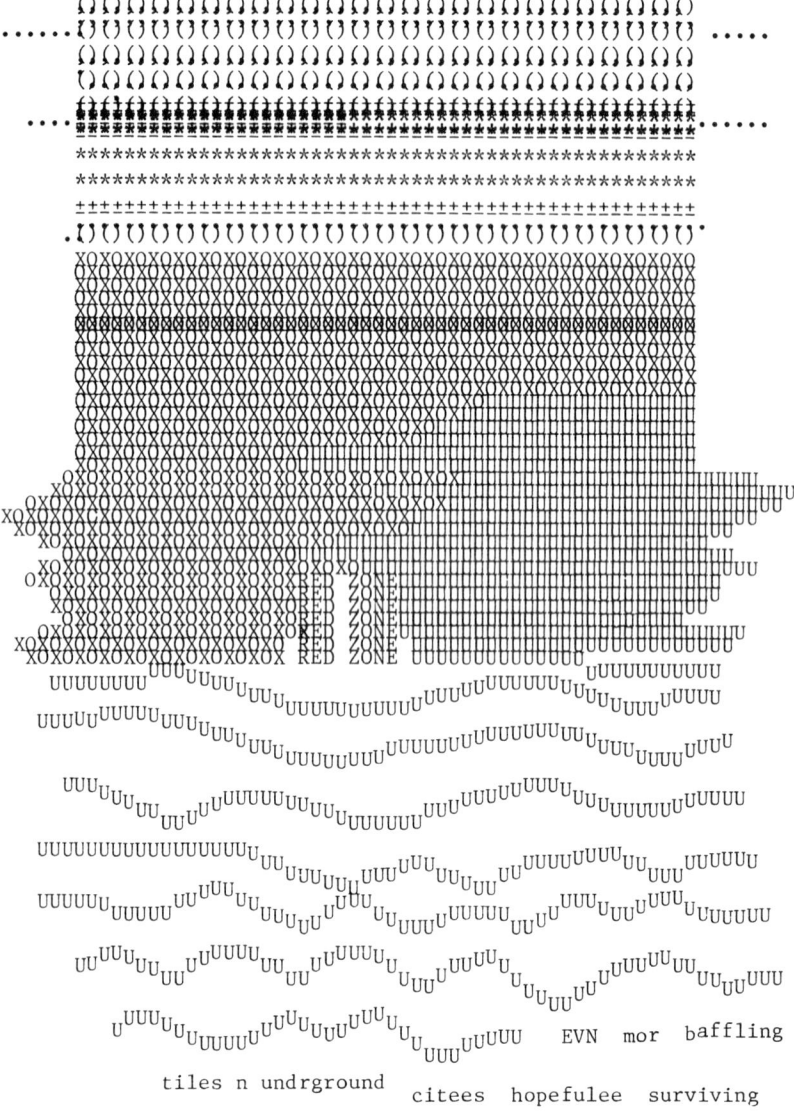

EVN   mor   baffling

tiles n undrground   citees hopefulee surviving

sept   16.90

Marilyn Bowering

Tranquille

I return to the bees:
to the cloud of them that razored the air
above the path to Roxana's house,

their white hives in two rows,
like a landing field below;

swaying like giant bells on
an invisible dancer;

or as if Mediterranean waves curled
and lipped at them.

Your bees, Gargoris, colonising
to the furthest reaches of the West,

the cold Pacific.

I had left you by then.
The liquidising melt

of skin on skin,

the slow casting glances
from sky to river as we turned

were adrift like messages
in bottles: I could not track them,

had no idea where or when
they would turn up.

Until this,
the great bee kingdom.

I ache to strip the scarves,
gloves, sweaters, hats, boots

I wear in brilliant air
so hard it cracks my skin,

and dance the ringing bee dance,
clasp the cutting bees around my wrists
for bracelets.

I ache for honey, pain, you.

The bees, in swarm, move off.
Roxana, trailing golden nets,
comes to gather them.

She, like some priestess
of that far off time,
is veiled, slow and sure,

virginal as the sky is, the sea,
the moon—whatever men have done.

This time I watched, Gargoris,
I felt the gold kernel kick

to life in my belly,
and turned to run:
I could smell the pines,

the blooded knife
you would have used

if I'd refused,
and sensed again the growing heart, limbs, brain,

of our son.
The myths are all of him.

I do not figure.

Roxana, carrying bees, murmurs:
Tranquille. Tranquille.

Fred Cogswell

The Quiet Sunshine . . .

The quiet sunshine in the late afternoon
touches the grey bark and bare buds as if
they yet were clad in summer, gilding them
above December snow. How these trees blend
with dark green spruce and golden tamarack
as I look at them through the west window.

Inside the same balance. By the window
I am as calm as is the afternoon,
in my own autumn, heedless of the rack
and fury of an approaching winter. If
sun-rays shone inside my brain, they would blend
with light outside. No storm would stifle them.

Such calms are *given*, and we must enter them
as if they happened every day. Window
is the link where inside and outside blend
into one timeless, spaceless afternoon
without visible distortion, as if
my being now were one with tamarack.

But here the very rhythm, *tamarack*,
makes my thought-chords sound a perverse anthem
that breaks my unity of mood as if
a thick snowball outside hit the window
with a thud that shattered glass, or, too soon
inside, the notes of jazz eclipsed the blend.

It's better only to be and not lend
our sense to mere particulars that rack
the brain with thought. Let the afternoon—
inside, outside, without a seam or hem—
be all-engrossing. Let the west window
vanish. Let there be no more need for *if*.

This *now* is beyond space and time, and if
we lose ourselves inside that cosmic blend
time and space will turn elastic, and oh,

easeful to our souls which have borne the rack
of the particulars that have dwarfed them,
like *window*, *tamarack*, and *afternoon*.

If silent chords can sound through the window
with no crack in thought, let us, here with them,
blend in one instant like notes in one tune.

Lorna Crozier

A Brief History of the Horse

1.

The brown horse grazing in pastures of sleep
is full of soldiers. Each has his own
corner of darkness, his corner of despair.
The soldiers feel the sway of the horse's belly
as she races night across the meadows.
All of them believe they are in the hold
of a ship that smells of grass and forgetfulness
though they can't understand her hours of stillness,
or the mad sound of flies eating her ears.
Each remembers being pushed through the pale
thighs of his wound away from the field
where he fell though he can't remember
the name of the country or the day or the year.
Sailors all, they have crossed oceans of clouds
to reach this green meadow at the end
of the twentieth century where someone
may unlatch a gate for the horse to enter,
open the door between her ribs and let the light
pick among their bones.

2.

The farm girl who rides the horse
after her chores are done
has no idea they are there.

If she did, she would not
squeeze her thighs so tight
around the horse's belly,
she would not ride so hard.

Sometimes she thinks
she hears voices
as she lays her cheek
along the horse's neck,
sometimes she has bad dreams.

Already longing for the city
she is bored with horses,
the feral smell of them
on her hands, along
the inside of her legs.

When she brushes the horse
wipes away the lather,
she does not know
it could be foam
from the sea
churned by drowning
or froth from the mouth
of a dying man.

3.

The horse without wings
grazes calmly in the meadow.
She has no need of eternity,
no need of bits or bridles.

What she knows beyond
the good sense of her hooves
no one can tell.

If we call her *ship*,
if we call her *nightmare*,
if we call her *history*,
she will not care.

When she wants to
she moves, flicks
at flies with her tail,

curls back her lip
and shows her yellow teeth.

When she wants to
she stands
absolutely still.

Don Domanski

Dragon

the man sat clothed in shade
bearded in hymns
reading his copy of the earth
making promises to the grass

at his feet a salamander moved sleep
a little further onto land

a spider drank her black syllable
from both worlds once again

the ferns in the shadows laboured
to turn their mind
their single drop of blood
to a single thought

the man sought the comfort of belief
sought the old word in the grass
with its bone-coloured heart
its candle-scented eyelids
its few brush-strokes of skin

the man read from
his copy of the earth
but a new word came
to sit on his shoulder
like a feline-bird

like an enormous cat
with feather-studded fur

its eyes tapered to red
its hands big with holding

its ears   its wings
its braided back
all mottled with graces

the grace of sleep upon wood
of idea upon stone
the grace of the appointed cloud
in the appointed breeze
bringing its coppery rain

and the man reading
the rain in his book
smiled at the word on his back

that unaffected flying cat
that terrible wingless bird
which like the serpent in the
grass of the book
stirred and stirred
and crackled in blue.

Marya Fiamengo

A Mandala of Birds
and Feathers

The unexpected felicity
of the heron propped
solitary by the irrigation pump.

The white-washed lace of ice
on a waste of wide water.

Black quail nimble
in the frozen orchard grove.

A mandala of birds and feathers
as visiting finch perch

on the mustard radiance
of a winter willow.

Chill wind, hoar frost
last words spoken

on a walk from southern darkness
into the migratory northern light.

Gary Geddes

Postcard from Duck Lake

There are no ducks at Duck Lake
when I arrive in late June,
the station wagon loaded down
with books and plants, two bicycles strapped
to the roof, wheels turning slowly in wind
off the reserve.

I think of Almighty Voice, facing
Middleton's cannon, then his own demons
in Duck Lake prison, a log and sod hut no bigger
than our last bedroom. Events large enough
to take the words out of his mouth.

I'm moving house again, heading east
into Quebec's disputed territories
with only the still small voice
of poetry at my disposal.

Not conscious of the treaty talks ahead,
lying in bed on Greene Avenue,
my infidelities spread out

on the patchwork quilt.
Peace talks? Not quite. Years
of sniping, guerrilla war,
embargoes.

I lift my voice unto the hills
and hear the absence
echo.

Ralph Gustafson

Ars Poetica

To Scriabin F$^{\sharp}$
At 383 vibrations a second
Was bright blue, Rimbaud saw
Vowels each as a different colour.
The true poet is as lavish
The harmonics of words transcends words.
Genetic allocation perhaps,
But the poem as it is is what
Is said: breath and the degree of breath
Are meaning—let the accents clash
As they will (if the rhythm is right),
Rough or smooth transference, whatever
Is meant for the mind is as it is heard.
Scan the text as you will, it isn't
Harmony. Poetry delights the meaning,
Never self-conscious, too various
In modulation, emotion has
Its own degree, not sloven,
Not constrained, the heart the temperate
Power, alert for the vowel, the consonant
Unobtrusive constancy:
Movement, resonance, heard silence!
English, grand unparalleled music!
Ignored, scratch for tin ears.

Image up against image, connectives taken
As understood (God and the course of existence),

That's one method, Miró, Pound, Klee,
A second is narrative with enlightenment of breathless
Insert, a going richness, Chopin, Velasquez,
Liszt, a third is as music (almost
Solely) whether or not the telling suffer,
Music! syntax to the devil if need be,
Narrative arcane or none, Stevens, Kandinsky,
All those who hate tin ears.
Ut doceat, moveat, delectet,
Shakespeare incomparable. So it exists, this poetry.

Brian Henderson

There Is a Kind of Music

THERE IS A KIND OF MUSIC
an unfinished music
to this constantly moving house
an opening and closing of breath
like a tide of shadows

Who would have guessed how much
we depend on listening for it
and on not hearing it

Death is a stagger in the rhythm
so you hear it for the second time
Birth is the first

It flies up like a child's cry
It is the home of blood, of birds
of sooty wing whose songs are hard

We come all this way to lose ourselves finally
and it's family we find ourselves doing it in—
not the father tongue my mother taught me—
but the house in a cradle, another language
an island the music moves
sweeps as if it had hands
and nearly comforts

D.G. Jones

blue girl

there is no wind, no moon, only
this print about Modigliani
about a girl he had something
to do with, in blue—whatever cafés,
rooms in Paris, nights
in Canada with no moon, only
the blue girl, the normally absent
painter, the young woman who writes
in some room about some
piece of paper . . . and the faint
sound now of some plane crossing
this blank space—possibly in
moonlight, in the jet-stream, the pilot
logging the hours, precise
location in air—it is winter
still, though mild, dark, silent now
and I do not know where to place
the blue girl or the writer
writing so intimately about the
blue girl she never, no more
than Modigliani ever, or I ever
knew

Patrick Lane

The White Bear Burning

He sits alone in the room of late autumn
with a great exhaustion upon him and he is lost
in the struggle of words, trying to believe
they will redeem, if not himself, then someone
lonelier, some woman wanting what little there is

of love, a child, some man, perhaps himself, who stares
through his fingers and finds them making a church,
a steeple, and repeats the oldest song of childhood,
ending it with the cry: *And here are the people.*

His room grows small with memory. The fire begins
to die and he rises and places on the embers
wood, vine maple, whose leaves in autumn
always promise glory and turn brown
before the blaze of colour can appear that could
bring back his earliest memories of the forest
when his ancestors looked amazed into the dark
and did not know themselves. Gone now
except on isolated farms or in old poems
where taciturn, reluctant men built walls
against their love, tearing down the dark,
turning the land into a story to be told.
His room surrounds the place where words
begin, the fire which batters back the cold.

Inert, the log remains, a dark thing on the coals,
and the man watches what he believes is death, the cold
come creeping as if the northern bear, old polar animal,
has come at last to claim him, walking web-footed
on the snow with a last burden, swaying there.
The bear is what the man calls from himself,
a great white animal who is the story
in his bones, the one he tells himself
in a room where the fire has died.

He waits then for the muffle of paws on ice
and, staring, sees the maple burst to flame,
the slow accretion of the years when it
pulled into itself all that the earth had offered,
and bursts, a blazing light, and it is as if the man
has turned to flame, his flesh leaping into fire.

He turns then to the hands he holds, each finger
locked together and opens them to his eyes, the myriad
beings lifting there, such praise as what he knew
when the bones of his mother held him in the cup
of her broad hips. Beside him, the huge animal,
its white fur radiant, sways to music
and murmurs to the man what the far wind knows

that falls out of the north: *consumed, consumed,*
his white head weaving words out of the light.

Snow falls upon snow, the maple burns, and somewhere
at the edge where the forest begins, a man
steps into the darkness of the trees, entering
the world, leaving behind him only a story to be told
around a fire to children who will soon go into dream,
how someday he will return, the one who left,
bearing in his hands a church, beside him
his companion, a white bear who will give to those
who weave above the flames in their last hours
a story whose very name is without fear.

Dorothy Livesay

At the Solstice

The way   OUT
is the same
as the way
IN   a CHOKING
This daylight
for both
is blinding
an onrush
of bleeding
DONT
        DONT LOOK
Before you
        LEAP

George McWhirter

Psalm for Don Stephens

We have grown old
and ripe,

truffled
and underworldly,

as pampered with the damp
and precarious

as a tuft
of moss,

kicked like a toupee
off the curbside

where we clung
growling

like velvet green
terriers,

dislodged
by a jogger's heel

or toe.
Haven't you seen them

like the church-goers
of a Sunday,

spilling
immortally

across the road,
defying any traffic

other than
what passes

between them
and their godliness?

This piety
pelts by

like the heaven-ripened
rain

past the slow
immaculate assumption

of a dog turd
by the slug.

Dead slow
and sweet,

from that same still—
the drip

that lays the dew.
Are these souls

too good to rot
and enter

a green and brown
bargain

with their maker
and the ground?

What quickens best?
The rain,

the perspiration
of creation.

The world does laps
at 0-1000 miles per hour.

Lie down in it a bit.
Was the earth not made

to do this racing
round for you.

Seymour Mayne

At Night the Dew

for Don Stephens

At night the dew
   shines like the patina
      on an eye

and everything tall,
   standing rooted,
      begins to dart from sight—

I flee with the trees, fronds,
   birds and flying mites
      and take shelter

resting upon the stone
   that sweats lightly—

my forehead filled
      with dreams of rungs

rising into blinding light.

"And he lighted upon the place, and tarried there all night, because the sun was set; and he took one of the stones of the place, and put it under his head, and lay down in that place to sleep." *Genesis* 28:11

Daniel David Moses

Blues for a Barn

The barn's alone. No house or shed
keeps it company. The weathered
boards with that ingrained red are bill

boards now facing the highway. How
appropriately pale, ghostly,
the words that pose *where will you be*

in eternity? None of us knows
how or cares to reply.
Nor will it go on our agenda.

We hurry by. The wind wanders
the fallow field beyond, too
despondent to do more than sigh.

Why is it it never knew who
they were, that farmer and his sons?
It settles down, wreathing the barn.

Erin Mouré

Holding Out Tomatoes
Vera Dorosowsky, 1915-1990

If any of us in our separate spaces cried out, in which of
our corridors. Holding out the tomatoes, or the two corn.
Holding out the flats of strawberries, jam berries. The
way she said the word "delicious," "I ate them with a
little salt," she'd say, "they were so delic*i*ous." Vera on
the back porch holding two tomatoes, look at what I've

got she'd say, jubilant & confidential, you wanted to BE
tomatoes, that red.

Vera who'd worked so many years in the houses of the
rich, it was so peaceful, she said, I wanted to clean them
Saturday too. She couldn't imagine resting. When I
found out she'd gone that morning I sat down at my desk
& took out the Oreos. I waited for the sound of the CBC to
come through the wall & it didn't. I waited for her
beauty to home in on me. I waited for her to arrive back
from Czechoslovakia with a new story. I'm not coming
back, she'd said, lifted into the ambulance. They'd
awakened her for the pills, & when they came in, she'd
gone. Now her clothes are in the hospital bag on the
back porch, a blue bag with the last things she wore, a
blue bag with the things she went with, a few cloth
things, that's all, the last things she knew, the last that
touched her.

P.K. Page

After Hearing *Satyagraha*, an Opera, by Philip Glass

*"Let not the thread of my song be cut when I sing." Rig
Veda II.28.1-9*

Glass, you shatter and imprism us.

Your line of music is repetitive.
And holy. Holy.
It is just as if
a Bach had filled this modern opera house
and made the busy still, the tightened loose.

Gandhi began it with a perfect phrase
high enough to come as a surprise
then sang it over, over.
And again.

Sang it not so much as a refrain
but more as if perfection were his aim.

There is a bird that sings in the same way.

■ ■ ■

       Tenor:
       Shall I be changed forever as I sing
       night after night the role they gave me? Sing
       myself to a Mahatma?
       Sing my hopes?
       The red strings of my heart
       joining your hearts
       the white strings of our hearts
       rising to heaven?

       Night after night attentive
       I shall sing
       the sacred rhythms in Sanskrit,
       repetition
       changing the living hardware in my head.
       The hardware in our heads.
       All heads. All hardware.
       Here.
       Then everywhere.

■ ■ ■

Changed. Is it catching? Could a major change
occur so simply? Mutation by a sound?
By sonic resonance?
The hundreds of us here who boo or cheer
dazed by stage magic, multiple images
and those repeating phrases
actions, notes.

(I think of all those substances so slow
to crystallize
which crystallize with ease
when they have done it once.
Have learned the knack.)

Don't speak. Don't speak. If only we could stay
still enough and quiet, we could keep
these neural pathways that the music cut.

■ ■ ■

How recreate an opera in this space?
Impossible. But gratitude to Glass
who filled the stage with warring armies clad
in panoply of battle and against
that oriental splendor placed the man
Gandhi—isolated, visionary—
the dust
of Africa—stage magic's dust—
making us cough, the choir
drowning our coughs.

I think continually of those who were truly great:
Tolstoi, Tagore, and Martin Luther King
high on a platform upstage.

Downstage war
is acted out. The holy color war.
The war that counts a man's
skin color more
important than
his heart's intention, more
important than his
education or
his thought.

His heart, his education, or his thought.
His heart, his education, or his thought.
His heart, his education, or his thought.

William Prouty

Night

The night Lady Macbeth died,
an Iroquois chieftain
plotted the death of enemies,
a child was destined for sacrifice,
and one man's gold
bought another man's death.

On such a night as this,
someone stole the ring
Antony gave to Cleopatra
and melted it down
to buy a slave.

On such a night as this,
someone burned the Library
at Alexandria. Someone was,
justly or unjustly, eliminated.

On such a night as this,
someone bombed Hiroshima.

Of course, it must be admitted
that on such a night,
fish slept softly off Zanzibar,
nightingales sang in the trees,
and the Aurora Borealis
danced the night away.
But these are inferior,
mindless things.

The night Lady Macbeth died,
human madness was diminished
    slightly
        temporarily.

Al Purdy

On My Workroom Wall

Photo of Gabrielle Roy with her much-
lived-in face a relief map with all the wrinkles
her face a banner in the wind
Two of Margaret Laurence whom I loved dearly
one looking bored the other alight with amusement
Don Coles' poem which says so much about the
lost 'Forests of the Medieval World' it loses me
all the poem's parts adjustable in your mind
Harold Ballard on the cover of *Saturday Night*
his cane spanking the world in geriatric rage
My sister-in-law at age twenty-two
so beautiful the photo sizzles despairingly
knowing this one chance was lost
Acorn of course
who lost himself in a dream of what he was
and became his own incredible dream
Me pissing behind the Owen Roblin tombstone
only the stream of piss visible in photo
presaging dry centuries oncoming
Poster of Atwood's breasts surmounted by
her Proteus-face which she objected to
(I think rightly) or would cancel the reading
Tiff Findley's verse from Euripides
which says "never that which is shall die"
pollyanna stuff but I like it
Eurithe as a fifty-year-old child in water
colour pretending she isn't there
but she always has been
Zerox of Milosz with cigar looking cynical
Gary Snyder poet-smug and Wm. Everson a dead prophet
Stone heads atop a Turkish mountain
peering from the past into now
alien as a toothbrush
Ben Johnson beating Carl Lewis in Rome
grinning back at him like a little boy
saying "Haw-Haw-Haw" without stopping
MacLeish's "You, Andrew Marvell"
—and I too follow shadows around the world

at Petra and Ecbatan and Sumer and Palmyra
and sleep in those ruined cities still
Two original Lawrence letters
both so alive he can't be dead
Three Kipling poems I like much
megaphones into silence
Much more and all of it
brief components of myself
and live in my own silences

Linda Rogers

Wedding Feast for One Fork

Your brother is blessing the dirty
water at Waikiki.
He opens a suitcase
full of condoms and pills,
some pictures of Jesus,
the Maharishi
and tells us how
he shops the cosmos
for bargains.

God is a swap meet, he says,
and the sun is high on dexadrine.

Your brother never sleeps
Daruma told him to
tear off his eyelids.
He is shaving his legs
and will put on glass
slippers to wear to the church
where your mother is getting married.

After the wedding,
the bride and groom
and your brother

will all get happy and go
into the plastic tide,
shopping for God.

In the dark, you will call me
your Japanese nun
and touch the cheek
I burned with an iron.
You will name my scars
and smell the bread on my hands,
the plumeria in my hair.

Your lips will be numb
from so much kissing and praying.

Tomorrow, we will watch
the sunrise in Ala Moana Park.
We will take the leftover
wine and cake,
a wedding feast for one fork
to mynah birds and derelicts, the only
Holy Men left in Paradise.

Heather Spears

Rumania on the BBC

How awful is the awful
happiness of the good,
we have already seen
the unspeakable
orphanage images and now
a cheery British team
repairing drains and painting ceilings
while from their evil cribs
children are filmed being lifted
and hugged, their mouths
stretching into what is necessary—

The speaker with the microphone
is very pretty, and very fast she wants to convey
happiness back to the viewers
some of whom have donated money

Now it is the cribs
hauled into the yard, their peeled
chewed yellow rods and bars
(probably lead, from the look of the kids)
pulled apart in proper fury,
stamped on, heaved piecemeal
up on the pile, their stained
mattresses following and folding
          —they burn like books.

Meanwhile back in the wards, rows of
new wooden cribs have replaced them
as if miraculously. Each child
is lifted proudly in. Toys are given.
Their heads stare as the team waves good bye.

Lola Lemire Tostevin

---

from Cartouches: hieroglyphs of a visit

1.

Thoth has as many faces
as he has names:
sun-god
son of the god-king
eldest son of Ra
hidden father
of all things
bull among stars

he is bird
falcon hatched

from the egg
great cackler

wears on his ibis head
the cusped moon

I am sitting in the veranda of the old Cataract hotel in Aswan jotting down
ideas for poems, writing my daily journal entry. The building is Moorish in
style and painted a deep rust-orange, a perfect location for *Death on the Nile*.
The veranda is silent as everyone watches the sun set behind the Aga Khan's
mausoleum on the other side of Elephantine Island, the moon already high in
the sky. It is believed that Thoth, god of the creative word, was conceived to
replace the setting sun. The moon is to day what speech is to writing.

2.

A♭
heart-soul

baby beetle crawls
from the belly of death
sits on the heart
weighed against
a feather

The heart and soul are depicted by neither a heart or a beetle but as one dancing
figure. *A*♭, heartbeat, body's rhythm.

After death, the heart, excised from the body, is weighed for lightness, mummified
and preserved in a jar in the custody of Tuamutef. In *The Book of the Dead*
there is a special text meant to replace this missing heart. Hieroglyphs in lieu
of a heart, an engraved stone to weigh the body down. An *a* for the absent
heart, a *b* for the absent soul. What other parts of me for an *abc*?

3.

Hatshepsut
your fluted
defacement
returns you
to space   you
with your face
behind you

your hacked wall
a peal of stillness

The guide informs us that the greatest structure of the Eighteenth Dynasty is Deir el Bahari, the funerary temple of Queen Hatshepsut, except he keeps pronouncing it Hot-Shit-Soup and everyone laughs. Constructed of pink granite terraces and columns, the temple is situated in a narrow cliff at the edge of Gourna mountain and unlike other temples it suggests the imprint of a singular mind. Makes visible the invisible space of the desert against the mountain. Hot-Shit-Soup was Egypt's only female Pharaoh, the guide says. On the walls of her birth house, reliefs that should celebrate her divine birth have been defaced. Throughout Deir el Bahari, the face of the only female Pharaoh has been chiselled out except where she is portrayed as a man. "It probably took more time and effort to obliterate her from the stone than it did to carve her in," the guide says.

4.

a bullet
puts into play
the bodies
of my name

a lion
a dove
a lion
a falcon

oh mummified me

Did Nietzsche know about hieroglyphs when he wrote "All this I am and want to be: at the same time dove, serpent, and pig?" Today we came to the end of the cruise, five days gliding the Nile. It's what tourists do. In Luxor, the oldest city in the world, merchants stand outside their shops luring tourists. "Mister, a thousand camels for your wife . . . Two thousand camels . . ." In one shop I have a gold cartouche made bearing the four hieroglyphs of my name. All this I am and want to be: at the same time lion, dove and falcon. A bird tears open its prey under blue desert skies.

Gordon Turner

The Pemberton–Mount Currie Valley

The schoolbus driver from
white-town Pemberton
tells the visiting coach:
  "One winter the Indians
   buried in twelve feet
   of snow sheltered
   their horses in the local
   gym. Every Saturday
   night at the hotel
   pub in Pemberton Indians
   are stacked drunk
   in the doorway waiting
   to be carted the five
   miles home in taxis."

Telling this to Albert
and Larry, Indian farmers
on the Birkenhead River
at the end of a tough
day of hauling rock
to the river to save
their land from being swirled
away   downstream
I notice the shrug come into
their manner. Finally Albert
speaks
as if
to the river
he's facing. His words fall
as slowly
as dust
settling
from the last
load
of rock:
  "A horse seeking the end
   of winter lies down just
   inside a blown-open gym

door and becomes legend
as dumb Indians wintering
their horses. We sleep where
we drunkenly fall; whites manage
to stumble as far as their own
doorsteps. In their town we are not
people, merely figures in their
nightmares or beer glasses on
a table. In their better
moments we take on the shape
of woven baskets or sockeye
salmon to be bought cheaply.

To change their image
of us is like striving
to keep this river from doing
its will. An eroding force
that's had its way
so long
can hardly be rip-rapped."

Miriam Waddington

A Man and His Flute

A man in a black coat
plays a song
on a black flute
in a concert hall.
He plays with his whole
body with his hands
with his trunk until
he becomes a tree and
his arm a branch;
his fingers are urgent

extensions that startle
the air in the leaves.

His song is obscurely
about a lemon
picked from an old tree
in another country then
brought home and cut
against the blue
of a winter sky.

The lemon and the
black flute and the man
in the black coat who
sways with the music
in the concert hall
takes the blue sky the
yellow lemon and the
cold sunlight of March
and turns it into an April
filled with the blueness
of hyacinth; winter turns
its back and melts away
in the runnelled snow piled
against frozen houses.

The man and his flute
play their song,
the audience is pierced
by the blueness of sky,
the audience hears
the snow melting,
the audience sees spring
approaching the audience
stands up the audience claps,
the audience dances.

The man and his flute
end their song,
a smell of cut lemon
fills the air.

from Music at the Heart of Things

artknot 30

plane
reflection
echo
projection
cave
film
ga(u)ze
scat
entrail
residue
page
leaf
pile

book
descent
ocean
reprint
track
screen
tulle
actual

■ ■ ■

artknot 31

emergency of maps
shape of puddles
fruit of words
pith of whales

■ ■ ■

artknot 32

In   that threads S fold:
you   D facto mythic yet:
more   her M red fire:
than   next K 'membered S_1:
you   line S_2 F edge.

■ ■ ■

artknot 33

Outside of Emily Carr's
lone piss-fir these throats
that are long in art and
free-standing poems wall
the provinces no more rail
yelling every spike a chink.

■ ■ ■

artknot 34

Glenbow's sensation of the body femin
ism made for thirst

some guy's art wire heart
post-marble still thinking nature/natural

titled I was made for having
lapped "at" her tears

Tom Wayman

Correcting 120 Essays on Poetry

My task is dry
as brittle paper
the red pencil
scratching scratching
—sand
caught between metal parts
forced to slide
open/shut

Sometimes what they have created
is strangely
beautiful:
a wooden sculpture
almost spherical
half the size
of a basketball
I run my palms and fingers
around and around it
notice a rough part
write: *awkward; could be smoother*
at this spot
Later they read my comment
Their eyes say
I know that

Or
what they hand in
is shaped in a rush
or crude
grotesque
because they were absent
or inattentive
when the directions were given
they did not know
were thinking of other problems, joys
I examine each of these constructs
just as gravely as the others
rotating them before me

on the desk
Such creations seem
a rejected version
a piece
left with the shavings and wood chips
under a workbench
after a false start
or dropped by mistake
My hands travel

across the surface
find a deep furrow
gouged
I write *you have a furrow*
here
But when the makers
hold again what they devised
they do not read
any words: their eyes
seek the letter
or number I attach
to this broken thing
When they read that
they nod
toss the malformed object
away

Phyllis Webb

Memo from Hubert Aquin, 1986

For the thin poets

who come out of the Blue
into this place of departure:
Je suis un peuple défait
qui marche en désordre
dans les rues qui passent
au-dessous de notre couche . . .

The next episode introduces
the round fat body of the
intertextual critic
reading "Hamlet"
comme-çi, comme-ça
under blue Canadian skies.

Point: Papa Doc was seen entering
the Allan Memorial Institute
followed by *son fils et sa femme*.
They vanish through the back door.
Erasure.

Is it all a mistake?
This Seventh Heaven,
this Ninth Circle of Hell?
We are fat or thin,
gathered in the netherworld.
Here we go round again,
around and about in
the *Opel bleue*—
*Vite, car je suis sur le point
de céder à la fatigue historique* . . .

Circulez. Circulez!

Dale Zieroth

Self-admonitions

Not to set up structures
that require completion;
not to imagine that the stronger light
of April, May, June and July
signals growth in him;
not to expect the earth to come roaring.
To be caught instead unable to make
the clean and jerk required by the day

—to be weak in a human way
one time too many,
friends noting his grump and sag
twice in one week,
the announcement of decline
in the clutch of the night sheets
still on his skin; but also this:
how to extend the head gently down
so the neck cracks and energy
flows into his legs
the moment he walks smiling into work.

Once he hankered for fall's
dark and glory, and the last days
in the race for silent white.
As a child he looked out
for the morning when, in the night,
the snow had arrived to present
the chance for tracks
criss-crossing into paths
that signaled where he's been
and continues to be going.

Now spring has taken on
direction: one more release
of colour up into the light;
and the promise of heat to come;
ground good enough to lie on and
sink into with nothing like fear.
Not to linger there
counting blades of grass; not imagining either
how clouds break and drift—
and whether they meet each other again
in this country; but to divine
in the scatter of the insect air
new wings approaching.

PART FOUR

Epilogue

The Masks of Don Stephens

David Watmough

Oddly enough, Don Stephens first lodged in my memory in a somewhat abrasive context. As a visitor to the UBC campus, I had made light of certain studies connected with James Joyce's *Finnegans Wake*. Being a serious young academic (this was in the mid-1960s) Don was highly protective of his scholarly turf and railed fiercely at my levity as he escorted me to the UBC Faculty Club where I was to be offered lunch.

The significance of this encounter lies not in the immediacy of his ire but in the words with which he clothed it. I was doing a disservice to the students who had been at the colloquium, he asserted, by poking fun at matters he and his colleagues were at considerable pains to communicate. If I wanted to play the fool then it should be elsewhere and not in the hearing of his students. Over the subsequent twenty-five years I have never known him to deviate from that attitude. Don loved his undergraduates and would take on all comers in their defence.

It is a commonplace in our psychology-conscious era to be aware of "persona" and to observe how many masks we are prone to adopt in varying and various circumstances. As it happens, I have never witnessed Don's teaching guise, never observed him in the classroom. But I can readily attest to some vivid and memorable masks this man has worn in a dazzling variety of contexts.

Let me start with Don Stephens the evangelist for Canadian literature. Had Don been more extrovert I think he would have been a less indefatigable crusader for this country's writing and the need to take it seriously.

When I first encountered his championing of our poetry and fiction and insisting on its critical place in academe, it was not a gallant fool rashly confronting his peers that I was observing. Instead I saw a nervous, emotional adversary of the entrenched academic establishment that was then so hostile to any kind of affirmation of Canadian letters—as often as unsure of himself as he was unwaveringly confident of his cause. Don, I soon came to realize, was the kind of person for whom the vision first struck—after which came the more arduous and costing task of casting around for the strength to assert and the means to implement it. I have thus always seen him as infinitely more intuitive than ratiocinative and thus fashioned from the less common kind of academic cloth.

But the required belligerency to promote CanLit in the face of the advocates of British and American letters did not come easily to one of Don's essentially amiable nature. Nor did it always make friends for one who is quintessentially a warm-hearted, gregarious man—even if he often affects to be the contrary.

Two scenes involving the vulnerable, unguarded Don Stephens jumble in the kaleidoscope of memory for me. One occurred in the Weald of Kent where he was on sabbatical with his wife and I was their house-guest.

At the first dinner there was much talk of home and we all three spoke fondly of Vancouver and those we had left behind. As Dor-Lou enquired about my roommate, Floyd St. Clair, whom I hadn't seen for the best part of a month, Don slipped away from the table. When he returned it was to announce in a voice now loud with excitement that there was a phone call for me.

When I took the receiver—to hear my roommate's voice in far away British Columbia—I was staring at Don just a few feet away. As great a pleasure as my partner's voice was the expression on Don's face. It was one of a little boy joyfully giving a gift. The incident would have done Alexander Graham Bell's heart good.

The other cameo was at the Stephens' bosky home on the edge of the University Endowment Lands in Vancouver's Point Grey. It was a small dinner party to celebrate the completion of their swimming pool, which appeared David Hockney brilliant in the evening sun. We all trooped outdoors to admire the suburban artifact of which Don was patently proud. To make conversation I asked our host how many lengths he was prepared to do each morning before departing for campus. His expression changed and he looked afar—I suspect as far away as those distant prairies on which he had grown up and which contained some particularly sad memories for him.

In a voice from another time he confessed he was unable to swim and that his wife, children, and his friends, would be the prime benefactors. He was certainly not suffused in self-pity but the expression he bore was the other side of that same youthful coin I had discerned amid that English landscape we had briefly shared a few years earlier. Don Stephens is a complicated man.

Laughter is something I invariably link to Don. However, his is a humour of practised accomplishment. The seasoned warrior for CanLit long ago discovered the use of evoking mirth as a means of achieving recalcitrant goals. I suspect that generations of students as well as we his friends have learned by laughing at Don's wit and concomitant *mot juste*.

I don't wish to imply that my friend has reduced the benison of laughter to a mere pedagogic technique. To the contrary, he is simply incapable of NOT seeing the humorous side of things. So that his laughter erupts (or he begins to shake with attempts to suppress it) at the most inopportune moments. I recall a memorial service we were both attending—or perhaps I should not recall, for the occasion Don turned hilarious for me with just one whispered comment of characteristic tartness.

Then that, after all, is the Don I salute here. A man who is not only a master in the vital business of deflation in a world overpopulated with human balloons, but has the demonic skill of enlisting his friends into his ever expanding cadre of debunkers of all modes of pretension.

For those who do not grasp the subtleties of Don's wit there might well be failure to understand that he is not only forever seeking to deflate the kinds of pomposity some would call endemic to his profession but also practising something far more personal.

Don Stephens is a complicated man. Bafflingly, this fellow who can wear his humour like a moat remains profoundly convivial and enjoys affection as much as the rest of us. He has indeed truly Prairie-style traits of gregariousness and simple warmth.

The same man who brought me a clump of primroses all the way from Cornwall's Porth Navas for our yard ("to remind you each spring of your Celtic heritage") can be one of the most belligerent protagonists of the Canadian fact when it is either being ignored or slighted. Yet he is no chauvinist brimming with anti-American vitriol. Don proudly flies the flag but he is the first to tell you of a fine Seattle restaurant or of an interesting bookstore in Bellingham.

Don Stephens not only has a Saskatchewan background but shares with his wife profound links with New Brunswick. There can be few Canadians who in recent years, due to familial circumstances, have more or less commuted from the Maritimes to the West Coast several times a year. Their roots are deep and they can (but rarely do) play the Canadian game of boasting their generations upon the soil of this realm. Yet as an immigrant who has only known their native soil since 1959 I have NEVER been made to feel alien in or irrelevant to the country we now share.

My friend is not only complicated but he is also foxy. Now my Webster defines such as "crafty," "wily," or "sly" but I have my own definition which removes the sting of those words. I perceive "foxy"—in the Stephenesque fashion—as someone intelligently shy. That is why, when I had decided as a conclusion to these reflections to ask Don five questions one day over lunch, I made sure his answers were spontaneous and with no subsequent time for him to salt them with scholarly caution and balance.

Right off the bat with my first query he provided that childlike directness which is never remote from the adult man.

DAVID: What is your most distinct childhood memory?
DON: There are two. One is when I was three or four going with my parents to see planes coming into Yorkton to land. In those days planes were not very common. I was with my sister. She is eight years older than I am. It was a sunny and warm day and as a great treat we were given ice cream cones. It was just a field where those planes were landing. On the edge of town. As I was munching the ice cream the plane started to smoke and it crashed into the ground. The pilot had taken up two other people. A friend of ours was the local doctor and he went running out to the plane which was maybe a block away and he came out of the plane all covered in blood. It just absolutely petrified me. Then during the War, they used Yorkton air force base to train Commonwealth fliers and I remember being terribly concerned about people on all these planes—similar to that one which crashed. That frequently comes back to me.

The other memory is when our next door neighbour's daughter was getting married in July. Her name was Gladys (terrible name!) Now my father—

DAVID: He was a lawyer?

DON: No, a teacher. They were *both* teachers. Now my father had this wonderful garden and he had promised Gladys some of his sweet peas for her wedding. This was around 1939-1940. Mother believed you picked cut flowers either before ten or after five. My parents on the day in question got up very early and I got up by 8:30 to see my mother carrying an immense bowl—the copper thing they used to put on the stove to boil clothes? *Full* of sweet peas. I can see her face behind that huge bunch of them. Now, whenever I see sweet peas mixed with baby's breath I think of my mother. She could put them into a copper pot and they'd look GREAT! Flowers are very, very important to me and I think that's because my mother loved them so much.

DAVID: What in your opinion is the state of CanLit today?

DON: I have a feeling it's not as good as it was. We have a lot of poets, novelists, and short story writers who aren't doing the kind of good stuff they were doing earlier. I'm still impressed with the likes of Gary Geddes, and Phyllis Webb. I like the poetry of Marya Hardman—or Fiamengo—but perhaps that's because she's a friend of mine. Atwood and Munro? Munro is good but could be better. And I wish Atwood would write more poetry. She's a far better poet than novelist or reflective short-story writer. Though sometimes when you talk to students they say she doesn't write very well. It's true she doesn't. At times she writes sentences you wouldn't let get by in an English 100 essay. But she does write good poetry and I wish she'd go back to it.

We need something else to happen. We are in a country where things seem to be standing still, waiting for things to happen. And, just as in the past, when something happens to the country it will happen to the literature also.

DAVID: Has retirement brought any surprises?

DON: Actually it is much more exciting than I thought it was going to be. I'm really enjoying it. Being at home, writing letters. Above all, editing a nineteenth-century Canadian novel for a new edition. By working on this critical work about the War of 1812 and Brock all my patriotism and nationalism are re-inforced.

One thing that does surprise me is that while I do miss my students at UBC I'm not half as interested in departmental affairs as I had expected to be. I hear about things happening but it's all remote. The only thing that gets me is when I hear about people being mistreated. That bothers me, upsets me. People not receiving the care and compassion which the academic world should represent is one of the reasons I decided to retire early. I found that very difficult before and I see it's still there.

DAVID: Born in Saskatchewan, having such special links with the Maritimes, and having lived your professional life in B.C., you must have a special perspective as a commuting Canadian.

DON: I probably do in some way. But don't forget I was brought up in a home of native New Brunswickers. My father came out West and my mother followed him. They always had a strong connection with the whole Maritime complex.

My mother's family had been in this country since 1759 and my grandfather had been with Wolfe on the Plains of Abraham as a blacksmith before going to the Chesapeake Bay area in the United States. Then in 1763 he and his wife came to the Maritimes BEFORE the Revolution. They were what we call The Planters. Some went to New Brunswick and others to Nova Scotia. They (my parents) thus brought me up in that kind of tradition.

People in this country haven't changed. They are far more generous, loving and compassionate than a lot of people give them credit for. The only difference between Vancouver, the Prairies, and New Brunswick is the quality of the light. When I waken in the morning in New Brunswick I know I am there by the way the light filters through the windows. On the prairie there's that special prairie light and in Vancouver even on the greyest kind of day there's a certain kind of light. Sometimes that light exposes beautiful things, sometimes not very nice things . . .

DAVID: Which do you rate higher in human significance—laughter or tears?

DON: It would have to be laughter, although I am a great crier! But I would like people to remember me for my laugh. Oh yes, I would like to be remembered for the jokes and the puns and so on and not for the tears.

So there you have it—from the lips of the subject himself. No one enters the Stephens' home without being made conscious of an abundance of flowers. No one can spend much time with Don without hearing a pun or an outrageous opinion—or both. Tears come quickly to him—then so does the ready rejoinder and the quizzical smile.

However rough-hewn, I hope I have gotten my sketch of this truly antinomic man accurate in balance as well as detail. For in his own appointed contexts my friend is a stickler for accuracy. On rising from the lunch table at the restaurant where I posed my questions he looked me fully in the eye. His final comment was: "Now I hope you have all the facts, David. For example, I don't want the rumour perpetuated that Diefenbaker was my godfather. He wasn't, you know."

Notes on Poets and Critics

Margaret ATWOOD lives in Toronto; her many works include the poetry collections *The Journals of Susanna Moodie* (1970), *Power Politics* (1973), and *Selected Poems* (1976), and such novels as *The Handmaid's Tale* (1985); she also edited *The Oxford Book of Canadian Verse in English* (1987).

Margaret AVISON has been a social worker in Toronto; her works include *Winter Sun* (1960) and *The Dumbfounding* (1966), and her *Selected Poems* appeared in 1991.

Earle BIRNEY—poet, novelist, and professor of medieval literature—founded the Creative Writing Department at the University of British Columbia; his works include the picaresque satire *Turvey* (1977) and *Collected Poems* (1975); *Last Poems*, edited by Al Purdy, appeared in 1991.

bill BISSETT is an artist and visual and sound poet who now lives in London, Ontario; he has produced many volumes, and his *Selected Poems: Beyond Even Faithful Legends* appeared in 1980.

Marilyn BOWERING lives in Victoria; she is the author of several volumes of poetry, including *Sleeping With Lambs* (1980) and *The Sunday Before Winter* (1984).

Dionne BRAND teaches at Guelph University; she is the author of *Chronicles of the Hostile Sun* (1984), a collection of essays on racism in Canada entitled *Rivers have sources, trees have roots* (1986), and *No Burden To Carry: Narratives of Black Working Women In Ontario 1920s-1950s* (1991).

Robert BRINGHURST lives on Bowen Island, B.C.; his several books of poems include *The Beauty of the Weapons* (1982) and *Pieces of Map, Pieces of Music* (1986), and his appreciation of Haida culture has led to several books, essays, and stories (in collaboration with the Haida sculptor, Bill Reid), and a book about Reid's work, *The Black Canoe* (1991).

Diana BRYDON teaches Canadian and Commonwealth Literature at the University of Guelph; she is the current editor of *WLWE* and the author of *Christina Stead* (1987) and other works.

Pauline BUTLING teaches at the Alberta College of Art in Calgary; she is preparing, with Roy Miki, a festschrift in honour of Phyllis Webb, and has recently edited a special issue of *West Coast Line* devoted to Webb's work.

Elspeth CAMERON teaches at the University of Toronto; she is the author of biographies of Hugh MacLennan and Irving Layton, and is currently preparing a biography of Earle Birney.

Fred COGSWELL is Professor Emeritus from the University of New Brunswick, where he edited *The Fiddlehead* from 1952 to 1967; he has published several collections of poetry, including translations from Quebec poets and a volume of his collected works, *A Long Apprenticeship* (1980).

Nathalie COOKE teaches at McGill University in Montreal; with Donna Bennett and Russell Brown, she helped prepare the second edition of Oxford's *An Anthology of Canadian Literature in English* (1990).

Lorna CROZIER teaches Creative Writing at the University of Victoria; her most recent book of poetry is called *Inventing the Hawk* (1992).

Wilfred CUDE lives in Back Bay, Nova Scotia, where he teaches and is active with Medicine Label Press; he is the author of *A Due Sense of Differences* (1980) and *The Ph.D. Trap* (1987).

Roy DANIELLS was for many years head of the English Department at the University of British Columbia; he was the author of books on Traherne and Mannerism, and two collections of poetry, including *The Chequered Shade* (1963).

Frank DAVEY is the Carl Klinck Professor of Canadian Literature at the University of Western Ontario; a poet and critic, he is the author of such works as *The Clallam* (1973), *The Arches: Selected Poems* (edited by bp Nichol, 1980), and *Surviving the Paraphrase* (1983).

Sandra DJWA chairs the English Department at Simon Fraser University. The editor of Carl Klinck's papers, and the author of *The Politics of the Imagination: A Life of F.R. Scott* (1987), she is currently preparing a biography of A.J.M. Smith.

Don DOMANSKI lives in Halifax, Nova Scotia; he is the author of *War in an Empty House* (1982), *Hammerstroke* (1986), and *Wolf-Ladder* (1991).

Susan Rudy DORSCHT teaches at the University of Calgary; she is the author of *Women, Reading, Kroetsch: Telling the Difference* (1991).

Geoffrey DURRANT is Professor Emeritus from the University of British Columbia; his books include *William Wordsworth* (1969) and *Wordsworth and the Great System* (1970).

Mary Jane EDWARDS teaches at Carleton University in Ottawa, where she is General Editor of the scholarly series produced at the Centre for Editing Early Canadian Texts; among other works, she has edited Frances Brooke's *The History of Emily Montague* (1985).

Marya FIAMENGO recently retired from the University of British Columbia; her most recent book of poetry is *Patience After Compline* (1989).

Gary GEDDES lives in Dunvegan, Ontario; he edited *15 Canadian Poets X2* (1988), and his *The Terracotta Army* won a Commonwealth Poetry Prize in 1984.

Bruce GRENBERG teaches at the University of British Columbia, where he specializes in American literature; he has published articles on Crane, Hemingway, and Fitzgerald, and is the author of a recent book on Herman Melville.

Ralph GUSTAFSON lives in North Hatley, Quebec; for many years he was Poet-in-Residence at Bishop's University in Lennoxville and a music critic for the Canadian Broadcasting Corporation; among his many books is a volume of selected poems called *The Moment Is All* (1983).

Dick HARRISON teaches at the University of Alberta; he is the author of *Unnamed Country* (1977) and the editor of *Crossing Frontiers* (1979).

Tom HASTINGS is a graduate student at York University, where he is specializing in post-colonial literature.

Brian HENDERSON lives in Toronto, where he is Publisher of the College and Trade Division of Oxford University Press; his books of poetry include *The Migration of Light* (1983) and *Smoking Mirror* (1990).

John F. HULCOOP teaches English at the University of British Columbia and has published on Browning, Tennyson, and Dickens; he edited and introduced Phyllis Webb's *Selected Poems* (1971), wrote *Phyllis Webb and Her Works* (1990), and is currently working on a biography of Timothy Findley.

D.G. JONES teaches at the University of Sherbrooke, where he has been active with the journal *ellipse*; his critical works include *Butterfly on Rock* (1970), and his several volumes of poetry include *A Throw of Particles* (1983).

Manina JONES teaches at the University of Waterloo; she has published articles on Robert Kroetsch and on issues relating to literary form.

A.M. KLEIN—author of *The Rocking Chair and Other Poems* (1948), *The Second Scroll* (1951), commentaries on James Joyce, and numerous other works—for many years edited the *Canadian Jewish Chronicle* in Montreal; his *Collected Works* are now appearing in a multi-volume edition, under the general direction of Zailig Pollock.

Robert KROETSCH is a Distinguished Professor at the University of Manitoba; he is a novelist, poet, and critic, whose works include *Badlands* (1975), *Labyrinths of Voice* (1982), and *Completed Field Notes* (1989).

Archibald LAMPMAN worked for the Post Office Department in Ottawa; his poems appeared in such volumes as *Among the Millet* (1888) and *Alcyone* (1899), and a volume of his collected poems is currently being edited by Bruce Nesbitt.

Patrick LANE recently moved from Saskatoon to Sidney, B.C.; he is the author of several works, including *Poems New and Selected* (1978), *Old Mother* (1982), and *A Linen Crow, A Caftan Magpie* (1985).

Irving LAYTON taught for many years at Sir George Williams University in Montreal and York University in Downsview, Ontario; he is the author of stories, essays, and many volumes of poetry, including *The Bull Calf* (1956), *The Swinging Flesh* (1961), and *For My Brother Jesus* (1976); a volume of *Selected Poems* appeared in 1977, and *Waiting for The Messiah: A Memoir* in 1985.

Dorothy LIVESAY, who now lives in Victoria, has been a social worker, reporter, English teacher, and writer-in-residence at several universities; two selections from her many volumes are *Collected Poems: The Two Seasons* (1972) and *The Self-completing Tree* (1986); *Right Hand, Left Hand* (1977) is a memoir.

George McWHIRTER is head of the Creative Writing Department at the University of British Columbia; poet and fiction writer, he is the author of *Catalan Poems* (1971), which won the Commonwealth Poetry Prize, *Fire Before Dark* (1983), *Cage* (1987), and other works.

Eli MANDEL taught for many years at the University of Alberta and at York University; among his numerous publications are such critical works as *Another Time* (1977) and *The Family Romance* (1986) and an anthology called *Contexts of Canadian Criticism* (1971); his several collections of poetry include *Life Sentence* (1981) and *Dreaming Backwards* (1981).

Daphne MARLATT is a poet and fiction writer who lives in Vancouver; her books include *Steveston* (1974), *Zócalo* (1977), *Ana Historic* (1988), and a selection called *Net Work* (1980).

Seymour MAYNE teaches at the University of Ottawa, and runs Mosaic Press/Valley Editions; a specialist in Jewish writing, he is the author of *Mouth* (1970), *Diasporas* (1977), and other works, and he has edited collections of the poems of Red Lane and Rachel Korn, and the prose of Irving Layton.

Daniel David MOSES was educated at the University of British Columbia and now lives in Toronto, where he is active with the Native organization called The Committee to Re-Establish the Trickster; his works include *Delicate Bodies* (1980) and *The White Line* (1990).

Erin MOURÉ works for Via Rail and lives in Montreal; her works include *Empire York Street* (1979), *Wanted Alive* (1983), *Furious* (1988), *WSW (West South West)* (1989).

W.H. NEW teaches at the University of British Columbia, and since 1977 has edited *Canadian Literature*; his recent publications include *Dreams of Speech and Violence* (1987) and *A History of Canadian Literature* (1989).

P.K. PAGE now lives in Victoria, after having spent many years in Montreal, Brazil, and Australia; she is the author of numerous volumes of poetry and prose, including *The Glass Air: Poems Selected and New* (1991) and *Brazilian Journal* (1987); she paints under the name P.K. Irwin.

William PROUTY is President of the Writers' Federation of New Brunswick and teaches at the University of New Brunswick in Saint John.

Al PURDY, who has travelled widely, now divides his time between Ameliasburg, Ontario, and Sidney, B.C.; he is the author of many volumes of poetry; *The Collected Poems of Al Purdy*, edited by Russell Brown, appeared in 1986.

Laurie RICOU teaches at the University of British Columbia, and is Associate Editor of *Canadian Literature*; he is the author of *Everyday Magic* (1987), the chapter on poetry in Volume IV of the *Literary History of Canada* (1990), and is currently working on a cross-border study of writing in the Pacific Northwest.

Lilita RODMAN teaches at the University of British Columbia, where she specializes in dialectology, Canadian literature, and technical writing; she is the author of *Technical Communication: Strategy and Process* (1991) and articles on English-Latvian language contact.

Linda ROGERS is a poet and children's writer who lives in Victoria; her several works include *Queens of the Next Hot Star* (1981), *Worm Sandwich* (1989), and *Woman at Mile Zero* (1990).

Stephen SCOBIE teaches at the University of Victoria; among his recent volumes are critical works such as *bp Nichol: What History Teaches* (1984) and several collections of poetry, including *McAlmon's Chinese Opera* (1980).

F.R. SCOTT lived in Montreal, where he was actively involved in politics and poetry, and taught law at McGill University; his *Essays on the Constitution* won the Governor-General's Award for Non-Fiction in 1977, and his *Collected Poems* appeared in 1981.

Carol SHIELDS is a novelist and critic who lives in Winnipeg; she is the author of *The Box Garden* (1977), *Swann: A Mystery* (1987), and *The Republic of Love* (1992).

A.J.M. SMITH, who along with F.R. Scott was active in the Montreal Movement in the late 1920s, taught for many years at Michigan State University; a volume of selected essays, *On Poetry and Poets*, appeared in 1977, and *The Classic Shade: Selected Poems* in 1978.

Christine SOMERVILLE teaches Canadian Literature for Capilano College's Extension program; she lives in West Vancouver and helps to run a mineral exploration company.

Heather SPEARS divides her time between British Columbia and Denmark; her works include several volumes of poetry—among them, *The Word for Sand* (1988) and *Human Acts* (1991)—and a science fiction novel, *Moonfall* (1991).

Clara THOMAS is Professor Emerita from York University and currently York University Libraries Canada Research Fellow; her several critical works include

Love and Work Enough: The Life of Anna Jameson (1967), *The Manawaka World of Margaret Laurence* (1976), and (with John Lennox) *William Arthur Deacon: A Canadian Literary Life* (1982).

Lola Lemire TOSTEVIN lives in Toronto; she has published several books of poetry, including *The Color of Her Speech* (1982) and *'Sophie* (1988)—and is currently preparing a collection to be called *Cartouches*.

Brian TREHEARNE teaches at McGill University in Montreal; he is the author of *Aestheticism and the Canadian Modernists* (1988).

Gordon TURNER teaches at Selkirk College in Castlegar, B.C.; his volumes of poetry include *No Country for White Men* (1979).

Miriam WADDINGTON, Professor Emerita from York University, moved to Vancouver in 1992; she is the author of fourteen volumes of poetry, the latest being *The Last Landscape* (1992); a volume of *Collected Poems* appeared in 1986.

Fred WAH teaches at the University of Calgary; his collections of poetry include *Selected Poems* (edited by George Bowering, 1980), *Breathin' My Name with a Sigh* (1981), and *Waiting for Saskatchewan* (1985).

David WATMOUGH is a novelist and short story writer who lives in Vancouver; his 13 volumes of works include *Vibrations in Time* (1986), *The Year of Fears* (1987), and *Thy Mother's Glass* (1992).

Wilfred WATSON taught for many years at the University of Alberta and now lives in Nanaimo; his *Poems: collected / unpublished / new* appeared in 1986.

Tom WAYMAN lives in Winlaw, B.C.; he is the editor of *Going for Coffee: Poetry on the Job* (1983) and the author of *Introducing Tom Wayman* (1980), *Inside Job* (1983), and other works.

Phyllis WEBB worked for many years for the Canadian Broadcasting Corporation; she now lives on Saltspring Island, B.C., and her several collections of poetry include *Wilson's Bowl* (1980), *The Vision Tree: Selected Poems* (edited by Sharon Thesen, 1982), and *Water and Light* (1984).

Lorraine WEIR teaches English and Comparative Literature at the University of British Columbia; she is the author of *Writing Joyce—A Semiotics of the Joyce System* (1989) and *Jay Macpherson* (1989), and is currently working on a study of Marshall McLuhan.

George WOODCOCK lives in Vancouver; he is the author of over fifty books, and from 1959 to 1977 edited *Canadian Literature*; among his works are *Anarchism* (1962), *Faces of India* (1964), *Canada and the Canadians* (revised 1973), *Gabriel Dumont* (1978), *Collected Poems* (1983), and an autobiography, *Beyond the Blue Mountains* (1987).

Dale ZIEROTH lives in North Vancouver and teaches at Capilano College; he is the author of *Clearing* (1973), *Mid-River* (1981), *When the Stones Fly Up* (1985), and other volumes of poetry.